A HISTORY OF ISLAM IN WEST AFRICA

GLASGOW UNIVERSITY PUBLICATIONS

A HISTORY OF ISLAM IN WEST AFRICA

By

J. SPENCER TRIMINGHAM

Published for the UNIVERSITY OF GLASGOW *by the*
OXFORD UNIVERSITY PRESS
London Glasgow New York

Oxford University Press, Amen House, London E.C.4
GLASGOW NEW YORK TORONTO MELBOURNE WELLINGTON
BOMBAY CALCUTTA MADRAS KARACHI LAHORE DACCA
CAPE TOWN SALISBURY NAIROBI IBADAN ACCRA
KUALA LUMPUR HONG KONG

FIRST PUBLISHED 1962
REPRINTED 1963, 1965

PRINTED IN GREAT BRITAIN

PREFACE

THIS book provides the historical background to my study of *Islam in West Africa* (Clarendon Press, 1959). The history of the penetration of a religious culture is essential as a means towards understanding its present-day manifestations. At the same time no attempt to present or interpret life in West Africa in the past will have validity without reference to the present. The two books are, therefore, complementary to each other.

Increasing interest in the history of Africa will I hope bring this study to the attention of readers other than those purely interested in the history of Islam. It must, however, be understood that this is a history written from a special point of view—the penetration and influence of Islam upon the region and the bare outlines of the history of Islamic political unities. I have provided few dynastic lists since these are more appropriate for histories of particular states, but have provided chronological tables for convenience of reference.

I wish to express my gratitude to the Publications Committee of the University of Glasgow, the Trustees of the Carnegie Trust for the Universities of Scotland, and the James Long Lecture Committee of the Church Missionary Society, through whose generous help the publication of this book has been made possible.

J. S. T.

CONTENTS

MAPS

ABBREVIATIONS

Afr. Af.	*African Affairs*, London.
Afr. Fr. R.C.	*Bulletin du Comité de l'Afrique Française: Renseignements Coloniaux.*
A.E.F.	Afrique Équatoriale Française.
A.O.F.	Afrique Occidentale Française.
Barth, *Travels*	H. Barth, *Travels and Discoveries in North and Central Africa* (1849–55), 5 vols., 1857.
B.G.A.	*Bibliotheca Geographorum Arabicorum*, ed. de Goeje.
Bull. Com. Ét. A.O.F.	*Bulletin du Comité d'Études historiques et scientifiques de l'Afrique Occidentale Française.*
Bull. I.F.A.N.	*Bulletin de l'Institut Français de l'Afrique Noire*, Dakar.
D. Isl.	*Der Islam*, Berlin.
Delafosse, *H.S.N.*	M. Delafosse, *Haut-Sénégal et Niger*, 3 vols., Paris, 1912.
E.I.[1], *E.I.*[2]	*Encyclopaedia of Islam*, 1st, 2nd ed., Leiden.
I.W.A.	J. S. Trimingham, *Islam in West Africa*, 1959.
J. Afr. Soc.	*Journal of the African Society* (now *African Affairs*).
J. Asiat.	*Journal Asiatique*, Paris.
J.R.A.I.	*Journal of the Royal Anthropological Institute*, London.
J.R.A.S.	*Journal of the Royal Asiatic Society*, London.
J. Soc. Afr.	*Journal de la Société des Africanistes.*
Marty, *Soudan*	P. Marty, *Études sur l'Islam et les Tribus du Soudan*, 4 vols., Paris, 1920.
Marty, *Guinée*	P. Marty, *L'Islam en Guinée: Fouta-Diallon*, Paris, 1921.
M.S.O.S.	*Mitteilungen des Seminars für Orientalische Sprachen*, Berlin.
N. Afr.	*Notes Africaines*, Dakar.
Palmer, *Sud. Mem.*	H. R. Palmer, *Sudanese Memoirs*, 3 vols., Lagos, 1928.
P.E.L.O.V.	*Publications de l'École des Langues Orientales Vivantes*, Paris.
R.M.M.	*Revue du Monde Musulman*, Paris.

I

The Expansion of Islam in North Africa, Sahara and Sudan

1. SOURCES

THE technique of prehistory is providing new material for the period before the coming of Islam. Archaeologists are beginning the task of clearing up problems posed by such regions as the important diffusion centre of Lake Chad. Most of this evidence is still too fragmentary and unrelated to be of much value as historical material. Although providing valuable information about general changes in material culture, this can rarely be related to any people known to history and is of little help, except indirectly, towards understanding the Islamic period.

The sources for the history of Islam in West Africa divide themselves into two categories: external and internal; and these again subdivide: the external into Islamic and European, and the internal into oral and written. For the earlier period there are scattered notices provided by the geographers and historians of the Islamic world, together with a few first-hand accounts such as that given by Ibn Baṭṭūṭa. Then, since the time European adventurers and explorers first landed on the shores of West Africa, there is a gradually increasing volume of travellers' accounts of varying value. Finally come oral traditions of the people themselves. These include collections compiled by local archivists in Arabic, together with contemporary chronicles. In addition, there is a rapidly growing mass of oral traditions collected and recorded by Europeans and Africans themselves during recent years.

The geographical and historical information provided by Arabic writers is often confusing. Early geographers, like al-Khwārizmī, were dependent upon Ptolemy and would place African names at random within his framework. Ibn Ḥawqal (A.D. 961) provides intriguing original comments, but his attitude towards Negro peoples can be gauged from the following quotation in the introduction of his *Ṣūrat al-Arḍ*: 'I have not described the countries of the blacks in the West, nor those of the Beja and other peoples of those latitudes because the characteristics of organized states, such as religious, cultural and legal institutions and stabilized governmental institutions, are utterly lacking among them.'[1] It is not until al-Bakrī that we get more copious new independent material. Subsequent writers were dependent primarily upon literary information and their material was compiled indiscriminately with little regard to the date and value of their sources which they sometimes mention but often omit. They rarely discriminate between different categories of information, incorporating material drawn from sources written perhaps centuries earlier with information derived, probably at second or third hand, from a contemporary traveller. The result is that it is often difficult to decide to what period a particular observation relates. Gāna town, for instance, was destroyed in A.D. 1240, and one has to decide from other evidence whether it still existed or the name was applied to another town in the fourteenth century when it is referred to by Abū'l-Fidā' and Ibn Khaldūn. Abū'l-Fidā' and Yāqūt, who compiled his geographical dictionary between the years A.D. 1212 and 1229, borrowed material relating to the Sudan from *al-'Azīzī* (a work which is lost) by al-Ḥusain b. Aḥmad al-Muhallabī who wrote in A.H. 375/A.D. 985; and he in his turn may have drawn upon still earlier written sources. A source of al-Bakrī, writing in A.D. 1067, for North Africa and the Sudan was the Spanish geographer Muḥammad at-Ta'rīkhī who died in A.D. 973. Ibn Faḍl Allāh al-'Umarī (*Masālik al-abṣār fī mamālik al-amṣār*, written 1342–9) is especially important for the state of Māli on account of the first-hand material he collected from people who had lived there. Ibn Khaldūn also obtained independent information relating to the history of Māli from 'a *faqīh* of the people of Gāna', whom he met in Cairo in 796/1393–4, and from people who had visited Māli. Difficulties arise from the fact that whereas for European countries many historical events can be checked from outside sources, until the eighteenth century we get very little help in this way, for even the relations of Sudanese states with North African rulers were very tenuous.

Muslim and early European travellers help us to penetrate the veil a little, but only a little. They were impressed by the bizarre and extravagant, by the pomp of Negro courts and the crudities of the people; they were interested in trade and commerce; they list the names of many peoples and villages; but of the life even of those they saw they tell us little. Ibn Baṭṭūṭa, living amongst his own people in the mer-

[1] *Opus Geographicum auctore Ibn Hauḳal*, ed. J. H. Kramers, Leiden, 1938, i. 9–10; quoted from al-Iṣṭakhrī, *Masālik al-Mamālik*, *B.G.A.* i. 4.

chant quarters of the capital of Māli and other towns, does not go beyond the surface. Sources being limited in this way to Muslim writers have tended to bias historians into regarding the states as fully organized Muslim kingdoms, whereas they were pagan in essentials, only the immediate court entourage and largely foreign trading communities even making a profession of Islam.

Turning to internal sources we find two types of tradition: oral and written. Oral tradition, with its epic tales, cult legends, and the mythology behind taboo and custom, has played a very important role in the transmission of cultural heritage, but its utilization by the historian is a subtle art. Never intended to be historical, myth is intermediary between oral archives and panegyric. It is not concerned with the preservation of concrete events, but is a mode of expression, making explicit feelings towards institutions which have their nucleus in historical happenings. The relationship of ruler to people is expressed by the myth of the saviour-founder of the state. It expresses something about the nature of kingship that could not be conveyed by a straightforward historical narrative. The emphasis in tradition, therefore, is quite different from that given by historical sources, and indeed corrects our vision. For example, the saga of Sun Dyāta, founder of the Māli empire, appears to have greater historical foundation, in spite of the remoteness of the event, than anything else in Māli tradition, whilst Mansa Mūsā, who figures so prominently in both native and external Arabic writings in consequence of his bizarre pilgrimage, is almost unknown to native tradition except as a magician who imported idols from Mecca. The historical mystery is important since it reveals what the world looks like through African eyes, but difficult to control and utilize.

Tradition, as the collective memory of a social group, is assured some form of continuity by its relationship to kinship and aristocracy. Noble families maintained professional archivists. In the Western cycle these are caste groups, called *dyēli* by Mande, *dyāru* by Soninke, and *gyeserē* by Songhay. Their function was to chant the genealogy, praise the noble deeds, and extol the exploits of the privileged. They transmitted to pupils of their own family the accumulated traditions of the lineage or clan to which they were attached. They were always spared in war and not reduced to slavery and thus often came to devote their talents to new masters. In course of time they spread legends far and wide, which probably accounts for the fact that legends concerning the origins of founders of ruling houses and the way they came to power (for example, Yemenite origins and snake-killing) bear a surprising resemblance. All these stories are traditions of noble and free clans and tell us nothing about how the people were formed and their subsequent history, though sometimes traditions of stable occupational groups, like fishers who retain priests of the river cult, help to elucidate their history. Whilst search for origins is not our concern we must point out that the adoption of Islam adds to the difficulty of utilizing oral tradition, since its influence tends to dilute and often wipe out memory of pre-Islamic tradition. Many Negro ruling classes like the Moorish tribes and Islamic immigrants claim Arab origins, hence traditions that they came from Yemen, which generally means from the east. The effect of Islam in this respect is unequal. Where adopted in the Sudanese mode, which is not incompatible with the coexistence of pagan institutions, tradition survives. But the imposition of an aristocracy drawing its authority from Islam means a new beginning and the elimination or distortion of pagan tradition. To add to the difficulties, this oral material is subject to the changes familiar to students of African history: interpolation, suppression, reformulation, and transformation of the ordinary into the miraculous; the whole forming a network from which it is difficult to disentangle the historical.

All this material has yet to be examined in respect of each clan as an organic whole formed over many generations in order to find the original nucleus around which the cumulation took place, for both nucleus and accretions have an historical basis. Had we been examining any one dynastic tradition in detail we should have had to probe into it more carefully, but since it relates mainly to the pre-Islamic phase it has been utilized little in this primarily phenomenological study, and then mainly where there is corroborative evidence, which generally means where it can be related to relevant events in history known from written Arabic sources. But it is easier to make use of this material in dealing with the influence of Islam than in parts of Africa where Islam has not penetrated.

Written tradition is rare for African history and is due solely to the influence of Islam which introduced a new category of archivists, the 'lettered'. Their work is of value only for the Sudan. The word *ta'rīkh* came into use through Moorish Arabic where it is employed for 'family genealogical history', and is so used in the Sahil and Sahara, all Moorish-Arab tribes having family records passing down the male line. The word is used by extension for any cumulative compilation. Two types of *ta'rīkh* are found. One of the functions of *qāḍī's* clerks was to produce regular *ta'rīkhs* which comprised, besides such things as inheritance inventories, commercial documents, deeds of manumission, formations of *ḥubus*, also lists of holders of offices. The anonymous *Tadhkirat an-Nisyān*[1] is a derivative of this kind of compilation, an alphabetical inventory of the various pashas, *almāmis*, and *qāḍīs* of Timbuktu-Jenne from 1590 to 1750, a collection of the notes of three or four generations of Songhay clerks.[2] The *Kitāb al-Fattāsh*[3] is of a different type. This is a chronological history of the Askiya dynasty of Songhay which incorporates legends and notes about earlier dynasties and ends in the year 1599, shortly after the Moroccan conquest. It is the work of three generations of the family of Maḥmūd al-Kāti (b. 1468) who began it in 1519 and whose grandson, Ibn al-Mukhtār, completed it about 1665. The *Ta'rīkh as-Sūdān*[4] by 'Abd ar-Raḥmān as-Sa'dī, completed in 1655, also incorporated early traditions and was in many sections drawn from earlier writers of whom Aḥmad Bābā (d. 1627)[5] was the most famous. Books of this type were arranged according to subject matter and to some extent chronologically as a series of disconnected facts, a succession of rulers, wars, dynastic intrigues, and rebellions; and, being modelled upon the few Islamic chronicles which filtered into the Sudan, show all the defects of their models; indiscriminate incorporation of legends and traditions, eulogies of the reigning dynasties and denigration of their enemies, and taste for biographies and obituaries of the *'ulamā'* class to which the compilers belonged.

Although portraying mainly one facet of the life of their age, the records of these African Muslim chroniclers, like as-Sa'dī and Maḥmūd al-Kāti, and the records of the Bornu and Hausa states, are invaluable; as are poems relating to historical events such as the *qaṣīda* in Pulār on the life of al-ḥājj 'Umar,[6] and local legends collected in the main by French and British administrators or written in Arabic by local clerics.[7] Although a large part of the history recorded in local chronicles consists

[1] *P.E.L.O.V.*, série iv, vols. xix and xx. These volumes also include the text and translation of al-ḥājj Sa'īd's *Ta'rīkh Sokoto*, biographies of the first three successors of 'Uthmān dan Fodio.

[2] See P. Marty, *Soudan*, ii. 281–2.

[3] *P.E.L.O.V.*, série v, vols. ix and x.

[4] *P.E.L.O.V.*, série iv, vols. xii and xiii.

[5] Author of *Takmilat ad-Dībāj* (or *Nail al-ibtihāj*) and *Kifāyat al-Muḥtāj*, two works supplementing the *Dībāj* of Ibn Farḥūn, and other works (see *G.A.L.* Suppl. ii. 715–16 and *E.I.*² i. 279–80).

[6] Muḥammad 'Alī Tyam, *La Vie d'El Hadj Omar*, ed. and transl. by H. Gaden, Trav. et Mém. de l'Institut d'Ethnologie, vol. xxi, 1935.

[7] For example: *Chroniques du Foûta Sénégalais*, transl. H. Gaden and M. Delafosse, 1913, and 'Traditions historiques et légendaires du Soudan Occidental', transl. M. Delafosse, *Afr. Fr. R.C.* 1913, pp. 293–306, 325–9, 355–68.

of sterile ruler lists, dynastic *coups-d'état*, and local wars, in the midst of them are found illuminating sidelights.

Wars of conquest and dynastic upheavals have caused the destruction of historical documents. The Fulbe conquerors of the Hausa states are said to have destroyed all the Hausa chronicles they could find, but it is doubtful if many existed except in the memories of professional traditionists. The Kano Chronicle[1] is an important survival, but little survived with the Zaria exiled dynasty in Abuja except a mere ruler list. ʿUmar, son of al-Kānemī, is also said to have burned the royal chronicles of Bornu. Whether this is true or not, those which survive are mainly fragments or reconstructions from memory, though these are important. North African sources throw light on the relations of dynasties, like the Saʿdians of Morocco, with Sudan states, but most of this is peripheral and not intrinsic towards understanding Sudan history.

For the nineteenth century collections of manuscript books and fragments are found in various European libraries, notably the Bibliothèque Nationale of Paris,[2] whilst collections are now being formed in Africa, at the Institut Français de l'Afrique Noir at Dakar and Ibadan University College.[3] This material, which is of considerable value for the detailed study of the *jihāds* of the religious adventurers of the last century, has yet to be edited and examined critically. A few have been published in uncritical editions like Muḥammad Belo's *Infāq al-Maisūr* (London, 1951). A. Brass's study of ʿAbd Allāh dan Fodio's *Tazyīn al-Waraqāt*[4] stands almost alone. These documents can be correlated with Hausa and Fulfulde traditions written down during the present century.

In addition, there are the records of skilled observers, of which the most valuable is that of Dr. Heinrich Barth (travelled 1850–4) whose work provided a basis for later historical studies. Many travellers' records are of negligible value owing to their short stay, ignorance of languages, and surface impressions, yet something may generally be gleaned from their works. Later works also have to be used with caution for they were affected by the writers' attitude toward 'ignorant

[1] *Ta'rīkh arbāb hadhā 'l-balad al-musammā Kanū*, transl. H. R. Palmer, *J.R.A.I.* xxxviii. 58 ff., and *Sudanese Memoirs*, iii (1928), 92–132. M. Hiskett (see 'Kano Chronicle', *J.R.A.S.* 1957, pp. 79–81) is preparing an edition based on manuscripts found in Nigeria.

[2] Notices on the West African manuscripts at the Bibliothèque Nationale are given in G. Vajda, 'Contribution à la connaissance de la littérature arabe en Afrique Occidentale', *J. Soc. Afr.* xx (1950), 229–37.

[3] See W. E. N. Kensdale, *Catalogue of Arabic Manuscripts preserved in the University Library, Ibadan*, fasc. i, 1955, fasc. ii, 1956; *J.R.A.S.* 1955, pp. 162–8; 1956, pp. 78–80; 1958, pp. 53–57.

[4] *D. Is.* x (1920), 1–73.

savages', by their contempt for and deprecation of local institutions and modes of expression, by the attitude of the 'official mind', by concentration upon political events which often passed over the lives of the cultivators, by stress on cities and consequently on surface Islam, the religion of cities.

Something should be said about plan, principles, and limitations. This study does not pretend to be more than it actually is, an attempt to utilize available materials in order to present the historical background of those Sudan regions which felt the impact of Islam. It is therefore a history, if it is not too great a licence so to style it, written from a particular point of view: an attempt to see in what way Islam has moulded the history of the Sudan.

The difficulties involved in writing a history of such a vast region are obvious. No dominant continuous political entity exists to give coherence and unity to the whole. The Sudan divides into two regions, western and central, each having its own underlying unity, whose history is not closely linked. The Guinea states in the south lie outside our sphere since they were not in contact with the Sudan states and were uninfluenced by Islam. In western Sudan the history tends to revolve around Māli and after its fall the innumerable Mande successor states. The indefinable, amorphous existence of Māli extended to the shores of the Atlantic where the Portuguese met chiefs who acknowledged it, although it is unlikely that those on the periphery paid tribute. Songhay, a large empire for but a short period, lies in an intermediate zone, more linked politically with the west and but slightly influencing the centre. In the central Sudan were a large number of small states of which that of Kanem-Bornu was the most influential, comparable in continuity, though not in stability, with that of the more unified pagan Mossi states of Upper Volta region.

Apart from the lack, meagreness, or unreliability of original sources, inequalities in the material pose problems. For certain periods (e.g. nineteenth century), states (the *askiya* dynasty of Songhay), towns (Timbuktu), or events (Moroccan conquest of Songhay), the material is more copious than for others where it may be lacking altogether. Great hiatuses exist in every period, including the nineteenth century, for there are many obscurities in the histories of adventurers like al-ḥājj 'Umar and the states they founded. These dynastic and regional histories have yet to be written. Selection rather than detail has often been necessary, though some disproportion of treatment has been unavoidable. The problem this raises is that statements are often made which are highly hypothetical, since they are based on insufficient evidence or individual interpretation. The difficulties do not end there, for historical movements have to be presented within a background of political and social institutions alien to Western readers and designated by Western terminology calling up different associations. In order to avoid the unbalanced view, it is necessary for the historian of Africa to have some acquaintance with related fields of study, especially cultural anthropology, in view of the help they provide towards understanding institutions in the past. This raises the question of *Geistesgeschichte* which cannot be clarified without considering material included in *Islam in West Africa*. Only as we see how Islam spreads and moulds the lives of Africans today can we see how this has been accomplished in the past. The two books are therefore complementary, and, had the history alone been attempted, material included in the other study would have been incorporated in order to show the influence of Islam upon social and cultural as well as political life. At the same time, whilst the great fact in the history of West Africa before the age of European penetration is the propagation of Islam, it is necessary, in view of the Islamic nature of the sources, to guard against giving it an influence disproportionate to the actual facts.

These considerations present a problem in organization and planning. It is obvious that the Sudan is not yet ripe for the historian and the result is not a history but a kind of historical compendium, having the characteristics of a mosaic built up into some form of coherent sequence. It will be clear that the attempt to harmonize such varied material from which pieces are missing without leaving too many gaps may have led to the formation of new patterns bearing little relationship to the original. The story of human life influenced by Islam as reconstructed in the following pages must be read with the greatest scepticism, or, at least, discretion and reserve.

2. SAHARA AND SUDAN BEFORE THE COMING OF ISLAM

Some reference to prehistory seems to be unavoidable and the material in this section is compiled from a relatively limited reading of scattered articles on the subject.[1] What appears most clearly is the fragmentary, incomplete, and confusing nature of the evidence. This is natural since the study of West African prehistory is still in its infancy.

[1] A summary of the prehistory of West Africa upon which I have drawn is given by Raymond Mauny in *L'Encyclopédie Coloniale: A.O.F.* 1949, i. 23–34, with a full bibliography up to that date.

Primary questions relating to changes in hydrography and climate are still the subject of controversy. Changes in techniques and the areas they covered are not well known. Few stratified deposits giving successive layers of occupation have yet been excavated, consequently the chronology of the techniques, being based on concordances with other regions, is largely conjectural. The material, therefore, gives the impression of a patchwork of scraps from which a related view of the whole is not yet possible.

The Sahara, now so arid and repellent, was formerly inhabited and carried rich and varied forms of life. Rivers once flowed from the massifs of Adrar, Ahaggar, Air, and Tibesti, forming extensive but shallow lakes around which the greatest concentrations of population were formed. Its fauna and flora included species which are now peculiar to tropical regions. In the Tihodain and Admer ergs[1] the bones of hippopotami, elephants, zebra, and buffalo have been discovered, whilst Neolithic man produced many pictographs depicting these animals. The only fossil man that has been thoroughly studied shows strong negroid characteristics and seems to belong to the early Neolithic period.[2]

Climate more than anything else has shaped the geographical aspect of the Sahara and consequently the occupancy of man, but account must also be taken of orographic movements which have raised or depressed the land. In Neolithic times the rivers of the Sahara flowed either into the Atlantic or depressions of which the Chad, one of four in the Libyan desert, is the last survivor. Considerable hydrographic change has taken place within relatively recent times as is shown by the dead beds of rivers and lakes. These changes were more significant in the southern Sahara (regions of Tawāt, Tishīt, Niger, and Chad), and the buckle form which the Niger and Senegal have taken is supposed to be due to 'captures'.

Although Neolithic man knew a different Sahara from that of the present day its favourable character should not be overestimated. It had a humid winter season when the valleys ran with water and filled the shallow lakes, followed by a dry summer season. Yet large areas were suitable for human habitation and since then it has progressively deteriorated although there is no evidence of any great climatic change.

[1] Ar. *'irq*, shifting dune masses.

[2] It was discovered by Besnard and Monod at Asselar in the valley of Tilemsi, 220 miles north-east of Timbuktu, and has been studied by M. Boule and H. Vallois, *L'Homme fossile d'Asselar*, Paris, 1932.

The continued desiccation that has taken place in the southern Sahara during the last three thousand years is accounted for by historical as much as climatic reasons: Berber pressure upon cultivators, ruinous methods of clearing land by fire, the ravages of goats, as well as the migration of cultivators in consequence of successive dry seasons.

Prehistorians tell us something about the succession of techniques, though their information is still vague since so few superimposed industries have been found and this implies a lack of continuously inhabited places. Little Paleolithic material earlier than what corresponds to the Acheulian has been found, but this technique is abundant in western and central Sahara, especially in the massifs of Mauritanian Adrār, Tibesti, Borku, and Ennedi. Elsewhere it is more dispersed and south of the Sahara has been found only at Dakar, in the Pita region of French Guinea, in the plateau region of Northern Nigeria, and a few other places. Within the fourth pluvial period an industry corresponding to the Mousterian but more complex has been found in the Dakar region, middle Senegal, Nema, and Mauritanian Adrār. The region south of the Sahara seems to have passed directly from this stage to the Neolithic, but the Sahara provides a number of techniques. One is similar to the Aterian culture widespread in North Africa and found *in situ* to the south of Tebessa. In the southern Sahara it has been found in Mauritanian Awkār, at In Jawak north-east of Gao, and other places. This Upper Paleolithic period, of relatively short duration (25000–12000 B.C.), was one of extreme aridity when man could occupy few parts of the Sahara. There is no discernible connexion between these people and their successors, but a Mesolithic industry appears to have marked the end of the Paleolithic (12000–7000 B.C.), though little is known about this stage.

Neolithic civilization, beginning about 7000 B.C. and characterized by the existence of settled agricultural societies, was widespread both in the tropical zone and in the Sahara, especially in the plains and around the great shallow lakes and river valleys. From the early Neolithic period derive many pictographs showing a Sudanese fauna. At a later period oxen make their appearance. Cattle are thought to have been introduced into Africa between the fifth and fourth millennium B.C. and it was during the period when the desiccation of the Sahara was becoming more pronounced that man, finding it increasingly difficult to live by fishing, hunting, and agriculture alone, became a stockbreeder. The nature of the land rendered the simultaneous cultivation of crops and the tending of herds impossible and pastoralism became the specialized occupation of distinct groups of whites and blacks. Thus appeared the division between pastoralists and cultivators characteristic of all subsequent history.

West Africa in Neolithic times has been divided into three bands. The first embraced western and part of central Sahara. Then came a transitional band corresponding to the Sahil of today but very much wider, stretching from 21° N. to 17° N. This was peopled by Negro cultivators, pastoralists, and hunters. After that came the tropical and sub-tropical zone. The majority of Neolithic deposits discovered have been in the Saharan and Sahilian zones where they are found in vast masses. There are a number of different techniques, one basically in the Capsian tradition is blended with Nilotic importations, and there seems to have been a steady stream of migrant fishers and cultivators from the Nile valley. The material discovered in the Sahara shows two main culture complexes, a nomadic herdsmen culture and an agricultural culture which presumably did not develop in entire independence. The first may be that of proto-Berbers and Zaghāwa primarily occupied with cattle-breeding, whilst the oases and more humid valleys were inhabited by sedentary Negro cultivators as is shown by the heavy implements, such as polished globular axes, fixed mortars for grinding corn, pestles and grinders or pounders, which have been discovered. It is clear that there were a number of different races. The occurrence of fine points in both the southern Sahara and northern Mauritania is not due to northern hunters descending south,[1] whilst a particular type distinct from any known whites and blacks occupied the country east of the Chad at this epoch.[2] The confusion of Saharan prehistory is due to the fact that a characteristic of its life has been the simultaneous co-existence, but not fusion, of peoples of different ethnic, linguistic, and cultural characteristics, and following specialized occupations, over which those with nomadic antecedents gained predominance.

The end of the Neolithic period is difficult to determine. It lasted longer in the tropical zone, especially in the forest country whose people lived in small isolated groups and had no relations with the north, whereas the Sahara and Sahil were open to radiations from other civilizations. Copper and bronze were little used and the material found cannot be dated, consequently West Africa viewed as a region is

[1] See P. Laforgue and F. Saucin, 'Nouvelles recherches sur les objets anciens de l'Aouker', *Bull. Com. Ét. A.O.F.* 1923, pp. 111–12.

[2] See H. Gaden and R. Verneau, 'Stations et sépultures néolithiques du Territoire militaire du Tchad', *L'Anthropologie*, xxx (1920), 513–43.

regarded as having passed directly from the Stone into the Iron Age without any defined intermediary bronze period.[1] Gold was the first metal known, but could not be utilized except for ornaments and as a means of exchange, in which connexion Herodotus (450 B.C.) speaks of the Carthaginians trading for it on the Atlantic shores. In the Sahara iron came into use between the establishment of the Phoenicians in North Africa (1100 B.C.) and the Carthaginian expansion. The Garamantes, who appear to be a Negroid-Hamitic nomadic people extending from Fezzān to Nubia with permanent settlements, made use of iron, for war carts in the Mycenaean tradition appear on pictographs, whilst Herodotus stated that 'the Garamantes hunt the cave-dwelling Ethiopians with four-horse cars'.[2] Iron is found in parts of West Africa as surface ore in an easily workable form and the technique was no doubt spreading as a specialized caste occupation from about the third century B.C. Stone naturally went on being used by some people until recent times owing to the rarity of iron, but that does not mean that the technique for working it survived. Pottery and megaliths[3] in advance of the existing Negro work of the localities where they were found point to former higher cultures, but probably do not go back to this period. The very interesting Nok culture which covered a wide area of the Niger-Benue valley and was distinguished by exceptionally fine terracotta figurines is thought to have lasted from 900 B.C. to A.D. 200.[4] These people had a knowledge of iron smelting though the tradition does not appear to have been long established.

[1] The introduction of the bronze technique seems to be later than that of iron though the copper mines of Akjouit were being exploited about this time and western Mauritania has provided examples of bronze arms (see R. Mauny, 'Un âge du cuivre au Sahara occidental', *Bull. I.F.A.N.* 1951, pp. 168–80). Weapons of copper and iron have been found in tumuli near Lotokoro and Gao along with stone implements (M. Desplagnes, *Le Plateau central Nigérien*, 1907, pls. xvii–xviii). On the So bronzes see Lebeuf and Masson Detourbet, *La Civilisation du Tchad*, 1950, pp. 176–80.

[2] Herodotus, iv. 183. R. Mauny has traced the pictographs to show that the desert was traversed by cars in two distinct zones: a western route from Morocco to Goundam by Zemmour and Mauritanian Adrār, and a central route from Syrtes to Gao by Fezzān, Ajjer, Ahaggar, and the Iforas. The *terminus a quo* for the use of war chariots is the invasion of the Peoples of the Sea (Rameses III, *c.* 1170), and the *terminus ad quem* the elimination of war chariots by cavalry in the fourth century B.C. The horse practically disappeared from the Sahara after the diffusion of the camel and St. Augustine refers to the kings of the Garamantes using bulls for their conveyance (*Op.* ed. Bassan, xvi. 526). It was reintroduced by the Arabs of the eleventh-century invasion.

[3] For example, the megalithic structures of Sin-Salum, Portuguese Guinea, Gambia, Zirt al-'Aish, and Niafunke region north of Masina. Artificial subterranean grottoes are reported from a number of places.

[4] See Reports of the Antiquities Service of Nigeria from 1952 to 1955, Lagos, 1955–6.

Rock pictures from this Libyco-Berber period differentiate three main Saharan groups corresponding to the Moors, Tuareg, and Teda of today. In western Sahara the pictures show figures armed with a spear and javelin and sometimes a round shield. In central Sahara, often associated with the Libyco-Berber script, are pictures of men wearing feathers on their heads and carrying a shield, sword, javelins, and sometimes a dagger suspended from the forearm. Both groups employed the horse. Also in the central Sahara are men armed with a long lance tipped by a broad metal point. In addition there appear to have been still other Negro groups as well as refugee groups belonging to other types of civilization. The Phoenicians introduced North Africans to the technique of arboriculture and this penetrated into Saharan oases but not into the Sudan. The traditions of present-day west Saharan Moors and of Sahilian Negroes recall the existence of a distinct cultural group, referred to as Bafūr, versed in the art of cultivating palms and constructing irrigation works, living alongside Negroes on an armed-peace footing. Upon these Berbers gradually imposed their hegemony. Negroes, mingling with proto-Berbers or Fulbe, formed new groups, among them the Wangāra (Soninke). Serer and Wolof, now living on the Atlantic coast of Senegal, formerly inhabited Mauritanian Adrār, where numerous ruins and pottery fragments show similar ornamentation to their present-day pottery.

In antiquity the Sudan provided Mediterranean lands with a certain amount of gold and slaves and in exchange received cloth, copper, and tools, though this traffic could not have been of great importance. Frequent rock pictures depicting oxen wearing a pack saddle show that they were employed in this traffic. The Phoenicians, active in North Africa from about the eleventh century B.C., were in direct touch with Negro peoples,[1] as were Cyrenians and Egyptians by Saharan and Nile routes. The trans-Saharan traffic, however, fell off considerably during the Roman occupation of North Africa when Leptis Magna in the Province of Libya took the place of Carthage (ruined 146 B.C.) as its main centre. Direct Egyptian, Punic, and Roman influences have been exaggerated. They were very fugitive, though peoples influenced by the derived Egyptian culture of the Nubians undoubtedly transmitted elements in the course of the continual westward migrations. It is

[1] Pliny's River Niger 'which separates Africa from Ethiopia' and upon which the Gaetuli border, was presumably a river in southern Morocco where lived the Melanogetules, Black Getules, Negroes dominated by whites (Ptolemy, iv. 6. 5).

necessary to avoid the fallacy of seeking to establish specific connexions with particular civilizations because they possess similar institutions such as ritual king-killing. Similarities do not necessarily mean direct borrowing, but more likely that both had a common source or were derived through the untraceable process of culture diffusion, passed on, diminuendo, by relays. It is obvious that Carthaginian commercial links led to the introduction of products of Mediterranean civilization such as beads, textiles, and copper goods, but this rarely led to change in material civilization since new techniques were not adopted. This fact accounts for many inexplicable cultural and historical reversals. If, for example, only one family owns the technique of iron, its elimination through disease or famine will deprive the whole group of its weapons. Two richer, more diversified, post-Neolithic civilizations formed through the interaction of many currents were that based on Garama in the Fezzān region and another in the south Sahil in the region where the state of Gāna appeared. But in general West Africa acted like a vast cul-de-sac, receiving, diluting, and finally assimilating or sterilizing foreign elements, and in this extraordinary culture complex it is not yet possible to disentangle the various strands in any satisfactory way.

Judaic and Christian influences are equally tenuous and unidentifiable. Jews established important colonies in North Africa and their religion even penetrated among Berbers, many tribes having sections which, without abandoning pagan beliefs, professed Judaism or Christianity. Some were agriculturalists in established *qṣūrs*,[1] and there are many references to Jewish communities in Saharan oases from the time of Eldad the Danite (A.D. 860–80) to the thriving community in the oasis of Tamentit described by Antonio Malfante in 1447,[2] which was eliminated through the activities of al-Majhīlī. Some settled in the Sudan and were absorbed.[3] Jewish influence in the Sahara and Sahil seems indisputable, but it does not precede the Christian era and cultural elements were so absorbed into local cultures that they cannot

[1] See Ibn Khaldūn, *K. al-'Ibar*, iv. 12–13.

[2] See the letter of Antonio Malfante in C. de la Roncière, *La Découverte de l'Afrique au Moyen-Âge*, Cairo 1922, i. 143–58. According to Ibn Khaldūn Tamantit was the most easterly of the *qṣūr* of Tawāt. Funerary inscriptions attest to the former existence of these communities. Other references to Jews in the Sahara, including some from Hebrew sources, are given by M. N. Slouschz, 'Un voyage d'études juives en Afrique', *Mém. Acad. des Inscriptions et Belles-Lettres*, xii (1913), 481–565.

[3] Maḥmūd al-Kāti describes (*T. al-Fattāsh*, pp. 62–63/119–20) a visit he paid to the ruins of an ancient Jewish town in the Tendirma region (Ra's al-Mā') which had been abandoned about A.D. 1500.

be isolated. Christianity never spread into western Sudan. Radiations penetrated Saharan Berbers and Blacks through political and commercial influence both from the north and from Nubia, but they were of no importance in the evolution of their cultures.[1]

Towards the end of the Roman period occurs an event which completely transformed the life of North Africa and the Sahara. This was the arrival of the camel. Although these animals were imported into Egypt with the Persian conquest of 525 B.C. they were long in making their appearance in North Africa and were only becoming numerous in the fourth century A.D. Their introduction enabled the formation of those great turbulent warrior Berber tribes with an immense range of activity who transformed the whole of Saharan life.

By the time Islam made its first inroads, the characteristic cultural groupings of the Sudan belt were already clearly differentiated. These were, proceeding from west to east: Senegalese (Serer-Tokolor), Soninke-Manding, Mossi-Gurma, Songhay, Nupe, Hausa, Kanem, and the Waday–Bagirmi–Darfur region. All present clear differences, having evolved separately and under different influences. Some were orientated towards Morocco, Tripoli, Egypt, or the Nilotic Sudan, whilst others in the south developed with a minimum of external contacts. The geographical isolation of West Africa is not, therefore, an historical isolation. Yet it was a real isolation in spite of continuous connexions with North Africa and Nilotic regions, and rarely did outside influences until the arrival of Islam result in radically new points of departure.

[1] Since Christianity gained so slight a hold upon northern Berbers we can scarcely expect it to have influenced Berber and Negro tribes in the Sahara and Sudan. M. ibn Abī Bakr az-Zuhrī (A.D. 1137) mentions Sudanese Berbers, that is Ṣanhāja of the Adrār and Ḥawḍ, islamized by the Murābiṭūn as once Christian (*Not. et Extr. de la Bibl. Nat.* xii. 642), but Ibn Khaldūn states specifically, 'This people was pagan and never adopted Christianity' (*Berbères*, tr. de Slane, i. 212). The Garamantes of Fezzān accepted Christianity as a political measure linking them with Byzantine authority in A.D. 569 (see *Chronica Joannis abbatis monasterii Biclarensis*, ed. Th. Mommsen, p. 212), as did a neighbouring people, the Maccurritae. From Fezzān, then far more fertile than now and traversed by important caravan routes, and from Nilotic Sudan where it had been adopted as the state religion of Makoria and Alodia (see my *Islam in the Sudan*), Christianity may have penetrated similar peoples in Borku for Ibn Saʿīd writes that, 'the part of Berkāmi [in Kawār, north of Lake Chad] which touches the Nubians, professes Christianity' (*Géogr. d'Aboulfèda*, ii. 218–19).

Through Berber tribes in western Sahara a few Christian terms were absorbed into Sudanese languages. For instance, in Wolof the word *tabaski dya* is a borrowing from Tuareg *Afasko* or *Tafisko*, 'spring', which in turn came from πάσχα; Wolof *bakar*, 'fault', through Tuareg *abekkaḍ*, 'sin', from Latin *peccatum*. The possession of Christian terms and symbols does not prove that they ever were Christian, merely that they absorbed foreign elements.

3. THE ISLAMIZATION OF THE BERBERS

The Berbers of the mountains and plains of North Africa and the Sahara were divided into three ethnic groups, Lowāta, Ṣanhāja, and Zanāta, each subdivided into vast numbers of smaller groups.[1] The majority had remained independent and little influenced by the civilizations which flourished along the shores of the Mediterranean, and the Arab conquest did not for some time change the situation.

As soon as they had conquered Syria the Muslim Arabs invaded Egypt where they were welcomed and in full control by A.D. 642. With Egypt as a base they began to extend their conquest westwards. Although accounts of the conquest of North Africa are confusing and unreliable in their details the general outlines, which alone we need to indicate, are clear.[2] In A.H. 27 the Caliph ʿUthmān authorized an expedition into Ifrīqiya under ʿAbd Allāh b. Saʿd who concluded a treaty with the Byzantine authority in 35 (656) in return for a heavy tribute. When Muʿāwiya came to power he sent ʿUqba ibn Nāfiʿ to undertake the serious conquest of North Africa. During his first period (A.H. 41–51), when he conquered Ifrīqiya and founded Qairawān, ʿUqba also took Ghadāmes and certain districts of Negroes (A.H. 42–43), presumably in the Fezzān region,[3] but clearly there was no permanent conquest of any part of the interior.[4] In his second period (A.H. 60–63) as *wālī* of Ifrīqiya ʿUqba's raids extended

[1] See the long list given by Ibn Ḥawqal, op. cit. i. 104 ff.

[2] R. Brunschvig has examined the 'historical' traditions collected by Ibn ʿAbd al-Ḥakam regarding the conquest of North Africa and has come to the conclusion that only the simple outlines represent authentic recollection. See R. Brunschvig, 'Ibn ʿAbdalh'akam et la conquête de l'Afrique du Nord par les Arabes', *Annales de l'Institut d'Études Orientales*, Algiers, vi (1942–7), 108–55. See also the important account of ʿUbaid Allāh b. Ṣāliḥ, translated and commented by E. Lévi-Provençal, 'Un nouveau récit de la conquête de l'Afrique du Nord par les Arabes', *Arabica*, i (1954), 17–43.

[3] See E. Lévi-Provençal, loc. cit., p. 38. Cf. the account of Ibn ʿAbd al-Ḥakam who mentions a campaign against the oases of Waddān, Fezzān, and Kawwār in the year 46/666–7; *Futūḥ Miṣr*, ed. C. C. Torrey, 1922, pp. 194–6.

[4] R. Brunschvig (loc. cit., pp. 120–2) calls attention to a previously unnoticed passage in Saḥnūn's *al-Mudawwana* (ed. Cairo, 1324–5/1906–7, i. 406), which bears on this question: 'They questioned Mālik concerning the Fezzānīs (*al-Fazāzina*) who are a race of Ethiopians (*jinsun min al-Ḥabasha*). He replied, "I am not of the opinion that one should fight them before having invited them to embrace Islam. . . . If they do not accept, one should invite them to pay the *jizya*, at the same time keeping to their religion; if they respond favourably one should accept it of them." That shows you the opinion of Mālik as regards no matter what people, because what he says of the Fezzānīs applies equally to the Slavs, Avars, Turks, and other non-Arabs who are not People of the Book.' This suggests that the conquest and islamization of Fezzān took place during the lifetime of Mālik in the second half of the eighth century under the early ʿAbbāsids, and not by ʿUqba who was just a raider.

to Morocco, but when on his return journey he was killed in a fight with the Berber chief Kasīla (68/682–3) the invasion collapsed and the Arabs had to evacuate most of the country. The Caliph ʿAbd al-Malik b. Marwān was determined to include North Africa within the sphere of the Arab empire and after two failures, the second associated with the Berber queen known to the Arabs as the *kāhina*, it was conquered by Ḥassān b. an-Nuʿmān between A.H. 82 and 90 (701–8) and effective resistance crushed in all accessible territory.

The conversion of the North African Christians of the towns and the mainly pagan Berbers of the hills and plains was the work of the second century of the *hijra*. The North African Church died rather than was eliminated by Islam, since it had never rooted itself in the life of the country. Although considerations such as the prestige Islam derived from its position as the religion of the ruling minority and the special taxation imposed on Christians encouraged change, the primary reasons for their rapid conversion were the less obvious ones deriving from weaknesses within the Christian communities. Among these were Christianity's failure to claim the Berber soul and its bitter sectarian divisions. The organized life of the Church disintegrated and could not hold its adherents against the stimulating effect of the new and vigorous Islam.

The conversion of the pagan Berbers was a slow process and they reacted against Arab feelings of racial superiority. From the beginning the Arab leaders recruited Berbers into their armies where they became Muslims simply by contagion and association. They formed the main body of the armies which, under Arab leaders, succeeded in subduing the Maghrib and later conquered Spain. Friction, however, arose between Arab and Berber whom the Arabs treated as inferiors. The ideas of the Khawārij, revolutionary schismatics like the Donatists, quickly won the allegiance of many Berbers and they inflicted such heavy defeats upon the Arabs that the authority of the *khalīfa* was eclipsed in North Africa. Internal divisions and incessant tribal rivalries so weakened the Berbers that the Arabs, after years of struggles, were able to reassert their rule over eastern but not western Maghrib; and for the Arab world, as for the Carthaginians and Romans, Morocco remained 'The Far West' (*al-Maghrib al-Aqṣā'*), independent except for the period between the conquest of Mūsā ibn Nuṣair (nominated *c.* 708) and the revolt of the Khārijite Maisāra in 739–40. Middle Maghrib became independent at the beginning of the ʿAbbāsid régime, but the Khawārij of eastern Maghrib after years of struggles were brought under control by Yazīd ibn Ḥātim (governor 772–87). All over the country new states under Arab or Berber chiefs rose and fell rapidly.

The Arab immigrants urbanized and married local women but had little influence upon the Berbers in general. Islam did not really begin to win them until it assumed the form of national movements and it was Berber opposition to the Arabs which assured the triumph of the Khārijite and Shī'ite reactions. Shī'ite ideas were propagated in A.H. 280 (A.D. 893) by the *dā'ī* Abū 'Abd Allāh ash-Shī'ī and were used by the Ketāma in a successful movement against the Arab governor which established (A.D. 910) the Fāṭimid rule of the *mahdī* 'Ubaid Allāh over a large part of Maghrib. After Abū Tamīm Ma'add al-Mu'izz extended Fāṭimid rule over Egypt in A.D. 969, leaving the Ṣanhājī, Bologgīn ibn Zīrī, in control of his North African states, the Berbers reintensified their internal struggles.

Ibn Khaldūn sums up the effect of the Arabs upon Berber life:

> After the formation of the Islamic community the Arabs burst out to propagate their religion among other nations. Their armies penetrated into the Maghrib and captured all its cantonments and cities. They endured a great deal in their struggles with the Berbers who, as Ibn Abī Yazīd has told us, apostatized twelve times before Islam gained a firm hold over them. These Arabs did not establish themselves in these parts as tent-dwellers nor as nomadic tribes because the need to maintain their authority did not allow them to occupy the open country but restricted them to the towns and cantonments. For this reason, we have said, the Arabs did not settle in the Maghrib and it was only in the middle of the fifth century [eleventh century A.D.] that they migrated in order to colonize it and disperse themselves in tribes and sections.[1]

A great revolution took place in the whole life of North Africa and the western Sahara from the middle of the eleventh century when Arabs of the Banū Hilāl and Sulaim were unleashed upon the country, but at the period when their migrations were beginning a measure of stability was achieved under the successive dynasties of the Murābiṭūn (Almoravids, 1056–1147) and the Muwaḥḥidūn (Almohads, 1130–1269) who went to the opposite extreme to Shī'ism and asserted their political consciousness through the medium of a reformist orthodoxy. The Murābiṭūn were responsible for the first definite attempt to extend Islam into the Sudan.

The legendary cause of the Hilālian invasion was that in A.D. 1045 al-Mu'izz ibn Bādīs, governor of Ifrīqiya, renounced Shī'ism and later

[1] Ibn Khaldūn, *Histoire des Berbères*, ed. de Slane, Algiers, 1847, i. 15–16.

proclaimed himself independent. The Fāṭimid *khalīfa*, al-Mustanṣir, having no means for enforcing his authority sent a message to the Banū Hilāl, then making a nuisance of themselves in Upper Egypt, stating, 'I make you a gift of the Maghrib and the rule of al-Muʿizz ibn Bādīs, the Ṣanhājī, the runaway slave. No longer will you be in want.'[1] Ibn Khaldūn writes of the effect of this invasion:

> After the Banū Hilāl and Banū Sulaim descended upon Ifrīqiya and the Maghrib from the beginning of the fifth century three hundred and fifty years of struggle ensued during which the countryside fell into utter ruin; whereas formerly the whole region between the Sudan and the Mediterranean had been well populated, as the remains of civilization, the debris of monuments and buildings, the ruins of villages and towns, bear witness.[2]

This great Arab invasion was the most far-reaching event in the history of Islamic North Africa. It led to the spreading of Arabs all over the country, their definite establishment side by side with the Berbers, and their coalescing with them, a process which took three centuries to complete. The Banū Sulaim stayed for a time in Tripoli, but the Banū Hilāl after overrunning Tunis spread farther westward. By the middle of the twelfth century they were dispersed over half the region and within the next century the Banū Hilāl pressed by the Banū Sulaim had reached the Atlantic.

These Arab tribes remained nomads. They had nothing in common with the Arabs of the first invasion who had settled in towns as the ruling aristocracy. They arrived as colonizers, in families, with their wives, children, and slaves, and spoke a distinct dialect of Arabic. They founded no states and their history belongs to the maze of Berber history. Their invasion caused a great dislocation and regrouping of peoples. Many Berber tribes withdrew from the plains to the Mauritanian uplands, others moved into the Sahara. The Berber language persists in groups in the Atlas uplands and especially among Tuareg in central Sahara, but in western Sahara the majority adopted the Arab language and institutions. During the twelfth and thirteenth centuries the Moors of Mauritania and Ḥawḍ were arabized and during the

[1] Ibn Khaldūn, *Berbères*, i. 18; transl. i. 33. Economic pressures lay behind this invasion for the real cause of the migration of the Banū Sulaim in A.H. 460 was probably the great famine in Egypt during the years 457–64 (1065–72); see al-Maqrīzī, *Mawāʿiẓ*, transl. Casanova, p. 282.

[2] Ibn Khaldūn, *Maqaddima*, Cairo ed., p. 150; transl. de Slane, i. 312; cf. pp. 66–67. This migration gave rise to the cycle of legends associated with the name of Abū Zaid al-Hilālī still current throughout North Africa and found also among the Shuwa Arabs of the Chad region.

fifteenth the Meshdūf and Berābish of Timbuktu region after the invasion of the Ḥassān, a branch of the Ma'qil, who belong to the second wave of invaders. Berbers became their subject *zanāja* and *zāwiya*, the latter so called because, being forbidden to carry arms, they found in the cultivation of Islam a compensation for their inferior status.

4. CONVERSION OF THE SAHARAN TRIBES TO ISLAM AND ITS SPREAD INTO THE SUDAN

During the half millenary of Roman control over North Africa the Sahara had proved an almost insurmountable barrier. However, the end of the Roman period saw the introduction of the camel. This was as revolutionary in its effect upon life in the Saharan sea as the discovery of the compass was upon maritime navigation. The camel gave a new mobility and an immense range of activity to the Berbers, caravan traffic developed,[1] commercial towns in the Sahil flourished, and the pressure of the lean wolves of the Sahara upon the Blacks increased. For the first time in history West Africa was in permanent contact with Mediterranean civilization. In this case it was the Islamic civilization and led to the spread of Islam in West Africa. The Arabs themselves took no part in its islamization, nomadic tribes did not arrive in North Africa until the middle of the eleventh century and were not interested in the propagation of Islam. The primary islamization of the Negroes is almost entirely the work of Berber merchants.

Over western Sahara roamed the nomadic white people known as the Ṣanhāja[2] who wore the face muffler called *lithām* by Arabs, whence their nickname *mulaththamūn*, 'muffled'. They inhabited the vast spaces of the Sahara from Mauritania to Ahaggar as far south as the Sudan, and their present-day descendants are the Moors of the west and the Tuareg of central Sahara. They were pagan and Muslim writers speak in conventional phraseology of their worship of the sun and eating of unclean flesh.[3]

These Ṣanhāja appear in the ninth century grouped into a vague

[1] 'Abd ar-Raḥmān b. Ḥabīb, independent governor of Ifrīqiya (127/745–137/755) at the end of the Umayyad and beginning of the 'Abbāsid period, had wells dug, or perhaps renovated, in western Sahara from the Jabal Bani region to Awdaghast (al-Bakrī, *Description de l'Afrique Septentrionale*, ed. de Slane, 2nd ed. 1911, pp. 156–7; transl. pp. 296–8). Elsewhere (p. 163) he says of the wells of Tezāmet in as-Sūs al-Aqṣā' at the beginning of the Gāna route, 'They are of ancient construction, although some assert that they were dug by the Umayyads.' We may take it that the route was reorganized.

[2] The Arab pronunciation of *azenūg*, pl. *idzāgen*; cf. Ibn Khaldūn, ed. de Slane, i. 194.

[3] Cf. al-Muhallabī, in Yāqūt, i. 400.

confederation consisting of the Lamtūna, Masūfa, and Godāla. Its formation may derive from their desire to control the Saharan trade-route which had at its terminals the strong states of the Zanāta in the north and Gāna in the south. The leading group were the Lamtūna who arrived in Mauritanian Adrār in the second half of the eighth century, then moved south to gain control of the caravan centre of Awdaghast.[1] In these regions lived many groups of black and white cultivators and the arrival of the nomads upset the whole western Sahara. Continually in search of pasturage they roamed over the most suitable regions occupied by Negro peoples, who either became their tribute-paying cultivators or were pushed towards the Senegal. Ibn Khaldūn preserves an echo of these struggles: 'They subdued those desert regions and waged the *jihād* against the Negro peoples who lived in them to constrain them to adopt Islam. Many complied but others elected to pay the *jizya*.'[2] Under Telāgāgīn (Tīklān) and especially his successor Tīlūtān (d. A.H. 222/A.D. 836–7)[3] they imposed their authority over both Berber and Negro groups of Mauritania, with the exception of Gāna, and it was some time before the two powers came into decisive conflict. Tīlūtān was succeeded by his grandson (?) al-Abrin b. Bulair b. Tibustan[4] (d. 287/900), but the dynasty collapsed under his son Temīn through internal troubles, the federation broke up (306/918–19), and Gāna became the dominant power, gradually

[1] Awdaghast was probably founded in the sixth century A.D. and may be identified with Tegdaost (cf. R. Mauny, *Not. Afr.*, No. 48). Ibn Ḥawqal says (i. 92) that the journey between it and Gāna took from ten to twenty days, and al-Bakrī (p. 168) confirms this when he writes that it lay some fifteen days west of Gāna in eastern Tagant. It is first mentioned by al-Ya'qūbī (*Kitāb al-Buldān*, composed A.D. 891/2, *B.G.A.* vii. 360; transl. Weit, p. 227). After describing the veiled Ṣanhāja he continues, 'Then one comes to a place called Ghasṭ, an inhabited valley in which are dwellings and a king of theirs who has neither religion nor revealed law. He raids the country of the Negroes, whose kingdoms are numerous.' Al-Muhallabī (see Yāqūt, i. 400), writing just before its conquest by Gāna, shows that it was a prosperous centre which must have been developed by skilled oasis people. He says that its people were converted to Islam by the *mahdī* 'Ubaid Allāh, first Fāṭimid caliph, 909–34. Al-Bakrī (op. cit., pp. 157–9, 168) gives an extended account of Awdaghast at the time when it was under the control of Gāna and just before it was captured by the Murābiṭūn. He also confirms that as well as being a prosperous caravan centre it was well cultivated by means of artificial irrigation. Its prosperity declined after the downfall of Gāna as is shown by the description of al-Idrīsī (p. 32/38). This provides an example of the part human beings have played in the impoverishment of the Sahara.

[2] Ibn Khaldūn, op. cit. i. 236/ii. 65; see also i. 237/ii. 67.

[3] According to Ibn Abī Zar' (*Rawḍ al-Qirṭās*, ed. Tornberg, 1839, p. 43) Tīlūtān could call upon 100,000 cameleers.

[4] According to Ibn Abī Zar' (op. cit., p. 43) he was the grandson of Tīlūtān and was called Al-Athar or Ilettan; see also Ibn Khaldūn, i. 236 (ii. 66). An alternative reading gives the date as A.H. 237/A.D. 852.

extending her rule. Between the years A.H. 350 and 360 (A.D. 961–71) the ruler of Awdaghast was a Ṣanhājī named Tīn Yarūtān whose sphere of influence had an extent of two months' journey, and to whom twenty Negro chiefs paid tribute.[1] He furnished Ta'rīn (or Ba'rīn), king of Māsīn,[2] with 50,000 camelmen to invade the Negro kingdom Awghām, whose king was defeated and killed, whereupon his women committed suicide in order to avoid falling into the hands of white men. This must refer to a conflict with Gāna or a tributary people because al-Bakrī shows elsewhere[3] that Awghām was a region just east of Gāna. However in A.D. 990 the Soninkes of Gāna, profiting by its internal troubles, captured Awdaghast.

During this century (tenth) the Ṣanhāja chiefs were converted to a nominal Islam and trading centres like Awdaghast with their large foreign population assumed the characteristics of Muslim towns. About A.D. 1020 the leaders of the Lamtūna, Godāla, and Masūfa, faced with the growing power of Gāna, again reunited for the purpose of common action. Their leader Tarsina, a Lamtūnī, may have been the first important Muslim Ṣanhāja ruler. He went on pilgrimage to Mecca, acquired the idea of a *jihād* to justify his campaigns against Negroes, but was killed fighting them (1023). At any rate he had sown the seed which was to be taken up by his successor, and son-in-law, Yaḥyā ibn Ibrāhīm, who, according to the rule by which command alternated between the two tribes, was of the Godāla. He also set off on pilgrimage with other Ṣanhājan chiefs in A.D. 1035.[4] On his return journey he asked a famous jurist of Qairawān, Abū 'Imrān Mūsā b. 'Isā (d. A.D. 1038), for a man hardy enough to come and teach his semi-pagan tribesmen the true doctrine. None of Abū 'Imrān's pupils was willing to take the risk, but he directed Yaḥyā to Wajjāj ibn Zalwī, head of a school of religion in the town of Naffīs[5] called *dār al-murābiṭīn*. Wajjāj persuaded one of his disciples called 'Abd Allāh ibn Yāsīn to go. 'Abd Allāh's mission amongst the Godāla had little success and

[1] Al-Bakrī, p. 159; transl. pp. 351–2. Ibn Ḥawqal, a first-hand authority since he visited Awdaghast in A.D. 951, calls him Tinbarūtān ibn Isfaishar, and states that his relationship with the ruler of Gāna was cordial (op. cit. i. 100).

[2] H. Barth says (*Travels*, v. 506) that the indigenous inhabitants of Shētu or Tishīt were the Māsina, a section of the Soninke Azer.

[3] Al-Bakrī, p. 180.

[4] Ibn Abī Zar', *Rawḍ al-Qirṭās*, 1839, p. 44. Ibn Khaldūn (i. 237) has 440/1048–9, which is obviously incorrect, probably derived from al-Bakrī's date (p. 164) for the launching of the *jihād*.

[5] *Rawḍ*, p. 46; at Melkūs according to Al-Bakrī (p. 175/364). At any rate in the region of Sijilmāsa (cf. Ibn Khaldūn, p. 268).

after the death of Yaḥyā they turned against him in consequence of his attempt to reform their customs. He set off towards the Sudan borderland with eight companions, including Yaḥyā ibn 'Umar and his brother Abū Bakr, who were Lamtūnīs, descendants of Telāgāgīn. The first was from the beginning leader of the party founded by 'Abd Allāh;[1] and constructed a *ribāṭ* or fortified fraternity centre[2] somewhere on the Atlantic coast of Mauritania.[3] The *ribāṭ* soon won a great reputation as a recruiting centre for a *jihād* and new followers, all Lamtūna, poured in. The subsequent history of the Murābiṭūn, as his followers came to be called, is an illustration of what militant Islam can accomplish, and in West Africa we have to wait until the nineteenth century for its repetition.

When his followers numbered a thousand 'Abd Allāh decided that the time had come to launch the *jihād*. He first directed his disciples to return to their own people as missionaries.

Go under the protection of God and warn your fellow-tribesmen, [he exhorted] teach them the Law of God and threaten them with His chastisement. If they repent and return to the truth and amend their ways, then leave

[1] Al-Bakrī, p. 364.

[2] *Ribāṭs* were fortified frontier posts whose guards were often effective propagators of Islam. Two early *ribāṭs* were those of Monastīr founded in 180/796 and Sūs founded in 206/821. Al-Ya'qūbī (A.D. 891) writes, 'From Sfax to a place called Bizerta is an eight days' journey. At every stage is a strong point, each close to the other, garrisoned by pious men and *murābiṭūn*' (*B.G.A.* vii. 350). Later these *ribāṭs* changed their character from centres for proselytization to centres of Ṣūfī teaching. Ibn Marzūq writes, 'In the terminology of the *fuqarā'*, *ribāṭ* means the act of devoting oneself to the holy war and frontier defence. Among the Ṣūfīs, on the contrary, it means, the place in which a man shuts himself up for the purpose of worship' (Ibn Marzūq, *Musnad*, ed. and transl. E. Lévi-Provençal, *Hespéris*, v, 1925). Al-'Umarī, in the middle of the fourteenth century, refers to 'the pious men who are called *murābiṭs*' (*Masālik*, p. 204).

[3] Al-Bakrī, a contemporary, does not mention the situation of this *ribāṭ*. The first mention is by Ibn Abī Zar' writing *c.* 723/1323, who, no doubt mistakenly, says the *ribāṭ* was founded by Yaḥyā b. Ibrāhīm and 'Abd Allāh with seven companions (*Rawḍ*, p. 48). He writes that it was situated on 'an island in the sea, to which at low tide one can cross on foot, but at high tide one must go by boat. It has trees of the same species as those on the mainland, together with land and sea game such as birds, animals and fish' (*Rawḍ*, p. 48). Ibn Khaldūn, however, may have been consciously correcting Ibn Abī Zar''s account when he wrote, 'They withdrew from the society of men into hills surrounded by the waters of the Nile, shallow during the summer but deep during the winter so that separate islands were formed into whose bush they went individually for their devotions' (op. cit. i. 238). The difficulty about this account is that summer is the rainy season, but the water would remain to isolate the island for part of the winter. Delafosse (*H.S.N.* ii. 34) seeks to reconcile the accounts by suggesting an island-peninsula near the mouth of the Senegal; and this is probable because Al-Bakrī writes (p. 171), 'Near Awlīl in the sea is an island called Iyūnī (Tidra?). At high water it is an island inaccessible from the shore, but at the ebb one can reach it on foot.'

them in peace; but if they refuse and persist in their errors and infidelity, let us invoke the aid of God against them and make war upon them until God decides the issue between us.[1]

Threats had no effect upon the Berbers, therefore in A.D. 1042 ʿAbd Allāh, placing Yaḥyā ibn ʿUmar at the head of his followers, threw them first against the pagan Godāla. One tribe after another was defeated and compelled to acknowledge Islam. The victories which attended this method of religious propaganda and prospect of booty quickly resolved the doubts of hesitants among the Lamtūna and the numbers of Murābiṭūn increased until they became such an effective fighting force that they could expand out of their own deserts and overwhelm established populations.

In response to the exhortations of Wajjāj, urging them to attack Sijilmāsa and the Maghrāwa, the force advanced northwards, subduing one Berber tribe after another. When the Maghrāwa of Sijilmāsa had been conquered in 446/1054–5, the Murābiṭūn turned south and took possession of Awdaghast then under the Negro kingdom of Gāna.[2] But the main body of the Murābiṭūn did not concern themselves for long about the Sudan and after the disastrous defeat and death of Yaḥyā b. ʿUmar by the Godāla at the battle of Tebferīlla in 448/1056–7,[3] ʿAbd Allāh turned towards his own country of Morocco and reduced Darʿa, Sūs, and the Maghrāwa kingdom of Aghmāt. He himself was killed in 450/1059[4] when fighting against the Berghawāṭa. Abū Bakr ibn ʿUmar, military leader since the death of his brother Yaḥyā, was confined to the desert by Yūsuf ibn Tāshufīn (1061–1106) who founded the Murābiṭ state. Yūsuf conquered Morocco and central Maghrib as far as the kingdom of the Ḥammādids and then went on to take control of Spain. Thus Islam carried the Berbers for the first time on to the stage of world history.

The motives behind this movement were various. The religious motive seems subsidiary, yet religion provided the initial impulse, a new unity, and the will to conquer. But the fact that ʿAbd Allāh b. Yāsīn was accompanied by Yaḥyā b. ʿUmar and other leaders and the rapidity of their recruitment of supporters shows that there was more to it than a 'retreat' for religious purposes. These Atlantic Berbers

[1] Ibn Abī Zarʿ, op. cit., p. 49.

[2] Al-Bakrī, op. cit., p. 168; transl. pp. 369–70.

[3] Al-Bakrī, op. cit., pp. 167–8.

[4] After his death the Murābiṭs chose Sulaimān ibn Addu as spiritual leader, and although when killed twelve months later he was not replaced, they did not immediately give up their pretensions of a religious conquest (cf. Ibn Khaldūn, *Berb.* i. 239).

were feeling hemmed in between the Zanāta who had gained control of the Moroccan oases and ruled from Sijilmāsa[1] and the powerful black kingdom of Gāna which had captured Awdaghast, their south Saharan centre. It was to the interests of both these powers to ensure the safety of the trade-routes which passed through the territories of Ṣanhāja tribes and Ibn Ḥawqal and al-Bakrī recount how caravans were waylaid and sacked. There is also the figure of the Lemṭī Wajjāj whose intrigues against the Zanāta must be taken into account. The whole affair seems to have been planned in his *ribāṭ* and from the very beginning 'Abd Allāh preached the *jihād*. This is the impression given by the account of al-Bakrī who was a contemporary of Ibn Yāsīn.[2] In 1054–5 the Murābiṭs had conquered the two termini of the main trade-route, Sijilmāsa and Awdaghast, and it was only when the Zanāta regained Sijilmāsa that the movement developed into a war of conquest. From then, if not from the first, the eyes of the Lamtūna were fixed upon Morocco rather than Negroland, and Abū Bakr with the Masūfa and Godāla only turned to the conquest of Gāna when Yūsuf ibn Tāshufīn showed that he intended to be sole leader.

The Murābiṭ dynasty, however, was destined to be short-lived. The transplanted nomads rapidly changed in settled and civilized lands, they scandalized the orthodox by their conduct and many Berbers were ready to revolt when a Maṣmūda called Ibn Tūmart proclaimed himself the Mahdī in A.H. 515 (A.D. 1121/2), and founded the 'unitarians' (al-Muwaḥḥidūn). He denounced the Murābiṭūn as infidels and anthropomorphists, declaring the *jihād* against them to be a religious obligation. Ibn Tūmart's successor, 'Abd al-Mu'min ibn 'Alī (527/1133–558/1163) of the Kūmya, a Zanāta tribe, destroyed the Ṣanhāja dynasties and established the rule of the Muwaḥḥidūn throughout North Africa from Syrte to the Atlantic. In the thirteenth century the empire of the Muwaḥḥidūn broke up in its turn and the Battle of Las Navas de Tolosa (1212) marked the end of these great Berber empires. Morocco fell to the dynasty of the Marīnids, central Maghrib to the Zayyānids (or 'Abd al-Wādids) whose capital was at Tilimsān, and eastern Maghrib came under the Ḥafṣids.

Now to turn to the penetration of Islam into the Sudan. After the conquest of North Africa trade continued to follow the ancient well-tried routes. Accounts given by Arabic writers make it clear that Islam made its first appearance through the operations of traders who formed

[1] Sijilmāsa, founded in 140/757–8, corresponds to the present-day oasis of Tāfilālt.

[2] Al-Bakrī, op. cit., text pp. 164–6; transl. pp. 354–6.

settlements in the commercial centres where they exchanged the manufactured goods of Mediterranean lands and salt of the Sahara for the raw material of the Sudan, gold, slaves, ivory, and gum. It spread southwards along the western trade-routes among Saharan Soninke and the ancestors of the Tokolor, and then eastwards up the valley of the Senegal. Islam, therefore, had already progressed among the Negroes before it was propagated by force, but before dealing with its penetration we must mention the Negro states which existed south of the Berbers.

Both light and dark-coloured pastoral tribes of the Sahara had been moving southwards and living freely amongst Negroes in all the borderland regions, often intermarrying with them. Certain of these gained a political and social influence within Negro tribes and it is possible that the aristocracies of some Sudan kingdoms were due to such a white or mixed family taking the lead.

The most important kingdom on the Senegal was that of Takrūr, whose people were ancestors of the Tokolor. Its formation may go back to the beginning of the Christian era. It occupied both banks of the Senegal. From the ninth to tenth centuries it was ruled by a dynasty (Fulbe?) which came from the Ḥawḍ via Tagant and were known as Dyā'ōgo, but from the end of the tenth to the thirteenth centuries it was a semi-independent dependency of the Soninke kingdom of Dyāra in the Sahil.

In the Ḥawḍ was the Soninke kingdom of Awkār, generally known as Gāna, which may have been founded as early as the fourth century A.D. and acquired cohesion and power in the ninth century. Its capital lay south of present-day Awkār. It appears to have been founded by Negroes who had been influenced by Mediterranean culture, whose subjects were Soninke. Gāna reached its zenith under a Soninke dynasty which came to power towards the end of the eighth century. One of the titles of the king was *gāna*, and it is this word that Arab writers gave both to the capital and the state. This Soninke kingdom was the most powerful in West Africa at the time of the Arab invasion of North Africa, stretching from the Niger in the east to the Takrūr of Senegal in the west, well into the Sahara in the north and into the territory of Mandinka peoples to the south. Its prosperity was mainly due to its control of the gold trade, and commercial interests led it to gain political control of the Lamtūna trading town of Awdaghast in A.D. 990 and install a Negro governor.

South of Gāna were a number of Mande chieftaincies. One of these had its capital at Jeriba, situated near the junction of the Niger and Sankarani, whose Keyta dynasty was to take the place of Gāna as the dominant power of the region. Another insignificant kingdom of a very different type, but also destined to found an empire after many centuries, was that of Kawkaw (Gao), founded in the seventh century in the valley of the middle Niger. The subjects, who belonged to various ethnic groups, came to be known under the general name of Songhay. East of the Songhay came a series of uncoordinated groups of peoples and village states who were to develop into the Hausa kingdoms. Beyond these in the basin of the Chad was the state of Kānem, founded by a family of the nomadic Zaghāwa who roamed all the desert between the territory of the *lithām*-wearers and the Nile.

The first currents of islamization into West Africa had an economic basis. The Arab conquerors of North Africa had no desire to conquer the Sahara and Sudan, but were concerned with the organization of the gold trade.[1] Ḥabīb ibn Abī ʿUbaida led an expedition against Negroes in A.D. 736,[2] and his son ʿAbd ar-Raḥmān organized the caravan-route to Awdaghast. The Rustumid ʿIbāḍī *imāms* of Tihert had trade relations with the Sudan.[3] Gold was the great attraction which drew Mediterranean traders into Sahilian towns like Awdaghast and Gāna. From the notices given by Arabic authors it is clear that by the end of the seventh century A.D. Muslims from Egypt, Ifrīqiya, and the Maghrib were attending markets in the Sudan, and in this they were but continuing the practice of pre-Islamic days. Many had settled in market

[1] M. Lombard shows ('L'Or musulman du VIIe au XIe siècle', *Annales*, 1947, pp. 143–60) that the undisputed economic supremacy of the Muslim world from the seventh to the eleventh centuries was due 'to the possession of gold and to the universally acknowledged value of its money'. Apart from the stocks gained through the overthrow of empires, the Muslim world could count upon receiving a continuous supply from the Sudan. After the Hilālian invasion of the eleventh century began to make itself felt, both the Maghrib and the Sudan became more and more isolated from the Muslim East, and its economic supremacy ended when the Maghribī states opened up their commerce to the Christian world.

[2] Ibn ʿAbd al-Ḥakam writes, ' ʿUbaid Allāh gave Ḥabīb b. Abī ʿUbaida al- Fihrī command of an expedition to Sūs and the land of the blacks. He won unbelievable successes and all the gold he wanted' (*Futūḥ Miṣr*, ed. C. C. Torrey, 1922, p. 217). We should take this to mean no more than that he raided Negro cultivators living in SW. Morocco, were it not for the fact that al-Bakrī (p. 179) states that Gāna was attacked by Umayyads and that the descendants of the raiders settled down there. Al-Balādhurī writes that ʿAbd Allāh ibn al-Ḥabḥāb, governor of the Maghrib, 'sent ʿAbd ar-Raḥmān ibn Ḥabīb . . . to the invasion of as-Sūs and the land of as-Sūdān. The victories won by ʿAbd ar-Raḥmān were unparalleled. . . . These people were known by the name of Tarajān' (*Kitāb Futūḥ al-Buldān*, transl. P. Hitti, p. 367).

[3] See Ibn aṣ-Ṣaghīr, in *Actes du XIVe Congrès International des Orientalistes*, Algiers, 1908, iii. 13; Ash-Shammākhī, *Kitāb as-siyar*, Cairo, A.H. 1301, pp. 213–14.

centres as local agents for their firms. Although these traders were little interested in proselytization it is clear that early in the eleventh century A.D. Islam had begun to spread amongst black peoples.

The first reference to its spread to the Niger is by al-Muhallabī (A.D. 985) who says that the ruler of Kawkaw or Kūkū had made a profession of Islam, possessed a royal mosque and an open space for the congregational prayer. Al-Bakrī, writing before the fall of Gāna and using information obtained from travellers, mentions many Negro peoples whose rulers professed Islam, whilst he shows that all trading towns, including pagan Gāna, had a Muslim quarter. In Gāna Islam was fully tolerated. Muslims held important posts at court and their quarter boasted twelve mosques. The king of Takrūr, Wār Dyābi (d. 1040–1), and his family became Muslim at the beginning of the eleventh century, and converted the neighbouring chieftaincy of Silla whose king was at war with the pagan Qalanbū. West of pagan Ghiyāru, where Muslim traders were settled, was Iresnā, situated on a nile, which was Muslim. South of Iresnā was Malel where Islam had been adopted as the royal cult. Kūgha, a depot town for the gold trade, was Muslim although all the surrounding people were pagan; whilst Qanmir son of Basī, chief of Alūkan (al-Waken?), was said to be a secret Muslim. The town of Kūkū, situated either in the Songhay region or central Sudan, consisted of two towns, one Muslim (presumably the foreign trading quarter), and the other, the king's town, was pagan, though the king himself professed Islam. Besides Muslim trading settlements al-Bakrī mentions Muslim Berber tribes, in particular the Medāsa, living amongst Negroes all along the desert region of the Niger bend, opposite Ra's al-Mā', at Bughat and Tādmekka.

It is not surprising, therefore, that 'Abd Allāh ibn Yāsīn, when he had made things too hot for himself in western Mauritania, should consider making for the country of the Negro Muslims (presumably Takrūr) in order to organize the malcontents among the Ṣanhāja for a *jihād* against Berber tribes. Ibn Abī Zar' writes, 'When 'Abd Allāh ibn Yāsīn saw their [the Ṣanhāja] aversion for him and their intention of sticking to their old ways, he purposed to leave them for the country of the Negroes who had adopted Islam, for Islam was already spreading among them.'[1] Yaḥyā ibn Ibrāhīm, however, persuaded him to set up his *ribāṭ* beside an estuary on the Atlantic coast.

It will be understood that Islam at this stage was the religion of foreign traders who were allowed full freedom of practice. The mer-

[1] *Rawḍ*, pp. 47–48.

chant in West Africa is always outside the religion of the state and people, whether he is a temporary or permanent resident. Where Islam was professed by the ruler it was merely as an additional religious safeguard, running parallel to his traditional religion but not displacing it, whilst the masses of the people did not and were not expected to adopt even a veneer of Islam. This is shown clearly in al-Bakrī's account of the conversion of the ruler of Malel.[1]

The first attempt to disseminate Islam in the Sudan by force came through the Berbers of western Sahara who had joined the Murābiṭūn movement, a secondary aspect of this movement being Berber reaction against Soninke supremacy over Awdaghast and the trade-routes. When 'Abd Allāh ibn Yāsīn left his *ribāṭ* in A.D. 1042 and his agents began to preach his militant gospel among the Berbers of the Adrār and Tagant, they were certainly in touch with the Negroes of Takrūr (Fūta Tōro) and Silla who were in active opposition to the Soninkes of Gāna. Many vassal peoples, amongst whom were Berber groups, were anxious to throw off the yoke of Gāna, and Islam made a ready appeal as a means towards effecting this. The king of Takrūr, Lebi, son of Wār-Dyābī, after he succeeded his father, went with contingents of troops to join the forces of the Murābiṭūn under Yaḥyā ibn 'Umar in his disastrous war against the Berber tribe of Godāla.

With the rise of the Murābiṭūn the conquest of Awdaghast (446/1054–5) was inevitable, but that of Gāna was almost fortuitous. Al-Bakrī wrote, at a time when the future of this movement born in the western desert could not have been foreseen, 'The leader of the Murābiṭūn today, that is the year A.H. 460 (A.D. 1067–8), is Abū Bakr ibn 'Umar. But their power is dispersed, not consolidated, and is based upon the desert.'[2] In 452 (1060) Abū Bakr had to break off the Moroccan campaign and return to the desert to deal with quarrels among nomadic Berbers, leaving his cousin Yūsuf ibn Tāshufīn in command in Morocco. 'After resolving their quarrels', Ibn Khaldūn writes, 'to distract them he led a raid against the Negroes to a distance of 90 days from their homeland.'[3] When he returned to Morocco he found Yūsuf indisposed to hand over authority and returned to the desert to wage war against the Negroes which eventually led to the conquest of the capital of Gāna (1076) and his own death in 1087.

The sack of Gāna ended the long period during which this kingdom had dominated western Sudan. Its fall led to the political triumph of

[1] See below, pp. 61–62.

[2] Al-Bakrī, op. cit., p. 170/373.

[3] Ibn Khaldūn, op. cit. i. 339–40.

Islam throughout the Sahil region between the Senegal and Niger. The Soninke of Gāna were compelled to adopt Islam and they not only did so *en masse* but began to spread it amongst the many peoples over whom they still ruled. Tributary peoples, like the Dyāra or Kanyāga (Soninke of the present-day Nyoro region), Gumbu (south of Kumbi), Sūsū (Soninke living between Gumbu and Bamako), and Dyākha or Dyā (Soninke of western Māsina), took advantage of the fall of Gāna to make themselves independent. The success of the Murābiṭūn forces also seems to have set in motion new migrations. Soninke spread over a vast area; Serer migrated towards Takrūr (Fūta Tōro), and across the Senegal into Baol, Salum, and Sin where they still live; Fulbe from Termes and Tagant also moved to Fūta Tōro.

Whilst in the north the triumph of this movement born in the western desert had established Yūsuf ibn Tāshufīn upon the throne of Morocco, in the Sudan the end came when Abū Bakr ibn ʿUmar was killed in Adrār fighting against rebellious Berbers in the same year that Yūsuf was beginning the conquest of Spain. With Abū Bakr's death the Ṣanhāja confederation of Mauritania broke up and the temporal power of the movement disappeared from the Senegal and Niger. Of the tribes who had taken part the Godāla continued to occupy the Atlantic shores, the Lamtūna remained in Adrār and Tagant, and the Masūfa in Ḥawḍ. Their subsequent history was characterized by interminable internal struggles, and the next great event is the arrival of the Arab tribes four centuries later. None of the central Saharan Berbers took part in these events. The movement left no enduring political system and the borderland nomads became subject to Negro kings. Ibn Khaldūn, writing (*c.* 1394) at a time when Māli had gained the ascendancy, illuminates the situation in the desert:

The tribes of *lithām*-wearers still live in our days in their ranges confined between the Negroes of the sands which border upon the Berberlands of the two Maghribs and Ifrīqiya. To this day they extend from the shores of the Atlantic in the west to the Nile in the east. Those who had gained control of Spain and Africa, who comprised but a small proportion of the Masūfa and Lamtūna, have perished . . .; eaten up by power, swallowed by their far-flung territories, and worn out by luxury, they were overwhelmed by the Muwaḥḥidūn. Those who had stayed in the desert remained as before, divided and disunited in word and deed; and they are now subject to the king of the Negroes, paying him the *kharāj* and supplying contingents for his armies. They extend like a fence eastwards parallel to that formed by the Arabs on the frontier of the two Maghribs and Ifrīqiya.[1]

[1] Ibn Khaldūn, op. cit. i. 260 (ii. 104).

The role of the Murābiṭūn in the islamization of the Sudan has been exaggerated. The peaceful penetration of Islam along trade-routes into borderland towns had begun before this movement was born. Traders were allowed full liberty by the tolerant Negro rulers both to practise and propagate their religion. Gāna and other towns possessed Muslim quarters, whilst the rulers of Takrūr and other states had become Muslims. The Murābiṭūn simply accelerated a process that had already begun, and their conquest was ephemeral because the attraction of Morocco was stronger than that of the Sudan. The role of Gāna in the Sahil and southern Sahara was taken over by the Mande empire of Māli, but its function was much greater than that of a buffer-state and it rapidly became the greatest Negro state Africa has ever known.

Islam continued to spread by peaceful means and the Soninke of Gāna have been of great significance in its propagation; the history of their dispersion, if it could be unravelled, would clear up many historical obscurities. Its acceptance by the peoples of the Sahil and Māsina is due primarily to their efforts. Their traders converted and blended with the commercial and industrious Mande Dyula who carried it to the edge of the equatorial forest. By the beginning of the twelfth century, less than fifty years after the preaching of ʻAbd Allāh ibn Yāsīn, Islamic traders had reached the south Sudan savanna and were on the verge of the routeless impenetrable forest. These Mande Dyula converted by Soninke of Dyākha became accustomed to penetrate to the edge of the forest to buy kola-nuts, and their settlements often became little states in the heart of the southern savanna among pagan peoples.

Commercial towns naturally were attracted to Islam. The king of Jennē, whose foundation may go back to the eighth century, joined it towards the end of the sixth century of the *hijra* (about A.D. 1200) and his example was followed by all its inhabitants, for the religion had made peaceful progress before he decided to change. Jennē rapidly became the greatest Muslim metropolis in the western Sudan. Its traders also began to make use of a Berber settlement near the Niger where it flows through the desert, called Timbuktu. As-Saʿdī claims that this town was founded about A.H. 490 (A.D. 1096/7) by the Tuareg Magsharen. It was, however, some time before the desert caravans began to use it, otherwise it would have been known to al-Idrīsī and later writers, but from the thirteenth century it rapidly grew, not only into a great emporium for the carrying trade with the north, but also into an important religious centre. Māli was now at the zenith of its power and influence, and in the second half of the thirteenth century it gained control of Timbuktu and exacted tribute from the Songhay kingdom. One king, Mansa Mūsā, became a legendary figure in the Muslim world in consequence of his pilgrimage to Mecca in A.H. 724 (A.D. 1324–5). The pilgrim traffic, which took the Saharan and not the west–east route, was organized, substantial, and closely associated with the slave-trade. Apart from the pilgrimages of named Negro rulers al-Maqrīzī mentions the arrival in Cairo of caravans from Takrūr (which to him is a general term for West Africa) in 743/1342–3 (over 5,000 pilgrims), 752/1351–2 (headed by a king and bringing a large number of slaves), 819/1416–17 (1,700 slaves and gold), and 835/1431–2 (headed by a king who died in the town of Tor).[1]

Little by little Islam gained ruling classes and urban peoples north of the Senegal and along the vast sweep of the Niger buckle. But although it became the imperial cult of these states it had little effect upon the cultivators who clung to their traditional religious beliefs and practices. The majority of the loosely organized Mande peoples were unaffected by Islam. East of them in the centre of the Niger bend the Gurmanshe and the two Mossi kingdoms (Wagadugu founded *c.* 1050 and Yatenga founded *c.* 1170), covering roughly all the region belonging to the basin of the Volta north of present-day Ghana, resisted Islam and blocked its extension to the south and east.

Islam was still slower in spreading among peoples of central Sudan. Yaʿqūbī (A.D. 889) says that ʿIbāḍite Berbers maintained slave-trading establishments in Fezzān and Kawār. These were in touch with Zaghāwa inhabiting all central Sahara who supplied them with slaves, and Islam was established among their ruling classes by the middle of the thirteenth century. It was also introduced into Kānem, a Negro state with a nomadic Zaghāwī ruling class, whose first Muslim chief lived towards the close of the eleventh or beginning of the twelfth century A.D. Islam was still later in entering the Hausa city-states. The Kano Chronicle shows that it was introduced into that town between A.D. 1349 and 1385 by Wangāra (*dyula*) from Manding, but it was never more than the religion of the trading class and the agriculturalists remained pagan until the nineteenth century.

Although sources relating to the introduction of Islam into western and central Sudan are so meagre and unreliable what is clear is the slow

[1] See *Not. et Extr. de la Bibl. Nat.* xii (1831), 637–8.

peaceful nature of its spread and the weakness of its impact upon Sudanese religious and social life. This is due to the peculiarities of its adoption as a class religion with a place within the ruling pagan social structure defined in such a way that its effect as a religious law and spiritual transformer was completely neutralized.

2

West Sudan States

I. THE SUDAN STATE SYSTEM

THE last chapter gave a general account of the penetration of Islam. This chapter is concerned with the history of the states which adopted Islam as the imperial cult.[1] The Sudan zone may be divided into three historical regions: the Senegalese chieftaincies, Soninke and Mandinka states between the Niger and Senegal, and the Songhay region of the upper Niger; all of which, together with central Mande peoples, were embraced within the sphere of the empire of Māli. These historical regions correspond to the main linguistic regions: West Atlantic (Serēr, Wolof, Fulbe, and Tokolor), Mande (Soninke and Mandinka), and the isolated Songhay language.

History in Africa is primarily family tradition. To write of kingdoms and empires implies the existence of centralized states, but it is necessary to take what Africans consider constitutes a political group. There were two levels of political relation: the local group and a ruling lineage. The real rulers of the Sudan were not kings and emperors but patriarchs of families, councils of elders, and chiefs of villages on the one hand, and the heads of superimposed clans on the other. The first, the heads of the basic unities of social life, were also political authorities, deriving their authority from their natural position in the community as heads of communal cults. In the other case, the state was not an expanded local community, but came into existence when a village chief or leader of an age-group or immigrant warrior clan gained control of a widening range of uncentralized village communities and formed a 'kingdom'. This type of political authority was superimposed without seriously impairing the authority of the other system. In the same way, as each individual had his status in the family defined according to age, sex, and filiation, so in the state each lineage had its hereditary status and role according to occupation: cultivators, fishers, hunters, craftsmen, traders, clerics, or griots. Hence one lineage could adopt Islam without affecting the rest of society. Kingship also fell into the lineage system, but since it also was a ritual as well as political office, the royal

[1] For a definition of the three main types of Sudan Islamic states see *I.W.A.*, pp. 138–43.

family cult had wider implications. It was important for the welfare of society as a whole as well as the ruling clan. The state of Māli was such a superimposed lineage, whether it consisted of the primitive community from which it originated and in which it ended or that amorphous political sphere called the Māli empire. The states had no names and were known to the Arab world by the ruler's title such as Gāna or Māli. As the ruling clan embraced more and more families and villages an apparently territorial arrangement entered into its composition, for the king appointed representatives or, in our terminology, provincial governors to maintain the ritual link and perform political functions on his behalf.

The Sudan concept of dominium is difficult to define. It was the reverse of an imperium if by that is meant a dominium which seeks to extend its form of civilization over diverse types of societies. It was not a political unity, nor based on territorial sovereignty. Thousands of political groups at all stages of development coexisted within the sphere of Māli. It is impossible to demarcate these spheres upon a map for the frontier did not exist. Nor was there any capital city, hence the very sites of the many villages where the ruler of Māli held court can only be conjectured. 'Empires' were spheres of influence, defined not by territorial or boundary lines but by social strata, independent families, free castes, or servile groups of fixed status regarded as royal serfs.[1] The ruler was not interested in dominating territory as such, but in relationship with social groups upon whom he could draw to provide levies in time of war, servants for his court, and cultivators to keep his granaries full. He held the allegiance of village groups or *civitates* who recognized his spiritual authority by paying tribute, for the collection of which he appointed agents to live in provincial villages. He possessed his 'royal domains' as did all noble clans and high officials, but the principle behind these was lineal, not territorial.[2]

Nor had these states ethnic or cultural homogeneity. There were no

[1] This is shown by Maḥmūd al-Kāti in his account of the inheritance of *askiya* Muḥammad from the *Sī* rulers, who again had acquired them by conquest from Māli; see below, pp. 78, 102, n. 6. Serf families were attached to a master, not a glebe, and *askiya* Muḥammad appears to have moved them about at will.

[2] All over West Sudan is found the belief that the first occupants are the 'owners of the land' (see *I.W.A.*, p. 144). They perform ritual duties on behalf of the community since they are in special relationship with the spirits of the land. The political chief, as guardian of community welfare, respected their office. Even in a long-islamized town like Jennē the institution survives. The *dugu-tigi* is the Bozo chief of a poor quarter, but political authority (*ku-ntigi*) has belonged to Soninke Nono ever since they gained control of the town in the twelfth century A.D.

tribal boundaries any more than geographical frontiers. For example, there was no Songhay people but only a number of kinship groups, possessing an inherited status (noble, freeman, serf, slave, blacksmith) and following different occupations (rulers, fishers, hunters, cultivators, and traders), who eventually adopted the same language and cultural characteristics, but never became a clearly defined unified people and never thought of themselves as subjects of a state, but only of their status relationship to the ruling authority.

The Sudanese 'empire' was an amorphous agglomeration of kin-groups having little in common except mythical recognition of a far-off suzerain. Within these empires were political, that is tribute-paying, units of various types above that of the village state, called *dyamāna* in Mande, over which Māli applied a system of protectorate. Within the protectorate the village group or the *dyamāna* maintained its own religious, social, and political institutions. In non-Mande regions chiefs retained their titles, as in the Jennē, Soninke, and Tokolor states. Account must be taken of the coexistence and overlapping of dynasties which makes the history of the Senegal region extremely confusing.

These steppe empires give the appearance of structural weakness and instability. They rose rapidly, expanded prematurely, and then either died away like Māli or suffered a catastrophic disintegration like Songhay. Songhay was not originally a kingdom. The region from which it emerged had a number of aristocratic classes with changing dynasties, who paid tribute to Saharan chiefs or the rulers of Māli or Mossi. But when a dynasty arose which formed a quasi-military régime, under a ruler basing his authority upon Islam, and drawing his troops from levies of the subjected, it lasted little more than a century and collapsed when faced with the invasion of a few hundred European musketeers. Māli, on the contrary, simply crumbled into its basic parts and its concept of sovereignty faded away, but the intrinsic organization of community life was left unimpaired by the collapse of the superstructure that had been erected. On the other hand, the Mossi states within the Niger bend in the Upper Volta region showed remarkable stability, ruled by dynasties which still survive. Their stability is not based upon ethnic unity which did not exist in any Sudan state, but derived from a centralized administrative system and political unity.[1]

[1] At the summit of the social structure was a conquering aristocracy (*nakomse*), headed by a sacred king in intimate communion with his ancestors. He was assisted by ministers of state (*nāba*) who held court offices or governorships. A warrior class maintained internal security and defended the state against invaders, for there were no physical barriers to deter aggressors. They checked the armies of Māli, Songhay, and the Arma. They did not seek to expand too

All north Sudan states, except the Mossi, adopted Islam as the imperial cult. This strengthened commercial links with North Africa, facilitated the introduction of new elements of material culture, and above all brought a written language and clerical class. But its adoption did not lead to either confessional nor cultural homogeneity and had no effect upon basic civilization. As the ruler cult Islam was analogous to the cults of lineage groups. It introduced new elements into the elaborate ceremonial which manifests the authority of the ruler such as the formal cortèges with which he proceeded to the *jāmiʿ* or *muṣallā* for Friday or festival prayer, but its adoption did not affect the mythic basis of the chief's authority, caused no breach between him and the community, and he never thought of imposing it upon his subjects.

2. THE STATES OF THE SENEGAL

The region with which we are concerned here is section one of al-Idrīsī's first clime in which are 'the towns of Awlīl, Silla, Takrūr, Daw, Barīsa, and Mūra (or Madara)'. This region is the southern part of *Arḍ Maqzārati 's-Sūdān* (Land of the Maqzāra of the Negroes).[1] The first section of the next clime to the north is also *Arḍ Maqzārati 's-Sūdān*, but here water is rare, it is largely uninhabited, and travellers are few. North of this was Qamnūriyya[2] which has the Atlantic in the west and the Desert of Nīsar in the east, through which desert travellers must pass from Sijilmāsa, Darʿa, and an-Nūl to Gāna. Qamnūriyya was more habitable and is of some interest to us because al-Idrīsī, whose information, where not derived from Ptolemaic legends, came from merchants, says that Negro settlements and towns used to exist there, the best known being Qamnūrī and Nighīra,[3] 'but desert tribes of Zaghāwa and Lamtūna inhabiting both flanks of this land, so

widely. The periodic progresses of their armies were concerned primarily about booty, but they kept other powers aware of their strength. In the nineteenth century the Fulbe states of Māsina and Gwandu arose to the west and east but the *jihād* leaders were forced to skirt their territory. Unlike other states they maintained no direct commercial links with North Africa and strictly controlled the activities of immigrants, Dyula traders, Hausa artisans, and Fulbe herders, the latter being under a minister of state, the *yār-nāba*. About the only breach was when Fulbe drove away the Gurmanshe chief of Liptako (*c.* 1700) and remained in control until incorporated in the sphere of Gwando (*c.* 1800).

[1] Al-Idrīsī, text p. 2. 'The *maqzāra* of the Blacks' implies that there was another *maqzāra* (of the whites?). In one place (p. 13) he uses the plural *maqāzara*. In the central Sudan he has a similar expression, *arḍ Zaghāwati 's-Sūdān* (p. 32). One wonders from where d'Anville got the *maczara* situated east of Timbuktu on his maps published between 1749 and 1777.

[2] This is al-Khwārizmī's Thamtūriqī or Thamnūrīqī adopted from Ptolemy's Θαμονδόκανα.

[3] Ptolemaic *Νίγειρα* (iv. 6. 27). Al-Khwārizmī places it on an unnamed river.

MAP 1

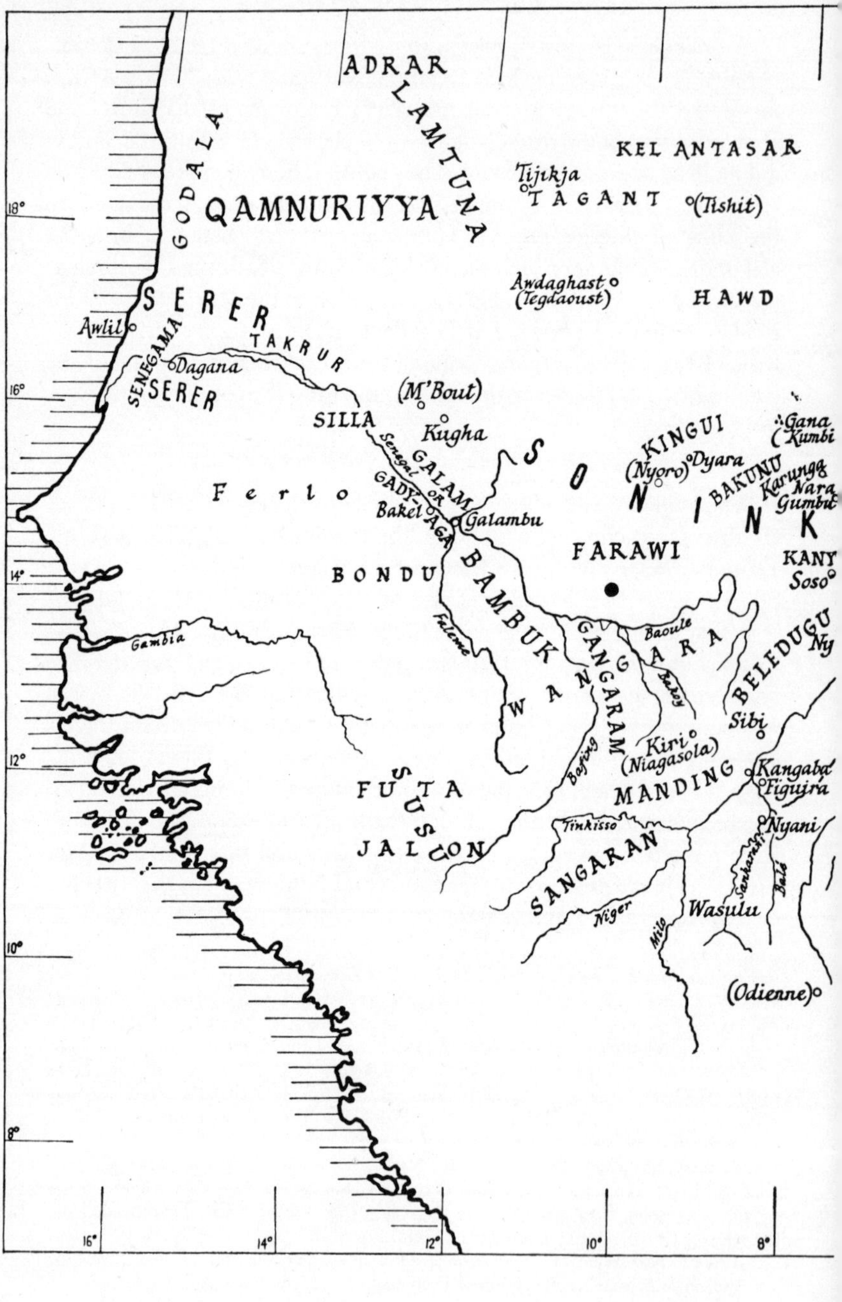

ADRAR
LAMTUNA
KEL ANTASAR
Tijikja
TAGANT
(Tishit)
GODALA
QAMNURIYYA
Awdaghast
(Tegdaoust)
HAWD
SERER
Awlil
SENEGAMA
TAKRUR
Dagana
SERER
(M'Bout)
SILLA
Kugha
Senegal
GALAM
OR
GADY-AGA
Bakel
Galambu
Ferlo
SONINK
KINGUI
(Nyoro)
Dyara
BAKUNU
Gana
Kumbi
Karunga
Nara
Gumbu
FARAWI
KANY
Soso
BONDU
BAMBUK
Faleme
Gambia
GANGARAM
WANGARA
Baoule
Bakoy
BELEDUGU
Ny
Sibi
Kiri
(Niagasola)
Bafing
MANDING
Kangaba
Figuira
FUTA
SUSU
JALON
Tinkisso
Nyani
SANGARAN
Niger
Milo
Wasulu
Sankarani
Bale
(Odienne)
18°
16°
14°
12°
10°
8°

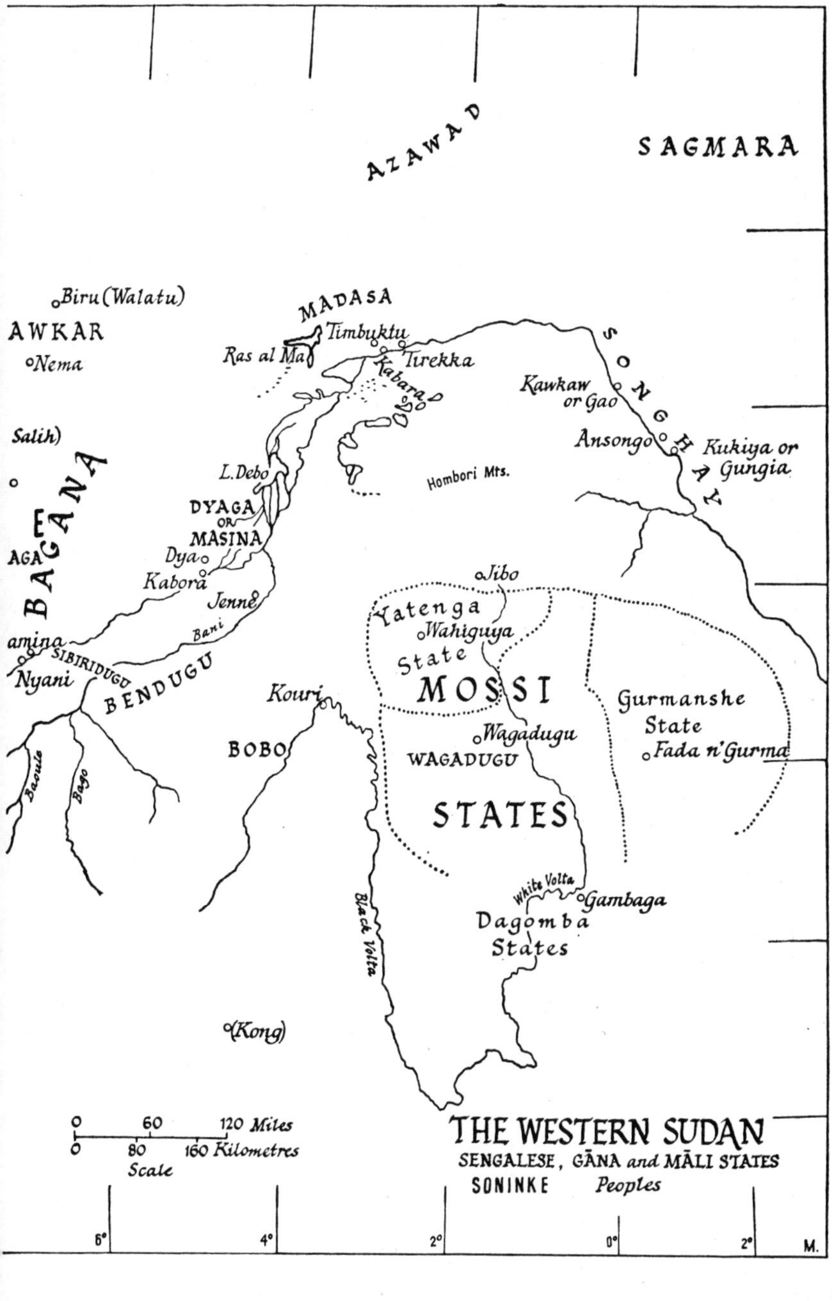

THE WESTERN SUDAN
SENGALESE, GĀNA and MĀLI STATES
SONINKE Peoples

penetrated this country, that is Qamnūriyya, that they eliminated most of its inhabitants and cut up and scattered the remnants. The inhabitants of Qamnūriyya, so the merchants report, claim to be Jews, but their beliefs are a meaningless confusion.' The distance from Qamnūrī and Nighīra to Silla was fifteen and twelve days respectively. He adds that formerly traffic with the Senegal towns was important, but now traces of the routes are beginning to be lost.[1] The Maqzāra we may take to be the ancestors of the Serēr, Tokolor, and Wolof. Elsewhere[2] al-Idrīsī distinguishes them specifically from the Ghāniyyūn, that is, the Soninke.

Al-Idrīsī's information shows the pressure of the Berber tribes upon Negro peoples inhabiting parts favourable for cultivation. Lamtūna and Godāla, with smaller groups of Gezūla and Wārith,[3] moved into Mauritanian Adrār and Tiris, then into Tagant and Ḥawḍ, where they found Soninke cultivators and met the influence of Gāna. In the ebb and flow of contact sometimes they subjected the Negroes, at other times they paid them tribute, but the pressure was unremittent, and eventually, between the eleventh and sixteenth centuries, they forced the Negroes across the river, except for those who cultivated the oases as *ḥarrāṭīn* or serfs.

In addition to the Berbers we have to take account of the interaction of Negroes with another race, the Fulbe, living in much closer contact. Serēr, Wolof, and Fulbe all speak related languages, and it is conjectured that the Fulbe, when a relatively small group, adopted the language of the Negroes among whom they lived. From this region they migrated all over the Sudan. These peoples retreated before the advance of the Berbers which was becoming strong in the tenth century and eventually they were all pushed across the Senegal. Also throughout the centuries the Berbers have been in contact with Soninke inhabiting the Sahara where remnants are still found in oases as *ḥarrāṭīn* and as the Azēr of Walāta, Tishīt, and Shinqīṭ (Azēr: Si-n-gede). As-Sa'dī reports a tradition that Shinqīṭ and Tishīt were founded by Azēr.[4]

Communication between North and Negro Africa was entirely by land. The Carthaginian Hanno (between 475 and 450 B.C.) probably did not penetrate south of Morocco and the settlements he founded there were merely ephemeral for no archaeological evidence of their

[1] Al-Idrīsī, op. cit., pp. 29–31.

[2] Al-Idrīsī, op. cit., p. 13, l. 12.

[3] Al-Bakrī, op. cit., (p. 171) mentions the Banū Wārith 'at the settlement of Nūl, the last outpost of Islam where the desert begins'.

[4] *T. as-Sūdān*, p. 22 (38).

existence has been found. Arab writers considered the Atlantic to be unnavigable, though they mention a few ships which adventured or were driven south of Gibraltar. Al-Masʿūdī relates[1] an account 'well known in Spain' of how a young man of Cordova called Khash-khāsh led a number of ships into the Atlantic and returned with great riches. Al-Idrīsī[2] mentions a party of merchant venturers (*mugharrirūn*) who sailed from Lisbon with the purpose of exploring the Atlantic and touched the mainland some distance beyond the straits of Gibraltar. Ibn Saʿīd[3] was told of the discovery of Cape Blanco by a passenger of a boat which was wrecked at Wādī Nūn (north of Cape Non), whose crew eventually landed and made their way inland to the salt market of Taghāza. Al-ʿUmarī also has an account of a vessel driven south from Spain and of the adventures of its company on the African mainland.[4] Such voyagers would report the lack of natural harbours, the dangerous surf, and mangrove swamps which fringed the rivers, but the main discouragement to navigation was the difficulty of the return journey. By sea, therefore, the Muslims did little towards the 'opening up of Africa', but by land they did a great deal and most of the Portuguese travellers' knowledge of the interior was derived from them.

On the coast north of the mouth of the Senegal was the town of Awlīl often referred to by Arab geographers, hence it must have been situated on an important trade-route to Morocco. It was celebrated for its saltmines, for salt was a basic commodity in the trade with Negroes and plays a role in history comparable with that of gold. Awlīl is first mentioned by Ibn Ḥawqal.[5] Al-Idrīsī makes it his starting-point in reckoning measurements, especially longitudes, in the Sudan. Islamic influence seems to have spread south along the coast to the Senegal (it is noteworthy that ʿAbd Allāh ibn Yāsīn chose to set up his *ribāṭ* in this region), then along its valley eastwards to influence the rulers of Takrūr. None of the *mamālik*, 'sovereignties', 'dynastic possessions', to adopt the terminology of Arab writers, situated north of the Senegal enjoyed the renown of Gāna, Māli, and Songhay, but that of Takrūr was eventually to extend its name to the whole of the Sudan. Its people

[1] Al-Masʿūdī, *Les Prairies d'or*, i. 258–9.

[2] Al-Idrīsī, op. cit., pp. 184–5, and his contemporary Abū Ḥāmid al-Andalusī (1080/1–1169/70), see E. Fagnon, *Extraits inédits relatifs au Maghrib*, Algiers ,1924, pp. 30–31, 72, 90–91.

[3] Cf. Abū'l-Fidā', transl. Reinaud, ii. 1, 215–16.

[4] Al-ʿUmarī, *Masālik*, pp. 82–83.

[5] Ibn Ḥawqal, op. cit., i. 92. Awlīl is generally identified with the peninsula of Arguin situated near Cape Blanco (see W. D. Cooley, *The Negroland of the Arabs*, London, 1841, p. 23).

were the first Negroes to embrace Islam and have remained fervent followers, so that the word Takrūr has become equivalent to west Sudan Muslim. Amongst Arabic writers of the Middle Ages the phrase *Bilād at-Takrūr* was equivalent to *Bilād as-Sūdān* for 'the region of Black Muslims'; al-Qalqashandī, for instance, calls the kings of Māli *Mulūk at-Takrūr*.[1] Al-'Umarī, however, is quite clear about its correct signification when he writes that the ruler of Māli 'is he whom the Egyptians have confused under the name of king of Takrūr; but if one addressed him so he would object because the Takrūr is only one of the regions of his empire. It is best to style him "Lord of Māli" (*Ṣāḥib Māli*) because Māli is the largest and most renowned region.'[2] We shall restrict the word Takrūr to the homeland of the Tokolor, that is, Senegalese Fūta.

The main kingdoms on the Senegal mentioned by al-Bakrī were: Ṣanghāna extending along both banks near its mouth, Takrūr, and Silla (Galam), between which and Gāna were many less organized groups of peoples. Al-Bakrī's description gives us the setting at the time Islam began its penetration. After mentioning that the territory of the Berber Banū Jaddāla (Godāla) borders on the land of the Blacks he continues:

The nearest Negro country to them is Ṣanghāna,[3] at a distance of six days' journey. Its capital consists of two towns lying on both banks of the Nile [Senegal] and its inhabited country extends to the Atlantic Ocean. Immediately after Ṣanghāna, to the south-west, on the banks of the Nile, is the town of Takrūr[4] inhabited by Negroes. These, like the rest of the Negroes, were once pagan and worshipped *dakākīr* (*dakkūr* in their language meaning 'idol')

[1] *Ṣubḥ*, v. 282, 286.

[2] Al-'Umarī, op. cit., pp. 53–54; quoted by Al-Qalqashandī, op. cit., v. 292.

[3] Ṣanghāna is mentioned by al-'Umarī (1342/9) as one of the *aqālīm* subject to Māli (p. 55); in the 'pilot Book' of the Medicis of 1351 as *Senegamy*; by Ca da Mosto (1455), Thevet, Marmol, and Pacheco Pereira as *Senega* or *Çanagudá*; by Maḥmūd-al-Kāti (*Ta'rīkh al-Fattāsh*, p. 39/68) in the sixteenth century as *Singilu*. The River Senegal derives its name from this district and not from the Ṣanhāja or Zanāja who are also mentioned by these writers as roaming about farther north. Ca da Mosto mentioned the Rio di Senega 'dividing a race which is called Azanaghi [i.e. *Azenūg*, arabized Ṣanhāja] from the first kingdom of the Blacks' (*The Voyages of Cadamosto*, transl. G. R. Crone, Hakluyt, ser. ii, No. 80, 1937, p. 18). P. Marty states that Moors use the word *Sanghāna* for the Wolof province of Cayor (*R.M.M.* xxxi. 415 n.) and M. Delafosse says that those of Trārza employ the term *Isongān* for the Wolof bank of the lower Senegal, and pronounce and write it quite distinctly from the name of the Zenāja (*H.S.N.* i. 57–58).

[4] Delafosse places the capital on the Senegal, a little to the west of Bakel (*H.S.N.* ii. 50). See also Bonnel de Mézières, 'Recherches de l'emplacement de Ghana et sur le site de Tekrour', *Mém. Acad. Insc. et B.-L.* xii (1920), pt. 1. A place called Tokoror on an island at Morfil is said to be the site of the former capital.

until the reign of Wār-Jābī,[1] son of Rābīs. This king joined Islam and introduced Islamic law. He enforced the religion upon his subjects, thus opening their eyes to the truth. He died in A.H. 432 (A.D. 1040/1). Today (*c.* 1067) the Takrūr are Muslims.

From Takrūr one travels to Silla,[2] which likewise consists of two towns lying on both banks of the Nile. Its people are Muslims having been converted by Wār-Jābī. From Silla to the city of Ghāna is a twenty-days' journey across a region inhabited by tribe after tribe of Blacks with whose pagan inhabitants the ruler of Silla is at war. The nearest are those of the town of Qalanbū,[3] a day's journey away. It [Silla] is an extensive and populous kingdom almost equal to that of Ghāna. The means of exchange of the inhabitants of Silla are *dura*, salt, brass rings, and fine cotton strips called *shakkiyya*.[4] They possess many cattle, but neither sheep nor goats. . . . Adjoining this country is the town [i.e. country] of Qalanbū, a day's journey away as has already been mentioned. It lies on the banks of the Nile and its people are idolaters. Near it is the town of Toronqa covering a wide area. Its people make the material called *shakkiyya* already mentioned, which is four spans in breadth.[5]

The next country to Toroŋqa is Zāfaqu,[6] whose people worship the serpent, the cult of which he gives an interesting description. Then comes the independent state of the Faruwiyyīn,[7] and finally Gāṅa.

Al-Idrīsī (A.D. 1154) adds to the information given by al-Bakrī. Naturally enough, since their information was obtained from traders, these writers based their descriptions on trading villages. After describing Awlīl and its export of salt up the Senegal he places Silla on the opposite side of Takrūr from the description of al-Bakrī, which is certainly incorrect:

From the island of Awlīl to the town of Sillā is a 16 days journey. Sillā, which lies on the northern bank of the river, is a well populated town, a

[1] Al-Bakrī transliterates the name Wār-Jāy (= Wār-Ndyāy) on p. 167. Both Wār and Ndyāy are the names (*yettōde*) of Wolof clans, but *wār* is probably a title.

[2] This Silla or Sila is not to be identified with the present village of Silla (Bosseya district in the centre of Fūta), whose foundation is not ancient (see Delafosse, *Chroniques du Foûta Sénégalais*, 1913, p. 296), though it was apparently near Galam (Galambu in al-Bakrī's text) at the confluence of the Falemē with the Senegal. The Soninke ruling class (Manna) of Silla, who had become Muslims, were independent of the rule of Gāna. They are now the Pulār-speaking Silbe; Soninke Sillaŋku, 'people of Silla'.

[3] The Tokolor of Fūta still call the Soninke of ⁿGalam, the country immediately east of Fūta, *galambo*.

[4] Arabic *shuqqa*, Ḥassāniyya *sheggē*, still used for long strips of locally woven cotton material. Barth (iv. 443; v. 30–31) reported the use of *sheggē* in Timbuktu and Hausaland for stuffs of calico.

[5] Al-Bakrī, op. cit., text pp. 172–3; transl. pp. 377–9.

[6] Dyafuko = Dyomboko?

[7] *V.ll.* Farawni, Farāwi, Farāwa, Barāwa. Ṭabarī (*Hist.* iii. 1428) mentions the Faruwiyya.

congregating point of the Blacks, and an important commercial centre. Its people are progressive. It is a dependency (*'amāla*) of the Takrūrī (the ruler of Takrūr) who is an independent sovereign, possessing slaves and troops, and renowned for his resolution, firmness and sense of justice. His country is secure, peaceful, and tranquil. The place where he resides is the town of Takrūr which is situated on the south side of the river, two days journey from Sillā by river or land. The town of Takrūr is larger than Sillā and its commerce is more extensive. The people of the Far West (al-Maghrib al-aqṣā) travel there with wool, copper and beads, and export gold and slaves. The food of the people of Sillā and Takrūr consists of millet, fish and milk products. Most of their animals are camels and goats. The ordinary people wear woollen *qadāwīr*, with woollen *karāzī* on their heads,[1] whilst the upper class wear cotton clothing and head wraps. . . . Travelling from Takrūr on the river eastwards for 12 stages one comes to Barīsā,[2] a small town without walls, more like a well populated village. Its people are itinerant traders subject to the ruler of Takrūr.[3]

These Negro peoples living north of the Senegal, whom we may call proto-Serēr, probably differed little in physical and cultural characteristics. Chieftaincies had emerged which extended their rule over a number of villages and of these Takrūr was the most important. The inhabitants of Takrūr[4] were influenced by Islam as well as by the stock and culture of Fulbe[5] and Soninke. The Soninke also became islamized

[1] These are arabized Berber names: the *qadwūr* (Berber *taghandar*) is a long, loose, sleeveless garment, and the *karziya* a woollen band which is rolled around the head (see Glossary to Idrīsī, op. cit., pp. 364, 375).

[2] *V.l.* Baransā. This place is probably al-Bakrī's Iresnā (يرسنى) which lies on a nile west of Ghiyāro 'inhabited by Muslims, though all the surrounding country is full of pagans. . . . From Iresnā the foreigners (*al-'ajam*) known as Nūnaghamāratah, who are merchants of gold, export negroes to all countries' (al-Bakrī, op. cit., pp. 177–8), which agrees with al-Idrīsī who may be indebted to him. De Slane (p. 387) translates the last sentence, 'Les nègres *adjem*, nommés Noughamarta, sont négociants, et transportent la poudre d'or d'Iresni dans tous les pays'; but with this rendering who are *as-sūdān al-'ajam*, 'detribalized Negroes'? Ibn Sa'īd (quoted by Abū 'l-Fidā', op. cit., p. 157) says that Barīsa lies on the north bank of the river.

[3] Al-Idrīsī, op. cit., pp. 3–4.

[4] It has often been stated that the earliest reference to the Tokolor is in the بدكرير of al-Ya'qūbī (A.D. 872), reading it as Tadhkarīr, i.e. Takārīr, but they are enumerated among the peoples under Kawkaw and could not be Tokolor.

[5] Al-Bakrī mentions (op. cit., p. 179) a people who appear to be Fulbe in the territories of both Gāna and Silla: 'In the territory of Ghāna we find a people called Al-Hunaihīn (*vll.* النهيين and الهميين) whose ancestors were the soldiers that the Umayyads [i.e. Ḥabīb b. Abī 'Ubaida, *c.* A.D. 736–9] sent against Ghāna in the early days of Islam. They follow the religion of Ghāna, but their members never contract marriages with Negroes. They are white of complexion and handsome. Men of the same race are found at Silla where they are known under the name of Al-Famān' (Al-Fellān?). 'White' may be taken to be the Sudanese 'red' and the *Fulḅē woḍāḅē* are characterized by endogamy and paganism..

Ibn Sa'īd has understood the difference between Tokolor and Fulbe, 'The capital of the

and affected by other cultural influences. The Wolof–Serēr groups, however, after a chief or two had toyed with the idea of Islam, rejected it, and in spite of their openness to its influence it was not until the nineteenth century that the Wolof ruling classes joined it, whilst even today it has gained little influence over the Serēr.

From the Islamic point of view Takrūr was the most important of these kingdoms, but we are forced to rely almost wholly upon tradition for its history,[1] for in the eyes of the Arab world it was insignificant compared with the great empires. The first dynasty of which tradition has preserved the memory is that of Dyā'ōgo, probably of foreign origin, who founded a chieftaincy about A.D. 850. This was overthrown (*c.* 980) by the Manna, a branch of the Nyakhāte clan of Dyāra, a Soninke chieftaincy situated between them and Gāna.[2] According to al-Bakrī, this ruling family of Takrūr was the first Negro family to join Islam. Islam spread among them before 'Abd Allāh ibn Yāsīn organized his *jihād*, and their alliance with his

Takrūr lies on both banks of the river and is called Takrūr. The inhabitants are divided into two categories, sedentaries who live in villages, and nomads who roam the open country, most of whose ranges are on the northern side of the river, whilst on the south they possess only a few settlements' (Abū'l-Fidā', text p. 161). The map of Angelino Dulcert (1339) distinguishes between Felle and Tochoror.

[1] See especially *Chroniques de Foûta Sénégalais*, transl. by Siré Abbas Soh and ed. by M. Delafosse, Paris, 1913.

[2] Although Dyāra is not accorded much recognition here and the Dyāwara remained refractory to Islam until the last century, it was an important state playing a considerable role in the history of the Sahil. The site of the town of Dyāra, which still exists, is situated in Kingui, north-east of Nyoro. Its Soninke Nyakhātē rulers gained their independence when Gāna was conquered by the Murābiṭs. They became tributary to the Kanyāga dynasty of the Sōsē and then to Sun Dyāta when he defeated the Sōsē. The Nyakhātē were replaced by the Mande Dyāwara about 1385. Legend concerns itself particularly with the saga of Daman Ngillē, father of the conqueror, Maḥmūd. The latter's son, Silamakan (1415–35?), is responsible for the widespread extension of the state over Bakhunu, Dyanguntē, Kussāta, and Kanyāga, whilst he received tribute from Galam, Gidimaka, Gidumē, and Dyāfunu. In these places the Dyāwara installed a governor with the title of *faren*. But the indigenous chiefs of both Takrūr and Dyāra appear to have received investiture for their fiefs, for a time at least, from the *mansa* of Māli with the Mandinka title of *farba*, whilst the nomad chiefs received the title of *sa-tigi*. By the beginning of the fifteenth century the Dyāwara were independent of even the nominal suzerainty of Māli. Their independence was respected by the *askiyas* of Songhay. Civil wars were their curse, dependencies threw off their allegiance, and in 1754 they came under the domination of the Bambara Māsa-Sī, retaining some measure of sovereignty over their small original area until Nyoro, the capital of Bambara Karta, fell to al-ḥājj 'Umar in 1854.

On Dyāra see *Fattāsh*, pp. 39–40 (70–74); M. Adam, 'Légendes historiques du pays de Nioro', *Revue Coloniale*, nouvelle série, Nos. 13–15 (1903), pp. 25–38; Delafosse, *H.S.N.* ii. 154–61, and *Traditions historiques du Soudan Occidental*, pp. 30–47 (Nyakhātē dynasty pp. 47–51); G. Boyer, *Un peuple de l'Ouest Soudanais: Les Diawara*, Mém. I.F.A.N. No. 29, 1953.

Ṣanhājan warriors was no doubt connected with their fear of the power of Gāna. We have seen how in A.H. 448 (1056–7) Lebi, son of Wār-Jābī, aided Yaḥyā ibn 'Umar in his war against the Godāla who lived north of Ṣanghāna and Takrūr, and how they suffered in the overwhelming defeat of Yaḥyā at the battle of Tebferīlla, when the combined armies were so crushed that the Murābiṭs ever after left the Godāla alone.[1]

Between the eleventh and thirteenth centuries the Wolof differentiated themselves from the Serēr, a process accelerated when the son of a Tokolor cleric called Ndyadyan Ndyay formed the Jolof state (*c.* 1360).[2] This state soon lost any Islamic traces it may once have had. Berber pressure was increasing, Soninke were moving in from the north and east, the area of Takrūr became more and more restricted, and it was made tributary by the Soninke state of Dyāra. In the thirteenth century, when Dyāra itself became tributary to Māli, Takrūr also acknowledged its suzerainty, although to all intents and purposes independent. Its weakness and unsettled state are shown by the rapid succession of dynastic changes. About A.D. 1300 the Manna were overthrown by the pagan Tondyon.[3] A hundred years later the Tondyon were replaced by a family of Fulbe coming from the Termes region (in the Sahil, north-east of Fūta), whence the new rulers were called Lām Termes, 'Chiefs of Termes'. A group of nomadic Lamtūna, the Lām Tāga (1450–1500?), founded another dynasty which in time became Fulbe. We have to take into account in this region of the coexistence of a number of dynasties whose interrelationships, since our sources are traditional, are extremely obscure. All this region was now split up into small chieftaincies. The Fulbe were found mainly on the right bank of the Senegal, whilst the left bank was controlled by the

[1] Al-Bakrī, op. cit., text pp. 167–8.

[2] Attention may be called to the existence of a state south of the Senegal embracing part of Ferlo which only became desert as a result of overcultivation and the displacement of cultivators by Fulbe. The kingdom is mentioned by al-Bakrī who, after describing Iresnā (Barīsa) on the Senegal, goes on, 'Over against this town, on the opposite bank of the river, is a great kingdom more than eight days' journey in extent, whose king carries the title of Daw. They fight with arrows. Behind that is a country called Malel' (op. cit., pp. 177–8; cf. also al-Idrīsī quoted below, p. 63, who in the text and on his chart places Daw on the Falemē). According to tradition this was the kingdom of Namandirï, the old name of Fūta south of the river. It was ruled by a family of the ^{n}Daw (Ostrich) clan (see H. Gaden, *Proverbes Peule*, p. 35, and *Chroniques de Foûta Sénégalais*, p. 123). On the other hand, it is just as probable that Daw was a Mandinka chieftaincy, the Do-dugu region with the ruling village of Tabu where lived the Konatē lineage.

[3] Mande *tō-dyō*, 'slaves of the age-group association (*flā-tō*)', implies that they were agents of the Māli.

Dyāwara, except for Tōro where a Fulbe chief had made himself independent. All these were subject theoretically to Māli. But between 1400 and 1450 there was a redistribution of power during which the recently founded state of Jolof dominated Takrūr. In 1558 Takrūr gained its independence under still another Fulbe dynasty, the Deniyankobē (Awlād Tengella), who were pagans. It was possibly during these wars that the kingdom of Namandiri (Daw?), south of the Senegal, was destroyed. During the subsequent period, to which we shall return, the rising power of Islamic sentiment enabled the Tokolor to throw off the yoke of their pagan rulers and in 1776 to form an independent Muslim theocratic state.

The influence of these Negroes of Takrūr, formed through the mixture of many ethnic groups, has been far more important than their actual numbers and political instability would make appear. Their language, through being adopted by the Fulbe nomads, has spread from the Atlantic to Darfur. Also, since they were the first Negroes converted to Islam, they have been missionaries extending it among Wolof, Susu, Mandinka groups, Fulbe, Hausa, and Kanuri. When Tokolor *tōrodḅē*[1] began their *jihāds* it was always in those parts where they hoped to find allies in the Fulbe, though their hopes have not always been justified, for in Takrūr proper and in Māsina they had no more bitter enemies than the Fulbe. Tokolor have conducted widely celebrated Islamic schools to which many strangers came for legal training; those who settled became naturalized *tōrodḅē*, but others returned to their homeland to extend the knowledge of Islam.

3. THE SONINKE EMPIRE OF GĀNA

The empire known to the Arabs as Ghāna was situated in the Sahil in country which is not now inhabited by Negroes. The region was clearly more fertile than it is today, but being situated on the borderland of interaction between white nomads and black cultivators its history reveals a state of constant tension and instability. Consequently the depredations of nomadic Berbers drove away the cultivators and it is now largely desert.

[1] *Tōrodḅē*, sing. *Tōrōdo*, 'mendicant', is derived from *tōrade*, 'to beseech (a favour)', used of intercessory prayer to God (Ar. *da'ā*), not 'to perform the ritual prayer' which is *dyuldē* (Ar. *ṣallā*). In Nigeria *Tōrodḅē* is often confounded with *torañkoḅe* (sing. *torañke*) and merely means any immigrant from Futa Toro. The Muslim party which triumphed over the pagan Fulbe was designated by this name Tōrodḅē and it has become the equivalent of Tokolor; whilst in the Senegal, *Denyankē*, the name for the pagan Fulbe influx under Koli, has become equivalent to *Fulḅē woḍāḅe*, the *tyeddo* or warrior party as opposed to the clerical party.

That the dynasty which originally ruled Gāna was of different origin from the Soninke inhabitants is probable, but we do not know who founded it nor when. As-Saʿdī says that the dynasty was of white origin,[1] but Maḥmūd al-Kāti gives various speculations as to its origin which shows that there was no clear tradition. The last king of this line who lived at the time of the *hijra* was replaced by a non-noble dynasty which arose from among their subjects.[2] The Muslims of the north never thought of the rulers as other than Negroes even when they acquired an ʿAlid origin, but if we are to judge by the claims of African Muslims we should imagine that all ʿAlī's descendants emigrated to Africa.

At any rate Gāna was in existence when the geographers under the patronage of the early ʿAbbāsids were compiling their treatises. Muḥammad b. Ibrāhīm al-Fazārī, who compiled a recension of the *Brahmasiddhānta* called *Kitāb as-Sindhind al-Kabīr* in A.H. 156–7 (773–4) for al-Manṣūr, mentions 'the territory of [the] Ghāna, the land of gold', and gives its size as equal to the Idrīsid state of Morocco. Al-Khwārizmī, though his *Ṣūrat al-Arḍ* is based upon Ptolemy, inserts in the interior of Africa a few names which are not derived from Ptolemy:[3]

[1] 'Mallī is a region of vast extent situated in the far west towards the Atlantic Ocean. Qaya-magha founded the first state in those parts and the seat of his government was Ghāna. This was an important city in the country of Bāghana. According to tradition their power was in existence before the *hijra*, 22 kings exercising the authority before it and 22 after it, making 44 in all. In origin they were of the white race, but we have no idea to whom they traced this origin. Their slaves [subjects] were Waʿkori [Wankore or Soninke]. When their dynasty came to an end people of Mallī, who were blacks in origin, succeeded to their power' (As-Saʿdī, *Sūdān*, p. 9).

[2] Maḥmūd al-Kāti writes, 'Malli rose to power only after the downfall of the dynasty of the Kaya-magha, rulers over the whole of the western region. The chief of Malli was one of his subject vassal chiefs. Kaya-magha means in the Wankore language 'king of gold', *kayhu* being 'gold' and *magha* 'king'. He was a powerful king and I understand, on trustworthy evidence derived from the *qāḍī* of Māsina, that the Kaya-magha were among the most ancient of rulers, of whom 20 reigned before the manifestation of the Prophet. The name of his capital was Qunbi which was an important city. Their dynasty came to an end during the first century of the *hijra*. Some predecessors told me that the last of them was Kanisaʿay who ruled in the time of the Prophet, and whose capital was called Kurunkaʿ which was the residence of his mother and remains inhabited to this day. . . . God brought their line to an end and made the most ignoble of their people lord it over their superiors and overcome them. They killed all the children of their kings, even ripping open the women to kill those in the womb. There is disagreement as to the tribe to which they belonged, some saying that they were Waʿkore (Soninke), others that they were Wangāra (Mandinka) which appears improbable, whilst others say that they were from the Ṣanhāja which seems to me more likely' (*Fattāsh*, pp. 41–42). 'Gold' in Soninke and Fulfulde is *kaŋŋe*. Kaya-maga may mean 'master of the land', as a general term applied at this late date to the descendants of the first occupiers; but see Delafosse in *Fattāsh*, transl. p. 75, n. 1. Koroŋga is a locality 22 miles north of Gumbu.

[3] See C. A. Nallino, 'Al-Ḫuwārizmī e il suo rifacimento della Geografia di Tolomeo', *Mem. R. Accad. d. Lincei*, ser. v, ii (1894), 27.

Mūrā, 'interior' Kūs (Kūs al-Wāghila),[1] 'Alwa, Fazzān (?), Zaghāwa, Ghāna, Kankụ (Gungia?), Jarmī the great, Jarmī of al-Ḥabash,[2] Donqola, and Sijilmāsa; as well as various Berber names, Tāqart (Tāhart?), Targha, and Kātama, in the western Sahara. Gāna is associated in particular with the gold trade and was under the control of the Negro chief of the Wagadu region[3] at the beginning of the Islamic era. Ibn Khaldūn was reflecting these early contacts when he wrote, 'When, after the conquest of North Africa, merchants penetrated into the western parts (of the country of the Blacks) they found no Negro kingdom more powerful than that of Ghāna whose domain extended westwards as far as the Atlantic.'[4]

The actual site of the capital is uncertain. Al-Bakrī places it in Awkār, but it must have been south of the region called Awkār today (south-west of Walāta) which was probably as unsuitable for settled life in those days as it is now. Presumably the word Awkār covered a much wider area to the south than it does today. It would be unlikely to be the actual name of the state, but merely the term used by the Berber merchants from whom al-Bakrī got his information. The only writer to name the town is Maḥmūd al-Kāti who says that it was called Qunbi,[5] and the fact that there is a place called Kumbi Ṣāliḥ in Wagadu led Bonnel de Mézières to initiate excavations there in 1914,[6] which has been followed by a number of other French expeditions.[7] These excavations have revealed the remains of a town of the Islamic period, some of whose houses were built of stone, not a very common practice in the Sahil, and suggests some unusual influence in the kingdom upon which it is to be hoped archaeologists will one day throw light. Though some of the evidence accords with indications given in al-Bakrī's account of the town, the assumption that this is the site of Gāna rests

[1] Al-Idrīsī situates Kūshat al-wāghila clearly in the Nubian kingdom of Maqurra (ed. Dozy and de Goeje, p. 19, transl. pp. 23–24).

[2] Mžik restored Jarmī madīnat al-kabīra to Jaira, probably Ptolemy's *Γειρέοι Αἰθίοπες* and Jarmī (or Jaramī) al-Ḥabash is his *Γαράμη μητρόπολις* (iv, cap. 6, 12). Ptolemy employs *Αἰθίοπες* for any dark-coloured people. Al-Idrīsī (p. 35) writes, 'In Fazzān is the town of Jarma and the town of Tasāwa. The Negroes call the latter Jarmī the little.'

[3] The Gāna region is called Wagadu by the Soninke, Bāghana by the Mandinka, and Awkār by the Berbers. *Awkār* signifies undulating sandy country and there are naturally many *awkārs*.

[4] Ibn Khaldūn, op. cit. i. 263 (ii. 109).

[5] *Ta'rīkh al-Fattāsh*, p. 41 (tr. p. 76). Cf. also the local traditions given by Delafosse, *H.S.N.* i. 259.

[6] *Mém. Acad. Inscr. et B.-L.* xiii (1923), pt. i, pp. 227–73.

[7] See P. Thomassey and R. Mauny, 'Campagne de fouilles à Koumbi Saleh', *Bull. I.F.A.N.* xiii (1951), 438–62; xviii (1956), 117–40.

on precarious grounds. It is not proved by archaeological evidence, no indications of a twin town have been found, *kumbi* merely means 'tumulus', and Maḥmūd al-Kāti simply says that Qunbi was the capital of the first dynasty whose last king at the time of the *hijra* was resident at Koronga.

Gāna was not the name of the country, nor of the capital, but one of the titles of the ruler.[1] The earliest Arabic writers meant by *Bilād Ghāna*, 'the country of [the] Ghāna', and even later writers are careful to point this out. Ad-Dimishqī writes, 'Amongst the countries of the Blacks is Ghāna whose capital is [in] Awkār. Ghāna is the dynastic name for he who rules over this country, just as Baghpūr is that of the ruler of China and Qāqān for the ruler of the Turks.'[2] Abū 'l-Fidā' and Ibn Khaldūn, both of whom were dependent upon Ibn Sa'īd, use Ghāna for the title of the king, for the name of the country, and for its capital. Other titles the king carried were *tuŋka*, a Soninke title applied to the rulers of the Bākyili dynasty of Galam as well as the Sīsē dynasty of Gāna and still a common Soninke word for a chief, and *magha* or *maghan*, 'master', 'lord'.[3]

The power and prosperity of the state of the Gāna were due primarily to its borderland position on the great commercial routes between Negroland whence came the gold, slaves, ivory, and ebony which were exchanged for salt, copper, blue pearls, hides, dates, and textiles of the north. To the Muslim world Gāna had the reputation of being one of the extremities of the world for the trader.[4] Yāqūt, whose material we may take to be based upon al-Muhallabī (A.D. 985), writes of its situation from the commercial point of view:

> Ghāna is a great town situated south of the Maghrib and contiguous with the land of the Negroes. It is the place where the merchants who wish to penetrate through the deserts into the gold countries foregather. If it did not exist access to these regions would be impossible because its situation is at the point of separation between the country of the Moors and that of the Negroes where they provision themselves.[5]

The power and prosperity of Gāna must not be exaggerated. It

[1] The word is employed in Soninke (*gāna*) and Mandinke (*kāna*) for 'war-leader'; see Delafosse, *La Langue Mandingue*, ii. 241.

[2] Ad-Dimishqī, ed. Mehren, p. 240.

[3] Cf. *kaya-magha* in the passages quoted above (p. 48) from As-Sa'dī and Maḥmūd al-Kāti. The Māli kings were probably all called *magha*, though the term is only applied to certain of them in our texts.

[4] Cf. al-Ḥarīrī, *Maqāma* of Iskandariyya, ed. Steingass, p. 65.

[5] Yāqūt, ed. Wüstenfeld, iii. 770.

probably reached the height of its influence in the ninth century when its sphere included the greater part of Ḥawḍ and Tagant as well as Awkār-Bāghana, having the Niger on the east and the Senegal and Baule to the south and west. Al-Ya'qūbī (writing A.D. 872), who regarded Kawkaw as the greatest of the Sudan kingdoms, says of Gāna, 'Its king is also powerful. In his country are the mines of gold, and under his authority are a number of kings, among them the kingdoms of 'Ām and Sāma.'[1] Other dependencies of Gāna mentioned later by al-Bakrī were Anbarā, Safnagu situated on a nile,[2] and Jāda (Dyāra?).

The prosperity of Gāna was closely allied with that of the unstable Lamtūna centre of Awdaghast. Ibn Ḥawkal, after describing Awdaghast as 'a pleasant place comparable with Mecca . . . in that it lies between two hills', writes that the direct route from Egypt to Gāna[3] had been abandoned in consequence of the sandstorms which had overwhelmed caravans and the attacks of brigands, wherefore the traders had taken to using the longer but safer route through North Africa to Sijilmāsa in southern Morocco where many merchants from 'Irāq resided. Thence the route went to Awdaghast which filled an analogous role on the Sudan border. He was amazed by the enormous transactions of these merchants and recounts how he saw in Awdaghast in A.H. 340 (A.D. 951) a cheque (*ṣakk*), which was officially certified for 42,000 *dīnārs*, drawn up by a man of Sijilmāsa on Muḥammad b. 'Alī Sa'dūn.[4] Ibn Ḥawqal also shows how much the prosperity of Gāna was dependent upon the trade link:

This king of Awdaghast maintains relations with the king of Ghāna. Ghāna

[1] Al-Ya'qūbī, *Ta'rīkh*, i. 219. 'Ām may be a mutilated form of Awghām or Anbarā which are mentioned later by al-Bakrī as situated respectively east and west of Gāna. Sāma is mentioned by Ibn Ḥawqal (i. 92, and *qabūl Sāma*, i. 61) who says that 'from Kūgha to Sāma is less than a month's journey'. Al-Bakrī writes (pp. 177, 178–9) that Sāma is one of the dependencies adjoining Gāna, its capital, Sāma-qanda, being four days' journey away. The people, who go about naked except that the women wear plaited leathern girdles, are called al-Bakam. They are very skilful archers using poisoned arrows. The eldest son inherits all the paternal property, which seems to show that they were not Soninke. They are obviously not the Baghāma of al-Idrīsī (p. 9) who are Berber nomads. Al-Idrīsī distinguishes between Sama-qanda and Shāma (cf. pp. 11, 12, 40) which he places in Climate II, section 2, among the Zaghāwa (p. 32/40). Sāma is a common place-name. That mentioned by Maḥmūd al-Kāti (p. 48/92) is probably the same as the Samakanda of Barth (iv. 369), but cannot be the Sāma of the earlier Arabic writers.

[2] Safnagu is mentioned by Barth (v. 487) in the Ra's al-Mā' region.

[3] Al-Hamadhānī (A.D. 903) writes, 'If one sets off from the land of the Ghāna for Egypt one passes through a Negro people called Kawkaw, then another called Maranda, then the Murāwa (Zaghāwa or proto-Hausa) until one reaches the oases of Egypt called Malsāna' (*B.G.A.* v. 68). Ālsāna is the name of a locality in the Dākhla group of oases.

[4] Ibn Ḥawqal, ed. Kramers, i. 61, 99–100.

is the richest king on the face of the earth by reason of the wealth and treasure of nuggets dug up (*at-tibr al-muthār*) in the past by his predecessors and by himself. He exchanges presents with the ruler of Kūgha whose wealth and prosperity is nothing like that enjoyed by the ruler of Ghāna. They exchange presents with ḥim [i.e. Awdaghast], for they are much dependent upon the kings of Awdaghast on account of their need to import salt from the Islamic regions for they cannot exist without this commodity. Sometimes the price of a load of salt in the interior and remotest parts of Negroland attains a value of between two and three hundred *dīnārs*.[1]

The power of the Ṣanhāja was derived from their control of the trade-routes for they levied toll on all caravans passing through their territory,[2] but in A.D. 990, probably because internal conflicts between the Ṣanhāja were upsetting the trade-routes, the Soninkē of Gāna took control of Awdaghast and installed a Negro governor. Seventy-eight years after this event al-Bakrī gives us the most interesting description of Gāna that we possess:

Ghāna is the title borne by their kings and the country is called Awkār. The king today, which is the year 460 (A.D. 1067–8), is called *Tunkā* Menīn who succeeded to the throne in A.H. 455. His predecessor was Basī who began to reign at the age of 85. His conduct was praiseworthy, he was a lover of justice and favourable to Muslims. . . . He was the maternal uncle of *Tunkā* Menīn for their customary law decrees that the king can be succeeded only by his sister's son, since there can be no doubt about him being her son, whereas he cannot be sure that his own son is really his. This *Tunkā* Menīn wields great power and inspires respect as the ruler of a great empire.

The city of Ghāna consists of two towns lying in a plain, one of which is inhabited by Muslims[3] and is large, possessing twelve mosques, one being a *jāmiʿ*, each having their *imāms*, muezzins and reciters (*rātibūn*). The town possesses jurisconsults and learned men. Water is obtained from sweet wells outside the town, around which they cultivate vegetables.[4]

[1] Ibn Ḥawqal, ed. Kramers, i. 101.

[2] Ibid. i. 102.

[3] That is the foreign quarter of Arab and Berber merchants.

[4] It is clear from this description that the town was not on a river but leaves open the question whether or not it was on a *wādī* which filled after the rains. He writes elsewhere (p. 180): 'After leaving Ghāna, travelling in the direction of the rising sun through country inhabited by Negroes, one arrives at a place called Awghām. . . . Four days further on one comes to a place called Ra's al-Mā' where one comes upon the Nile issuing out of the country of the Negroes. Along its banks live tribes of Berbers called Medāsa who are Muslims. The opposite bank to them is inhabited by pagan Negroes. From there, following the Nile for six days, one comes to the town of Tīreqqā.' Yāqūt (iv. 919) describes the Medāsa, a Ṣanhāja people, as part pagan, but we do not know the date of the source of his information (al-Muhallabī?).

The royal city is six miles from the foreign quarter and is called *al-Ghāba*.[1] The area between the two is covered with habitations. Their houses are constructed of stone and acacia wood. The king's residence comprises a palace and conical huts, the whole surrounded by a fence like a wall. In the king's town, not far from the royal court of justice, is a mosque for the use of the Muslims who visit him on missions. Around the royal town are huts, groves, and coverts where live the magicians who control their religious rites, and where they keep their idols (*dakākīr*) and bury their kings. These groves are protected by guards who permit no one to enter or find out what goes on in them. There also are situated the king's prisons and once a man is incarcerated in them he is never heard of again. The interpreters of the king are chosen from the Muslims, and likewise his treasurer and most of his ministers.

None of those who belong to the imperial religion may wear tailored garments except the king himself and the heir-presumptive, his sister's son. The rest of the people wear wrappers of cotton, silk or brocade according to their means. Most of the men shave their beards and the women their heads. The king adorns himself with female ornaments around the neck and arms, on his head he wears gold-embroidered caps covered with turbans of finest cotton. He gives audience to the people for the redressing of grievances in a hut around which are placed 10 horses bedecked with golden caparisons. Behind him stand 10 slaves carrying shields and swords mounted with gold. On his right are the sons of his [vassal] kings, their heads plaited with gold and wearing costly garments. On the ground around him are seated his ministers, whilst the governor of the city sits before him. On guard at the door are dogs of fine pedigree, wearing collars of gold and silver adorned with knobs, which rarely leave the presence of the king. The royal audience is announced by the beating of a drum, called *dabā*,[2] made out of a long piece of hollowed-out wood. When the people have gathered, his co-religionists draw near upon their knees sprinkling dust upon their heads as a sign of respect,[3] whilst the Muslims clap hands as their form of greeting.

Their religion is paganism and the cult of idols.[4] When the king dies they construct a large hut of wood over the place of burial. His body is brought on a scantily-furnished bier and placed in that hut. With it they put his eating and drinking utensils, food and drink, and those who used to serve him with these, and then the entrance is secured. They cover the hut with mats and clothing

[1] 'Forest' or 'grove', so called by the foreigners because of the sacred groves.

[2] The word *daba* is still the name for these drums in Soninke (*taba* in Mande) according to Delafosse, *H.S.N.* ii. 43.

[3] Ibn Baṭṭūṭa (iv. 407–8), Ibn Khaldūn (transl. iv. 343–4), al-ʿUmari (pp. 67–68), Maḥmūd al-Kāti (p. 11), and Portuguese (Marmol, iii. 79) report this dusting ceremonial at the courts of Māli, Songhay, and Jolof.

[4] The various indications of their religion given by al-Bakrī dispose of the statement of az-Zuhrī that the inhabitants of Gāna were Christians before A.H. 469 (A.D. 1076–7) when they embraced Islam; cf. MS. Bibl. Nat., No. 1873, fo. 5, l. ١٣; *T. as-Sūdān*, p. 42 n.; *Not. et Extr.* xii. 642.

and all the assembled people pile earth over it until it resembles a considerable hill, then they dig a ditch around it allowing only one means of access to the heap. They sacrifice victims to their dead and offer them fermented drinks.

The king levies a tax of one *dīnār* of gold for each donkey-load of salt which is imported and 2 *dīnārs* on any exported.[1] He takes 5 *mithqāls* for each load of copper and 10 for each load of merchandise. The best gold of his country comes from the town of Ghiyārū which is 18 days journey from the capital[2] over country intensively inhabited by Negro tribes. If any nuggets of gold are found in any of the mines of his country the king appropriates the best of them, leaving only the gold dust for the people, otherwise gold would be so abundant that its value would depreciate. Nuggets vary in weight from an ounce to a pound. It is reported that the king possesses a piece of gold the size of a large stone.[3] The town of Ghiyārū, in which many Muslims live, is situated 12 miles from the Nile. Ghāna is an unhealthy and sparsely populated country. Few newcomers escape the sickness which is prevalent during the growing season and many strangers succumb during the harvest season.[4]

We have mentioned that in A.D. 990 the Soninke rulers of Gāna had taken direct control of Awdaghast and that the Murābiṭūn, formed from people who were its former rulers, were concerned to secure this important caravan terminal. Al-Bakrī writes:

[1] Salt came from the mines of Tātentāl (Teghāza region?) and Awlīl on the Atlantic coast (al-Bakrī, op. cit., p. 171).

[2] Delafosse reads Gadyara for غيارو (*H.S.N.* ii. 44). Ibn Ḥawqal (i. 61, 64) has *Gharyū*; al-Idrīsī *Ghiyāra* (p. 6). This was not actually in the gold-bearing area but a merchant village. Elsewhere (p. 179) al-Bakrī says that the most prolific gold mines are in the neighbourhood of Kūgha. All the Arab writers mention the trade in gold. Yāqūt (i. 821–2) gives one of the most interesting accounts, since he describes the whole organization from the departure from Sijilmāsa and Dar'a to the silent bargaining with the extractors. See also Mas'ūdī (iv. 93) and al-'Umarī (pp. 70–72). The gold came from the region which other Arab writers call Wangāra (hardly the Qanqāra of al-Bakrī, p. 164/362, which is in the desert). According to al-Idrīsī (p. 8) it formed an island 300 miles long by 150 wide, surrounded by streams. The eastern part of the region between the Falemē and Bakhoy is still called Gangaran (Gãgarã or Gbãgarã, 'hole in the ground', i.e. gold mines). It is this word which was corrupted by Arab authors to Gangāra or Wangāra and perhaps applied by extension to the Soninkē of Mauritania and Ḥawḍ (cf. Qanqāra of al-Bakrī (p. 164/362) in the middle of the desert). Ibn Baṭṭūṭa passed through the village of Zāgharī (Dyāga) inhabited by Negro traders called Wanjarāta (iv. 394). Later the Arabs applied the term to Mande generally. Maḥmūd al-Kāti (*Fattāsh*, p. 38) distinguished in the seventeenth century between Malinke and Wangāra, regarding the former as warriors and the latter as traders (*dyūla*), though both were of the same origin. Today Wangāra and Wankore (Wakore) are used by Fulbė and Songhay as equivalent to Soninke and Malinke. In Hausa and the Gold Coast the Wangāra are the Mande Dyula.

[3] The size of this nugget keeps on increasing. With al-Idrīsī (text p. 7) it reaches the size of a boulder of 30 rotls to which the king tethered his horse. Ibn Khaldūn reports (i. 266–7) that this boulder, now in the possession of the king of Māli, weighed a ton and was sold by Mansa Dyāta (1360–73).

[4] Al-Bakrī, op. cit., pp. 174–7.

In the year 446 (A.D. 1054–5) ʿAbd Allāh ibn Yāsīn attacked Awdaghast, a populous country with a large capital in which there were many markets, palm groves and henna trees as large as olive trees. It used to be a residence of the king of the Blacks who is called Ghāna before the Arabs entered [the country of the] Ghāna. It is a solidly built town with fine residences, and lies two months journey from Sijilmāsa and 15 days from Ghāna. Zanāta and Arabs lived in this town in a state of mutual hatred and opposition. They were very wealthy and possessed many slaves, some having a thousand or more. The Murābiṭūn declared all that they found of women and goods to be lawful booty. ʿAbd Allāh ibn Yāsīn killed a mulatto from Qayrawān called Zabāqra who was renowned for his piety, virtue, zeal in reciting the Qur'ān, and for having accomplished the pilgrimage. The Murābiṭūn acted with such severity against the people of Awdaghast because of their allegiance to the ruler of Ghāna.[1]

At this time Gāna seems to have been having difficulties with tributaries. King Tārim of Anbarā (or I-n-Barā), six days west of Gāna on the route to Kūgha and Takrūr, was in rebellion against its authority.[2] This was no doubt a consequence of the ferment caused by the rise of the Murābiṭūn.

The energies of the Murābiṭ movement were directed primarily towards the north and it was only when Abū Bakr b. ʿUmar returned to the southern desert in 1062 that, in order to absorb the restless tribesmen, he directed their energies against the Negro kingdom. Even so a long struggle ensued before the Soninke capital was finally captured in 469/1076–7. Many of its people were massacred and those who survived were forced to join Islam. We do not know whether the king was left on the throne, but it seems clear that his widespread empire broke up and its constituent chieftaincies gained their independence. As we have seen, the fortunes of the Murābiṭūn quickly declined through tribal rivalries, Abū Bakr was killed in 1087, and the whole organization of the desert tribes collapsed. The Soninkes of Gāna recovered their independence, but they did not regain the position they had lost, although the commercial importance of the capital was maintained. At the end of the twelfth century its sphere of rule did not encompass more than its original nucleus in Awkār and Basikunu. About this time al-Idrīsī, writing at the Sicilian court (548/1154), gives an account of a place which he calls Ghāna:

The towns of this [second] section of the first climate include Malel, Ghāna, Tīreqqa, Medāsa, Saghmāra, Ghiyāra, Gharbīl, and Samaqanda. . . . From

[1] Ibid., p. 168; transl. pp. 369–70.
[2] Ibid., p. 179.

the town of Malel to that of Ghāna the great is about 12 days' journey across a soft, sandy and waterless waste. Ghāna consists of two towns situated on the two banks of a sweet river. It is the most extensive and thickly populated town in the country of the Negroes, and has the most wide-spread commerce. It is the goal of the richest merchants from all the surrounding countries and those of western Maghrib. Its inhabitants are Muslims and its king, so we are told, claims descent from Ṣāliḥ b. ʿAlī b. Abī Ṭālib.[1] His name alone is employed in the *khuṭba* although he is in allegiance to the ʿAbbāsid caliph. The king has a *qaṣr*[2] on the border of the Nile which is well and solidly constructed. Its dwellings are ornamented with various embossed designs, dawbs, and sun-blinds of glass beads. This palace was constructed in the year A.H. 510 (A.D. 1116–17). The territory he rules adjoins that of Wangāra so renowned for the quantity and quality of the gold it produces.[3]

Al-Idrīsī has been taken to task for mistakes in this account, but it contains nothing inherently improbable. The main difficulty, his statement that the capital was on a river 'on which they have canoes for fishing and communication between the two towns', raises the question as to whether the old capital had been abandoned and the Gāna was actually resident in a riverside town or whether al-Idrīsī has confused the town with the capital of another country which has taken the place of Gāna as the dominant power. Subsequent writers also place Gāna on a river. Ibn Saʿīd (1240) says specifically: 'Ghāna has a nile which is own sister to the nile of Egypt and falls into the Atlantic at $10\frac{1}{2}°$ long. and 14° lat. N. The difference of latitude between its mouth and Ghāna is about 4 degrees. Ghāna lies on the two banks of its nile and consists of two towns, one inhabited by Muslims and the other by pagans.'[4] Dela-

[1] Ibn Khaldūn (*Prolégomènes*, transl. de Slane, i. 115–16) reports this claim with scepticism, remarking that no Ṣāliḥ is found among the descendants of ʿAbd Allāh the Fāṭimid. We would suppose his white ancestors to have been of the Ṣanhāja for Ibn Khaldūn says, 'the Ṣanhāja claim to stand in the same relationship to Abū Ṭālib that the Maghrāwa do to ʿUthmān ibn ʿAffān' (*Berb.* ii. 3) were it not that no writer says that the rulers were Berbers.

[2] *Qaṣr* here meaning a group of houses surrounded by a wall.

[3] Al-Idrīsī, *Description de l'Afrique et de l'Espagne*, ed. Dozy and de Goeje, 1864, pp. 5–7. Awdaghast also declined with the decay of Gāna. Al-Idrīsī describes it as 'a little town deficient in water, with a scanty population and a miserable trade in camels' (p. 32).

[4] Abū 'l-Fidā', text 1840, p. 157. These references to the Nile become clearer when we realize that Ibn Saʿīd thought of three sister rivers issuing from a great lake, Kūrī (i.e. the Chad) in central Africa; Nīl Miṣr falling into the Mediterranean, Nīl Ghāna (the combined Senegal and Niger) falling into the Atlantic, and Nīl Maqdishū falling into the Indian Ocean (see Ibn Saʿīd in Abū 'l-Fidā', pp. 151–4, 163). The Niger probably once formed two distinct rivers of which the upper lost itself in an inland delta, the large alluvial plain which is now the Ra's al-Māʾ region, and the lower Niger born in Adrār of the Iforas which flowed into the Atlantic. The two basins were closely adjacent and the result was a capture at Tosaye. The decline of Gāna may well be associated with the joining up of the two rivers for this would totally alter the character of the Wagadu region which, in Ibn Baṭṭūṭa's time, was complete desert.

fosse[1] interprets these texts as applying to the first of the capitals of Māli on the upper Niger. But capitals were very unstable. The residence of the Gāna, wherever situated, was referred to by the same name. The old capital, being too exposed to Berber raids, was probably abandoned as the royal residence. The post-Islamic ruins of Kumbi Ṣāliḥ show that this place was a white trading city, later superceded by Walāta. Its change of status, no longer a capital city, led to confusion. If still situated inland the confusion probably arose because travellers referred to both the Senegal and Niger as *Nīl Ghāna*, 'the River of [the] Ghāna', but since trading relations were continuous someone would surely have corrected the error. There were no doubt many cities of the Gāna, but the indications are that it was on the Senegal or a tributary rather than the Niger.[2] Even Maḥmūd al-Kāti, who says the capital was Qunbi, mentions that the last Kaya-magha who ruled in the time of the Prophet had his capital at Koronka which still existed in his day.

Al-Idrīsī's contemporary, Abū Ḥāmid al-Andalusī, writes (1162) of the importance of the gold-salt trade, but adds little of value:

> Some of the kings of the Negroes have embraced Islam, those of five tribes, so they say, the nearest being Ghāna in whose sands sprouts gold of the finest quality in great profusion. Merchants carrying mineral salt on camels set off from a town called Sijilmāsa, the last town of the lower Maghrib, passing over sands as over seas, having with them guides who navigate the deserts by means of the stars and prominances, and carrying with them six months provisions. When they arrive at Ghāna they barter the salt for an equal weight of gold,[3] sometimes they sell it for double its weight or even more, depending upon the greater or smaller number of merchants. The people of Ghāna are the most renowned (or best behaved) and best looking of Negroes, having straighter hair and full of intelligence. They go on pilgrimage to Mecca. As for the Fāwah (*v.l.* Qitāwa), Qūqū (*v.l.* Qūqah), Malī, Takrūr and Ghadāmis, they are vigorous people, but their country is unblessed and unproductive. They have no revealed religion and are not intelligent. The worst of them are the Qūqū.[4]

Ibn Khaldūn gives the following account of the end of the kingdom:

> The domination of the people of Ghāna weakened and their power declined, whilst that of the 'muffled ones' of the Berberland adjoining them to

[1] *Bull. Com. Ét. A.O.F.* 1924, p. 479.

[2] On the *Weltkarte* of al-Idrīsī as reconstructed by K. Miller (*Mappae Arabicae*, Band I, heft 3) Gāna is situated slightly above the confluence of the Falemē and the Senegal.

[3] Al-Bakrī (op. cit., p. 174/381) says that the Farawī used to exchange gold for an equal weight of salt.

[4] Abū Ḥāmid, *Tuḥfat al-Albāb*, ed. G. Ferrand, *J. Asiat.* ccvii. 41–42.

the north increased. They overcame the Negroes, plundered their territories, imposed upon them the *kharāj* and *jizya*, and forced many of them to join Islam. As a result they declined and the authority of the rulers of Ghāna dwindled away and the neighbouring Negro people of Ṣūṣū conquered and enslaved them, and annexed their territory. Next the people of Māli, increasing in population, gained the ascendancy over the Negro peoples of those regions. They conquered the Ṣūṣū and took control over all they possessed, both their original territory and that of Ghāna, as far as the Atlantic in the west.[1]

Delafosse has been able to fill in this account with the aid of local traditions.[2] One Soninke chieftaincy which gained its independence after the sack of Gāna by the Murābiṭs was that of the Soso, founded towards the end of the eighth century, whose territory lay in Kanyāga between Gāna and Manding.[3] From 1076 to 1180, according to tradition, this region was under a pagan Soninke dynasty known under its clan-name of Dyari-so. During the reign of Banna-Bubu (*c.* 1100–20) Fulbe made their appearance in the region and members of the royal clan took wives from the Sō or Ferōbē clan, whose descendants were known as *Sōsē* and the town and state *Sōso*. This, of course, is purely conjectural. In 1180 a Soninke soldier called Dyāra Kantē overthrew the dynasty. He was succeeded by Sumāguru (or Sumāhoro) Kantē (*c.* 1200–35) who conquered Gāna.[4] This event, the pillage of their goods, and unsettled conditions led the merchants of Gāna to emigrate to the wells of Biru (*c.* 1224) where an important commercial centre called Walāta developed and replaced Gāna as the caravan terminal.[5] Ibn Baṭṭūṭa gives a long description of Walāta when it was the most northerly outpost of the Mandinka empire, but inhabited mainly by Masūfa Berbers.

After taking Gāna Sumāguru Kantē conquered Manding. He is reported to have put to death eleven members of the dynastic line, but one of the Keyta clan, called Sun Dyāta, survived to mobilize an opposi-

[1] Ibn Khaldūn, *Berb.*, ed. de Slane, i. 263–4.

[2] See *Traditions historiques et légendaires du Soudan Occidental*, traduites d'un manuscrit arabe inédit par M. Delafosse, 1914; and *H.S.N.* ii. 162–70.

[3] Ibn Khaldūn writes (i. 263), 'It is reported that adjoining them (Ghāna) on the east is another people called Ṣūṣū or Sūsū. After them comes a people called Māli, then the Kawkaw or Kāghū.' A town called Sosso still exists in Kanyāga, north of Beledugu. Al-Qalqashandī quotes Ibn Khaldūn as saying that the people of Sūsū were called *al-Ankāriya* (v. 283): Wangāriya? Ibn Khaldūn, however, says that the people of Māli are called Ankāriya (i. 263; v. l, *'Ibar*, Cairo ed., vi. 200, *Ankāwiya*).

[4] H. Barth conjectured that this took place in A.H. 600/A.D. 1203–4; *Travels*, iv. 585.

[5] Walāta, Ibn Baṭṭūṭa's Īwālāten, is a berberization of Mande *wa-la*, 'shady spot'. *Biru* is the Soninke plural of *birē* which means the same as Mande *wa*, 'shelter', used by semi-nomads in the Sahil, and by extension 'an open-air market'.

tion. About A.D. 1235 he defeated Sumāguru, freed Manding, and pressing northwards captured the capital of Gāna (A.D. 1240). Thus Mandinka of Māli replaced the Sūsū clan as rulers of Gāna country.[1] This was not the complete end of Gāna.[2] It continued as a separate tribute-paying ruling line. Al-Qalqashandī quotes al-'Umarī (1342):

Shaikh Sa'īd ad-Dukkālī reported[3] 'No one in his [the Māli's] empire is accorded the title of king except the ruler of Ghāna who is really only his deputy, although a king.' It seems as though the ruler of Ghāna and no other retains the title of king simply because he has not been dispossessed of it [the kingdom?] and his control over it is complete. But we read in the *Ta'rīf*,[4] 'As for Ghāna he [the ruler of Māli] does not actually rule it, but it is as though he possessed it. He gives up control because of the gold-fields[5] within and beyond it to the south. We have already described how, when Islam is propagated and the call to prayer proclaimed in the lands of the gold-fields, the supply of gold diminishes.[6] It is for that reason, because he is a Muslim, that

[1] Al-'Umarī does not mention Sūsū in his list of territories under Māli rule during the reign of Sulaimān (1341–60). This leads al-Qalqashandī (v. 286) to speculate as to whether it had disappeared as a separate political unit. According to tradition the royal family of the Sōsē and their adherents fled to Takrūr where they founded a local dynasty which lasted until overthrown by Wolof in 1350.

[2] Ramón Lull (*Blanquerna*, transl. E. Allison Peers, 1926, pp. 356–7) mentions the visit of 'a gentile (i.e. heathen) who came from a southern land which lies within the regions of the desert, and from a city which is called Gana.... The people of that land are very many, and they are black, and have no law.' He also refers to a Vatican mission which, about 1283, 'journeyed southwards, and found a caravan of six thousand camels, laden with salt, leaving a town by name of Tibalbert, and going to that country wherein is the source of the river Damiata. So many people did this messenger find here, that in fifteen days all the salt was sold; and these men were all black, and adore idols' (ibid., p. 374). Tabelbalet, an advance-post of Mediterranean commerce with the Sudan since Carthaginian times, lies deep within the desert between Ghadāmes and In Salah (cf. al-'Umarī, p. 202).

[3] Abū Sa'īd 'Uthmān ad-Dukkālī, whom al-'Umarī met in Cairo, had spent thirty-five years in Māli and travelled widely there.

[4] Al-'Umarī's *At-Ta'rīf bi 'l-Muṣṭalaḥ ash-Sharīf*.

[5] *Manābit adh-dhahab*. The first mention of this vegetable gold is by al-Hamadhānī (*B.G.A.* v. 87), 'Gold grows in the land of Ghāna in the sand just like carrots. It is harvested at sunrise.' Al-'Umarī, although giving an account of the gold root plant (op. cit., pp. 70–72), also gives a reasonable account derived from Mansa Mūsā himself, 'The sultan told me, said az-Zawawī, that he had in his empire pagan peoples whom he did not make to pay the tax on infidels, but employed them in the mines extracting gold. He told me also that the mines of gold consist of pits which they excavate to approximately the depth of a man and collect the gold from the bottom.'

[6] Al-'Umarī writes elsewhere (al-Qalqashandī, *Ṣubḥ*, v. 287), 'Under the control of the sultan [of Māli] is the gold-bearing country (*bilādu maghārati 'dh-dhahab*) which is the land of the primitives. Every year they send him gold as tribute. If he wished he could take control of them, but the kings of this state have learnt by experience that if they conquered one of their towns and propagated Islam there and instituted the call to prayer, the collecting of gold diminished and finally ceased, whilst in the neighbouring heathen lands it increased. Therefore they contented themselves with exacting obedience and payment of a fixed tribute.'

the ruler of Māli leaves it [semi-independent] and every year derives from it a large fixed tribute.'[1]

The Gāna referred to here is not in the old region but on the northern border of the gold-bearing area. When Ibn Khaldūn obtained information about Māli from 'Uthmān, *faqīh* of the people of Gāna, it was merely the name of a district.[2]

A widespread dispersion of Soninke ensued in consequence of these three successive disasters, the increasing desiccation of the region, and their commercial tendencies. They played an important role as propagators of Islam.[3] Those of Gāna spread it into dependencies such as Dyāra, Galam (Bakel), and Māsina, especially among the people of Dyā or Dyākha. Ibn Baṭṭūṭa, who passed through Zāgha (Dyākha) in 1352, remarks that 'its inhabitants are of long-standing in Islam; they show great devotion and zeal for study'.[4] From Dyā went out a movement of *dyula* who carried Islam eventually to the northern border of the forest region where they founded centres like that of Bēgo, not far from the southern winding of the Black Volta, from whence went out the founders of the trading village.states of Bonduku and Kong.

4. THE MANDINKA EMPIRE OF MĀLI

The renown of Gāna as a Sahilian gold-trading state has tended to confuse history, for south of it were the nuclei of what was to become a great empire far surpassing it in power and range of influence. The Mandinka plateau (Manding, Khaso, Bambuk, Gangaran, Wasulu, &c.) differentiated by its relief, intermediary position between the upper Senegal and upper Niger, and type of population, has played a great role in history. It was the centre of an indigenous Negro state called Māli[5] whose foundation owed nothing to the intrusion of whites.

[1] Al-Qalqashandī, *Ṣubḥ*, v. 292–3.

[2] Ibn Khaldūn, *'Ibar*, vi. 200.

[3] Although Soninke traders went into the Northern Territories of present-day 'Ghana' (Wangāra is the name by which *dyula* are known there) they had nothing to do with the migrations of the Akan. It is ironical that Gāna, title of a desert monarch, should have been adopted by Gold Coast politicians to provide a mythological tradition for the new state. The origin of this myth is due to the speculations of Europeans on the basis of local traditions that the Akan stock, to which the Ashanti and Fanti belong, is connected with the kingdom of Awkār, for which there is no historical foundation whatever.

[4] Ibn Baṭṭūṭa, transl. H. A. R. Gibb, p. 323; French ed. iv. 394–5; cf. *T. as-Sūdān*, p. 10/19–20; *Fattāsh*, p. 52/100, n. 7.

[5] On the terminology M. Delafosse writes, 'Le mot *Mandé* est prononcé généralement *Manden* ou *Manding* ou encore *Manen* ou *Maning* par les gens de langue mandingue et *Mali* ou *Malli* par les gens de langue peule, d'où les deux noms de "Mandingues" (pour

Its history as an empire, in the sense in which the term is employed for these states embracing large numbers of subject states of diverse populations, was one of the most glorious in Africa. Situated in full savanna it was firmly rooted in an agricultural population, well provided with natural resources, including control of the gold-bearing area, important for commercial relations with North Africa.

The dynasty which founded Māli was one of a number of Mande chieftaincies.[1] It appears to have begun as a small chieftaincy in the hills on the right bank of the upper Niger, upstream of modern Bamako, the region known as Jeliba, formerly Tubla. The date of its evolution from an agglomeration of independent family communities into a state with a ruling monarch surrounded by functionaries is unknown, but it was in existence in the tenth century A.D. An early capital was Jeriba situated near the junction of the Niger and the Sankarani. The Malel[2] mentioned by al-Bakrī and al-Idrīsī was no doubt a Mandinka chieftaincy, but not necessarily the one which grew to become the Māli empire, for, as Monteil has shown, three lineages existed in northern Māli.[3] Its position is clearly west of Daw, between the Falemē and the Niger. Al-Bakrī, who was a contemporary, gives the following account of the conversion of the ruler of Malel which is of interest from many points of view:

Behind it [the kingdom of the Daw] is a country called Malel, whose king is known as *al-Musilmānī*. The reason for his being so called came about in this way. Year after year his country was afflicted with drought. The people tried to obtain rain by making many sacrifices of cattle to such an extent that they almost exterminated the breed, but achieved nothing except dearth and distress. Now the king had staying with him as a guest a Muslim who passed his time reciting the Qur'ān and studying the *sunna* of the Prophet. The king complained to this man about his people's sufferings. He replied, 'O king, if you only believed in God almighty, acknowledged His unity and the mission of Muḥammad, and believed in all the articles of faith, then I would pray on

Mandenga) et de *Malinké* que nous donnons aux habitants du Mandé. De tout temps ce mot a servi à désigner le pays que nos cartes appellent encore "Manding" entre le Haut-Niger et la ligne de partage des eaux du Bakhoy et du Bafing.' Delafosse, 'Traditions historiques et légendaires du Soudan Occidental', *Afr. Fr. R.C.* 1913, p. 297; offprint p. 19.

[1] Ch. Monteil writes, 'Traditions place the oldest known Mali on the right bank of the upper Ba-khoy with its capital at Dakadyala near the present-day Nyagassola. Again we are told that Narena was the capital of Naré fa Maghan, father of Sun Dyāta who was born there; that Tabu was the capital of *mansa* Konaté of Do-dugu; and, finally, that Sibi was the chief place of Séndugu or Siéndugu, fief of the Kamara.' *Bull. Com. Ét. A.O.F.* xii (1929), 305–6.

[2] 'Malel' is a Fulfulde term for 'Mande'.

[3] The Tara-urē with their seat at Dakadyala, the Konatē at Tabu in Do-dugu, and the Keyta in the same region at Narena.

your behalf for relief from what you are suffering and from what has befallen you. Thus you could bring universal benefit upon the people of your country and thereby incite all your enemies and adversaries to envy.' He persisted with him until he agreed to embrace Islam, and that in sincerity. He taught him to recite easy passages from the Book of God and instructed him in those obligations which even the most ignorant should know. He waited until Friday night, then told him to make a total ablution, clothed him in a cotton robe which he had by him, and they went together to a rise in the ground. There the Muslim with the king on his right began to pray throughout the night that God's will be done, the Muslim doing the petitioning and the king repeating the 'amen'. As dawn began to break, behold, God envelopped the land with abundant rain. In consequence of this the king ordered the destruction of the idols and the expulsion of the magicians from his country. He is sincerely attached to Islam, as are his heir and courtiers, but the people of his kingdom remain idolators. Since that time their kings have borne the title of *al-Musilmānī*.[1]

According to Shaikh 'Uthmān, *muftī* of the people of Gāna, whom Ibn Khaldūn met in A.D. 1393/4, 'the first of their [Māli] kings to join Islam was Baramandāna[2] . . . who made the pilgrimage, an example followed by his successors'.[3] Bar-Mande-na might be a title, 'Chief of the Mande', but there is no evidence for identifying him with the king of Malel mentioned by al-Bakrī.

Al-Idrīsī (–1154) places Malel in the country of the Lemlem, the term Arab writers used for 'primitives',[4] whose organization was so simple that they could not unite to defend themselves or retaliate. He shows that as a result of the demand for slaves in North Africa the Sahilian states were no longer contented with the reduction of prisoners of war to slave and eventually serf status within their own communities but made a regular practice of raiding these uncoordinated Lemlem to obtain slaves for sale to northern merchants:

The people of Barīsā (or Baransā), Sillā, Takrūr and Ghāna make raids

[1] Al-Bakrī, op. cit., p. 178. We need not take seriously the statement of Ibn Abī Zar' (op. cit., p. 61) that the Murābiṭ empire embraced the Mountains of Gold, nor the echo of this in the statement of Leo Africanus that the people of Melli were 'the first that embraced the law of Mahumet, at the time when the uncle of Ioseph, the King of Moroco (i.e. Yūsuf ibn Tāshufīn), was their prince, and the government remained for a while unto his posterity'; transl. J. Pory, Hakluyt Society, 1896, iii. 823.

[2] Barama N'dana? Al-Maqrīzī provides Sarbandāna and Sarmandāna as alternatives; see *Not. et Extr. de la Bibl. Nat.* xii (1831), 637.

[3] Ibn Khaldūn, op. cit., ed. de Slane, i. 264; ed. Cairo, vi. 200.

[4] Al-Bakrī's Demdem (p. 183) on the Niger between Kawkaw and Tadmekka, were cannibals. Ibn Sa'īd (in Abū 'l-Fidā', p. 153) mentions 'the Namnam, brothers of the Lemlem in origin'. In Pulār *nyāmde* means 'to eat'.

upon the country of the Lemlem, taking its people captive and transporting them to their own lands where they sell them to immigrant merchants who take them to all quarters. Only two small towns are found in the whole of the lands of the Lemlem, and they are no more than villages. The name of the one is Malel and that of the other Daw, the distance between the two being a four days' journey. The inhabitants, according to the reports of the people of that region, are Jews, but most are steeped in infidelity and superstition. It is the practice of the people of Lemlem country when they reach puberty to scarify the face and temple by branding, as their tribal mark. The inhabited part of their country extends along a stream which flows into the Nile. Beyond them to the south no inhabited country has been reported. The land of Lemlem adjoins Maqzāra on the west, Wangāra on the east, Ghāna on the north, and uninhabited country on the south.[1] Their language [Mandinke?] is different from that of the Maqzārans [West Atlantic group] and of the Ghānians [Soninke].[2]

During this period the ruler of the town of Jennē was converted to Islam. This town is situated on the River Bani in the middle of the inundated plain of the central delta of the Niger. It is not mentioned in any identifiable way by the Arab geographers for it was much less important, from the commercial-Islamic point of view, than Dyā, situated on the Dyāka, the western arm of the Niger. According to a very late source, as-Saʿdī, Jennē was founded in the middle of the second century of the *hijra* (*c* A.D. 767) when the Nono, Soninke from Dyā, superimposed themselves upon the Bozo fishers of the region and with whom they soon intermingled.[3] A date between 1100 and 1200 appears more probable. It appears that Islam was well established through trading contacts before it was adopted by the ruler. As-Saʿdī, himself at one time (1627–37) *imām* of Jennē, gives the tradition current in his day:

The people of Jenne were converted to Islam towards the end of the sixth century [*c.* A.D. 1200]. The sultan Kunburu[4] was the first [ruler] to adopt it and his people followed his example. When he had decided upon taking this

[1] The region of *bowal*, laterite plains where cultivation is difficult.

[2] Al-Idrīsī, op. cit., p. 4. His contemporary Abū Ḥāmid also mentions a Malī (*J. Asiat.* ccvii. 42). Elsewhere (p. 6) al-Idrīsī says that Malel 'is a small town like a comprehensive village, without walls but situated strategically on rising ground of red earth which protects its inhabitants against sudden incursions by other Negroes. They get their water from a murmuring spring flowing from a mountain lying to the south, which is slightly bitter. West of this town on the banks of the stream, from its source to the point where it joins the Nile, are many Negro peoples, entirely naked, who marry without dowry or proper rites.' It is these who are raided for slaves and sold to traders 'by the file' (*qiṭāran*).

[3] See as-Saʿdī, op. cit., p. 12 (23); Ch. Monteil, *Djénné*, 1932, pp. 30–32.

[4] Or Kan-bara. This appears to be a Mandinke name or title.

step he ordered that all the *'ulamā* [i.e. Muslims] who were in the country should be assembled. Their number came to 4,200. In their presence he declared his allegiance to Islam and ordered them to petition God that He grant three requests to the town; that everyone who fled to it from his homeland in straitened circumstances and destitute might find these transformed into plenty and ease; that the foreigners who inhabited the town might outnumber its nationals; and that God might dissipate the patience of those who came there for trade so that, filled with ennui, they might sell their goods at the lowest rate and the inhabitants reap the profit. They read the Fātiḥa over these three petitions, which, as anyone may bear witness with his own eyes today, were accepted. After the king had joined Islam he demolished his palace and replaced it with a mosque dedicated to the service of God almighty.[1]

As in all these states Islam became the royal cult, as it was that of the trading community, but the people continued to practise their old religions. These were practised in Jennē itself until the sixteenth century when a zealot, Fodē Muḥammad Sānu the Wankorī, destroyed its sacred grove.[2] Jennē paid tribute to Māli and later became a great centre of Islam in the Sudan, far outshining Timbuktu whose prosperity was largely dependent upon that of Jennē.

Tradition preserves the names of few Mandinka rulers before Sun Dyāta. One of them, Mūsā Keyta, nicknamed Alla-koy (*c.* 1100), is said to have performed the pilgrimage four times. The history of Māli begins with Sun Dyāta, 'the lord lion'. About A.D. 1224, as we have seen, Sumāguru Kantē, lord of Sūsū, conquered Manding. Tradition records that he put to death eleven of the ruler's twelve sons. The twelfth, Sun Dyāta,[3] escaped the massacre because he was a cripple. Triumphing over his infirmity he waged a guerilla campaign, raiding Tinkasso, Sangaran, and towards Fūta Jalon. In this way he built up a trained army and returned in triumph to take control of Manding in 1234. Sumāguru Kantē prepared to meet the challenger and a battle took place at Kirina, near Kulikoro, when the king of Sūsū was defeated and killed. The traditional saga of Sun Dyāta represents the struggle between the two as a contest between two magicians. Sun Dyāta stole from Sumāguru the secret of poison-archery at a distance (Mande *korte*) by means of which he was able to kill his enemy.[4] Having subdued and annexed the people of Sūsū, Sun Dyāta advanced

[1] As-Sa'dī, op. cit., pp. 12–13 (23–24).

[2] Ibid., p. 17 (31).

[3] Ibn Khaldūn (i. 264) calls him Mārī Jāṭa, adding that '*mārī* means an *amīr* of royal descent, and *jāṭa* means lion'. *Māri* really means 'little master'.

[4] See M. Delafosse, *Trad. hist. et légend. du Soudan Occid.*, pp. 25–29.

northwards into Gāna, and plundered its capital (1240). His allies had in the meantime taken possession of Gangaran and the gold-bearing district of Bãmbuko.[1]

Sun Dyāta now claimed tribute from peoples inhabiting an expanse of country with which the former Sahilian kingdom of Gāna, whose wealth was largely derived from commerce and not actual control of the gold-bearing districts, could not compare. It extended well into the Sahara in the north, reached the upper Senegal in the west, and the upper Niger in the east. That such conquests were possible we know from the exploits of the adventurers of the nineteenth century. Important as were gold-extraction and commerce, the economy of this vast state was securely based on a foundation of agriculturalists. The rulers changed their capitals frequently, but the royal residence was never transferred to a trading city and the ruler always lived among the cultivators.[2]

Sun Dyāta was almost certainly brought up as a pagan, but a reference in the travels of Ibn Baṭṭūṭa shows that one of the family was converted to Islam about this time. 'A trustworthy person informed

[1] See A. Aubert, 'Légendes historiques . . . recueillies dans la Haute-Gambie', *Bull. Com. Ét. A.O.F.* 1923, p. 415.

[2] There has been a great deal of discussion about the site of the capital of Māli, but the site has little real significance in Sudan history for the residence of the ruler was continually changing. The name Kāba given by all Sudanese to the capital was the village of Kangaba which has always been the ritual centre of state and people, and where there is a sanctuary where septennial cult ceremonies which draw together representatives of the various Mande peoples are still held (see G. Dieterlen, *La Religion Bambara*, pp. xiii–xiv). J. Vidal was told by *dyeli* of the Keyta family of four villages which were successively royal residences: Dyeliba-koto (Dyeriba), Nyani, Mani-kura near Figuirà, and Kangaba (Kāba). But tradition mentions other places earlier than Dyeliba in the regions of Kri Koroni and Wanda. Ch. Monteil (*Les Bambara du Ségou et du Kaarta*, p. 12) gives traditions which situate the capital at Dakadyala, Tabou, Kunfange, Figuira, Kangaba, and Nyani. A passage in *Fattāsh* says (p. 38/66; cf. p. 56/108): 'The town which was formerly the seat of government of the ruler of Māli was called Jāriba [Dyeriba], and another was called Yani' [Nyani?]. Their inhabitants could get water only from the river Kala, to reach whose bank they had to travel quite a distance, going early in the morning and returning in the afternoon.' The upper course of the Niger upstream of the region of inundation is called the River of Kala, and Nyani was situated on the left bank of the River Sankarani, a little to the north of Balandugu. Ibn Khaldūn says that Māli was the name of the country and not that of the capital. The capital, he was told, was called Balad Banī or Yīy. The same name appears in al-'Umarī's *Masālik* in the manuscripts of which it can be read Binī, Bitī, Binā, and Bitā, and it is a question of reading a badly written سى as Yani or Nyani. The identification rests merely on the fact that tradition gives Nyani as a capital. For this discussion see Delafosse, *H.S.N.* ii. 182; idem, 'Le Gana et le Mali', *Bull. Com. Ét. A.O.F.* 1924, pp. 479–542; J. Vidal, 'L'Emplacement de Mali', *Bull. Com. Ét. A.O.F.* 1923, pp. 251–68, 606–19; J. Gaillard, 'Niani, ancienne capitale de l'empire Mandingue', *Bull. Com. Ét. A.O.F.* 1923, pp. 620 ff.; Ch. Monteil, 'Les Empires du Mali', *Bull. Com. Ét. A.O.F.* xii (1929).

me', he writes, 'that Mansa Mūsā gave three thousand *mithqāls* on one day to Mudrik ibn Faqqūṣ, whose grandfather was responsible for the conversion to Islam of his own grandfather, Sāraq (or Nāre) Jāṭa.'[1]

Little except their names is known about the immediate successors of Sun Dyāta. We are told that Mansa Walī (Ule, 1255–70) went on pilgrimage during the reign of aẓ-Ẓāhir Baybars (1260–77). Then came Mansa Wātī and Mansa Khalīfa who was weak-minded and an archer who used to amuse himself shooting at his subjects (by *korte* or invocation-shooting?) so that they rose and killed him. These three are said to have been sons of Sun Dyāta, but now the succession changes to the female line. Ibn Khaldūn writes, 'After him [Khalīfa] came Abū Bakr who was a grandson of Mārī Jāṭa in the female line, they elected him as king according to the custom of outlandish peoples whereby sisters or sisters' sons succeed to the inheritance.'[2]

We do not know when Songhay first paid allegiance to Māli, probably during Sun Dyāta's spectacular expansion, but about this time (*c.* 1275) a new dynasty was formed there by an adventurer from Māli; perhaps he was a Songhay royal hostage, as tradition says, or the Māli intendant gained control during this time of troubles. However, its independence did not last long. In 1285 the throne of Māli was seized by a freed slave of the royal family called Sabakura (or Sākūra) who followed the royal custom of pilgrimage but was killed on the return journey at a place called Tājūrā (*c.* 1300).[3] According to Ibn Khaldūn, Sabakura was one of the most powerful of the rulers of Māli. He acquired new territories and made raids as far as Takrūr in the west and Songhay in the east. One of Ibn Khaldūn's informants, al-ḥājj Yūnis, Sudanese interpreter in Cairo, said that he took Kawkaw, but another, Shaikh ʿUthmān, attributes its capture to Saghamanja, general of Mansa Mūsā.[4] He may have gained control of the copper mines at Tākedda for Mansa Mūsā refers to them as the most important source of revenue in his dominions. The decline or destruction of

[1] Ibn Baṭṭūṭa, iv. 419–20. Mansa Mūsā was the grandson of a sister of Sun Dyāta.

[2] Ibn Khaldūn, op. cit. i. 264. The normal succession in Māli, as Ibn Khaldūn himself shows, was through the paternal line, and this unusual procedure implies some dynastic trouble.

[3] According to Ibn Khaldūn the pilgrimage took place when al-Malik an-Nāṣir (1298–1308) was on the throne. Tajura, if not a mistake for Tājawa the Zaghawī centre, is, as C. F. Beckingham has suggested (*Bull. S.O.A.S.* 1953, pp. 391–2), more likely to be the coastal town of that name in Tripolitania than that on the Red Sea, since in those days all pilgrims travelled by Saharan routes.

[4] Ibn Khaldūn, i. 264. Al-Maqrīzī (transl. Gaudefroy-Demombynes, in the *Masālik* of al-ʿUmarī, p. 89) also says that Sabakura took Kawkaw.

Tirekka dates from this time for the merchants of Jennē diverted their commerce to pass through Kabara on the Niger bend, and an arid Berber settlement a few miles inland called Timbuktu became their emporium where caravans were assembled for the Saharan crossing. This settlement was essentially a port and never became very populous because it was not the centre of an agricultural population like Jennē.[1]

After Sabakura the succession reverted to the legitimate line with Gaw, a son of Sun Dyāta, who was succeeded by his son Muḥammad. The next king, Abū Bakr II, was in the line of succession from Sun Dyāta's sister.[2] Mansa Mūsā, his successor, when in Cairo mentioned that power was transmitted by heritage but did not specify by what line. He describes how his predecessor (he does not say father) sent an expedition consisting of 200 canoes down the Senegal to explore the Ocean. Only one returned to relate how the rest of the fleet had been overwhelmed in a storm. The king would not believe this and equipped another fleet of 2,000 canoes of which half were filled with provisions. He led it himself, after conferring the power upon Mūsā, and none of them ever returned.[3]

The most famous king of Māli in the Arab world was Mansa Mūsā (1312–37) who was able to build upon the conquests of Sabakura. His significance in the history of Māli has been exaggerated by reason of the fantastic pilgrimage which he made through Cairo to Mecca in A.H. 724 (A.D. 1324–5). In consequence the fame of Māli was proclaimed from Andalusia to Khurasan, and the names of Mansa Mūsā and Māli made

[1] Tirekka then held the trading position later attained by Timbuktu (see al-Bakrī, pp. 180–1). Al-Idrīsī writes (p. 8), 'Tīreqqā is a large and well-populated town though without walls or any other kind of enclosure, in allegiance to the Lord of Ghāna. From Ghāna to Tīreqqā, following the course of the Nile, is a six days journey.' Following the suggestion of Delafosse (*Fattāsh*, transl. p. 239 n., and *H.S.N.* ii. 70) A. Bonnel de Mezières claimed to have found it at Arnassey, a village on the Niger 25 km. to the east of Timbuktu (see his 'Découverte de l'emplacement de Tirekka', *Bull. Sect. Géog. Com. Trav. Hist. et Sc.*, Ministère Instr. Publ. et Beaux-Arts, 1914, pp. 132–5).

The date of the foundation of Timbuktu is uncertain. As-Sa'dī says that it was founded in A.H. 490 (A.D. 1096–7) by Tuareg Magsharen (probably the Imajer'en or aristocratic class). 'Never did the worship of idols profane it', he asserts. 'Never did any man prostrate himself on its soil except in prayer to God the Merciful' (op. cit., p. 21; transl. p. 36). We need not take this statement seriously for there is evidence of the performance of pagan cults in this town, but that it began as a settlement of Berbers is possible. The name is Berber *Tī-n Bukt*, 'the place of Bukt'. It was long before the desert caravans began to make use of it otherwise it would have been known to al-Bakrī and al-Idrīsī. Leo Africanus (Hakluyt, iii. 824) says that it was founded by a Mansa Sulaimān in A.H. 610 (A.D. 1213/14), which is unlikely though Sun Dyāta must have controlled the region. The real development of Timbuktu began about 1300 when the traders of Dyā began to make use of it instead of, or as well as, Tirekka.

[2] Ibn Khaldūn, op. cit. i. 264.

[3] Al-'Umarī, op. cit., pp. 74–75; al-Qalqashandī, op. cit., v. 294–5.

their appearance on fourteenth-century European maps.[1] Mūsā took with him a vast quantity of gold and disbursed it lavishly. In consequence of his visit, al-ʿUmarī tells us, the value of gold depreciated very considerably in Egypt.[2] The vast crowd of dignitaries and slaves who accompanied him naturally lost their heads at the sight of the wonders of the Cairene markets. At first the merchants preyed upon their ignorance of the value of the goods, but the Sudanese soon discovered that they were being rooked. Al-ʿUmarī writes, 'They have now reached the point that if they see the greatest of the princes of learning and religion and hear that he is from Cairo, they handle him roughly and have an unfavourable opinion of him as a result of the bad behaviour of his compatriots towards them.'[3] So great was Mūsā's extravagance that he had to borrow from Cairenes, some of whom accompanied him on the return journey in order to collect their loans.[4]

Tradition has credited Mūsā with conquests which were made by earlier rulers. According to as-Saʿdī Songhay was subdued whilst he was away and he himself gained control of Timbuktu after his return.[5] Maḥmūd al-Kāti makes no mention of any conquest of Timbuktu and his account of Mūsā's departure for the pilgrimage by way of this town makes it clear that it was already under the control of Māli. According to the fragment translated by Houdas[6] Māli was in control of Timbuktu earlier than the time of Mūsā. We read,

> At this epoch [time of *sī* ʿAlī Kolon *c.* 1275] the king of Māli possessed at Timbuktu a well-known royal residence on the place called *mā-dugu* where the meat-market of the people of Timbuktu is today. Beside and to the north of this residence was the royal mosque . . . *Mā-dugu* [Mande 'the land of the master'] is the name given in the country of the Takrūr to every royal residence wherever situated.

Besides his creditors Mūsā brought back with him to the Sudan a number of Arab and Berber adventurers, among them an Andalusian poet, Abū Isḥāq Ibrāhīm as-Sāḥilī, whom tradition credits with the

[1] On the *Mappa Mundi* of Angelino Dulcert (1339) a road through the Atlas is described as leading to the king of the gold mines, *Rex Melli*. This is the first reference to Māli on a European map. On the Catalan Atlas made for Charles V by Abraham Cresques in 1375 appear the names of Cuitat de Melli, Tenbuch, and Geugeu; whilst in the middle of the Sahara is drawn the figure of a king holding a sceptre in one hand and a nugget of gold in the other, with the legend, 'This Negro lord is called Musa Mali, Lord of the Negroes of Guinea.'

[2] Al-ʿUmarī, pp. 78–79. Arabic writers naturally provide much information about this pilgrimage; see al-ʿUmarī, pp. 70 ff.; Ibn Baṭṭūṭa, iv. 431; Ibn Khaldūn, ed. de Slane, i. 264–6; al-Maqrīzī quoted in the translation of al-ʿUmarī, pp. 89–93; As-Saʿdī, *T. as-Sūdān*, p. 7; al-Kāti, *Fattāsh*, pp. 33–37.

[3] Al-ʿUmarī, op. cit., p. 79.

[4] Ibn Baṭṭūṭa, iv. 431–2.

[5] As-Saʿdī, transl. p. 14.

[6] *Fattāsh*, p. 335.

building of mosques and other buildings at Kawkaw, Timbuktu, and elsewhere, which were adorned with the battlemented terraces and pyramidal towers characteristic of the Sudanese style, and alleges that these were the prototype of this style. But at most Abū Isḥāq merely adapted the form of the Sahilian house to more pretentious buildings.[1] Ibn Khaldūn was told by one of these adventurers in Mūsā's entourage, a Berber called Abū ʿAbd Allāh al-Ma'mar, that Abū Isḥāq only built an audience hall in the capital.[2]

Although al-ʿUmarī writes of Māli (1342–9) during the reign of Sulaimān his information relates primarily to the empire ruled by Mansa Mūsā. He was told that in length it extended from Tūrā on the Atlantic to Mūlī, wherever these places were. Ibn Baṭṭūṭa, who travelled through the country during the reign of Sulaimān, confirms that Mālian rule extended beyond Kawkaw to the district of Mūlī in the country of the Līmiyyīn.[3] Al-ʿUmarī gives precise indications of the various territories subject to Māli.[4] They included Ghāna, Zāgūn (or Zāfūn), Toronkā (or Tirekkā),[5] Takrūr, Sanaghāna, Bānbughū,[6] Zarqaṭabanā (or Zaranṭābanā), Bītrā, Damūrā (or Darmūrā), Zāghā, Kāborā,[7] Barāghuri (or Barāghudi), and Kawkaw. He also mentions white Berber tribes in the southern Sahara, Antaṣar,[8] Yantarʿarās, Meddūsa, and Lamṭūna, who paid allegiance to Māli.

[1] The so-called 'Sudanese style of architecture' is not Sudanese in origin but is characteristic of the early Mediterranean civilization and remains of the style exist in South Arabia and southern Morocco (cf. H. Terrasse, *Kasbas berbères de l'Atlas et des Oases*, Paris, 1938). As Th. Monod remarks, 'C'est dans ce monde-là qu'est née l'architecture soudanaise. Quand on prétend que le Granadin de Moussa Ier l'a apportée au Niger au XIVe siècle, ou que les Songhaï l'ont directement empruntée à l'Égypte, on dit des bêtises. Mais on en dit de plus grosses encore en l'imaginant autochtone et africaine.' *L'Hippopotame et le philosophe*, Paris, 1946, p. 179.

[2] Ibn Khaldūn, i. 265. As-Sāhilī settled down at Walāta and died in A.D. 1346 at Timbuktu where Ibn Baṭṭūṭa (iv. 431) paid a visit to his tomb.

[3] Ibn Baṭṭūṭa, iv. 395.

[4] Al-ʿUmarī, pp. 54–56, 59–60; al-Qalqashandī, v. 286–7.

[5] The word can be read either way. Toronqa is mentioned by al-Bakrī, p. 173.

[6] Bāmbugu, part of Bambuk (canton of Kundian), but no doubt the term for the whole of Bambuk between the Faleme and Bafing which included the auriferous mountains of Tāmbawula (Tambaura). The region is said to have been conquered by Amari Sonko, general of Sun Dyāta, and a Mandinka dynasty was established there in the time of Mansa Ule (c. 1255) by Mūsā Son Koroma Sissoko with Kundian as capital (see Delafosse, *H.S.N.* ii. 183–4). Islam became the imperial cult, but tradition records that the clerics of the country, having tried to get control of the gold mines, were all killed and the old cults again became predominant (cf. Delafosse, *H.S.N.* ii. 361), probably the episode to which al-ʿUmarī refers (see above, p. 59, n. 6).

[7] Ibn Baṭṭūṭa passed through Zāgha (= Dyāga) and Kāborā, which was not the Kabara port of Timbuktu but probably situated near Dyafarabi (cf. *T. as-Sūdān*, p. 13/25).

[8] Al-Bakrī places (p. 164) the Banī Yantasar of the Ṣanhāja in control of the watering places of the great desert between Darʿa and Gāna.

Al-ʿUmarī had his special interests. He gives accounts of the fauna and flora of Māli and of the dress and ceremonial of the court, but says little about how these territories were governed, except that Gāna was practically independent and that the Māli found it expedient to leave the Lemlem of the gold-producing country of Bambuk alone provided they sent a large annual tribute of raw gold. All gold found in the country belonged to the king[1] and this was used for trade with the north, the upkeep of the court, and rewards to his servants, but all the normal business transactions of the country were in shells (*wadaʿ*) from whose importation the merchants derived considerable profit.[2] Mansa Mūsā mentions the copper mine at Zkra which he says brought in more revenue than anything else.[3] Mansa Mūsā maintained diplomatic relations with North African states. He sent a deputation to the Marīnid sultan of Fez, Abū 'l-Ḥasan (1331–51), headed by two Mandinka notables and an interpreter belonging to the Masīn, with presents; and the sultan reciprocated with an embassy headed by ʿAlī b. Ghānim of the Maʿqil, which arrived in the reign of Sulaimān.[4]

Mansa Mūsā gave Māli certain characteristics of an Islamic state by constructing mosques and instituting the Friday prayer ceremonial. But Islam was not allowed to interfere with the collection of gold. When its propagation was pursued in the land of the pagans the supply ceased and the propaganda was accordingly called off. Al-ʿUmarī writes,

> Magic is widely practised in this country. They make use of it for every-

[1] This continued to be the rule in the Bambara successor states of Segu and Kārta whose rulers employed it for ransoming prisoners and negotiating royal marriages (see V. Paques, *Les Bambara*, 1954, p. 42) and in Khaso (see Ch. Monteil, *Les Khassonké*, p. 322).

[2] Al-ʿUmari, pp. 75–76, 202; al-Qalqashandī, v. 292.

[3] Al-ʿUmarī, pp. 80–81. We may well be sceptical of this statement. Both gold and salt were much more important. Copper was rather an article of importation. Variants of Zkra are Ḍkra and Nakwā, which Gaudefroy-Demombynes reads Tigidda. But Tākedda was situated on the western side of Air and it is very unlikely that the authority of Māli extended so far. Ibn Baṭṭūṭa, who passed through Tākedda in 1353, writes, 'The inhabitants of Takedda are wholly absorbed in trading. Every year they travel to Egypt for the purpose of importing the various types of beautiful materials and other goods which are to be found there. They live luxurious and easy lives and try to rival each other in the number of male and female slaves they possess, as also do the people of Māllī and Īwālāten. . . . The copper mine is situated on the outskirts of Takedda. The ore is extracted from the ground and brought into the town where it is smelted in their houses by their slaves. . . . The copper is exported from Takedda to the town of Kūbar (Gobir) in the country of the pagans, to Zaghāy, the country of Bornu, Jūjuwa (Gaoga?), and the country of the Mūrtabūn' (Ibn Baṭṭūṭa, iv. 439–41). G. Brouin (*N. Afr.*, No. 47, 1950, pp. 90–91) gives a description of ruins situated about 25 km. east of Tagidda n'Tesemt which are of Arab origin, and where small blocks of mineral copper in its native state, as well as fragments of smelted copper, have been found. This place may have been the ancient Takedda.

[4] Ibn Khaldūn, i. 266; ii. 394; Ibn Baṭṭūṭa, iv. 409.

thing even when—and I mean this literally and not allegorically—they hunt the elephant in the country of the heathens under their rule. Continually they bring cases concerned with the question of sorcery before the king. One of them will claim, 'So-and-so has killed my brother or my son by sorcery,' and the sultan passes sentence of punishment on the murderer and puts the sorcerer to death.[1]

In Cairo Mansa Mūsā learnt for the first time that the number of wives should be limited to four. He told Ibn Amīr Ḥājib, Governor of Cairo,

that among the customs of his people was this that when one of his subjects has brought up a pretty girl he hands her over to the king as a servant for his bed without marriage just as we do with a slave. I said to him, 'This is not permitted to the Muslim by law.' He said, 'Not even to kings?' I answered, 'Not even to kings, ask the *'ulamā*.' Then he said, 'By God, I did not know that. I renounce it from this moment.'[2]

Little is known about the next king Maghan I (1337–41) who had acted as regent whilst Mūsā was on pilgrimage.[3] About this time, or possibly towards the end of Mūsā's reign, Timbuktu was pillaged and burnt by the army of the northern Mossi kingdom of Yatenga,[4] who, however, made no attempt to occupy the territory. It must have been an unimportant place since Ibn Baṭṭūṭa, who passed through it later, says little about it except that 'most of the inhabitants belong to the Masūfa, *lithām*-wearers'.[5]

Sulaimān (1341–60), brother of Mūsā, reorganized the empire and his financial measures, taken to enable the state to recover from the extravagances of Mūsā, made him disliked. For this period there is an exceptional amount of material for, in addition to that of al-'Umarī, we have the first-hand account of Ibn Baṭṭūṭa and material collected by Ibn Khaldūn. Al-'Umarī writes of Sulaimān:

There accrued to him all the lands of the negroes which his brother had conquered and brought within the orbit of Islam. He built mosques of worship and convocation and minarets, and instituted weekly prayers, gatherings and the call to prayer. He attracted jurisconsults of the rite of Imām Mālik to his country, and was himself a student of *fiqh*.[6]

[1] Al-Qalqashandī, v. 291.
[2] Al-'Umarī, p. 72; al-Qalqashandī, v. 296.
[3] Al-'Umarī, p. 73.
[4] As-Sa'dī, *T. as-Sūdān*, p. 8/16–17.
[5] Ibn Baṭṭūṭa, iv. 430–1.
[6] Al-'Umarī, p. 53; al-Qalqashandī, v. 297. Delafosse's statement (*H.S.N.* ii. 193) that Sulaimān performed the pilgrimage seems to be based on al-Maqrīzī's reference in his *Sulūk* to the pilgrimage of a king of Takrūr in 752 (1351–2) who sought and obtained permission to be exempted from paying his respects to the sultan (*Not. et Extr.* xii. 638). But there is no reason

Sulaimān maintained cordial relations with the Marīnid sultans of Morocco. When the deputation arrived soon after his accession he received it with honour and on its return sent envoys to thank the sultan. Ibn Baṭṭūṭa shows that he maintained his authority over the Berber tribes of the southern Sahara. Ibn Khaldūn relates how he met in 754/1353 at Biskra an ambassador from the chief of Tākedda who gave him some information.[1] Tākedda was governed by a muffled Zanāgī who was in friendly communication with the chiefs of Wargla and Zāb, but recognized the suzerainty of Māli 'like all the other Saharan countries known as al-Malastīn'.[2] Tākedda was the capital of the Tuareg of that region and an important caravan town on the route from Wargla-Zāb to the Sudan, through which all the Negro pilgrims passed. That very year, Ibn Khaldūn was told, a caravan of 12,000 loaded camels went from Cairo through Tākedda to Māli.[3]

When Sulaimān heard of the accession of Abū Sālim (1359–61) he sent a congratulatory deputation to Fez with presents, but at Walāta they were overtaken by news of the death of Sulaimān and of rival parties in conflict over the succession. Sulaimān's son Qasā[4] was proclaimed, but a son of Maghan I called Māri Djāta (or Māli Dyāta) disputed his succession[5] and nine months of civil war ensued before Māri Dyāta's party defeated and killed Qasā (1360). Māri Dyāta immediately ordered the deputation to proceed to Fez and among the presents included a giraffe which caused a sensation when it arrived safely after the hazardous crossing. He is said to have been a bad king who oppressed his subjects and dissipated the wealth accumulated by the frugal

to suppose that this king was Sulaimān, especially since Ibn Baṭṭūṭa, who was in Māli the following year, makes no mention of it and in fact implies that Sulaimān had no personal acquaintance with the wider Islamic world. Many kings of Kānem went on pilgrimage about this time (see al-Maqrīzī, Hamaker, p. 207).

[1] The Tākedda referred to here cannot easily be identified with the copper-mining place through which Ibn Baṭṭūṭa passed and may have been confused with Tādmekka, although al-ʿUmarī (pp. 94–95), writing about the same time as Ibn Khaldūn, says that the last was an independent Berber kingdom.

[2] *V.l.* Mathīmīn.

[3] Ibn Khaldūn, ii. 73; transl. iii. 287–8; cf. i. 266 (ii. 116).

[4] *V.ll.* Fanbā and Qanbā.

[5] Ibn Baṭṭūṭa records an episode (iv. 417–19) which appears to refer to Māri Dyāta II, son of Maghan, and if so shows that he was already a pretender to the throne in the reign of Sulaimān. The chief wife of Sulaimān, daughter of his paternal uncle, had the title of *qāsā* and was co-ruler, her name being mentioned with his in the *khuṭba*. During Ibn Baṭṭūṭa's stay in Māli she was thrown into prison along with one of the *farārīs* or generals. The reason for this was that the *qāsā* had been plotting against Sulaimān and had sent one of her slaves to Dyāṭa, paternal cousin of Sulaimān, who was in exile in Kan-burnī, urging him to overthrow the sultan and informing him that she herself and all the army commanders were ready to accept him as ruler.

Sulaimān, selling the celebrated nugget, regarded as one of the (sacred?) treasures of the kingdom, to Egyptian merchants for a low price. Finally, 'he was attacked by sleeping sickness (*'illat an-nawm*), a disease which frequently affects the people of that region, especially those in high places', and died within two years of its onset.[1]

The next king, Mūsā II (1373/4–87), was good intentioned but fell completely under the control of his chief minister, Māri Dyāta, who kept him secluded and was the real ruler. He levied troops, initiated campaigns, and subdued territories to the east within the boundaries of Kawkaw. The Tuareg ruler of Tākedda (read Tādmekka?) had apparently repudiated the authority of Māli for he went on to reduce it. Mūsā II was succeeded by his brother Maghan II who was killed a year later and the *ṣandiki* or *wazīr*,[2] who was the husband of Mūsā's mother, seized the throne. He also was killed in less than a year by a descendant of Māri Dyāta. Then another pretender, Maḥmūd, a descendant of Mansa Gaw or Wali arrived from the country of the southern pagans in A.H. 792 (1390) and seized the throne as Mansa Maghan III. Here Ibn Khaldūn's narrative comes to an end. Apart from these brief accounts of the rulers he provides little information about the state. He was told by Ibn Wāsūl that 'the capital of the king of the people of Māli, Balad Bnī [read Nyani], is extensive, well-watered, and thickly populated for cultivation. It is a commercial centre and at the present day a station for trading caravans coming from the Maghrib, Ifrīqiya, and Egypt, to which merchandise is imported from all quarters.'[3]

These quarrels between rival claimants to the throne heralded the decline of Māli as a great power. Soninke states freed themselves from vassal kings or governors appointed by Māli. Maḥmūd al-Kāti writes of Dyāra: 'Then the Ahl Kanyāga gained control in those parts. They repudiated the authority of the Malli-koy, killed his *amīr* [vassal king or governor?] and replaced him, and there ruled over them the sons of Dyāwara, surnamed Kanyāga.'[4] Its dependencies were now subjected to attacks by Mossi, Tuareg, and Songhay. About 1400 Bonga, king of the Mossi of Yatenga, raided eastern Māsina as far as Lake Debo. About the same time *sī* Mādogo of Songhay began the conquest and permanent control of tribes subject to Māli, including three Bambara

[1] Ibn Khaldūn, i. 266–7. His informant, Ibn Wāsūl, a native of Sijilmāsa, had at one time been a *qāḍī* in the land of Kawkaw.

[2] So Ibn Khaldūn translates the title (i. 268), but Ch. Monteil has shown that it is actually *dyon sandigi*, chief of slaves.

[3] Ibn Khaldūn, i. 267; transl. ii. 116.

[4] *Fattāsh*, p. 39 (70).

tribes.[1] In 837 (1433–4) Akil ag Malwal, chief of the Tuareg Magsharen, gained control of the Saharan dependencies Arawān, Walāta, and Timbuktu without encountering resistance.[2] At Timbuktu they confirmed the Māli governor, Muḥammad Naḍḍī, a Ṣanhājī, and exacted tribute for forty years until it was conquered by *sī* 'Alī in 1468. In 1450 the states of Māsina and Mīma (between Māsina and the lakes) were independent[3] for a short while until *sī* Dāndi (d. 1465) conquered Mīma.[4] *Sī* 'Alī of Songhay continued the conquest of dependencies begun by his predecessors, annexing Jennē (between 1465 and 1473), and gained control of part of the zone of inundation. In the west and south Māli's sphere of influence remained considerable. Diego Gomez (1457–60) was told by Wolof at the Gambia that the *būr* Māli controlled all the interior. Cadamosto (1455–7) tells us that the Mandinka of the Gambia regarded the emperor of Māli as their overlord,[5] but we may take this to mean no more than that Mandinka families were settling along that river, not that the hegemony of Māli reached the lower Gambia. There followed a period of vast incursions by the Mossi. In 1477 Nāsere, *moro-nāba* of Yatenga, crossed the Niger, ravaged Māsina, penetrated into Bāgana, and pillaged Walāta (1480). We next find the Portuguese seeking to establish relations with Māli. Its ruler, suffering through the conquests of *sī* 'Alī Ber, Mossi war progresses, and troubles in the west with the Wolof who had gained control of Takrūr, sent an embassy to establish contact with a Portuguese fort (Mina?) to ask for aid. John II sent two delegations, one by the Gambia which failed to get through, and 'also, by way of the fortress of Mina he sent to Muḥammad ibn Manzugol [Mansa Ulē?], grandson of Mūsā, King of Songo, one of the most populous cities of that great province which we commonly call Mandinga'.[6]

In 1498–9 *askiya* Muḥammad annexed Bāgana despite the resistance

[1] *Fattāsh*, p. 55 (107).

[2] *Sūdān*, p. 9 (17).

[3] *Fattāsh*, p. 81. Mīma is mentioned by Ibn Baṭṭūṭa (iv. 425, 427) as on a canal on the route from the capital of Māli to Timbuktu. It is a region between the Faguibine and Debo.

[4] *Fattāsh*, pp. 42–43 (81).

[5] *Voyages of Cadamosto*, transl. G. R. Crone, 1937, p. 67; repeated by Valentim Fernandes, *Description*, Bissau, 1951, pp. 34–35.

[6] *Da Asia*, bk. iii, transl. G. R. Crone, Hakluyt, lxxx. 144. This may be a different Mandinka chieftaincy for Binger states in an account of Ngokho, south of Sikaso, that this town 'serait la plus vieille ville que l'on connaisse par ici. Jadis elle était capitale et composée de deux villes : celle où habitait le roi s'appelait Nsogona, Nansogona ou Nséguéna. Autour de cette ville il y avait de nombreux bosquets sacrés' (*Du Niger au Golfe de Guinée*, 1892, i. 235).

of its Mandinka governor, ʿUthmān, and the chief of the Fulbe of Māsina, Demba Dondi. In 1500–1 he took Zalen (Dyāra) against the opposition of *qāma* Fati Qalli, the representative of the king of Māli at the court of the king of Dyāra.[1] 'He sacked the town, pillaging the house of the sultan of Mallī and carrying off his family.' In 1506–7 the *askiya* took Galam and penetrated to the borders of Takrūr. Māli had now lost all its northern dependencies.[2]

In 1530 a Fulbe leader called Koli tried to get control of Bambuk and raided part of western Mandeland, and Muḥammad II of Māli sent a new appeal to the Portuguese which led to a mission in 1534.[3] At the same time the local Mandinka chief of Bambuk (Gime Sossoko), finding Māli unable to help him against Koli, made himself independent. In 1542/3 *askiya* Isḥāq I raided Bendugu, one of the vassal states of Māli.[4] Next, his brother Da'ūd set out against Māli town; the king fled but returned when Da'ūd left after occupying the town for a week (1545–6).[5] After his succession to the throne the same Da'ūd made other expeditions against Mandinka countries,[6] but they were never occupied or even controlled by Songhay. As-Saʿdī records that, after the conquests of *askiya* Muḥammad and his sons, what was left of Māli 'split into three sections each having its ruling family claiming the sultanate. But the two generals[7] repudiated their authority and made themselves independent in their respective domains.'[8] After the collapse of Songhay in 1591 all its vassal states asserted their independence, but there was no one in Mandeland capable of emulating the exploits of Sun Dyāta. When Mansa Maḥmūd of Māli sent an expedition against the Moroccans in Jennē in 1599 neither of these generals, nor the rival chiefs of Kara-dugu and Ben-dugu, would join him, and he was only helped by minor chiefs like Ḥamadu Amīna, Pulo chief of Māsina, who was directly interested in making himself independent of the new conquerors. The Moroccans, although they

1 *T. as-Sūdān*, p. 75 (124–5).

2 Leo Africanus, who visited Māli as a boy in 1507, adds nothing new. He describes the capital as a large village of 6,000 fires and says that Islam flourished and that teaching was done in the mosques. He writes, 'Izchia [*askiya* Muḥammad] subdued the prince of this region, and made him tributary, and so oppressed him with grievous exactions that he was scarce able to maintain his family' (Hakluyt, iii. 823). *Askiya* Muḥammad, however, did not have any control over Manding proper.

3 De Barros in Hakluyt, lxxx. 143–4.

4 As-Saʿdī, p. 96/159.

5 Ibid., p. 98/161.

6 Ibid., p. 103/169–70.

7 As-Saʿdī has written earlier (p. 10/20) that the ruler of Māli had two generals (*qā'idān*, military governors?); one, entitled Sanqar Zūmaʿ, over the south, and the other, Faran Surā, over the north.

8 As-Saʿdī, p. 11/21.

received reinforcements, had the greatest difficulty in resisting this attack, the canoes even penetrating the town. The Moroccans owed their successful resistance primarily to their firearms, and Maḥmūd and his allies returned home.[1] Māli was now reduced to the status of a petty chieftaincy, contracted almost to its original nucleus. The next period until 1670 marks the final stage in the decline of the reduced Māli kingdom, which was hastened by the rise to power of the Bambara states of Segu and Karta.[2]

The organization of the Mandinka empire. Little is known about the territorial, fiscal, and judicial organization of Māli, more about court ceremonial which especially interested Arabic writers. A great political advance was made when Sun Dyāta exchanged his career as chief of an age-group association and raider for that of an empire-builder, a change which involved the substitution of primitive ideas of the exercise of power for those of a sphere of protected communities. The Māli empire was a zone of influence. It had a centralized core, divided into provinces or feudal estates over which members of the royal family were placed, where administration was direct. Such a governor (*dyamana-tigi* or *mānsa*) appointed district chiefs (*kāfo-tigi*) in charge of a number of villages (*dugu*) under village chiefs (*dugu-tigi*). Beyond the *dugu* all political unions (*kāfo* means 'to unite') were unstable associations. The *dugu-tigi* was the religio-political chief, but if as frequently happened a political chief were placed over the village he was known as *ku-ntigi*, whilst the *dugu-tigi* remained religious chief. The Mansa Māli himself, whose sacred character rendered him too remote, probably took little direct part in the administration.

Within the empire the various chieftaincies which had been incorporated remained not merely visible but practically independent throughout its history, and most continued to exist after the concept of the supreme divine ruler faded away. When conquest brought other peoples under its hegemony their rulers were recognized and their organizations respected. Rulers of such protectorates were invested by the *mānsa* with their authority and given a Mande title, the sign of fealty being the swearing of allegiance and payment of tribute. To some at least the *mānsa* appointed a Mandinka resident called *fāri-ba*, 'great chief', whose main function was to keep an eye on the ruler and ensure that tribute was collected and transmitted to Māli. Residents could if necessary claim troops from the local ruler. Ibn Baṭṭūṭa writes that Kābarā and Zāgha (Dyāga) situated on the Niger, 'have chiefs who

[1] As-Sa'dī, pp. 182/278–80. [2] See below pp. 147–8.

pay allegiance to the king of Māli';[1] and describes briefly the investiture ceremony of a vassal Tuareg chief by the governor of Timbuktu, *faribā* Mūsā, acting on behalf of *mānsa* Sulaimān, 'He invested him with a robe, turban and drawers, all of which were dyed, and made him be seated on a shield which was then raised upon their heads by the chiefs of the tribe.'[2] Al-'Umarī says that the southern Berbers were 'governed by elders (shaikhs) except for the Yantaṣir who were governed by their own kings under the suzerainty of the Lord of Māli'.[3]

Other regions besides Manding proper seem to have been under direct administration. Ibn Baṭṭūṭa writes that Īwālāten, 'the first province of the blacks', was governed by a *nā'ib* of the sultan called *fariba* Ḥusain and that the *mushrif* (intendant or comptroller) of the town itself was known as *manshā jū*,[4] which Delafosse has suggested is probably *mānsa dyõ*, 'royal slave'.[5] A town like Walāta, so important for the commercial connexions of the empire with North Africa, would naturally tend to be administered directly. There appears to have been a tendency in some parts for the governor to encroach upon the civil functions of the local ruler who, however, retained his socio-religious functions.

The intricacies of inter-relationship are shown in Maḥmūd al-Kāti's account of the state of Mīma.[6] He says there were twelve great chiefs of whom the principal was the *Mīma-kono*. Among other chiefs was the *Tuki-firi-sōma*, probably the 'master of the soil', before whom the chief of Māsina had to remain standing and cover himself with dust when taking the oath of allegiance. Jennē possessed almost complete independence. As-Sa'dī, who is biased in regard to Jennē, maintains in one place that it retained its independence against repeated Māli attacks,[7] but elsewhere implies that it was subject to Māli, being divided into three provinces, Kala, Bendugu, and Sibiridugu, each of which had twelve district chiefs whose titles he enumerates.[8] Maḥmūd

[1] Ibn Baṭṭūṭa, op. cit. iv. 395.

[2] Ibid. iv. 430–1. This shield ceremony was a Berber and Teda custom, also observed in Bornu until discontinued when Shaikh 'Umar abolished the Saifī line; see Barth, *Travels*, ii. 270.

[3] Al-'Umarī, pp. 59–60; al-Qalqashandī, v. 286–7.

[4] Ibn Baṭṭūṭa, iv. 385–6.

[5] M. Delafosse, *H.S.N.* ii. 194.

[6] *Fattāsh*, pp. 42–43/81.

[7] *Sūdān*, pp. 11, 13–14; transl. pp. 21, 25–26.

[8] Ibid., pp. 9–10/19–20. The titles consist of the names of their districts followed by Songhay *koy*, 'chief'.

al-Kāti shows definitely that Jennē paid allegiance to Māli. Its chief was not even allowed to see the *mãnsa*, but had to pay the tribute to the queen (-mother: *mā-na*?) whose fief it presumably was. He recounts how a ruler of Jennē, in revolt against Māli, raided canoes conveying soi-disant *sharīfs*, who had followed *mãnsa* Mūsā from Mecca, on their journey from Timbuktu to Nyani.[1] Jennē does not appear to have had a Māli intendant like other protectorates. It was admirably protected by a network of waterways and it took *sī* ʿAlī several years to reduce it.

The foundation of the state, the power of the ruler, was based on an inheritance from his predecessors, not of a geographical, but of a human domain of serf clans or castes. It cannot be compared with the European feudal system because there was no indissoluble tie between man and land. This is shown by Maḥmūd al-Kāti who, after describing the defeat of *sī* Bāro of Songhay by *askiya* Muḥammad, writes, 'Thus he found himself master of the twenty-four tribes composed of slaves,[2] not of freemen reduced to slavery.'[3] He states that the twenty-four tribes which he enumerates had been conquered by *sī* Mādogo from the ruler of Māli.[4] Of three of these who were *bãmbara* (i.e. pagans) he writes:

> These were the domestic serfs of the Malli-koy. Ever since they belonged to him it was the custom that none of them should marry unless the king provided 40,000 cowries for the parents-in-law in order to hinder the wife or her children from claiming their liberty and to ensure that they and their children should remain the property of the king. . . . The dues [of the three tribes] since the time they became his property was 40 cubits [of land cultivated] for each husband and wife.[5]

So with other tribes; for instance, fishers had to provide ten bundles of dried fish; the caste called *tyindiketa*, 'which means in their language [Mandinke] "cutters of grass", had the duty, from the time of the Malli-koy to that of the *sīs*, of cutting grass for the horses'.[6] They were also thatchers of the royal houses. *Arbi* serving the royal household

[1] *Fattāsh*, p. 37/64–65.

[2] *Ariqqā'*, normally used for newly caught slaves, but here referring to serf peoples.

[3] *Fattāsh*, p. 55/106.

[4] Ibid., pp. 55–58/107–13; cf. pp. 14–15/19–22.

[5] Ibid., p. 56/107–8. Evidence of the identification of domain with clans is found elsewhere (cf. the distribution of estates on p. 71/136–7). These tribes of household slaves were normally inalienable property, though al-Kāti records (p. 56/109) that 'askiya Muḥammad took some of their children and bought horses with them'.

[6] *Fattāsh*, pp. 56–57/109.

directly as servants and cultivators, whose young men formed the *mānsa's* personal bodyguard and acted as special messengers, were relieved of such dues.[1] This system provided the ruler with large bodies of people upon whose service he could rely. Although the ruler's power was based on this form of slavery it was not strictly a slave-state. All the political apparatus was superimposed and the break up of the state did not lead to any dislocation of the basic patterns of society.

Ibn Baṭṭūṭa, though rather contemptuous of Negroes chiefly because Sulaimān at first took no notice of the famous traveller, was, after his experience of corrupt administrations, impressed by the impartiality with which justice was administered. They were more averse to committing injustices, he says, than any people he had come across, the sultan not forgiving any of his servants guilty of such acts,[2] and he describes the destitution of the governor of Walāta for that reason.[3] He also speaks of the admirable state of public security in the time of Sulaimān. The safety of travel in southern Sahara was a great achievement. From Walāta where the authority of Māli began it was unnecessary to travel by caravan, for 'there is complete security in their country, neither traveller nor native having anything to fear from robbers or men of violence'.[4]

In the early days of Māli succession to the throne often passed through the female line, whilst the majority of later rulers are recorded as being of the paternal line, but we can place little reliance upon the source of our information (Ibn Khaldūn). At any rate the possibility of a double line of succession widened the possibility of pretenders and dynastic troubles were frequent.

In the middle of the fourteenth century, the period when information is most copious, the ruler gave audience in two places. One was in the entrance-hut (*qubba*) to his compound,[5] whose window-openings were furnished with woollen curtains which were drawn to indicate the opening of a session.[6] The other was in the open air in a special place of council where a picture is given of the *mānsa* at an audience seated upon a three-tiered dais[7] covered with silk and cushions and flanked by elephants' tusks. He is wearing a golden skull-cap bound by a turban of gold brocade, a red gown, and a twenty-sectioned pair of

[1] Ibid., p. 57 (111).
[2] Ibn Baṭṭūṭa, iv. 415, 421.
[3] Ibid. iv. 416; cf. pp. 414–15.
[4] Ibid. iv. 421.
[5] This is the traditional audience-chamber of the Sudan.
[6] For a description of the audience see Ibn Baṭṭūṭa, iv. 403–8.
[7] Both Ibn Baṭṭūṭa and al-ʿUmarī use the Mandinka word *bembē*.

drawers. Beside him are his arms, a sword, spear, bow, quiver, and arrows, all in gold; behind him two standards are displayed and thirty Turkish *mamlūks* bought in Cairo, one carrying a silken parasol surmounted by a golden bird. Around him in a wide arc are seated the army commanders, whilst the cavalry chiefs face him. Beside him in constant attendance stands the executioner, together with the Interpreter or Herald, a most important member of the court since he is the intermediary between ruler and people. In addition there are drummers, dancers, and griots,[1] two horses harnessed for immediate service, and two goats to give protection against the eye. Both writers also describe the rigorous and complicated ceremonial or magical ritual involved, with its obligations upon those being received of semi-nakedness, prostration, dusting, and a peculiar gesture of homage (similar to *ḍarb al-jūk*). The *farārīs* (army commanders) provide a chorus of approval expressed by twanging their bowstrings. Practically all this was indigenous, or at least pre-Islamic; contacts with Mamlūk and North African courts having merely added minor details to the native pattern.[2]

The expenses of the court and administration were met by a system of taxation (a tithe on crops and livestock), tribute from dependent states, revenue from tolls and customs, slave-raiding, and the spoils of war. Officials deducted a proportion of the taxes and tribute they collected for their expenses. The *mānsa* distributed to officials and military commanders gifts of serf domains, gold, horses, and robes of honour. Decorations for valour consisted of golden bracelets, collars, and anklets representing ascending orders of chivalry, but the most important was the Order of the Pants, 'each time they perform a deed of valour the king invests them with wide drawers, and at each fresh exploit their width is expanded'.[3]

Islam occupied a minor place in the organization of the state. It had

[1] The Mandinka word *dyeli* or Soninke *dyāru*, *dyālu*, is mentioned by Ibn Baṭṭūṭa under the form *jālī*, pl. *julā*. On the function of the *dyālu-tigo*, the chief of the griots among the Khasonke, see C. Monteil, *Les Khassonké*, pp. 302 and 332. In the last century no Mandinka chief of Sankaran or Toron would travel without his *mori-kē*, cleric who acted as secretary, chaplain, doctor, and diviner; and his *fina-kē* or griot, who was charged with diplomatic missions. In this region *fina* is the name of an endogamous clan of griots who are masters of ceremony at the various *rites de passage*.

[2] The parasol, golden bird, standards, and executioner were probably borrowed from the Fāṭimid or Mamlūk courts; see Qalqashandī, *Ṣubḥ*, iv. 7.

[3] Al-'Umarī, p. 66. A. G. Laing, visiting Sōlimana in 1822, wrote, 'The width of the trowsers is a great mark of distinction among the Mandingoes; hence the common expression among them, Koorté Abooniato, "large trowsers", which is synonymous with "great man"' (*Travels in Western Africa*, 1825, p. 130). The practice was in use in the Bambara kingdom of Segu.

been accepted as the imperial cult and in consequence was regarded as an Islamic state by the Maghribīs, but it was little practised outside the immediate entourage of the *mānsa* and the white trading community. Many rulers gained notoriety through their pilgrimages to Mecca. They valued Islam as a link with North African countries with whom essential commercial relations existed. Ibn Baṭṭūṭa provides many indications of the adoption of Islam in this limited way: the institution of the *jāmiʿ* with its chief *imām*, Friday *khuṭba* with mention of the ruler's name, and Qur'ān schools. Both the *jāmiʿ* and chief *imām's* house were places of refuge[1] where the *qāsā*, Sulaimān's co-ruler, found asylum after her treason had come to light. Among qualities of the people of Nyani he commends:

Their punctilliousness in observing the prayer sequence, their assiduousness in attending congregational prayers and in bringing up their children to observe them. On Fridays so great is the crowd that unless one goes early to the mosque it is impossible to find a place. Consequently it is customary for a man to send beforehand his slave-boy with his prayer-mat which he spreads out in a place befitting his master's rank and reserves it until he arrives. . . . Another of their good qualities is their concern for learning the Qur'ān by heart. If their children show negligence in this duty they put leg-shackles on them and do not free them until they have memorized it. On the day of the festival I visited the *qāḍī* and found his children going around in shackles, so I asked him, 'Arn't you going to set them free?' but he replied, 'I shall not do so until they have the Qur'ān by heart.'[2]

He received his first audience after the recitation of the entire Qur'ān at a condolence party held at the palace after the death of Abū'l-Ḥasan, sultan of Morocco.[3] The Friday and *ʿīd* prayers were important occasions in the capital for the display of the ruler's pomp and majesty.[4] Ibn Baṭṭūṭa writes:

I was present in Māli on the occasion of both *ʿīd al-aḍḥā* and *ʿīd al-fiṭr*. The people went out to the *maṣallā*, which was near the palace of the sultan, wearing fine white garments. The sultan, wearing the *ṭailasān* on his head, rode there on a horse. None of the negroes wear the *ṭailasān* except at the two festivals, with the exception of the *qāḍī*, the *khaṭīb*, and the jurisconsults who wear it always. On this festival occasion they precede the sultan chanting,

[1] Al-Kāti mentions clerically ruled towns which served as cities of refuge, among them Kunjōro in the kingdom of Kanyāga (Dyāra region) and Dyāra (Dyā) within Māli where even one who had killed a relative of the king was safe from his vengeance; *Fattāsh*, pp. 179–80 (314–15). The author of *Tadhkirat an-Nisyān* (p. 140/228; cf. also p. 21/34–35) in the middle of the eighteenth century says that the house of the chief *imām* of Timbuktu was regarded as an asylum, but that the Moroccan soldiers did not respect these conventions.

[2] Ibn Baṭṭūṭa, iv. 421–3. [3] Ibid. iv. 400. [4] Ibid. iv. 409–13.

'There is no god but Allāh' and 'God is great'. Before the sultan are standards of red silk. On arrival at the *muṣallā* the sultan enters a tent which has been erected in order to prepare himself. Then he goes on to the prayer-ground and the prayer and sermon are performed. Afterwards the preacher descends from his block, sits before the sultan and declaims for a long while. Beside him is a man with a spear in his hand who explains to the people in their own language the preacher's discourse which consists of admonition and warning, eulogy of the sultan and exhortations to persist in obedience to him and pay him his dues.

Following this Ibn Baṭṭūṭa describes the military review witnessed by the royal entourage, seated according to strict protocol, after which the interpreter-griot and his assistants sing praises of the sultan to the accompaniment of music, dancing, and acrobatic feats. This took place every Friday as well as on festivals. The commanders are invited to break the fast at the palace where Ibn Baṭṭūṭa was shocked to observe that each was attended by twenty or more entirely naked female slaves who carried the food from his own house.[1]

From his account the dualism of the imperial cult characteristic of this stage of islamization is quite clear. He gives an account of the griots (*dyēli*), clothed in garments of feathers with wooden masks whose beak is painted red, performing their rites at the court on the day of the *'īd*.[2] *Mānsa* Sulaimān, devout Muslim though he was, saw nothing incongruous in providing a delegation of cannibals from the gold country with their customary flesh. 'I was informed', says Ibn Baṭṭūṭa, 'that this was the normal practice when a delegation visited him.'[3] Al-'Umarī refers to the practice of magic and sorcery throughout Māli and Ibn Baṭṭūṭa to their eating of flesh unclean to Muslims.[4]

Islamic law was scarcely observed,[5] but since the principle of personal status was recognized *qāḍīs* functioned in the towns. Probably they only tried cases involving foreign Muslims. With the decline of Māli Islam disappeared from the Mande regions, except for Dyula and Soninke trading colonies. During its decline, when kinship and mystery cults held undisputed sway in all successor states, teachers from the region sought new lives far outside its boundaries. Many Islamic communities in northern Nigeria attribute their conversion to missionaries

[1] Ibn Baṭṭūṭa, iv. 423. [2] Ibid. iv. 413–14. [3] Ibid. iv. 428–9.

[4] Ibid. iv. 424.

[5] Ibn Baṭṭūṭa mentions the existence of 'Ibāḍites called Ṣaghanaghū (Sangha?), but only among the whites, 'The orthodox Mālikites among the whites are known as *Tūrī*' (iv. 395). This is the Soninke word for 'stranger', and the word has spread widely. In Hausa *ba-tūre* (pl. *tūrāwa*) is applied to non-Berber white North Africans, Arabs, and Europeans. Mande *sūra*, 'whites', generally derived from Arab. *Ṣūr*, 'Tyre', 'Phoenicians', is no doubt the same word.

from Māli. Wangāra settled in Kano and Katsina at the end of the fourteenth century and a Zaria king appointed a Māli cleric to the chieftainship of a pagan district in A.D. 1500. Thus, in spite of the weak position of Islam as a kinship cult Māli contributed to the islamization of West Africa.

The consequences of Māli's hegemony over a vast area for more than two centuries (1238–1468) show themselves in various ways. It facilitated the expansion of peoples. Dyula trading colonies have been mentioned, but movements of agriculturalists were considerable. It also aided the shading of feelings of ethnic exclusiveness and the widespread diffusion of mystery-cult societies. A feature of 'primitive' communities and particularly in the forest region is that each locality is peopled by one ethnic group hostile to infiltration by others. But it is characteristic of the northern Mande world for different peoples to have learnt to live side by side. Mandinka areas show strong uniform characteristics. Manding absorbed diverse elements and moulded them into one culture so that traditions of origin disappeared, leaving only ethnic tradition, the so-called 'biological patriotism'. When travelling through areas of Mandinka penetration one notices the juxtaposition of villages of different elements. Thus in the interior of the Gambia Protectorate Manding, Soninke, and Fulbe villages are found adjacent to each other, the first two Muslim and agricultural, the Pulo village pagan and having stock-rearing as well as agriculture. In western Guinea many ruling families of Ṣerēr, Mende, and Vai are of Manding origin and it is through them and settlement of traders and clerics that Islam has penetrated these peoples.

5. THE SONGHAY EMPIRE OF KAWKAW

With Kawkaw we move into central Sudan, the third section of al-Idrīsī's first clime (*iqlīm*), of which he writes, 'The best known places are Kūgha, Kawkaw, Tamalma, Zaghāwa, Mānān, N'jīmi, Nuwābiyya, and Tājawa.'[1] The central Sudan therefore stretches from the middle Niger to Waday beyond Lake Chad. We are concerned here only with the state associated with the town of Kawkaw and the Songhay inhabiting the banks of the middle Niger. They are included here instead of in the next chapter because their migration trends were up the Niger and the history of Kawkaw as a short-lived great power is more associated with the west than with the east.

The cradle of the Songhay kingdom is the banks of the Niger from

[1] Al-Idrīsī, p. 10.

the present Nigerian frontier upstream to Gao, the traditional Dendi region, though not the Dendi of present-day maps. This stretch of the river was little influenced by northern civilizations and had no towns except Gungia on the northern Songhay fringe which became the seat of a ruling clan.[1] This town appears to be mentioned by al-Khwārizmī (Kankū?). North of this a market-centre grew into the important commercial town of Kawkaw[2] from which trade-routes radiated to North Africa by Kidāl in Adrār of the Ifoghas, to Egypt by Air, and to Kānem. As in the Nile valley, the Niger with its tributaries and deltas from Lake Debo right round to Tillaberi allowed for the settlement of cultivators in full nomadic regions. Arabic writers show us that the right bank of the Niger bend which was the most favourable for flooding was the domain of Negro cultivators, whilst the left bank was inhabited by Berber nomads more or less islamized, though there is no reason to suppose that this bank was completely devoid of villages of Negro fishermen and cultivators.

We need not speculate about their traditional history which is obscured in myth. Like other Sudanese peoples the Songhay[3] are not a homogeneous group. We get a picture of peoples clinging to the banks of the Niger and its tributaries, along some of which, as tumuli and the remains of villages show, cultivation was formerly possible. These comprised sedentary cultivators (*da*) of various ethnic groups, probably related to the Gurmanshi-Mossi, hunters (Gow) ranging the bush country, and fishers and harpooners (Sorko) who had apparently migrated from the east (Chad region?). These Sorko, who were divided into two main clans of Faran and Fono, grew in numbers and authority, establishing more and more settlements along the river banks, and because of their mobility dominated the cultivators. The *ta'rīkhs* preserve a tradition of a river beast which surfaced periodically and imposed orders and taboos upon the people of Kukiya or Gungia.[4] This

[1] Songhay *gungu*, 'island'. The site is unknown, though Delafosse (*H.S.N.* ii. 60) conjectures that it was one of the islands near present-day Bentia. See also L. Desplagnes, *Le Plateau Central Nigérien*, Paris, 1907, p. 82.

[2] Also called *Gāo* or *Gawo*, which is the name in Songhay and Hausa for the *acacia albida* (Arab. *ḥarāz*). The name of the town is spelt Kawkaw, Kāghu, and Kā'o in the Arabic script (see *Fattāsh*, transl. p. 330). In Tamāhaqq the town is still called Gaugu.

[3] The word Songhay (Sõŋai) designates, not the people, but the country, the riverain region from Gao southwards to Dendi. The people are referred to as *Sõŋai bor'ey*, *Sõŋoytye*, or *Sondankye*, ethnic names of recent formation. The word first appears in the *Fattāsh* (*Sunghay* or *Sughay*) where it is used both of the country and its inhabitants. The Sõŋoytye are especially the descendants of *sī* 'Alī.

[4] The earliest accounts of the myth are found in *Fattāsh*, pp. 30–31 (49–51); *T. as-Sūdān*, p. 4 (6–8).

beast was killed by a stranger with a harpoon, the weapon of the Sorko, and he became the first *zā* or *dyā*.[1] Delafosse places this event about A.D. 690.[2] A late literary source[3] dates the beginning of the dynasty from the middle of the fourth century A.H. (*c*. A.D. 960), but a date towards the middle of the third century, about A.D. 850, seems probable. Delafosse conjectured that the founders were Christian Lemṭa Berbers, but the only evidence for this is propinquity and a statement of the unreliable Leo Africanus.[4] Arabic writers do not imply that the rulers claimed to be Berbers or whites. Al-Masʿūdī (A.D. 943) speaks of Kushites who migrated westwards, leaving behind in East Africa the Nūba, Beja, and Zinj, as containing Zaghāwa and Kawkaw amongst others.[5]

The Sorko were the spearhead of the migratory movement up the river. Organized communal fishing and river trade meant control of the river banks and trading villages became political centres. They continued right up the river as far as the Mopti and Jennē region where they mixed with Mande. Whether they actually founded Kawkaw or not the *zā* were in control of it, and as a commercial centre it became more important than Gungia, a congregating point for caravans to Tādmekka or Tākedda and then North Africa or Egypt. Al-Yaʿqūbī (A.D. 872) regards Kawkaw as the most important of the Negro states and shows that it was organized in the normal Sudan fashion:

Kawkaw is the greatest sovereignty of the Negroes, the most important and influential, to whom all the kingdoms pay allegiance. Kawkaw is the name of

[1] The traditional name of the stranger-founder of the dynasty, *zā* Alayaman, is derived, by an Arabic rationalization, from *jā'a min al-Yaman*, 'he came from Yemen'. Ibn Khurdādhbih (first draft 232/846, *B.G.A.* vi. 89) mentions a king of the naked negroes called Zāghī b. Zāghī, but his country is more likely to be Gāna than Kawkaw since it seems to be situated near the Atlantic.

[2] *H.S.N.* i. 240–1. Delafosse is following Barth who suggested A.H. 60/A.D. 679–80; *Travels*, iv. 579.

[3] Author of the fragment (translation but not the Arabic text in Appendix 2, *Fattāsh* p. 329) written in the time of the puppet *askiya* of Timbuktu, Da'ūd b. Hārūn (1657–69), but based upon earlier material.

[4] *H.S.N.* i. 192–3. Referring to the first *askiya*, Muḥammad b. Abī Bakr, Leo writes, 'The king of Tombuto that now raigneth, called Abuacre Izchia, is a Negro by birth: this Abuacre after the decease of the former king, who was a Libyan borne, slue all his sons and so usurped the kingdom'; transl. J. Pory, Hakluyt, iii. 820; cf. p. 823. We see no reason to believe that the *zās* and *sīs* belonged to the same dynasty. If Libyan is taken to mean non-Negro black Saharans like the Zaghāwa the statement is probable. It is unlikely that the Lemṭa were Berbers. Al-Yaʿqūbī writes, 'Between Zawīla and the "centre" of Kawwār and in the vicinity of Zawīla in the direction of Awjila and Ajdābiyya, are a people called Lemṭa who resemble Berbers in some respects' (*Buldān*, p. 345).

[5] Al-Masʿūdī, iii. 1–2, 37–38.

the capital. Subject to this (king) are a number of kingdoms which pay him allegiance and acknowledge his overlordship although they are rulers over their own states. Among them is the kingdom of Maraw which is extensive, whose king has a capital called al-Ḥayā; and the kingdoms of Murdiya, al-Harbar, Ṣanhāja, Nadhkarīr, Al-Zayānīr, Arwar, Taqārūt. All these are dependencies of the kingdom of Kawkaw.[1]

Obviously Kawkaw's commercial relations brought it into contact with Muslims. Abū Yazīd (Makhlad b. Kaidād), the famous Khārijite revolutionary of Ifrīqiya, was born in Kawkaw (*c.* 260/874) when his father, a Zanātī trader, was residing there.[2] Yāqūt, after remarking that 'Kawkaw is both the name of a people and of a country of the blacks', quotes al-Muhallabī (A.D. 985) who shows that the ruling class made a profession of Islam at that early date:

Kawkaw lies in the first climate-band and its latitude is 10°. Their king makes a profession of Islam before his subjects, and most of them follow his example. He has a city on the Nile, east of it, called Sarnāt, which has well-stocked markets and upon which caravans converge continuously from every quarter. He also has a city to the west of the Nile where he lives with his body-guard and confidants. It has a mosque where he performs his prayers. The sanctuary for congregational prayer lies between the two cities.[3] In his city is a palace where no one resides or even enters except eunuchs (?), all of whom are Muslims. The king and his chief ministers wear gowns and turbans. They ride horses bareback. His dominion is more populous than that of the Zaghāwa, but the territory of the latter is more extensive. The wealth of the people of his country lies in flocks and herds. The storehouses of the king are extensive, most of them being used for storing salt.[4]

This account, if it refers to Kawkaw at all, implies that the rulers were not Songhay but more likely Zaghāwa, the black nomads who roamed the desert to the north-east and were familiar with horses, whilst most of the people were animal breeders.

As-Sa'dī relates a tradition that *zā* Kosoy, the 15th ruler of the dynasty, was the first to be converted to Islam, and states that he transferred his capital from Gungia to Kawkaw in A.H. 400/1009–10.[5] He adds, 'He was called in their language *Muslim Dam*, meaning "he has

[1] Al-Ya'qūbī, *Ta'rīkh*, i. 219–20. There are many alternative readings of all these names. The Marawiyyīn are mentioned on p. 217 and in his *Kitāb al-Buldān*, p. 345.

[2] Ibn Khaldūn, *Berb.* transl. iii. 201.

[3] Reading *madīnatain* for *madrasatain*.

[4] Quoted by Yāqūt, *Mu'jam al-buldān*, iv. 329. Al-Bakrī (p. 183) also says that salt was used as money.

[5] As-Sa'dī, *T. as-Sūdān*, p. 3 (5).

islamized voluntarily without compulsion".' According to the fragment already referred to, which was based upon earlier writers including Maḥmūd al-Kāti whose *K. al-Fattāsh* in its present form has no account of the *zās* and earlier *sīs*, he was called Kusho (or Kotso) Muslim,

It was during his reign that circumcision was introduced into Gāo by his orders. He entrusted this charge to a man called Ṣalāḥ ad-Dīn who had come to this country from the east. It was this man, so they say, who converted the people of Gāo to Islam; but that is not strictly correct because Islam existed among them earlier judging by what I have read on this matter in an autograph manuscript by our master, the jurisconsult and *qāḍī*, Maḥmūd b. al-ḥājj al-Mutawakkil Kāti, where these words occur, 'Praise belongs to God! The islamization of the people of Gāo took place between 471 and 475 (1078 and 1082).'[1]

Maḥmūd, therefore, believed that *zā* Kosoy lived about A.D. 1100. The list of *zās* in this fragment does not differ in any significant way from that of As-Saʿdī.

Al-Bakrī's account of Kawkaw (*c.* 1050), which he situated on the right bank,[2] is also full of difficulties, and it is possible that it refers to some other town in the central Sudan which had a different ruling class from that of the people, for he says they dressed like Negroes and worshipped idols like the Negroes:

Between Tādmekka and the city of Kūkū (or Kawkaw) is a nine days' journey. The Arabs call its people al-Bazarkāniyyīn.[3] It consists of two towns, that of the king and that of the Muslims. Their king is called *Qandā*.[4] Their dress is like that of the Negroes, consisting of loin-cloths, skins, and whatever else they fancy, according to their means. They worship idols like the Negroes. When the king sits down[5] the drums are beaten and it is the custom for the Negro women to dance [the hair-dance] with their plaited dangling tresses.[6]

[1] *Fattāsh*, pp. 332–3.

[2] Local legend also agrees with the Arab writers in placing Kawkaw on the right (*gurma*) bank at this period; see *Fattāsh*, p. 329.

[3] Persian *bāzargān*, 'merchant'. No satisfactory explanation has been offered for this word. If read *barankānī* (see Dozy, *Noms de vêtements*, 1845, pp. 68–71) it might mean 'weavers' or 'embroiderers'. The *barazakanya* of Katsina (their quarter is mentioned by Barth, ii. 556) are specialists in leather, coats of mail, horse-trappings, and the like (cf. H. R. Palmer, *Sud. Mem.* iii. 80 n.).

[4] *Qandā* is no doubt a title. The ruler of Kebbi in the sixteenth century was entitled *kanta*. De Sacy (*Not. et Extr.* xii (1831), 656) has *Firawz*.

[5] 'Sits down' to eat a meal of a ritual nature for the prosperity of the land? Normally one would take *julūs* to mean 'holds an audience', but the rest of the passage makes this impossible.

[6] It was characteristic of the Tēda, Kānembu, and Nilotic Nubians to arrange their hair in rat-tails, and reminds one of the hair-dance in the Nilotic Sudan.

No one is free to go about the town until he has finished eating and the remains have been thrown into the Nile, whereupon they (the attendants) assemble and shout so that the people may know that he has finished. Whenever a new king succeeds to the throne he is invested with a ring, a sword, and a Qur'ān which, they claim, the Amīr al-Mu'minīn sent for this purpose.[1] Their king is a Muslim for none but a Muslim may reign. . . . The commerce of the people of Kūkūland consists of salt which is employed as money. It is extracted from underground mines at Tūtek (or Tawtek) in Berberland, carried to Tādmekka and from there to Kūkū.[2]

Nothing indicates that this town is Kawkaw. Since Kūka, 'baobab', is a common name for a settlement or market village in central Sudan al-Bakrī's description probably relates to a town which has disappeared. Tādmekka,[3] a Berber town in Adrār of the Iforas, probably on the site of Taholas or I-n-Tedeini rather than As-Sūq,[4] is more than nine days from Kawkaw. Ibn Ḥawqal describes its people as berberized Negroes.[5] Al-Bakrī describes it as better-built than either Gāna or Kūkū. Its inhabitants were veiled Muslim Berbers who obtained their grain from the country of the Negroes.[6] Ibn Sa'īd says that in his time (1240) it was under the control of Kānem,[7] but this is clearly a mistake for Tākedda.

Arab writers appear at times to have confused Kūgha, Kawkaw (Kāghū in Ibn Khaldūn), and Gungia. The Kūgha which al-Idrīsī mentions as the first place in this section was a dependency of Wangāra (Mandeland south of Gāna). It is not the same Kūgha as the trading-town in the country of gold mentioned by al-Bakrī,[8] but it might be

[1] The Maghrāwa rulers of Sijilmāsa acknowledged the Umayyad caliphate of Cordoba until its fall. It must have been through some such link that the rulers of Kūkū formed relations with Spain.

[2] Al-Bakrī, p. 183. The Banī Tūtak are mentioned by Ibn Ḥawqal, i. 103.

[3] Tādmekka is the Saghmāra of al-Idrīsī (pp. 6, 10) whom al-Bakrī regards as a tribe, 'The Nile, after leaving Tīreqqā, turns towards the south into the land of the Blacks. One travels about three days to the country of the Saghmāra, a tribe of Berbers belonging to the territory of Tādmekka. Over against them on the opposite bank is the town of Kūkū' (al-Bakrī, p. 181). It has been suggested that the word Saghmāra is Issakamāren, Negro serfs of the Tuareg.

[4] See *Not. Afr.*, No. 51 (1951), pp. 65–69.

[5] Ibn Ḥawqal writes (i. 105): 'As for the Banī Tanmāk, kings of Tadmaka, and the tribes derived from them, it is said that their origin was Negro, whose skins whitened in the north, but others say they are from the Ṣanhāja.'

[6] Al-Bakrī, p. 181.

[7] Abū 'l-Fidā', text p. 127; transl. ii. 219.

[8] Ibn Ḥawqal's remark (i. 92; c.f 101) that Kūgha was a month's journey from Gāna would agree with an identification with Gungia. Al-Bakri's Kūgha (p. 179) was 15 days *west* of Gāna (6 days to Samaqanda, then 9 to Kūgha). Al-Idrīsī says (p. 10) that Samaqanda was

identified with Gungia (Kūkiya). Whilst Kūgha is a dependency, Kawkaw is independent. Al-Idrīsī's account of Kawkaw is full of difficulties. He puts it 20 days' camel-march north of Kūgha through the country of the black Baghāma Berbers:

The town of Kawkaw, one of the most renowned in the land of the Negroes, is large, situated on the bank of a river coming from the northern region. . . . Many Negroes say that this town of Kawkaw lies on the bank of an inlet,[1] whilst others say that it is on a river which falls into the Nile. But what is certain is that this river flows until it passes Kawkaw for many days and then peters out in the desert in the soft sand. . . . The king of Kawkaw is an independent monarch, the *khuṭba* being pronounced in his name. He has a large bodyguard, a considerable retinue, generals and armies, complete with uniforms and fine decorations. They ride horses and camels, and are brave and overawe the neighbouring tribes who surround their land. The common people wear merely skins to hide their nakedness, but their merchants dress in tunics and gowns with turbans around their heads and ornaments of gold. The nobles and notables, who wear the *izār*,[2] have dealings with the merchants and sit in with them and advance them goods in return for a share in the profits.[3]

The ruling class of this town, wherever it was situated, are clearly not Songhay, but probably Zaghāwa or Baghāma; nor is the town situated on the Niger. It appears that they raided the Zaghāwa for al-Idrīsī writes elsewhere[4] that the Zaghawī town of Shāma 'is sparsely populated because most of its inhabitants have been transported to the town of Kawkaw, sixteen days' journey away.'

But wherever this Kawkaw was situated we now have direct evidence that the rulers of this stretch of the Niger were Muslim since the discovery of royal steles in 1939 at Sané, 10 km. north of Gao. Under their Arabic names these rulers cannot be equated satisfactorily with kings in the traditional list.[5] Some steles are carved in relief on

well east of Gāna, and Kūgha 10 days east of Samaqanda and a month and a half from Gāna. Both say that it was a dependency of Wangāra, though al-Idrīsī adds that 'some blacks make it a dependency of Kānem'. It is, of course, not Leo's Gaoga. We know that a hundred years later Kānem's influence extended as far as Tādmekka (?).

[1] *Khalīj*, here probably a brush-covered dried-up river bed. See p. 38 (44–45) on conflicting evidence about the river of Kawkaw.

[2] *Uzur* (sing. *izār*) here seems to refer to the head-wrap, a derivative of the Tuareg mouth-veil, which is worn today by notables of the Songhay and Hausa.

[3] Al-Idrīsī, p. 11. Al-Idrīsī's contemporary, Abū Ḥāmid, who wrote in 1162, contributes little if his Qūqū (or Qūqah) refers to the Sorko or Songhay, 'They are the worst type of blacks. All the blacks can be utilized as servants and labourers but not the Qūqū who are useless except for war' (*Tuḥfat al-Albāb*, in *J. Asiat.* ccvii. 43).

[4] Al-Idrīsī, p. 34.

[5] See *T. as-Sūdān*, p. 3 (4–5); *Fattāsh*, transl. pp. 332–3.

marble in Kūfic characters, and are the work of an Andalusian sculptor called Ya'īsh, whilst others are of cruder local workmanship.[1]

Ibn Sa'īd provides no new information, saying, surprisingly, that 'the ruler is a heathen, having flanking him on the west the Muslims of Ghāna, on the east the Muslims of Kānem. Kawkaw has a river from which it derives its name, the town being situated to the east of its river.'[2]

The *zā* rulers of Kawkaw came under the hegemony of Māli possibly as early as the time of the conqueror Sun Dyāta (1230–55), but the link must have been very loose. In a late document (the seventeenth-century fragment) we read:

> As for the limits of the authority of the *juwa* they stretched in the west to Kīma and Na'na'. Timbuktu and the region beyond, up to Mīma, formed part of the domain of the Tuareg and of the Malli-koy; occasionally the Mossi invaded this region and made raids.[3] In the east the authority of the *juwa* extended up to the country of the Zerma.[4]

[1] See J. Sauvaget, 'Les Épitaphes de Gao', *Bull. I.F.A.N.* xii (1950), 418–40. These epitaphs show that the rulers were Muslims and were linked with Almoravid Spain, but the names cannot be equated satisfactorily with the native lists of rulers. Many of the epitaphs record only the Muslim and not the native name, but where this is given it does not appear to be Berber, e.g. 'Māmā b. Kamā b. Ā'ī, known as 'Umar b. al-Khaṭṭāb'. M. Sauvaget has worked out the relationships of certain of the people mentioned:

Rā'ī (Ā'ī)

- 'Abd Allāh
  - Abū 'Abd Allāh Muḥammad (d. 494/1100)
- Abū Quḥāfa
  - Abū Bakr (d. 503/1110) married Sawā (d. 502)
    - Namī (daughter)
- Kamā or al-Khaṭṭāb
  - Māma or 'Umar (d. 514/1120)

There is an epitaph to 'Ā'isha bint al-malik Kūrī who died in 511/1117 and the 13th *zā* of the traditional lists was Jata-Korē (*Fattāsh*, p. 332) or Kū-Korai (*Sūdān*, p. 3). Such an identification would support a suggestion that *zā* Kosoy was Abū 'Abd Allāh Muḥammad and the invention of Muslim names (related to the first *khalīfas*) for his father and uncles was due to a conscious islamization after the Murābiṭ episode.

A collection of inscriptions from the Niger formed by G. de Gironcourt and deposited by him in the Académie des Inscriptions have not yet, so far as I know, been edited. Van Berchem writes that this material, which ranges from the beginning of the twelfth to the first quarter of the fifteenth century A.D., constitutes 'une source précieuse, et entièrement nouvelle pour l'histoire de l'Islam au Niger' (*Missions de Gironcourt en Afrique Occidentale: Documents Scientifiques*, Paris, 1920, p. 355).

[2] Abū 'l-Fidā', p. 221. Al-Qalqashandī (v. 285) has *yuqātilu* for *yuqābilu*.

[3] The same document says that the king of the Mossi warred against the 24th *zā*, Barai (*c.* 1220). The campaign lasted for four months before the Mossi withdrew (*Fattāsh*, p. 333).

[4] *Fattāsh*, p. 334.

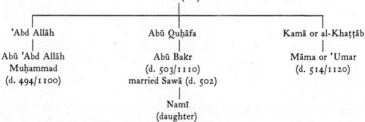

About 1275 a new dynasty replaced that of the *zā*. As-Saʿdī writes, 'Then came the *Sonni* line, of which the first, ʿAlī Kolon, with God's help, severed the rope of the dominion of the people of Malli over the people of Songhay.'[1] He relates how two of the sons of *zā* Yasi-boy, called ʿAlī and Salmān, employed in the service of the king of Māli as chiefs of military expeditions, escaped to Songhay. ʿAli freed the country and ascended the throne as the first *sī* or *sonni*. He therefore regards them as legitimate continuators of the line of the *zā*. Another source, however, corrects this explicitly.[2] The writer gives a list of the *zās* (which he orthographs *juʿa*, *juwa*, or *jā*'), three of whom reigned after Yasi-boy—Bāro, Dūro, and finally the 28th *zā* Bisi Bāro (or Bēr):[3]

> With him their authority finished, no *juwa* having reigned after him. Their dynasty is extinct and their descendants are called *Juwa-bēr-banda*.[4] Those who give the name of *Juwa-bēr-banda* to the princes of the *su'i* commit a grave error. . . . The first who reigned over these countries with the title of *su'i* was the *su'i* ʿAlī Golom (this word being also written *siʿi* . . .),[5] who was born in Malli and had risen in the service of the king of Malli. He was very brave, energetic and valiant. He left the king of Malli for reasons which would take too long to recount here.

According to this account the *sī* dynasty was a new one founded by a Mande adventurer. Maḥmūd al-Kāti implies that he was a Soninke when he writes, 'Know that the *Shī*, askiya Muḥammad, and *mōri* Hawgāro . . . are all of the same origin.'[6] Barth, followed by Delafosse, suggested that the date of ʿAlī Golom was about 1335 on the ground of the statement of Ibn Khaldūn of its capture by Mansa Mūsā's armies, followed by the *mansa*'s visit on his return from pilgrimage in 1324/5,[7] but this fragment says: 'After *si* ʿAlī Golom reigned the *si* Salmān Nāri, then *si* Ibrāhīm Kabayao, ʿUthmān Gīfo, and Mākara Komsū. It was under the reign of the latter that the Malli-Koy, Ganko Mūsā passed through the country, performing the pilgrimage to Mecca. This was in the year 720 (1320).'[8]

[1] As-Saʿdī, op. cit., pp. 3 (5–6), 5–6 (9–12).

[2] This is the fragment already quoted which was first utilized by Ch. Monteil in his reconstruction of the history of this period (*Les Empires du Mali*, 1930, pp. 79–80).

[3] As-Saʿdī (p. 3) has a different order: (27) Yāsi-boy, (28) Dūro, (29) Zenko Bāro, (30) Bisi Bāro, (31) Bada. See list in Appendix, p. 238.

[4] 'Posterity of the great *juwa*'; cf. *Fattāsh*, p. 333, n. 4.

[5] As-Saʿdī writes *sonni*. Maḥmūd al-Kāti quotes: 'The meaning of *shī* is *koy-banandi* [tax-collector] that is '*khalīfa* of the sultan', or 'his substitute' (*Fattāsh*, p. 43/82), which supports the theory that he was appointed by Māli.

[6] *Fattāsh*, p. 48 (93–94).

[7] Cf. *T. as-Sūdān*, p. 7 (14); Barth, *Travels*, iv. 590.

[8] *Fattāsh*, p. 335.

If we accept this account ʿAlī Golon must have reigned about A.D. 1275. Kawkaw's freedom from vassalage to Māli, if real, did not last long, for one of Ibn Khaldūn's informants told him that the usurper Sabakura raided towards Kawkaw (*c.* 1295), though another as we have seen attributed its capture to Saghamanja, one of Mansa Mūsā's generals.[1] No doubt Māli's effective influence over this region fluctuated. Al-ʿUmarī (1342) includes Kawkaw among the dependencies of Māli, and says that its 'inhabitants are of the tribes of Yartēn'.[2] Ibn Baṭṭūṭa, who spent a month there in 1353, implies that Kawkaw was within the sphere of Māli. He travelled from Timbuktu to Kawkaw by canoe, staying on the way at a village whose chief, *farba* Sulaimān, judging by his title, was the Māli intendant, and then on to Kawkaw which he describes as 'one of the finest and largest towns of the Blacks, and also the best provisioned, having much rice, milk, chickens and fish, as well as the incomparable *ʿattābi* (striped) cucumber. As in Māli cowries are used in business transactions.'[3] He does not say that Kawkaw was the seat of a ruler and we may conjecture that the *sī* resided at Kukiya. He also says that Mūli, situated east of Kawkaw, is the last province of Māli.[4] Since he does not mention religion, except to say that one of his hosts was '*imām* of the mosque of the whites', we may take it that it bore what he had come to expect in the Sudan, the outward signs of Islamic profession by the ruling class and merchants whilst the people remained pagan.

Foundation of the Songhay empire. Māli's control of the northern Niger bend and the trade-routes was weakening in the time of Mūsā II (1373–87), for his powerful minister Māri Dyāta had to make an expedition to subdue territories near Kawkaw and bring the Tuareg of Tākedda (Tādmekka) under control. But by the time of *sī* Mā Dogo (Muḥammad Dāʿo, *c.* 1420) who ravaged Māli territory, subduing amongst others a number of Bambara tribes,[5] it was free from any nominal allegiance and beginning the process by which it was to become a great empire. Sulaimān Dāma (or Dāndi, d. 1465) conquered

[1] Ibn Khaldūn, op. cit., i. 264.

[2] It is not clear whether these are Berbers or Negroes. They may be the Wartanīs of Yāqūt (*Muʿjam*, iv. 919). Gaudefroy-Demombynes (p. 57, n. 2) reads *Yrtān* as *Ydnāns*, identifying them with the Idnānes who moved to the Azawād region in the tenth century. Today the Idnāsen live east of the Niger between Bourem and Gao (A. Richer, *Les Oulliminden*, 1924, p. 59). The *Ṣubḥ* (v. 285), however, has *Sukkānuha qabāʾilu yarnān min as-sūdān*, implying that they were blacks.

[3] Ibn Baṭṭūṭa, op. cit. iv. 435.

[4] Ibid. iv. 395.

[5] *Fattāsh*, p. 55 (107).

the province of Mīma in Māsina whose king had become independent of Māli.[1]

The founder of the Songhay empire was the 15th *sī*, ʿAlī (1464/5–1492), son of *sī* Mā Dogo whose warlike exploits may have inspired his son. The Māli empire was in full decline. In consequence of internal weaknesses and pressure from the earlier *sīs*, Tuareg and Mossi, it was disintegrating into its constituent parts. ʿAlī made an attempt to reconstruct this empire from its eastern periphery by military power alone without making use of Islam. The empire he founded was solidly established by his successor, *askiya* Muḥammad, who made full use of Islam as a factor of consolidation.

ʿAlī's first objective was Timbuktu, then controlled by the Tuareg who had taken it from Māli in 1433. Having secured it (1468) he set to work to make himself master of the rich and populous region of the upper Niger. Maḥmūd al-Kāti writes:

> He was always victorious. He directed himself against no country without destroying it. No army led by him in person was put to rout. Always conqueror, never conquered, he left no region, town, or village, from the country of the *Kanta* to Sibiri-dugu without throwing his cavalry against it, warring against its inhabitants and ravaging them.[2]

He subjected the whole Niger bend as far as Jennē,[3] and, in the Gurma hinterland, northern Yatenga, Hombori, and Banjāgara. The most formidable power he had to face was the Mossi state of Yatenga, and although he won notable victories and led raids deep into Mossi country

[1] Ibid., pp. 42–43 (81). Maḥmūd al-Kāti's information corrects the statement of as-Saʿdī that their sphere of rule did not extend beyond the limits of Songhay until the conquests of ʿAlī the Great.

[2] *Fattāsh*, p. 43 (82). The country of the *Kanta* is that of the Zerma, and Sibiri-dugu is probably the Bambara region south of Jennē and west of the Mossi. Elsewhere we read (p. 73/140) that 'Sibiri-dugu marks the boundary between our territory [i.e. that of *askiya* Muḥammad] and that of the sultan of Māli'.

[3] Jennē, an independent city state, tributary to Māli, was conquered by *si* ʿAlī in 1473 (*T. as-Sūdān*, pp. 14–15; *Fattāsh*, p. 50). He treated it generously and left the chief in control subject to the payment of an annual tribute. Inclusion in the Songhay empire and the security of the trade-routes enhanced its prosperity. As-Saʿdī wrote, 'It is one of the great markets of the Muslim world. One comes across traders in salt from the mines of Taghāza and others who bring gold from the mines of Bīṭu (or Bayṭ). . . . It is by reason of this blessed city that caravans converge upon Timbuktu from all quarters' (text pp. 11–12; transl. p. 22). He also writes of the number and prosperity of the villages of agriculturalists in the Jennē state. But in addition to its trade the town acquired renown as a centre of Negro Islamic culture in contrast to Timbuktu which was largely non-Negro. Jennē's prosperity continued until the Moroccans took it in 1591 and so oppressed its merchants by their exactions and misrule that many migrated.

he made no attempt to reduce it.[1] We need not concern ourselves with the details of his conquests, but the problems he had to confront as a result of them are of interest.

His empire was divided into two distinct parts, the eastern and western parts of the great Niger bend. The rich former dependencies of Māli were separated from the Songhay homeland and man-power reserve by the desert, the Hombori mountains, and the strong Mossi kingdoms. The problem of unification he never solved. He never had a fixed capital, but was forever on the move. He sought to link Songhay with Māsina by conquering the small tribes of Hombori and taking a slip of territory from Yatenga. He was awake to the dangers inherent in Fulbe penetration and their influence in Negro courts and harims:

> He hated no enemy more bitterly than the Fulbe. He could not see one, whether learned or ignorant, man or woman, without wanting to kill him. He admitted no learned Pulo into the administration or judiciary. He so decimated the Sangare tribe that the remnant which survived could have been gathered under the shade of one tree.[2]

ʿAlī had no use for Islam, the religion of urban communities. Its learned men constituted a state within a state and were critical of rulers for their lukewarmness in Islam and indulgence in pagan rites. Confident in his own power, ʿAlī did not need their support and refused to compromise with a religion which involved paying allegiance to a law higher than himself. After gaining control of Timbuktu he came up against the Islamic particularism of white traders in its most acute form, and when its people intrigued with Tuareg he dealt with them with characteristic brutality. On the other hand, the people of Jennē, though they had put up a long and determined resistance, accepted his conquest and he treated them generously. The chroniclers assert that ʿAlī was a Khārijite,[3] but all this means is that in their opinion he was a heretic or a pagan. He treated Islam as a joke as the account of the

[1] The Mossi states had achieved cohesion during the previous century. There was a large-scale Mossi movement at this time which had almost the character of a tribal migration. Nāsere, *moro-naba* of Yatenga, the northern Mossi state, led a great raid which lasted for some years. He crossed the Niger near Mopti in 1477, penetrated Bāghana and pillaged Walāta in 1480. On its return *sī* ʿAlī fell on the Mossi army, put the king to flight, captured the booty it had accumulated, and then carried the war into Yatenga where he pillaged the royal residence (1483). But ʿAlī could do no more than raid, he could not reduce the unified Mossi state (see *Fattāsh*, transl. pp. 85–86, 89, 90, 92; *T. as-Sūdān*, transl. pp. 112–13, 115).

[2] *Fattāsh*, p. 44 (83–84).

[3] Khārijism existed among Berber tribes (cf. Ibn Baṭṭūṭa, iv. 394, on ʿIbāḍites in the Sahil) as it does today in the Mzab in the stony desert of southern Algeria, but they were closed-in communities and ʿAlī would hardly have been attracted by their austere manner of life.

mockery he made of the prayers showed.[1] The hatred the *'ulamā'* bore him has compromised their accounts for they endow him with all the vices and none of the virtues of a Negro conqueror, and their constant refrain is 'he persecuted the learned and pious'.

'Alī died under mysterious circumstances[2] and the line which he represented went into exile with his son Abū Bakr Dā'o (or Bāro), who reigned only a few months before power was seized by one of 'Alī's generals, Muḥammad Tūrē, although he was supported by only one of the great Songhay or Mandinka chiefs.'[3]

The Askiya dynasty (1493–1591). Muḥammad Tūrē ibn Abī Bakr, who was of Soninke origin,[4] took his title of *sikiya* or *askiya* as his dynastic title.[5] His great achievement was the consolidation of 'Alī's conquests, which included the whole of the Niger valley from Jenne to Gungia, the hinterland of Hombori and northern Yatenga, but such was the respect which 'Alī had inspired for the Songhay fleet and cavalry that the task was not difficult.

The *askiya*'s rule did not extend much south of Gungia. Abū Bakr Dā'o, after his defeat, fled to the Ayoru region[6] in the Songhay homeland where he maintained himself until about 1500 when the *askiya* reduced the region and imposed a governor. The *sī* families then moved into the arid Anzuru region. The *askiya* also tried to eliminate the descendants of the old *zā* princes. In 1505 he led a disastrous expedition against Bargu (region of the Bariba south of Songhay) installed in fortresses,[7] the ruins of which are visible today. In this campaign:

> Many of the best and bravest *zā-bēr-banda* perished. Seeing this 'Umar Komzāgho, the Askiya's brother, wept and exclaimed, 'Do you wish to annihilate Songhay?' 'No', he replied, 'I wish to preserve Songhay. These you

[1] See *T. as-Sūdān*, p. 67 (110).

[2] See *Fattāsh*, pp. 51–52 (98–100), and *T. as-Sūdān*, p. 71 (116), where it is stated that his body was embalmed.

[3] Cf. *Fattāsh*, pp. 53 (102), 55 (106), and fragment pp. 338–9.

[4] Al-Kāti (p. 59/114) says, 'His father was surnamed Arlūm, a clan of the Silla, said to belong to (Fūta) Toro.' Muḥammad was then aged 50 (p. 58/113). Tūrē means 'elephant' in Soninke.

[5] The form *askiya* came from the prefixing of the Arabic or ancient Berber definite article. The first syllable of the compound *sikiya* may be related to the old dynastic title. Maḥmūd al-Kāti says that the title was not first assumed by Muḥammad but was in use under the *sī* dynasty, and refers to an expedition sent by *sī* 'Alī under an *askiya* Baghna (*Fattāsh*, pp. 45–46/88–89).

[6] *Fattāsh*, p. 55 (106). According to the fragment (p. 338) *sī* Bāro was killed.

[7] *Fattāsh*, pp. 69–71 (133–7); *T. as-Sūdān*, p. 76 (125). Al-Bakrī (p. 182) writes about the anthropophagous Damdam south of Kawkaw who have 'a stronghold in which is an idol in the form of a woman whom they regard as a goddess and visit on pilgrimage'.

MAP 2

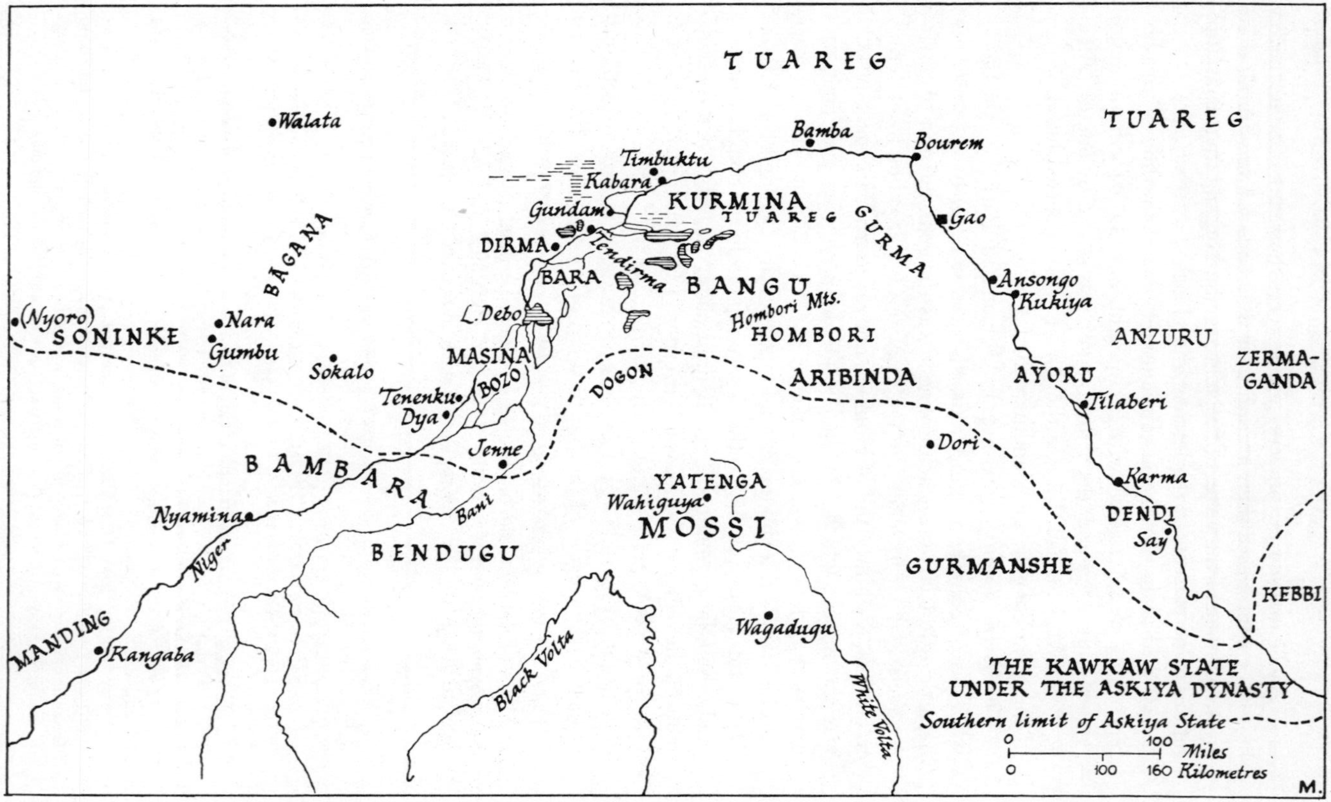

TUAREG
TUAREG
Walata
Timbuktu
Kabara
Bamba
Bourem
Gao
Gundam
KURMINA
TUAREG
GURMA
DIRMA
Tendirma
BARA
BANGU
BAGANA
Ansongo
Kukiya
(Nyoro)
SONINKE
Nara
Gumbu
L. Debo
Hombori Mts.
HOMBORI
ANZURU
MASINA
Sokalo
ZERMA-
GANDA
ARIBINDA
AYORU
Tenenku
BOZO
DOGON
Tilaberi
Dya
Jenne
Dori
BAMBARA
YATENGA
Karma
Wahiguya
Nyamina
Bani
MOSSI
DENDI
Say
Niger
BENDUGU
GURMANSHE
KEBBI
MANDING
Kangaba
Wagadugu
Black Volta
White Volta
THE KAWKAW STATE
UNDER THE ASKIYA DYNASTY
Southern limit of Askiya State
0 100 Miles
0 100 160 Kilometres
M.

have seen fall would have made life difficult for us in Songhay had they remained. It would have been impossible for us to deal with them in this way with our own hands, therefore I brought them here so that they might be decimated and we relieved of them, since I knew they would not escape death.'[1]

Muḥammad's political astuteness led him to reverse the attitude of ʿAlī towards Islam and to pander to the vanity of the *ʿulamāʾ*. As the chroniclers could not find anything too bad to say of ʿAlī so they covered Muḥammad with praise:

He cared for the *ʿulamāʾ*, holy men and seminarists; he made many acts of almsgiving, and performed both the obligatory and the supererogatory duties of religion. Although one of the most intelligent of men he showed humility before the *ʿulamāʾ*, offering them slaves and wealth in order to assure their interests in the welfare of the Muslims as well as assist them in their submission to God and for the practice of the cult. He eliminated all the innovations, forbidden practices and bloodshedding characteristic of the *shī*, and established Islam upon sure foundations.[2]

Although Muḥammad, as an alien usurper, made use of Islam to reinforce his authority there is little evidence to support the claim that he initiated a wave of islamization. Maḥmūd al-Kāti the elder, in his account of the struggle with *sī* Bāro,[3] shows him sending messengers, of whom Maḥmūd himself was one, inviting *sī* Bāro to embrace Islam, thus following the rules of the *jihād*. His plundering expedition against the Mossi in 1498 is the only one recorded as a *jihād* by as-Saʿdī:

He took with him *mōri* Ṣāliḥ Jawara, commanding him to make it into a *jihād* for God's cause. He raised no objections and explained all the rules for the *jihād*. Therefore the *askiya* asked the Sayyid to act as his messenger to the king of the Mossi. He agreed and went to that country bearing a letter from the *askiya* inviting him to embrace Islam.[4]

The king of the Mossi, having consulted the ancestors, rejected the demand, and, after describing the expedition, as-Saʿdī adds, 'In this region this raid is the only *jihād* undertaken in the way of God.'

Although a Muslim of deeper conviction than his predecessors Muḥammad was lenient towards pagans under his rule and there is no record of his compelling peoples like the Bambara to join Islam. Each people, following Sudanese practice, retained its own organization, customs, and domestic religion upon which their communal identity

[1] *T. as-Sūdān*, p. 76 (125).
[2] *Fattāsh*, p. 59 (114–15).
[3] *Fattāsh*, pp. 53–54 (103–5).
[4] *T. as-Sūdān*, p. 74 (121–3). See also *Fattāsh*, p. 70 (134–5).

was based. Even though many made it a profession Islam had little effect upon the lives of the ordinary people. Muḥammad's work for Islam was primarily the fostering of Timbuktu as a centre of learning[1] and the establishment of Islam as the imperial cult throughout his empire. Once he felt his rule to be consolidated he decided to perform the pilgrimage to Mecca.[2] Whilst there (1497–8) he gave a hundred thousand *dīnārs* in gold as alms and for the endowment of a hostel for Sudanese pilgrims. At the same time he made an astute political move which added to his status among the *'ulamā'* by getting the Sharīf al-'Abbās to invest him with the caliphate of the lands of the Blacks (*Khilāfatu bilādi 't-Takrūr*).[3] A nephew of the Sharīf nicknamed aṣ-Ṣaqlī visited him at Timbuktu in 1519 where he married and left behind him a clan of what soon became negroid *shurafā'*. Muḥammad also met such people as 'Abd ar-Raḥmān as-Suyūṭī and al-Majhīlī, the reformer of Tilimsān, with whom he corresponded on questions of Islamic law and who visited him in Kawkaw in 1502.[4]

On his return from Mecca he embarked upon a number of expeditions, of which those in the west (e.g. Bāghana, old Gāna region, in

[1] The role of Timbuktu as a centre of Negro Islamic learning must not be exaggerated for Jennē was more important. 'The University of Sankorē', which has been compared with al-Azhar, did not exist. Sankorē was simply the quarter where the majority of the teaching clerics had their houses, though some *fuqahā'* taught in the mosque there (cf. *Tadhkirat an-Nisyān*, p. 54/85). The number of Qur'ān schools in Timbuktu at the epoch of the last *askiyas* was 150, which is very little when you consider that the majority of clerics were teachers and classes very small (cf. *Fattāsh*, pp. 180–1/315–16). It is noteworthy that under Māli and the earlier period of Tuareg rule the *imāms* of the chief mosque were Negroes. Afterwards all those appointed were whites (see *T. as-Sūdān*, p. 57/92), and from then on Timbuktu continues to be dominated by whites. It never became a real city-state, and its people, derived from heterogeneous sources, separated by caste-like distinctions, never formed a unity or achieved a form of municipal government. It was generally dominated from without, under governors provided by Māli, Songhay, Tuareg, Morocco, Moors, and Fulbe. Its greatest bane was the Tuareg tribes who kept it in a continual state of insecurity, yet its citizens never organized themselves as a unit against their terrorism. Islamic law was only operative through outside controllers investing its *qāḍīs* with judicial authority. It was not clerically governed, though the role of the clerics in its life, especially that of the Kunta in the nineteenth century, was considerable.

[2] See the account of Maḥmūd al-Kāti who accompanied the *askiya* in *Fattāsh*, pp. 12 (16), 16–17 (25–27), 65–69 (124–32); *T. as-Sūdān*, pp. 72–73 (119–21).

[3] *Fattāsh*, p. 12 (16); *T. as-Sūdān*, p. 73 (120).

[4] *Fattāsh*, p. 69 (132). Muḥammad b. 'Abd al-Karīm al-Majhīlī (d. 1532) is notorious for his instigation of a massacre of the Saharan Jews of Tawāt in 1492. See his biography by Aḥmad Bābā of Timbuktu, *Takmilat ad-Dībāj*, *J. Asiat.*, sér. v, vi (1855), 393–8; ed. Cairo, A.H. 1329, pp. 330–2. Many of those who escaped fled to the Sudan where they were well received by the *askiya* (*H.S.N.* i. 219). Al-Majhīlī influenced the Sudan in other ways since it was he who initiated 'Umar b. al-Bakkā'ī of the Kunta, the propagator of the Qādiriyya in the Sahil (see I.W.A., p. 94 n.).

1498–9) led to permanent control. He defeated *qāma* Fati Qalli, general of the ruler of Māli, in 1500/1, captured the town of Zalen (Dyāra), pillaged the palace of the ruler and carried off his family,[1] but Māli proper remained independent. In the east, whilst he gained control of the route to Air,[2] his expeditions into Hausaland were mere raids and those into Bergo south of Songhay were disastrous. His interest in the east was mainly concerned with the trade-route. About 1513 he raided the Hausa state of Katsina.[3] Shortly afterwards (1514–15) he defeated Muḥammad al-ʿĀdil, Tuareg sultan of Agadez. In this expedition he was assisted by *kanta* Kotal, a Hausa chief, who in 1516/17 quarrelled with him over the spoil, defeated Muḥammad's troops at Tara (near Gaya?), and went on to form the large kingdom of Kebbi.[4]

The equilibrium of the empire was maintained by his successors on the foundations he had instituted, in spite of perpetual dynastic revolutions, without any difficulty until it was finally and irrevocably shattered by barbarian soldiery, when it dissolved into its constituent parts. But during its existence a relative peace prevailed, cultivators prospered, and traders circulated freely.

Having become blind Muḥammad was deposed at the age of eighty-five (1528) by his son Mūsā, exiled by Muḥammad Bengan to an island in the Niger, set free by Ismāʿīl, and died in 1538. The subsequent history of succession to the throne is a series of fratricidal struggles, palace revolutions, and *coups d'état*. Eight *askiyas* occupied the throne between 1528 and 1591, but the history of their reigns is beyond our scope. Among them only Da'ūd, whose long reign (1549–83) emphasized the mediocrity of the rest, is worthy of comment. Da'ūd was successful in containing the Tuareg; he established posts in the Sahara, and assured for a time the security of the trade-routes. A pious Muslim, 'he was the first to form treasury storehouses, including libraries. He employed scribes to copy manuscripts which he sometimes presented to the *ʿulamā'*. The *gisaridonke*, Dako ibn Bukar Faṭa, told me that having learnt the Qur'ān by heart he went on to read the whole of the *Risāla*, taking lessons from a shaikh daily for an hour or so after midday.'[5]

[1] *T. as-Sūdān*, p. 75 (124–5).

[2] The *askiya*'s expedition of the year 906 (1500–1) seems, from the reference to Tilẓa = Tadeliza, then the chief Tuareg centre in Air), to refer to Air rather than Ayoru (*Fattāsh*, p. 70/135; *T. as-Sūdān*, p. 75/124).

[3] *Fattāsh*, p. 77 (147). Probably Katsina Laka, south of Zamfara.

[4] *T. as-Sūdān*, p. 78 (129–30). On the *kanta* see below, p. 134.

[5] *Fattāsh*, p. 94 (177–8).

The whole structure of the empire collapsed when the cupidity of Aḥmad al-Manṣūr adh-Dhahabī, Sa'did sultan of Morocco, was stirred by the reputed wealth of the Sudan and signs of weakness in the empire to send an expeditionary force of Europeans to conquer it. The bravery of the Negroes was no match against their discipline and firearms, and the army of *askiya* Isḥāq II was defeated and Kawkaw captured in 1591. Maḥmūd al-Kāti ascribes the downfall of Songhay to the disastrous war between Muḥammad Bāni b. Da'ūd (1586/7–1588) and his brother, the *balama* Ṣādiq,[1] and to defiance of the laws of God by indulgence in immorality and pagan rites which reached its zenith in the reign of Isḥāq,[2] but it was mainly due to the fact that no one was astute enough to realize the value of firearms as did Idrīs Alawma of Bornu.

We may conjecture that the restricted state of the *zās* and *sīs* was organized on normal Sudan lines with its various grades of population headed by a tax-farming noble class. Maḥmūd al-Kāti says that the titles of *balama*, *Benga-farma*, and *Kurmina-fāri* existed from the time of the *sīs*.[3] *Sī* 'Alī, as he extended his domains, appointed provincial governors such as the *Dendi-fāri*, governor of the provinces downstream from Kukiya, or confirmed conquered chiefs such as the ruler of Jennē on the same lines as the state of Māli.[4] He created the province of Dirma in the region between Timbuktu and Jennē. His flotilla chief, *hī-koy*, was an old Songhay official, as was probably the *Tondi-fāri*, 'governor of the mountains' (a title borne at one time by the future *askiya* Muḥammad), whose task was to keep subdued the people of the Hombori region.[5]

The definitive organization of the empire won by *sī* 'Alī was the work of the first *askiya* who showed great administrative talent. He reorganized the whole administrative, fiscal, and military set-up of the agglomeration of peoples who had come under his control. Apart from the Gao region, which was under direct administration and where a large part of the people were of serf status, the empire was decentralized into provinces over which he appointed members of his own family or favourites. He left few vassal kings except in subordinate sub-provinces. The main provinces were: Dendi, the most southerly, situated south of Kukiya, whose neighbour was the powerful *kanta* of Kebbi; Bal, north of the river around Timbuktu, controlling the caravan-

[1] *Fattāsh*, p. 126 (230–1).
[2] Ibid., p. 152 (272); see also *T. as-Sūdān*, p. 144 (224).
[3] *Fattāsh*, pp. 62/118, 45/86, 54/103–4.
[4] Cf. *Fattāsh*, p. 54/103–4.
[5] On these offices see *Fattāsh*, pp. 88–90.

routes as far as the saltmines of Taghāza; Benga, the lake region on the right bank of the Niger south of Timbuktu, under a *Benga-fāri*, 'governor of the Lake', one of the great dignatories who had the right of being heralded by drums when entering Gao. Kurmina, mostly on the right (*gurma*) bank but having Tendirma on the left bank as capital, was the most important province and ranked as the granary of the empire. Its governor was entitled *Kurmina-fāri* (or *Gurman-fāri*) and in the *Fattāsh*[1] is accorded the title of *kanfāri*, 'superior chief'. Besides these there were scores of minor governors, sometimes subordinate to the great dignatories, sometimes holding independent posts. The relationship between the different officials is difficult to elucidate and appears to vary considerably. South-west of Kurmina were the two provinces of Dirma (town of Dire) and Bara, situated to the north of Lake Debo; Aribinda, that part of Gurma facing Gao (right bank between Bourem and Gungia), had an Aribinda-fāri, so with Bāghana and Shā'a or Sama. Most of the great officers had Mande titles affixed to their charges, whilst district officials had the Songhay title *koy* affixed. There was a Timbuktu-koy, but Kabara, the port of Timbuktu, had its own *farma* subject to the governor of Bal.

Apart from provincial governors the great central officials of the state include: the *balama*, comptroller-general (governor of Bal?), an important military post; the *fāri-mundyo* (lit. 'inspector of cultivation'), the chief tax-collector; *sāo-koy*, chief of forests; *hī-koy*, chief of the navy; *korey-farma*, minister in charge of whites; *waney-farma*, minister of property; *hari-farma*, minister of the water who policed the rivers, lakes, and fisheries.

The *askiya* régime was more despotic than normal Sudanese states with their elaborate system of checks upon the ruler's power. Provincial governors were not hereditary feudatories, but were appointed and dispossessed by the *askiyas* at will. They had no place in the internal government, but being royal princes and commanding large armies of serfs were a factor of instability, intriguing and seeking to seize the throne or install their own candidate. There appears to have been no council to appoint the successor as in the normal Sudan state and the death of every *askiya* was the signal for a time of troubles.

There is little sign that the *askiyas* were of the divine-ruler type like the *zās*, though when in audience they were treated as sacred or taboo chiefs with prostration and dusting.[2] At audiences there was the usual

[1] Cf. *Fattāsh*, pp. 85/160, 116/212.

[2] Cf. *Fattāsh*, p. 184, 193; Leo Africanus, op. cit. iii. 824–5.

elaborate protocol by which each official had his exact precedence, uniform, headdress, ornaments, and number of drums. Al-Kāti writes of *askiya* Da'ūd 'giving his customary Friday audience; the eunuchs, numbering about seven hundred, standing behind him, each clad in a silk dress. Whenever the *askiya* wanted to spit or expel one of them hastened to extend his sleeve into which he spat and then wiped his mouth clear of the phlegm.'[1] Only the *dyina-koy*, or commander-in-chief, had the right of being seated on a carpet and of using flour instead of dust. All must remove their headgear before dusting with the exception of the *kurmina-fāri*. No one could address the *askiya* directly by name except the *gisaridonkēs*,[2] but there was a *wandu*, 'interpreter' and master of ceremonies, 'whose function is to repeat the *askiya's* words to the people'.[3] Muḥammad and his successors never became true rulers of the Songhay, although Gao was the capital, for the Songhay were not a people but a number of clans many of whose free groups migrated into the creeks and swamps of Dendi where they maintained their independence. The Niger gave his empire its only unity and his power was largely based upon the mobility given him by the possession of a fleet. Hence the importance of the *hī-koy* and port officials like the *Kabara-farma*.[4] Muḥammad had broken the old dynastic links and needed Islam as a new spiritual base. His armies were composed of serf tributaries of many races, for he built up a regular army instead of calling for levies like *sī* 'Alī. The symbols of investiture, which in fact counted for little, were Islamic, consisting of the tunic, turban, and sword with which the first *askiya* was invested by the Sharīf of Mecca. Although the *sīs* carried away the old sacred insignia the *askiyas* possessed some native symbols: a drum, twelve standards, and the *din-tūri*, a brand from the first fire lit in the country.[5]

The revenue of the state was derived from state or imperial domains (that is, state-serfs),[6] regular contributions sent by governors, and tri-

[1] *Fattāsh*, p. 114 (208–9); cf. p. 116 (212).

[2] *Fattāsh*, p. 11/13–14.

[3] *T. as-Sūdān*, p. 101/167; cf. pp. 203, 206; *Fattāsh*, transl. pp. 198, 205, 259, 261.

[4] On the vast fleet which existed at Gao alone at the time of the Moroccan conquest see *Fattāsh*, pp. 150–1/270.

[5] See *Fattāsh*, transl. pp. 16, 161–2, 273–5.

[6] These human fiscal domains, which include the Sorko and Arbi, are enumerated; cf. *Fattāsh*, pp. 140–2 (prohibition of marriage with Sorko and Arbi who are the property of the king), 107 ff. The same writer, after enumerating the personal agricultural estates the *askiya* possessed 'in every region which paid allegiance to him', goes on, 'the produce he obtains from these amounts in some years to over 4000 *ṣunniyya* (a measure of capacity, Songhay *sunnu*, 200–250 litres). In each of the villages we have mentioned the prince has slaves and a *fanfa*. Some of these *fanfa* had under them 100 slaves employed in cultivation, whilst others had 60

bute from vassal states.[1] Each district or town had its collector of taxes called *mundyo* (a Pulo word), the chief collector being the *fāri-mundyo*. Provincial chiefs drew their main revenue from taxes on free cultivators, nomads, or traders passing through or operating within their domains.[2] Commerce flourished under the *askiyas*, for the dynastic struggles did not disrupt communications or cause internal instability. Inspectors were placed in charge of important markets and the system of weights and measures unified. Salt was the staple exchange commodity and control of the main source, the mines of Taghāza, was essential, but cowries were the general currency. North African luxury goods were plentiful. The state bought horses from there to improve the local breed, for cavalry were an important, though not a basic, element of military power. The cavaliers were armed with spears, swords, and javelins. Coats of mail and brass helmets are mentioned, but no fire-arms, otherwise the Moroccan attack would not have had such a demoralizing effect upon the Songhay army.

50, 40, or 20. The word *fanfa*, which takes the plural *fanāfī*, designates "chief of slaves", but it is also used to designate the "master of a canoe" ' (*Fattāsh*, pp. 94–95/178–9). The *fanāfī* were slaves themselves and though they accumulated large estates these were inherited by the *askiya* (see the account of Mūsā Sagansāro from whom *askiya* Mūsā inherited 500 slaves, 14 granaries of cereals, 7 herds of cattle, 30 herds of sheep, 15 horses and their harness, together with clothing, household goods, and weapons (*Fattāsh*, pp. 102 ff./190 ff.). These human domains were technically inalienable, but we read of many gifts to clerics and others (see gift of large bodies of *zenjī* by Muḥammad I and Da'ūd, *Fattāsh*, pp. 38, 214).

[1] It was not clear who was the chief treasurer. A *kalissi-farma* is mentioned (p. 136). The *khaṭīb* or Friday preacher, one of the most important people in Gao, may have been treasurer in the early days for Muḥammad I drew funds from *khaṭīb* 'Umar for his pilgrimage (*T. as-Sūdān*, p. 73/119). One *khaṭīb* held in addition the post of chief *qāḍī* which was normally a distinct appointment.

[2] A deed of exemption from such taxes is quoted in *Fattāsh*, pp. 72–73/138–41.

3

Central Sudan States

I. CHARACTERISTICS OF THE CENTRAL SUDAN

By the central Sudan we mean the region stretching between the Songhay of the middle Niger and Waday lying beyond Lake Chad, which is orientated partly towards the Niger and partly towards Lake Chad. The northern part consists of parched steppe where nomadic herdsmen circulate among sedentary peoples who combine stock breeding with their basic cultivation. Its geographical position and lack of natural barriers has allowed the continual influx of new peoples from the north and east who after dominating or mixing with former inhabitants have formed new cultural groups. Consequently its civilization, though basically Sudanese, is a mosaic of Nigritic, Hamitic, and Semitic elements. Lake Chad region in particular was a point of concentration upon which cultural currents from North Africa, Egypt, and Nilotic Sudan converged; and it in turn formed an important centre of culture diffusion. It is associated with a population known as the So or Saw who, migrating from the Nilotic region (?), settled among paleonigritic 'little red men', the *gwaigwai* of Hausa folklore. The term So, although it now belongs to the realm of myth, is useful since it was used by nomads for those inhabitants of the Chad region (other than paleonigritics) who had a well-defined civilization, which from the historical point of view is centred in the walled town state, divine kingship with ritual murder, and elaborate hierarchization of political organization. The So languages belonged to the Chado–Hamitic linguistic group, represented today by the languages of the Hausa, Kotoko, Buduma (Yedima), Bolewa, Musgu, and many others.

A third influence is that of the central Saharan nomadic Zaghāwa often mentioned by Arabic writers.[1] They may be classified as negroid Kushites and were spread over a vast area of central Sahara and northern Sahil from Fezzān to Nubia.[2] They facilitated the diffusion of

[1] They are first mentioned by al-Khwārizmī, though his map (Codex Spitta 18, Strassburg, in Miller, *Mappae Arabicae*, i. 1. 12) shows the Zaghāwa, Farān, and Ghalwa living near a river (Atbara?) issuing from a lake (Tana?) east of the Nile into which it falls.

[2] Al-Mas'ūdī (*Murūj*, iii. 1–2, 37–38) regards them as belonging to the Kushites who migrated westwards, leaving behind in East Africa the Nūba, Beja, and Zinj, and comprising

Nubian culture into central Sudan and influenced the history of the region since they founded, or at least provided dynasties for, Kanem and certain Hausa states (Gobir) in the Sahil, giving them a different outlook from that which characterized city-states where the So civilization was relatively unmodified. Berbers were also present to add to the confusion, but it is only later that they come to predominate in south-central Sahara and narrowed the Zaghāwa domain.

Though the state of Kanem was founded by Zaghāwa they adopted the civilization of the autochthones. In their retreat, the Kotoko–Logon region south of Lake Chad, the So have left behind them the remains of their civilization and live in tradition through their long resistance to Bornuan expansion. They first moved south of Lake Chad about the end of the tenth century.[1] Archaeological evidence[2] reveals three successive cultural strata in the Kotoko–Logon region apart from that of the 'little red men'. The two oldest, who buried their dead, the first in the soil, the second in urns, offer close resemblances. The third have adopted Islam and its burial customs. Islam began to spread into the northern So towns of this region in the sixteenth century and reached the southern in the eighteenth. Ceramic art and bronze technique were highly developed, but degenerated under Islamic influence. Indications of their religious beliefs provided by clay effigies of ancestors or culture heroes show that their cultural inspiration was African in spite of the fact that their material culture reveals both northern and Nilotic influences.

Although so important culturally the So peoples did not found important states but were organized in small town groups. For this reason they appear in history mainly as objects of Kanemi or Bornuan raids

the Zaghāwa, Kawkaw, al-Qarāqir, Madīda, Marīs, al-Mabras, al-Malāna, al-Qumāṭī, Duwaila, and al-Qarma. Ibn Sa'īd says that the Zaghāwa and Beja belong to the same stock (see Abū 'l-Fidā', p. 159). Ibn Khaldūn regards them as a section of the Ṣanhāja Berbers (ii. 64). At any rate they were distinct from both Berbers and Sudan blacks, like the Teda of today who are probably their descendants. Al-Idrīsī (p. 32), writing of the land of the negroid Zaghāwa (*arḍ Zaghāwati 's-Sūdān*), shows that they are different from Berbers when he says (pp. 33–34) that in the country of the Zaghāwa, 'there is a nomadic tribe called Ṣadrāta which is said to be Berber but resemble the Zaghāwa in all their customs and have become one of their races'. Ṣadrāta is probably the present-day Sawāta in Air on the route to Ghāt with which the second ruler of Katsina, Rumba Ramba, was at war about A.D. 1150 (see Katsina kinglist in H. R. Palmer, *Sud. Mem.* iii. 79).

[1] Teda traditions collected by Angus Buchanan (*Sahara*, 1926, quoted by H. R. Palmer, *Sud. Mem.* i. 2–4) point to the So being in the oases of Bilma, Tadjere, and Fashi in the seventh century A.D. since it was from them that the Zaghāwa had to obtain permission to install themselves.

[2] See J. P. Lebeuf and A. Masson Detourbet, *La Civilisation du Tchad*, 1950, pp. 173–5.

and absorption. From the historical point of view it is simpler to regard the So as a civilization. The reason for their disappearance is that each town had its separate government, therefore a power like Kanem-Bornu could deal with them one by one. The last struggle with Bornu from the fourteenth to the sixteenth century corresponds to the period when many were assimilated. Some have been completely absorbed into the Kanuri, whilst many survive as the Kotoko, Musgu, Bolewa, and others.

This same town element is found among the Hausa. These form no ethnic unity. In the twelfth century their country was filled with hundreds of town and village states under chiefs who were cult officials (*sarkin tsāfi*). New elements (Zaghāwa and Kanembu) in the state organization brought out of this nebulous mass by the sixteenth century a dozen or more important states taking their name from that of a central city. As they expanded by conquest or peaceful means over formerly independent walled towns (*birnis*) they acquired the characteristics of confederacies. They were well organized with relatively stable dynasties. They had their distinctive traditions, splendid courts, hereditary nobility, administrative hierarchies, differentiation of status and prerogative, and a complicated system of etiquette. Village organization was similar but on a smaller scale. Political supremacy and cohesion lay largely in regal and city cults.

Their history begins with the arrival of immigrants and their often prolonged struggle to gain control of the So city cult. Their eventual incorporation was symbolized by the provision of virgins and infants to be immured in the walls. New dynasties had their own myths (snake and *dōdō* killing), sacred symbols (chain of Tsuede, founder of a Nupe dynasty at the end of the fifteenth century), and the *mūnē* of the Kanem kings. They had to observe peculiar rituals and taboos. Thus the Nupe king could dress only in white, eat only food prepared by his wives, must not be seen eating by strangers, and no one could be killed in his presence or even in the place where he was residing.[1] This 'divinity' could apparently be acquired by an immigrant dynasty as it became indigenous, and in Kanem the process of change can be seen from a nomadic chieftain, representative of the *jamā'a*, to a divine ruler hedged about with etiquette and constrained to observe irksome taboos, ending in a synthesis of the nomadic and the native elements. Their unitary organization, mutual hostility, and intermediate position between Songhay based on the upper Niger, Bornu based on the Chad,

[1] See S. F. Nadel, *A Black Byzantium*, p. 87.

and Jukun-Kwararafa based on the Benue, meant that the independence and sphere of the Hausa states was precarious and restricted. The one attempt made in the sixteenth century by the *kanta* of Kebbi to form a great state failed under his successors.

Islam was introduced into Kanem from the north and into the Hausa states from the western Sudan. The two most important trade-routes were: Ghadāmes–Air–Katsina and Tripoli–Fezzān–Kawār–Chad; whilst a third route went from Cyrenaica through Kufra to Waday. Commerce in slaves is noted at an early date. Al-Ya'qūbī (A.D. 889) writes that 'Ibāḍite Muslims of Zawīla:

> export slaves of the Mīriyyīn, Zaghawiyyīn, Maruwiyyīn and other races of the blacks who, owing to their vicinity, they take captive. I have been informed that the kings of the blacks sell their own people without justification or in consequence of war. . . . Below Zawīla at a distance of fifteen days' journey is a centre called Kawār in which are Muslims from various tribes, though Berber in the majority, who export blacks.[1]

Kanem was situated south of Kawār and north-east of the Chad, in a region which had long connexions with the Garamantes of Fezzān. Islam, penetrating from Fezzān, Cyrenaica, and Egypt, was more successful in winning its nomadic rulers than those of the Hausa towns. It came to these not from the north but through a stream of Wangāra and Pulo traders and clerics from western Sudan. Rulers gave clerics a place in the religious hierarchy without in any way displacing the power of the native cults. At Kano, founded towards the end of the tenth century, the first Muslim ruler appears in 1370, but he was followed by six pagans. Kebbi and Katsina had rulers calling themselves Muslim in 1510 and Zamfara not until 1640. Adopted parallel to the city, dynastic, and local cults Islam's spiritual influence was negligible outside the heterogeneous commercial communities. On the other hand, its cultural, and especially linguistic, influence was considerable.

One state, Kanem-Bornu, compares in some respects with the greater empires of western Sudan. In longevity its dynasty exceeds those of the Mossi states; in fact it has the longest Muslim dynastic tradition in Africa. In consequence of its early acceptance of Islam, which enabled it to acquire a written tradition, the main phases of its history are known. The religion made its first inroads in the eleventh century during the reign of Ḥumē and by 1250 there were sufficient

[1] Al-Ya'qūbī, *Kitāb al-Buldān*, *B.G.A.* vii. 345. The presence of Muslims in Kawār is accounted for by the extensive pure salt deposits, an essential commodity for trade with the Sudan.

Kānemī students in Cairo to justify the founding of a *riwāq*. About the same time the dynasty began to base itself upon Islam, a change denoted in tradition by the killing of the snake-king and opening of the *mūnē*. A rival and related lineage, the Bulāla, gained control of Kanem and at the end of the fifteenth century the dynasty was compelled to migrate west of Lake Chad into Bornu, then inhabited by uncoordinated So peoples. They carried their religion with them and made use of it to consolidate their state. Bornu has no ethnic tradition because its peoples have no ethnic unity. Within the Kanuri are the remains of many groups and the unification of their culture was a long process, not helped by the nomadic element in the ruling class. The ruling line of Zaghawī origin maintained the nomadic idea of unity, based on birth. In this respect they contrast with the Hausa and So peoples whose tradition is linked with a founded walled village. The Kanuri are not people of a state, but members of a particular clan, and those over whom they ruled, though they gradually adopted the Kanuri language and certain cultural elements, remained separate peoples.

West of the Chad, besides the Kanem and Bulāla states, grew up those of Waday and Bagirmi. These states lie on the periphery of our historical region, but the outlines of their history may be traced since they influenced that of the Chad region. Islam did not reach Bagirmi until the end of the sixteenth century and was not preached in Waday until the seventeenth.

Sources. The early history of the central Sudan and the beginnings of the penetration of Islam are even more obscure than that of western Sudan and we have to rely far more than is wise upon historical myth, distorted by reflection through a thousand mirrors. The information furnished by Arab geographers, who had only the vaguest idea of its topography, is meagre. There are two main reasons for this: the fact that there were no great states except Kanem to claim their attention and the nature of the trading relations. The west Sahil ports and Sudanese trading towns were full of white traders, but in the centre their number was considerably less until the eighteenth and nineteenth centuries, for they operated mainly from intermediary Saharan centres. Although from an early date there were relations between the Chad region and North Africa and Nubia, no known trade relations existed with Hausaland, then a no-man's-land, the domain of hundreds of separate village groups, but with no important towns or states. Northern traders were only found in borderland places like Air, Kawār, and Kanem, and the latter is the only state about which the Arabs provide information. When Hausa settlements eventually became commercial centres direct connexions with North Africa became more important, though transcontinental west–east commerce remained in the hands of Sudanese. Arab writers mention the names of many peoples and villages, but it is a hazardous proceeding to seek for correspondences between these and mythical or contemporary peoples. Often we cannot tell whether they refer to villages, districts, or ruling clans. In any study of African history one must bear in mind not only the migratory nature of the cultivators who, when they had exhausted one area by their slash and burn methods, moved to a virgin tract, but also the extreme sparseness of population to which oral traditions of the appropriation of unoccupied land by first settlers testify, as they do in other parts to the existence of 'masters of the land' when immigrants arrived.

Local manuscript sources, although fairly considerable for Bornu, are unreliable. This is due to the far-reaching dynastic changes which characterized the Sudan especially during the nineteenth century. It is said that the Fulbe, seeking to wipe out the former dynastic tradition, destroyed all Hausa records upon which they could lay their hands, but it is doubtful if there were many written chronicles. 'Umar ibn Muḥammad al-Amīn is also said to have destroyed those of Bornu after an attempt to restore the Saifī line in 1846.[1] Many of the surviving chronicles are recent. European administrators encouraged local scribes to write out ruler lists and genealogies based on oral tradition or remembrance of destroyed chronicles. Others are copies of repeatedly written lists, for rough handling, the climate, and white ants did not allow manuscripts to last long.

The chronicles of the Hausa and Bornu states are often little more than dry ruler lists[2] chanted by the official griot or praise-singer at ceremonial gatherings, to which it is rarely possible to attach external events until the nineteenth century. One of the genuine survivals, the chronicle of the wars of *mai* Idrīs Alawma of Bornu,[3] though a rather

[1] See H. Barth, *Travels*, ii. 255. Later Rābiḥ followed the same practice. Many Dawra records were lost when Sarkin Damāgaram seized the insignia and archives of Nūḥ when in exile after the *jihād* (see Palmer, *Sud. Mem.* iii. 132). Those of Gari'n Gabas were destroyed by fire in 1921 (ibid. iii. 134).

[2] See, for example, the *Dīwān* of the *mais* of Bornu which was first utilized by Barth (*Travels*, ii. 633–71). It has been translated by Sir H. R. Palmer, *Bornu Sahara and Sudan*, 1936, pp. 90–95. The original manuscript obtained by Barth is in Hamburg. It was printed from a bad transcription in the edition of Imām Aḥmad's *Wars of Idrīs Alawma*, Emir of Kano's Press, 1930, pp. 130–7, together with facsimiles of four pages of another manuscript list of the *mais*.

[3] *Ta'rīkh Mai Idrīs wa ghazawātihi*, by Imām Aḥmad al-Barnawī, ed. H. R. Palmer,

savage record of this ruler's warlike activities, provides valuable side-lights on the history and life of the period. Few records of the Hausa states survived, but that of Kano[1] is sufficient to show what important material they might have provided. Few of the texts of these documents have been published, and none in critical editions, and we have to rely to a large extent on translations.

For Bornu, first-hand documents are found in *maḥrams*. The consolidation of Islam there is associated with the emigration and settlement of clerics from other regions. These were welcomed and many were granted *maḥrams* or 'letters of hereditary privilege' in recompense for services rendered. They state that *X* and his descendants are *ḥarīm*, 'set apart' or 'privileged', that is exempted from taxes, military services, hospitality charges, and the like.[2] Naturally these documents were carefully preserved by the families concerned who sought to get them renewed by subsequent rulers, though this increased the possibilities for interpolation and falsification of date and origin and consequently they have to be used with caution.[3]

2. THE STATE OF KANEM–BORNU

Kanem was founded by the black Saharan nomads whom Arabic writers call Zaghāwa. They are of little importance today and exist under that name only in northern Waday, but during the ninth century their territory covered a vast area. They were encountered by traders passing through the central Sahara and on that account receive special attention from Arab geographers. Ibn Khaldūn includes them among the *mulaththamīn*, but this does not mean that they were Tuareg

Kano, 1930; and translated in two parts, 'The Kanem Wars', in *Sud. Mem.* i. 15–72; and 'The So Wars', under the title of *History of the First Twelve Years of the Reign of Mai Idrīs Alooma of Bornu (1571–1583)*, Lagos, 1926.

[1] Translated by H. R. Palmer, *J.R.A.I.* xxxviii. 58 ff. and *Sud. Mem.* iii. 92–132. The references which follow are to this last translation although I have sometimes retranslated passages from a photograph of the manuscript (transcribed in 1929) in the possession of Sir Richmond Palmer. The authorship is unknown. It appears to have been compiled by a Hausa and Arabic-speaker from tradition related to him by a Hausa praise-singer and brought up to date with an account of the Fulani rulers, ending in the middle of the reign of Muḥammad Belo (1883–93). It is clear that the author had not followed the normal scholastic training for the Arabic is strange and notably free from the usual pious terminology.

[2] The *askiya* dynasty of Songhay also issued *maḥrams*, but few survived its downfall except one or two preserved in the *ta'rīkhs*; see *al-Fattāsh*, pp. 72–73/138–41.

[3] Sir H. R. Palmer has translated many in his *Bornu Sahara* and *Sudanese Memoirs*. They are, however, difficult to control since we have few copies of the originals, owners being jealous about letting them out of their hands for photographing. Palmer gives a facsimile of one in *Bornu Sahara*, pp. 40–43. Most of those seen give the appearance of being copies.

for other Saharans wore the muffler. They are first mentioned by al-Ya'qūbī (A.D. 872). After describing the eastern blacks, Nūba, Beja, Ḥabash, and Zinj, he writes:

The blacks who went westwards migrating towards the Maghrib split up the country, forming a number of kingdoms. The first is that of the Zaghāwa who inhabit the place called Kanem. Their dwellings consist of huts of reeds. They have no use for towns. Their king is entitled *Kā-karah*. Among the Zaghāwa is a type called Hawḍīn (?) who have a king from the Zaghāwa. There is another kingdom called Mallel which is at enmity with the [Zaghawī] ruler of Kanem. Their king is called Mayūsī [or Mai Wasī]. Then there is the kingdom of the Ḥabash[1] who have a city called Thabīr. The king of this city is called *Maraḥ*. Adjoining them are the Qāqū [or Alqāqū] except that they are dependent,[2] the king of Thabīr being their king. Next comes the kingdom of Kawkaw.[3]

Ibn Ḥawqal (A.D. 961) was probably referring to one of these Zaghawī settlements situated on a trade-route when he wrote that 'from Fezzān to Zaghāwa is a two months' journey'.[4] Shortly afterwards al-Muhallabī (A.D. 985) wrote that the Zaghāwa were composed of many tribes and had only two towns Mānān and Tarāzakī, both belonging to the first climate, that is the southern Sahil. They had a divine king:

They exalt and worship him instead of God. They imagine that he does not eat for his food is introduced into his compound secretly, no one knowing whence it is brought. Should one of his subjects happen to meet the camel carrying his provisions he is killed instantly on the spot. He drinks with his intimates a beverage which is concocted from millet laced with honey. . . . Most of his subjects are naked except for skin waist-wrappers. They subsist upon the products of their cultivation and the stock they own. Their religion is king-worship (*'ibādatu mulūkihim*), believing that it is they who bring life and death, sickness and health. They [the Zaghāwa] belong to the cities of al-Bilmā'.[5] The capital of the country of Kāwār lies in a south-easterly direction.[6]

[1] Not, of course, Ethiopia. The middle radical is unpointed and the word may be read Ḥbsh, Ḥnsh, Ḥysh, or Ḥtsh.

[2] Reading *ma'ūlūn*. The translation of this sentence is uncertain, perhaps 'in subjection'.

[3] Al-Ya'qūbī, *Ta'rīkh*, i. 219–20.

[4] Ibn Ḥawqal, ed. Kramers, i. 92; cf. p. 64.

[5] *Wa hiya min madā'in al-Bilmā'*. This sentence is awkward. *Hiya* one would expect to refer to the preceding *diyānatuhum*. If emended to some such phrase as *wa hiya min dīn Abī 'l-Bilmā'*, 'these beliefs are derived from the religion of Abū 'l-Bilmā'', it would read better.

[6] Quoted by Yāqūt, *Mu'jam*, ii. 932–3. Elsewhere (iv. 230) Yāqūt writes: 'Kāwār is an extensive region situated south of Fezzān beyond its oases, It has many towns, among them the *qaṣr* of Umm 'Īsā, Abū 'l-Bilmā', and al-Balās; the largest being Abū 'l-Bilmā'. The colour of its inhabitants is yellow and they dress in woollen garments. In their country are market-places, running streams and many palm groves. They have a king who is vassal to the king of the Zaghāwa.'

MAP 3

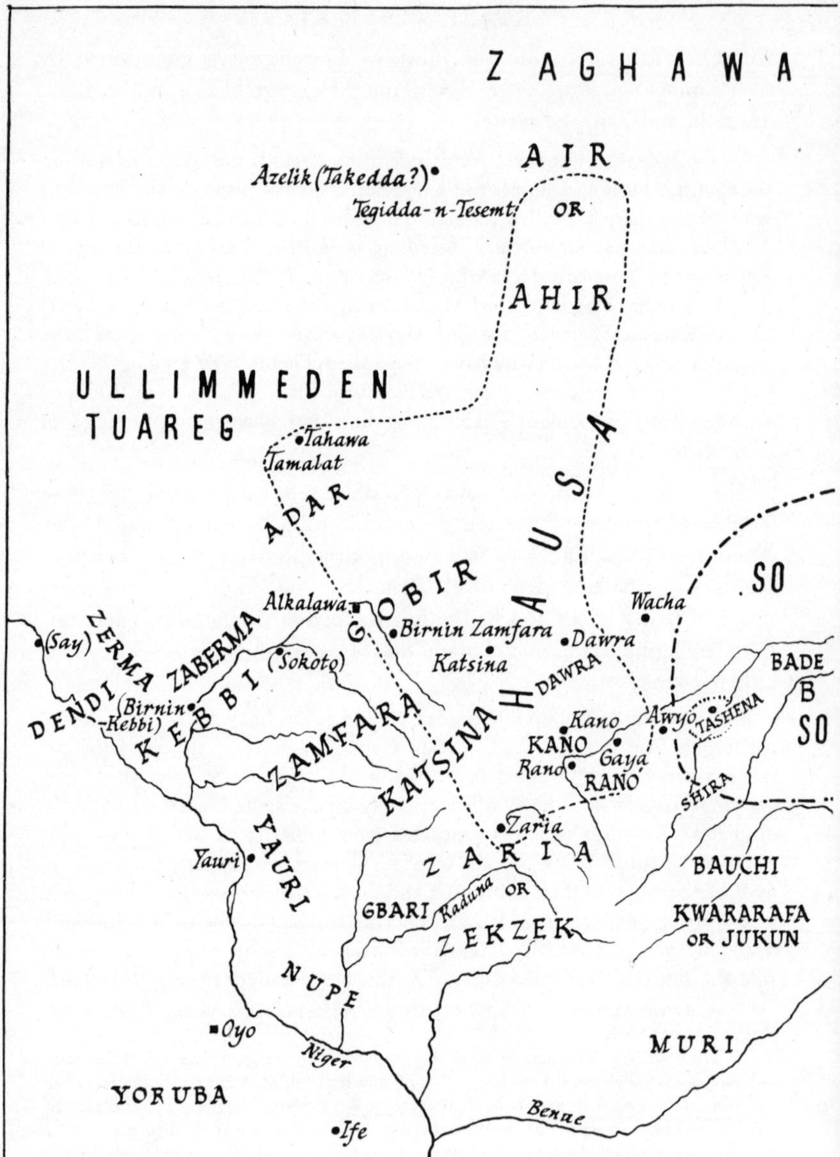

ZAGHAWA
AIR
OR
AHIR
Azelik (Takedda?)
Tegidda-n-Tesemt
ULLIMMEDEN
TUAREG
Tahawa
Tamalat
ADAR
HAUSA
GOBIR
Alkalawa
Birnin Zamfara
Katsina
Dawra
DAWRA
Wacha
SO
BADE
B
SO
(Say)
ZERMA
ZABERMA
DENDI
(Sokoto)
(Birnin-Kebbi)
KEBBI
ZAMFARA
KATSINA
Kano
KANO
Gaya
Rano
RANO
Awyo
TASHENA
SHIRA
Zaria
ZARIA
OR
ZEKZEK
Kaduna
GBARI
YAURI
Yauri
BAUCHI
KWARARAFA
OR JUKUN
NUPE
Oyo
Niger
MURI
YORUBA
Benue
Ife
Benin

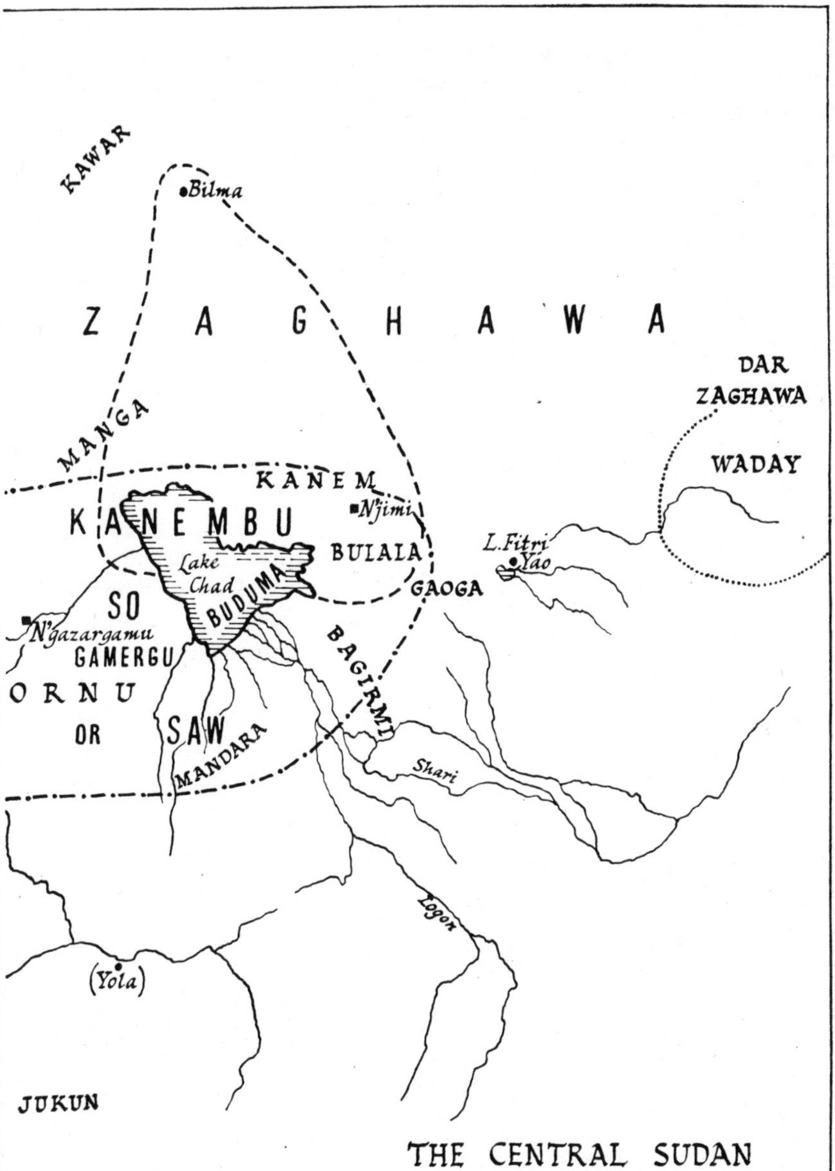
KAWAR
Bilma
Z A G H A W A
DAR ZAGHAWA
MANGA
KANEM
N'jimi
WADAY
KANEMBU
BULALA
L. Fitri
Yao
Lake Chad
SO
BUDUMA
GAOGA
N'gazargamu
GAMERGU
BAGIRMI
ORNU
OR
SAW
MANDARA
Shari
Logon
(Yola)
JUKUN
THE CENTRAL SUDAN
Kanem circa 1300
Bornu circa 1800
KANEMBU = Peoples
BORNU = States
0 100 200 Miles
0 150 300 Kilometres
Scale
M.

Al-Bakrī says that the land of Kanem was forty days' journey from Zawīla. He appears to give the name of Kanem to the whole south Saharan region where Zaghāwa nomadized, of whom those of Kanem proper were only an insignificant section. He adds that the inhabitants were idolatrous blacks amongst whom lived Umayyad refugees from 'Abbāsid persecution.[1]

The sketch of the region given by al-Idrīsī shows that there was no one power dominating it. Tribes of Zaghāwa occupied the desert and acted as guides to travellers. Proceeding eastwards from Kawkaw he mentions Tamalma,[2] Mānān 12 days,[3] N'jīmī 8 days, Tājawa 13 days,[4] then Nuwābiyya on the borders of Nubia 18 days. He says that Mānān belonged to the land of Kanem and that the chief resided there. Apparently it was merely the dry-season centre, north-west of N'jīmī, for the semi-nomadic ruling class, since it was small in size and commercially unimportant. N'jīmī, which later became a kind of capital, was situated in Kanem proper, east of the Chad.[5] It was 'very small, sparsely inhabited by a subservient population'. Six days north of N'jīmī and eight days from Mānān was the 'town' of the Zaghāwa (Kawār or Borku region?) 'embracing many districts and well populated',[6] whose inhabitants in the time of Ibn Sa'īd had joined Islam and fallen under the control of the Kanemi king.[7]

Legend carries the dynasty which was to rule Kanem back to Dūgū (*c.* A.D. 800) who is made to descend from Saif ibn Dhī Yazan, whence the ruling line is known as Saifī or Yazanī. The early pagan section is

[1] Al-Bakrī, p. 11; transl. p. 29. Whether there is any truth in the Umayyad legend we do not know. It may derive from the name of the first Muslim ruler, Umē or Ḥumē.

[2] Elsewhere al-Idrīsī has the spelling Talamla. He includes it in the third section of the second climate and his statement that it was one of the towns of Kāwār shows that it was well within the desert region (pp. 39–40).

[3] *V.l.* Māqān. Mentioned earlier by al-Muhallabī and later by Ibn Sa'īd as Mātān (Abū 'l-Fidā', p. 163), situated 'in the direction of the angle of the lake known as Buḥairat Kawarī (i.e. Chad), having to the south of it the capital of Kanem, Khīmī (Jīmī)'.

[4] Tājawa (Bīr Naṭrūn?) is the most easterly Zaghawī region. Al-Idrīsī writes that Tājawa is 'the capital of the Tājawiyyīn who are *majūs*, having no (revealed) religion. Their country adjoins the land of the Nūba. In it is also the town of Sāmina (*v.ll.* Samiya, Samta) which is small. Certain travellers who have visited Kawwār have reported that the governor of Bilāq who commands under the king of the Nūba, made an expedition to Sāmina, burnt it down, laid it waste, and dispersed its inhabitants to all quarters' (p. 13/15–16; cf. p. 40/47). Bilāq was not Philae but an important commercial town, the seat of the governor of al-Abwāb, in the Christian Nilotic kingdom of 'Alwa and was situated at the confluence of the Atbara and the Nile (cf. al-Idrīsī, text p. 20).

[5] The ruins of N'jīmī still exist 35 miles east of Mao.

[6] Al-Idrīsī, p. 12/15.

[7] Abū 'l-Fidā', p. 159.

referred to as the Dūgāwa or Banī Dūgū, which, as Barth recognized, was probably a different dynasty. None of the early chiefs have Arabic names and the legend was probably acquired with the change of dynasty. Whether any of the chieftaincies mentioned by al-Ya'qūbī represent this naissant dynasty we cannot tell, but his account serves to show that it was only one among many political groups. The statement in the Bornu chronicle that the first Muslim ruler was Ḥumē or Umē (*c.* 1085–97) may mark the beginning of a new dynasty. This is confirmed by a Bornu *maḥram* or letter of privilege given by Ḥumē to one Muḥammad ibn Mānī who is said to have introduced Islam.[1] Ibn Mānī's descendants became hereditary chief-*imāms* of N'jīmī and later N'gazargamu. No doubt there were interludes of pagan chiefs, though there is mention of early rulers going on pilgrimage, a characteristic of the early stage of conversion of Negro rulers. Al-'Umarī says[2] that the religion was first introduced by a descendant of the Umayyads (Ḥumē?) called al-Hādī al-'Uthmānī which links with al-Bakrī's statement about a settlement of Umayyads in Kanem. Al-Maqrīzī says the first Muslim ruler was one Muḥammad who can clearly be identified with Dūnama Dabalemi,[3] though the *Kitāb al-Istibṣār* which was written in A.H. 587 (A.D. 1191) dates the conversion of Kanem after A.H. 500 (A.D. 1106–7).[4]

Islam it is clear was establishing itself between 1085 and 1240 when Ibn Sa'īd's account shows that the religion was firmly established among the ruling class. Confirmation of this comes from the fact that between A.H. 640 and 650 (A.D. 1242–52) Kānemī Muslims established a Mālikī *madrasa*-hostel called Ibn Rashīq in Cairo,[5] from which we may conjecture that they had received teachers from the Egyptian capital, or it may be as a result of Kanembus going on pilgrimage.

The nature of the authority which the Saifīs exercised over an

[1] H. R. Palmer, *Sud. Mem.* iii. 3.

[2] Al-'Umarī, op. cit., p. 45; *Ṣubḥ*, v. 281.

[3] Al-Maqrīzī (H. A. Hamaker, *Specimen Catalogi*, 1820, p. 206) gives him his Islamic names: 'The first of their chiefs to adopt Islam was Muḥammad [i.e. Dūnama 1221–59], ibn Jabal [read Jīl or 'Abd al-Jalīl, also called Salma, 1194–1221], b. 'Abd Allāh [1174–94], b. 'Uthmān [Bīri 1151–74], b. Muḥammad Dūnama Umemi [1097–1151], b. Abī [or Ubayy; i.e. Ḥumē or Umē Jilmi 1085–97].'

[4] *Kitāb al-Istibṣār fī 'Ajā'ib al-Amṣār*, ed. von Kremer, 1852, p. 52; transl. Fagnon, p. 61.

[5] *Khiṭaṭ*, ed. Wiet, iii. 2 (1922), 266. Al-Maqrīzī also includes it in his section on *madrasas* and remarks that 'it has acquired great renown in the countries of the Takrūr and most years they send money for its upkeep' (*Khiṭaṭ*, ed. Cairo, 1326/1908, iv. 195).

increasing number of nomadic tribes and settled cultivators was that of overlords who received tribute in exchange for protection against other marauders. But a slow process of social and political change was in progress. We see the beginnings of the transformation of the chief from a purely nomadic shaikh to a Sudanese king and his country from a sphere where the ruling group had acquired grazing rights (as shown by al-Yaʿqūbī) towards the formation of a Sudanese type of feudal kingdom through the adoption of the Chadian civilization and the fusion of the various heritages. Its basic structure as a genuine Sudanese state were laid down during this period and it endured for the next seven centuries in spite of the disruptive tendencies inherent in its nomadic heritage which led to civil war and eventual transfer to Bornu. That nomadism still ruled the life of the dominant group is shown by indications in Arabic writers, by the fact that they must marry into nomadic tribes (especially the Tomagra, a noble Teda tribe); and that, as the *girgam* or genealogical list shows, all the rulers were buried in different places, none being buried at N'jīmī except ʿAbd Allāh b. Kaday (1321–42).[1] Al-ʿUmarī also records that the troops of the Kānemī army wore the *lithām*.[2] During this time there began the process by which the Kanembu were formed through the mixture of the Zaghāwa with autochthonous So. The early rulers were regarded as 'red' like all Saharan nomads, but the chronicle records that Tsilim (or Salma) ibn Bikur (1194–1221) was the first 'black' (*tsilim*) *mai*.[3] The language was also being transformed into the related Kanembu and Teda dialects.

Humē's son Dūnama, during his long chieftaincy (1097–1150), began the process of building up the power of his tribe in Kanem. He is said to have performed the pilgrimage twice and was drowned in the Red Sea when undertaking a third.[4] During the reign of Salma they gained control of the Zaghāwa tribes and the trade-routes northwards to and including Fezzān.[5] In Salma's reign the break up of the old reli-

[1] See Palmer, *Sud. Mem.* iii. 36–37.

[2] Al-ʿUmarī, op. cit., p. 43.

[3] Palmer, *Bornu Sahara*, pp. 91–92, 179.

[4] *Dīwān*, text, Kano, 1930, p. 131; Palmer, *Bornu Sahara*, p. 91.

[5] Ibn Saʿīd in Abū 'l-Fidā', p. 126; al-Maqrīzī, *Ilmām*, p. 24. In 1183 a Turkish adventurer, Sharaf ad-Dīn Qaraqosh, overthrew the Berber dynasty of Zawīla and it was no doubt in order to protect the trade-routes that Salma extended Kanembu control over Fezzān. It was administered by a tributary black dynasty resident at Traghen where there is the tomb of a *mai* ʿAlī and where names of streets and other localities are still in Kanembu. Kānemī control over Fezzān lasted for a century (except for the Qaramān episode) and was brought to an end about 1310 when a Moroccan *sharīf*, al-Muntaẓar b. Muḥammad, who founded Murzūq, expelled the Kanembu.

gion began. A *maḥram* belonging to the Kānemī tribe N'galma Duku records:

The learned Imām ʻAbd Allāh Dili ibn Bikuru read with the son of the king called Mabradu ibn Salma a hundred and fifty books. Therefore the Sultan built the plastered Mosque, and roofed it with clay. . . . He established this Faki as the Imām of the Mosque. And when the Faki advanced to pray he saw the two exalted treasures under the 'unapproachable lotus bud' [i.e. the seventh heaven]. One of the treasures came down to earth in the time of the king Salma ibn Bikuru, and killed the snake.[1]

About this time N'jīmī became the capital.[2] Ibn Saʻīd gives a long list of the peoples of the region, but in view of the widespread movements of population it would be pointless to quote his description unless one were prepared to go into inconclusive speculations about the habitat and present-day affinities of the various peoples.

The reign of Dūnama Dabalemi ibn Salma (1221–59) was full of wars. Ibn Khaldūn says that the rulers of Kanem 'maintained friendly relations with the Ḥafṣid dynasty since its foundation'[3] and it was in alliance with them that Dūnama fought against the Qaramān who had gained temporary control of Zawīla. In 655 (1257) he sent a rich present, which included a giraffe, to the Ḥafṣid, al-Mustanṣir.[4] Ibn Khaldūn refers to him as 'king of Kānem and lord of Burnu', but that was no doubt the title by which he was known in Ibn Khaldūn's day.

During this Dūnama's reign the clash with the Bulāla which had begun in the twelfth century intensified and he inflicted upon them a severe defeat. Sudanese rulers such as the *mais* had now become could not allow a nomadic group, even though derived from the same stock, to disrupt the life of their cultivators and challenge their own authority. Islam also appears to have been a factor of division which local tradition indicates by linking the beginning of the troubles with Dūnama's opening of the local Pandora's box. This was the *mūnē* or *sacrum* of the royal authority, 'whose nature was known only to God most high'. Ibn Fartuwa says that the Banī Saif possessed something covered and

[1] Palmer, *Bornu Sahara*, p. 19.

[2] Ibn Saʻīd in Abū 'l-Fidā', pp. 159, 163.

[3] Ibn Khaldūn, ed. de Slane, i. 262; transl. ii. 109. Ibn Saʻīd, a contemporary, says definitely that Fezzān was under the control of Kanem, as was the Berber trading town of Tādmekka (mistake for Tākedda?); Abū 'l-Fidā', p. 127 (cf. transl. ii. 219). The Ḥafṣids were a Berber family in control of Tunisia and Tripolitania from 1228 to 1347.

[4] Ibn Khaldūn, i. 428; transl. ii. 346–7.

hidden upon which victory in war depended.[1] It was called *mūnē* and no one must open it. The same chronicler with insight compares it with the *Sakīna*.[2] According to tradition this sacrilegious act alienated a branch of the ruling clan later known as the Bulāla.[3] This act meant the refutation of the old imperial cult and a change in attitude towards the divine ruler was the result. It shows that al-Maqrīzī was probably right in regarding him as the first genuine Muslim ruler. The Bulāla had gained an ascendancy among autochthones of the Fitri region where they formed a ruling caste similar to the rulers of Kanem, the traditions of both going back to the same ancestor. They appear to represent a pagan reaction against the islamizing tendencies of the Saifī house and it was only later under different conditions that they became Muslims. Their bid for power made a clash between the two houses inevitable. To the south expansion was difficult among the peoples of the marshes and rivers of the Kotoko–Logon region, but some Kanembu were already moving to the fertile banks of the Yo on the other side of the lake, a region which came to be known as Bornu, where they mingled with So tribes.[4] The chronicles show that wars against the various So peoples were continuous and an echo of them reached Ibn Sa'īd who writes that 'the Sultan of Kanem is famous for taking the *jihād*',[5] whilst al-Maqrīzī says that the Mābina, whose most numerous group was called the Kālkīn (So N'galaga?), was invaded from al-Jīmā (N'jīmi?) in A.H. 650 (A.D. 1252–3) by the king of Kanem

[1] H. R. Palmer, *Sud. Mem.* i. 70, 71–72. Sir Richmond writes, 'The factor regarded as essential to preserve the efficacy of the Mune and similar *sacra*, which were and are still, in some cases, jealously guarded by the Hausa and Jukon chiefs, is "covering". When the peoples in question became Muhammadans, a copy of the Qur'ān itself did duty as the "hidden *sacra*", as in the case of the *sacrum* called *Dirki* . . . which was opened and destroyed by the last Hausa Sariki of Kano about 1807. . . . At Katsina, similarly, a *kudandam*, or round house, which had been carefully closed for years, was opened by the last Hausa Sariki; while at Wukari there still exists a sacred and carefully guarded forked staff or spear, which is identical in its supposed qualities with the Bornu "Mune" and is called "Aba Kindo", which means, or perhaps connotes rather, "something occult". A Zaghawi of Wadai stated that the Zaghawi name for a sacred Qur'ān, covered with skins like the Kano *Dirki*, was Māni. When asked whether Māni was anything else but the Qur'ān, he stated that among the pagan Beli and Zaghawa, Māni was a "ram" which was kept in a cave (*kurkuri*) with other sacred objects. . . . Māni is the mythical ancestor of several Kanembu tribes or peoples, and at Kano a deity once worshipped at Dāla is called Amane in the Kano Chronicle' (H. R. Palmer, *The Bornu Sahara and Sudan*, 1936, p. 185).

[2] Qur'ān ii. 249, Heb. *shekīnā*. The opening of the *mūnē* is also mentioned in the *dīwān* of the rulers of Bornu (transl. H. R. Palmer, *Bornu Sahara*, pp. 90 ff.).

[3] The name is said to derive from an ancestor called Bilāl. Their name for themselves is Magge or Maggode.

[4] See the traditional account in Palmer, *Sud. Mem.* ii. 64.

[5] Al-Maqrīzī, *Ilmām*, p. 27.

who 'slaughtered and enslaved'.[1] Jājā (Kākā of other writers, and the modern Gāga), which became the capital of Bornu,[2] was tributary to Kanem: 'Jājā is the seat of a separate state which has under it towns and provinces. It now belongs to the Sultan of Kānem so celebrated for his prosecution of the *jihād*. . . . East of it in the angle of Lake Kawarī (Chad) is al-Maghazā, the industrial centre of the Sultan of Kānem.'[3] That the Kānemīs did not find it easy to conquer the So is shown by the fact that we get a succession of their chiefs killed whilst fighting against them during the middle period of the fourteenth century.

Al-'Umarī, who does not mention Bornu in the *Masālik*, writes, 'The king of Kānem is Muslim and independent. His country is a great distance from Māli. The capital of his kingdom is called Jīmī. His sphere of rule begins towards Egypt at a town called Zella[4] and terminates in the sense of longitude at a place called Kākā.'[5] In the *Ta'rīf*, however, al-'Umarī refers to Kākā as the capital of a separate kingdom (*bilād al-Burnū*).[6] He says, 'The ruler of Kanem comes from a family which is of longstanding in Islam. Among them have been some who have pretended to an 'Alid descent from the sons of al-Ḥasan. They follow the rite of ash-Shāfi'ī. The formula for correspondence is the same as that for the ruler of Bornu.'[7] Ibn Baṭṭūṭa has confused the province with Kanem when he writes that Bornu 'is forty days' journey from Tākedda. Its inhabitants are Muslims. They have a king called Idrīs who never shows himself to his people and never speaks to them except from behind a curtain. From it are exported fine slave-women, youths, and saffron-coloured materials.'[8] This again points to the semi-divine character of kingship.

[1] H. A. Hamaker, op. cit., p. 206.

[2] Al-Qalqashandī, v. 279, 281.

[3] Abū 'l-Fidā', p. 163. *Dār as-sinā'a* may mean 'naval base'.

[4] A Zella (an alternative name for Zawīla? cf. G. F. Lyon, *Travels*, 1821, p. 217) in the Fezzān region is mentioned by Abū 'l-Fidā' (text p. 129; transl. ii. 180, 182) as an independent state (cf. Ibn Khaldūn, transl. i. 91). There circulated a legend that the power of Kanem once stretched to Daw in Dongola, but this can mean nothing more than that Zaghawī raiders ranged as far as the Nile, as a branch called the Bedāyāt still do today.

[5] Al-'Umarī, p. 43; cf. al-Maqrīzī, *Khiṭaṭ*, ed. Wiet, iii. 2, 265.

[6] Al-'Umarī, *At-Ta'rīf bi 'l-Muṣṭalaḥ ash-sharīf*, Cairo, 1312, p. 29.

[7] *Ṣubḥ*, v. 281. The Bornuans are now said to follow the Shāfi'ite rite, whereas in the *Masālik* the author said they were Mālikites.

[8] Ibn Baṭṭūṭa, iv. 441–2 The reference is to Idrīs b. Ibrāhīm (Nikāle), reigned 1343–66. Al-'Umarī also mentions that the *mai* 'is never visible to anyone except on the occasion of the two *'īds* at the time of the daybreak and afternoon prayers. During the rest of the year no one, even though he be an *amīr*, may address him except when he is behind a screen' (*Ṣubḥ*, v. 281). This ceremony of audience was witnessed by Denham in 1824 (Denham and Clapperton, *Travels and Discoveries in Northern and Central Africa*, 3rd ed. 1828, i. 231–3), who gives

We have seen that Ibn Khaldūn, writing towards the end of the century, regards Kanem and Bornu as being under the same ruler, but shortly afterwards when al-Qalqashandī was compiling his book, he was informed by an envoy from Abū ʿAmr ʿUthmān b. Idrīs in the year 794 (A.D. 1391–2) to the court of aẓ-Ẓāhir Barqūq that Kākā, which he says is 40 miles from N'jīmī, was the capital of Bornu and that Kanem had fallen to the Bulāla.[1] The real struggle with the Bulāla began in the reign of Da'ūd ibn Ibrāhīm (1366–76) when one Jīl ibn Sikuma was at their head, and continued until ʿUmar ibn Idrīs (1384–8) finally abandoned Kanem and moved to Gāga (Kākā) in Bornu where immigrants from Kanem had long been mingling with So. Ibn Fartuwa says that Da'ūd b. (Ibrāhīm) Nikāle fled from Kanem to Bornu.[2] In the *Kanem Wars* he writes, 'We heard from Shaikh Dūnama b. Ruskū that the period between the date on which Sultan Da'ūd left Sīma (N'jīmī) and the date of Sultan b. Idrīs b. ʿAlī's re-entry was 122 (Islamic) years exactly.'[3]

This change of fortune is confirmed by al-Maqrīzī (d. 845/1442) who writes:

> The king of Kānem about the turn of the seventh century (A.D. 1300) was al-ḥājj Ibrāhīm (Nikāle 1290–1311), descended from Saif ibn Dhī Yazan. He had his capital in Kānem, and Kānem is the seat of the government (*or* the motherland) of Bornu. After him ruled his son al-ḥājj Idrīs (1343–66); then his brother Da'ūd ibn Ibrāhīm (1366–76); then ʿUmar (1384/5–1388/9), son of his brother al-ḥājj Idrīs; and lastly his brother ʿUthmān ibn Idrīs (1390–1422) who reigned a little before the year 800 (1397/8). But the people of Kānem rebelled against them (the rulers) and they forsook (their country). Nūbī remained under their sovereignty (reading *mamlaka*) and these are Muslims who fight on behalf of the people of Kānem. They have twelve kingdoms.[4]

Al-Maqrīzī has not included all the *mais* in this account for many were killed in wars with the Bulāla, So, and Arabs after very short reigns.

a drawing of the lattice-curtained cage called *fanādīr* (plur. of *findīr*), mentioned in the *Dīwān* (text in *Ta'rīkh Mai Idrīs*, p. 132, l. 1). Other terms were *tatatuma* (in Kanem) and *daghil*, Ar. 'place of retirement'; the *daghilma* was the 'master of ceremonies' at court. See also Barth for Logon (iii. 288–90) and Bagirmi (iii. 412).

[1] *Ṣubḥ*, v. 279–81; viii. 116. This envoy may also be the source of al-Maqrīzī's information on Kanem.

[2] *Bornuan Wars*, p. 3; transl. Palmer, p. 10.

[3] *Kanem Wars*, pp. 54–55; transl. *Sud. Mem.* i. 17.

[4] Extract from al-Maqrīzī in H. A. Hamaker, *Specimen Catalogi*, 1820, p. 207. The meaning of the Arabic in the last section is obscure. In the Chad region the Shuwa Arabs refer to Muslim blacks as *Nūba*, sing. *Nūbai*. The transference of the dynasty to Kākā is also confirmed by al-Qalqashandī (*Ṣubḥ*, v. 279; viii. 116) on information he obtained in 1391.

There were actually fourteen or more *mais* in the hundred years from al-ḥājj Ibrāhīm to ʿUthmān ibn Idrīs, but he is accurate as regards the succession of the main figures.

The Bulāla were now the rulers of Kanem and had their headquarters at Gaw (or Yaw) a little north of Lake Fitri, and it may be this which is the kingdom of Gaoga of Leo Africanus. Later, when the Bornuan kingdom became strong, the old ruling house once again conquered Kanem, but the Bulāla remained virtually independent and later dominated the region which came to be known as Waday.

As al-Maqrīzī shows, the old Saifī line in Bornu lived a harried nomadic life, but they did not abandon their dynastic feuds. The Bulāla wars died down after 1390 although they did not cease. Arabs now joined in and al-Qalqashandī quotes a letter from Abū ʿAmr ʿUthmān b. Idrīs[1] to al-Malik aẓ-Ẓāhir Barqūq in A.H. 794 (1391–2) in which he complains of the raids of Joḍām who had killed his brother, the former chief, ʿAmr (ʿUmar) ibn Idrīs b. Ibrāhīm, and carried off many of his subjects, fellow Muslims, men, women, and children.[2] Settlement among So and proximity to the Hausa states led to many struggles. Yet the strength of the old organization and the growing nucleus of settled Kanuri cultivators devoted to the ruling house enabled it to revive and expand. The fact that a *mai* called Kanje b. Jamshīsh in 843/1440 sent to Tawāt to renew former relations[3] and that ʿAbd Allāh Burja, Sarkin Kano, paid Bornu tribute[4] shows that its rulers were becoming more powerful.

The real founder of the new kingdom was ʿAlī (Ghāzī) ibn Dūnama (1476–1503) who brought the dynastic wars to an end, established an administrative system, and, as symbol of the new stability, founded (*c.* 1484) a capital, N'gazargamu,[5] on the River Yo. He exacted tribute from the Hausa states in the west including Kano.[6] Leo Africanus

[1] Known as Biri b. Idrīs, reigned *c.* 1390–1422/3.

[2] *Ṣubḥ*, viii. 116.

[3] Letter dated A.H. 843 (A.D. 1440) to the Kunta *murābiṭīn* of Tawāt translated in A. G. P. Martin, *A la frontière du Maroc, les oases sahariennes*, Algiers, 1908, p. 122; cf. Palmer, *Sud. Mem.* ii. 4. Perhaps Kadai b. ʿUthmān, but there is doubt about the date, for ʿUmar ash-Shaikh who seems to be referred to died *c.* 960/1552–3 (cf. Marty, *Soudan*, i. 22–23) according to Kunta tradition. The Kano Chronicle states that Pulo shaikhs from Mali after visiting Kano went on to Bornu (1452–62), but they were no doubt on pilgrimage.

[4] According to the Kano Chronicle, *Sud. Mem.* iii. 109.

[5] Also called Gasreggomo (Qaṣr Gomo) and Birnin Barnu, 'the stronghold of Bornu'. It was west of the Chad, near Guidam in British Bornu, and remained the capital until 1811. It was built of baked bricks and its ruins are described by Denham and Clapperton (i. 348–51) and Barth (iv. 22–25), and H. R. Palmer (*Bornu Sahara*, pl. xxv, p. 232) gives a photograph of the remains.

[6] Kano Chronicle, *Sud. Mem.* iii. 112.

mentions what appears to be an invasion of the Kwararafa which led the king of Bornu to obtain horses in exchange for slaves from the merchants of Barbary.[1]

In his reign the chief *imām*, 'Umar Masbarma (d. 918/1512) ibn 'Uthmān, tried to get the ruling class to observe the minimum of Islamic practice:

> The Sultan 'Alī ibn Muḥammad Dūnama went every day to Masbarma 'Uthmānmi to hear him reading and explaining the Qur'ān and the traditions until he became a true Muslim. Masbarma ordered him to marry four wives and to put away his other women. He did so. Masbarma ordered him to place many slave girls in his house and told him that there would be no harm even if he had a thousand, but that he must divorce the free women in excess of four. He also ordered the chief men of Bornu to do likewise, which order some obeyed and some did not.[2]

Under his successor, Idrīs Katagarmabe (1503–26), Kanem was reconquered,[3] but the Bulāla were allowed to remain as tributary independent rulers, and continually threw off even that nominal recognition before they were ejected by the Tunjur about 1750.

The reign of Idrīs ibn 'Alī (1570–1602), known as Idrīs Alawma, was the highlight of the period, though this is primarily due to the fact that we know so much about him since his chief *imām*, Aḥmad ibn Fartuwa, wrote accounts of his wars both west and east of the Chad, whereas we have little information about subsequent rulers. In consequence of this chronicle he is chiefly famous for his campaigns, though his *imām* also eulogizes him as a just and wise ruler. Early in his reign he went on pilgrimage and discovered the value of firearms. He imported Turkish musketeers and this altered the whole character of his campaigns.[4] Another innovation was his employment of Arab camelry. He subdued many of the walled So towns in and around Bornu. He attacked and defeated Tuareg tribes and raided the stockaded villages of

[1] Transl. J. Pory, op. cit., iii. 833.

[2] Transl. by H. R. Palmer, *Sud. Mem.* iii. 158. 'Umar's father appears to have been an immigrant from the Nilotic Sudan.

[3] Ibn Fartuwa, *Ta'rīkh Mai Idrīs*, p. 54; *Sud. Mem.* i. 17.

[4] *Bornuan Wars*, text p. 4; transl. p. 45. This was a little before firearms appeared in the western Sudan with the campaign of Jūdar in 1591. According to the Kano Chronicle Kanajeji (1390–1410) was the first to introduce *lifidi* (quilted armour), coats of mail, and iron helmets into Kano (*Sud. Mem.* iii. 107). The use of this so-called Crusader armour did not begin to spread widely in the region from the Chad to Sennar until the early eighteenth century. It was apparently derived from that of the Egyptian *mamlūks*, but local armourers quickly learnt to make it, though it remained costly and was only worn by chiefs and their special retainers.

Kano state, though his attack on the city itself failed. Most of his campaigns were similar raids and did little to extend the effective area of his rule, but his main achievement was the political unification of the various tribes who inhabited Bornu and consequently the gradual increase of the Kanuri nucleus. East of the Chad he defeated the Bulāla in successive campaigns, though he never subdued them and was content to reach an agreement whereby Kanem remained independent and the frontier between their respective spheres was carefully defined.[1] This is a unique instance of the acknowledgement of frontiers in any Sudanese state, although in practice it was ignored.

Idrīs is more significant from the Islamic viewpoint than as a genuine empire builder. In the old Kanem kingdom only the ruling class and a number of clerical families had been Muslims, and during the time of troubles their Islam evaporated. Idrīs did a great deal to revive it as the state religion. Imām Aḥmad says that in his time all the notables became Muslims.[2] He began the process of substituting the *sharīʿa* for customary law in certain spheres. He separated the administration of justice from the executive, taking legal decisions out of the hands of the political chiefs and setting up *qāḍī*'s courts.[3] He was the first to construct brick mosques in his territories,[4] and when in Mecca he had a hostel built for Bornuan pilgrims. His *imām* shows that he was scrupulous in carrying out the Islamic regulations regarding the conduct of war,[5] unlike the Bulāla liberating the freemen among the captives. At the same time the regulations regarding the invitation to the enemy to embrace Islam were not applied. His wars were *jihāds* only in the terminology of his *imām* chronicler. There is little record of the defeated being expected or forced to become Muslims, and its spread was the normal result of its being the state religion. Imām Aḥmad, after mentioning the state of insecurity caused by the Bīnāwa tribe during the reigns of Idrīs's predecessors, writes, 'A few days after Idrīs succeeded to authority over the country of Bornu, Ghamaru, the chief of this people, came to offer allegiance and become a Muslim sponsored by Idrīs. After him one Naṣr surnamed Bultu also joined Islam with a few of his people, but most of the Bīnāwa did not become Muslims', which means did not submit. Later Bultu converted many, that is he

[1] *Kanem Wars*, p. 73; transl. *Sud. Mem.* i. 30.

[2] Loc. cit., p. 57; transl. i. 18.

[3] *Bornuan Wars*, p. 13; transl. p. 20. In fact, their function was little more than to act as legal councillors to the great chiefs.

[4] Loc. cit., p. 27; transl. p. 33.

[5] *Kanem Wars*, p. 82; transl. i. 36.

got them to abandon their raiding and become regular soldiers or merchants, through peaceful propaganda.[1] Most of the tributary states east and south of the Chad threw off any ties of allegiance after Idrīs's death.[2]

Although we know so little about them none of his successors seem to have had his ability, and the tendency of the following centuries was towards stagnancy and decline. None are worthy of record in this outline. Famines, due in part to the general insecurity, were frequent, as were attacks from the Tuareg of Air in the north and Jukun in the south. Control of the Saharan routes was lost after 1700. Fulbe settlers began to increase and expand, and there are frequent accounts of their increasing boldness in attacking small tribes.

In the Kanem–Bornu state we see the change in the conception of chieftaincy from that of the shaikh, a *primus inter pares*, of a nomadic tribe encamped among tributary cultivators, to a Sudanese despot exercising direct rule over his own people and holding the indirect allegiance of a varying range of semi-independent peoples. For long the chief was in continual movement save when occupying his unstable dry-season centre. No important commercial towns developed in either Kanem or Bornu, presumably because of the endemic state of insecurity. The region was a complex pattern of small Negro agriculturalist communities among whom moved groups of nomads. The cultivators were also in a state of perpetual movement, due to this political insecurity, the state of the rains, and their cultivation methods. The ruling clan were for long content simply with acknowledgement of their suzerainty by the payment of tribute. But gradually there formed around it a stable core of Kanembu and later in Bornu of Kanuri, which nucleus grew gradually to form a homogeneous 'national' population upon whom the rulers could rely as their people.

As in western Sudan no strict frontiers existed, but dominion consisted of a graduated sphere of influence over villages or nomadic tribes, and naturally the political situation was very fluid. The distinction between subjects and vassals was very clear. There was a sphere which came under direct administration, over which the *mai* appointed members of his family as governors. Vassal tribes were both within and around this nucleus, but there was a political difference. The vassal groups within the state were deprived of their own chiefs except at the village level and came under direct administration. These incorporated So groups gradually adopted the Kanuri language and uniform cultural

[1] *Bornuan Wars*, p. 33; transl. pp. 38–39.

[2] *Sud. Mem.* iii. 162.

characteristics,[1] to which Islam in time gave a characteristic stamp, although many of these groups remained and still remain distinctive within the Kanuri.[2] It is similar to the more widespread process of linguistic and cultural assimilation which was proceeding in Hausaland. On the other hand, the outer vassal peoples retained their own rulers, language, and cultural characteristics. They were not expected to become Muslims, and, although speaking allied languages, remained distinctive peoples. But there was nothing stable about their position; borderland villages were raided, chiefs killed, and a district officer responsible to the *mai* appointed. The difference is seen in the distinction between taxation and tribute. Block tribute was levied on vassals, but those directly administered were assessed by families, the tax being paid to the village chief and passed on through the district chief and governor to the *mai*, each intermediary taking his share. Judging by the account of the wars of Idrīs Alawma an important source of revenue was derived from slave-raiding.

It is impossible to tell how the Kanem state was organized and not a great deal is known about that of Bornu, for, though titles did not change greatly during the centuries, the functions they carried did. A characteristic of Chad states was the cosmogonic division of the country into four regions corresponding to the four points of the compass, and it appears that in Kanem there was the west (*futē*) ruled by the *galadi-ma*,[3] east (*gidin*) under the *mastre-ma* or *hira-ma*, north (*yeri*) under the *yeri-ma*, and the south (*anum*) under the *kaiga-ma*.[4] But any such division was soon obscured as the state developed. All great offices were given to members of the ruler families who maintained their own forces. The *māgira* or queen-mother was very influential; Biri ibn Dūnama (1151–74) being imprisoned by the *māgiri* of his time. There was originally a supreme council of twelve great dignatories, derived from the nomadic stage, presided over by the *mai*. The state maintained no regular army, but relied upon the feudal system of levies. These

[1] The Gamergu, for example, were once an important So tribe living south-west of Lake Chad who were conquered by Idrīs Alawma (*Bornuan Wars*, transl. pp. 12, 29). Those in the plains brought under direct administration were assimilated, but those pushed back into the Mandara mountains maintained their independence (Barth, op. cit. ii. 362–3).

[2] For example, the Dietko, formerly an important (Teda?) tribe living west of N'jīmi, who migrated (*c.* sixteenth century) to the banks of the Yo in Bornu, the Dagra (17,000), Manga (32,000), Mober (11,000), though now speaking Kanuri in the main, are only partially assimilated. See G. Nachtigal, *Sahara et Sudan*, French transl. 1881, i. 528.

[3] Governor of the western provinces, rather than an adoption from Arabic *jallād*, chief of police in Egypt.

[4] H. R. Palmer, *Bornu Sahara*, pp. 159–62.

elements of disunity account for the centuries of dynastic troubles. After the settlement and reconstitution of the state in Bornu with a fixed capital, a stable administrative and military system developed. The titles of the great dignatories, deriving from their old territorial commands in Kanem, were retained, but their power was neutralized since title and authority were separated. Recipients of the honorific titles were attached to the court and they appointed *chima-gana* to administer their fiefs. The real offices were given to servants of the *mai* who were often freedmen and slaves.[1]

3. THE HAUSA STATES

The Hausa, today one of the largest linguistic groups in Africa, do not form an ethnic unity but are the result of a complex historical process which extended the range of a common language and culture. Their history is bound up with the fortunes of a number of city states which were formed during the eleventh and twelfth centuries. Traditions indicate that their distinctive cultural characteristics arose from an intermingling of diverse elements from the north (Saharan nomads like Baghāma and Zaghāwa) and east (Nilotic Sudan elements) with the autochthones. The culturally dominant people belonged to the So cycle of civilization characterized by matrilineal succession in the ruling class and walled towns, who had fused with patriarchal autochthones. Later strains produced the ruling class associated with the proto-historical and historical period of these states. The village-state tradition was in existence before the arrival of these last immigrants connected with the Abayajidda legend.[2] The mother of the personified

[1] The *wazīr* of Idrīs Alawma, for instance, was an assimilated member of the So N'gizim· *Bornuan Wars*, pp. 33–34; transl. pp. 28–29. Imām Aḥmad refers to these dignatories as *akābir al-'ālam* and *arbāb ad-dawla*.

[2] The Kano Chronicle refers to the formation of many villages before the arrival of Bagoda, first *sarki* of Kano (*c*. A.D. 1050), e.g. 'The *sarkis* of Gano, Dab and Debbi came to Hausaland nine years before Bagoda' (*Sud. Mem.* iii. 100). *Bagudi* is employed by the Daza of Borku for 'chief'. Numerous legends witness to the diverse elements confounded in the ruling class as well as the people. A type of tradition that may have a foundation of fact is related of the Darnekāwa who came originally from the Bornu region and founded the town of Kufan Kanāwa in the hills of Washa (now in French Niger). Famine forced them to abandon the place and migrate to Kano where they founded a new town (see M. Brouin, 'Le Pays de Ouacha', *Bull. Com. Ét. A.O.F.* xxi (1938), 469–70). Upon these village states an alien group imposed themselves and we find the same legend as in Songhay. Dawra when under the ninth queen, Dawra-ma, was menaced (*c*. 980–1020) by a snake. A white called Abayajidda (arabized as Abū Yazīd) made his appearance, killed the snake, married the queen, and begot seven sons who founded the 'seven Hausa' (Hausa *bakwai*): Biram, Katsina, Zegzeg, Kano, Rano, Gobir, and Dawra. These legends vary considerably; for different versions see Barth, *Travels*,

Hausa towns is said to have belonged to the Deggāra, a once powerful Kanuri–Berber tribe,[1] and the Abayajidda legend implies the substitution of patrilineal for matrilineal succession.[2]

The Hausa political unit was the *birni*, the walled or stockaded village, as distinguished from the *gari* or *ḳauye*, village, hamlet, or collection of compounds. The *birni* is peculiar to the central Sudan. Its wall marked a geographical divide enclosing a large self-sufficient community, with trade, industry,[3] and a large area of open land for cultivation. Its inhabitants could support a long siege and the people of surrounding hamlets came within its walls when hostile armies were around. The Hausa states were formed when one *birni* secured the acknowledgement of a widening circle of hamlets and then of other *birnis*, and developed into a capital town whose head (*sarki*) changed from a village to a city chief with an elaborate court and official hierarchy. The other *birnis* became subordinate chieftaincies. Political unity had a spiritual bond embodied in the foundation myth and divine king, with town and regal deities, state and religious hierarchy, symbols, taboos, and rituals.

The Kano Chronicle shows that it was long before the superimposed groups gained control of the city cult. The political element in So culture was based on uncoordinated self-governing village units and it was the new-comers who provided the organization which led to the towns and villages where they settled becoming capital cities embracing a widening circle of villages. The So element ensured the maintenance of the village cult and consequently the social organization. The imposition of alien rulers seems to have been accomplished without conflict[4] until there were hundreds of these village states, though they were not entirely separate since they owed allegiance to a capital city.

ii. 71–72; M. Belo, *Infāq al-Maisūr*, pp. 17–18; O. Temple, *Notes on the Tribes . . . of the Northern Province of Nigeria*, p. 406; H. R. Palmer, *Sud. Mem.* iii. 132 ff. The dynasties certainly go back to this epoch. The Kano Chronicle (*Sud. Mem.* iii. 97–132), for example, gives the names of 43 rulers from Bagoda, grandson of Abayajidda, until they were dispossessed by the Fulbe in 1807, though it does not enter the sphere of history until the reign of Yāji (*c.* 1349–85).

[1] Established in Barth's time north of Muniyo; *Travels*, ii. 72.

[2] See *Sud. Mem.* iii. 132–4, 137.

[3] Barth gives a list of the names of the various quarters of Kano and Katsina which show both industrial and trading connexions (*Travels*, ii. 120–3, 555–6).

[4] For instance in the Kano Chronicle we read: 'The nineteenth Sarki was Yakubu [A.D. 1452–63], son of Tasāfi. He was a good Sarki. In his time Agalfati came to Kano; he was Sarkin Gaya, and son of Sarkin Machina. Gaya came with his three brothers who became Sarkin Hadejiya, Sarkin Dal and Sarkin Gayam' (*Sud. Mem.* iii. 110). Agalfati was a son of the chief of Mashina, north-west of N'guru, Gaya was east of Kano, and Gayam in Zegzeg.

Originally the Hausa region stretched farther north than it does today. For long they also occupied the regions of Damergu and the massif of Air whose southern part is more humid than might be expected from its latitude. These Hausa were subject to the same Berber pressure as the west Saharan Negroes. For a time the meagre resources sufficed for both, but as pressure increased through the Banū Hilāl movement the Hausa were displaced, with the exception of those who became Tuareg servile tribes, and settled in the region where Hausa states had already been founded.

The fortunes, power, and spheres of influence of these states varied enormously throughout the centuries. Gobir, the most northerly, as a result of centuries of conflict with Tuareg, gained a reputation for warlikeness. Its ruling class appears to have been of a different origin (Zaghāwa?) from the rulers of the other states. Tradition brings them from Bilma in Kawār to Azben (Air) where the state formed and grew in power (eighth to twelfth centuries A.D.). In the fifteenth century under Tuareg pressure they moved to Gobir.[1] Biram and Dawra, both traditionally the original state, remained small and peaceful, being regarded to some extent as immune from the attacks of their neighbours. The records of Kano give evidence of the settlement of a small alien group (*c.* A.D. 1000), gradually winning wider authority over the natives, scheming to gain the secret of their cult, until finally Tsamia (A.D. 1307–43) obtained it by force and gained their full allegiance.[2] Kano became known as a manufacturing centre, but at this time Katsina (Kashna) was more important commercially. The first of a succession of dynasties in Katsina was founded in the twelfth century A.D. by Kumayo whose village was not far from the present Katsina town. But there also appears to have been another Katsina Laka situated north of Zaria in the Chāfi (Kwotarkoshi) region.[3] During the period A.D. 1200–1300 the Durbāwa dynasty of northern Katsina was unimportant, but the Wangāra dynasty in Katsina Laka was powerful and its king Korau (*c.* A.D. 1200–60) conquered the northern state. Succeeding kings built a capital there, joined Islam (1320), and the town became commercially prosperous, especially after the fall of Kawkaw. The state of Guangara mentioned by Leo Africanus about 1500 was probably this state of Korau founded by Soninke, hence the

[1] This is confirmed by the Kano Chronicle (*Sud. Mem.* iii. 111) which records that in the reign of Yaʿqūb (1452–63) the Asbenāwa came to Gobir.

[2] *Sud. Mem.* iii. 103–4.

[3] Still said to be a strong centre of the cult of the god Chumburburai, the Tsunburbura mentioned in the Kano Chronicle.

name of Wangāra. Its dynasty disappeared at the beginning of the sixteenth century and thus there were no annalists to preserve the record of its rulers.[1]

The sites of these towns were fairly stable, but not as the residences of rulers any more than in Māli. This was due to the fact that the rulers had a different cult from that of the people and only when they succeeded in gaining control of the city cult did they become settled. The rulers of Zegzeg or Zazzau (from *c.* 1370), however, founded their own capital. Early rulers had their centres according to tradition[2] at Rikochi, Wuchicherri, and Turunku, before Zaria city was founded (*c.* 1536) in the transitional zone between the Sudanese and Guinean types of savannas. Traditions centre around the exploits of a queen Amīna or Āmina who seems to be an historical personnage. Said to be the daughter of Bakwa Turunka, a Tokolor from Fūta Tōro, she lived at the time of the 15th *sarki* of Kano, Da'ūd Bākon Dāmisa (1421–38).[3] Zaria remained the capital until the Fulbe conquest when the dynasty transferred itself to the rock of Zuba in the south-west of the old state where it still survives. In spite of this instability the dynasties were not normally nomadic as in Kanem, and the rulers were buried in their own towns.

Farther west was the state of Zamfara, whose ruling class and ethnic composition was quite different from that of the other states. At one time powerful, its ancient capital of Dutsi (Zurmi district) remained the royal burial place (twenty-three kings being buried there) even after the capital was transferred to Birnin Zamfara (founded by Buḳuruḳuru, *c.* 1300) near the present town of Isa. Out of these states a soldier of fortune formed the kingdom of Kebbi at the beginning of the sixteenth century. In addition, there were hundreds of other village states, sometimes independent, but more generally within the sphere of influence of one or other of the more powerful. Bornu exercised hegemony over those in the east, among them Shira, Tashena,

[1] Wangāra merchants continued their operations throughout the centuries. Barth wrote (*Travels*, ii. 82) that in his time, 'almost all the more considerable native merchants in Katsina are Wangarāwa (Eastern Mandingoes)'.

[2] Palmer, *Sud. Mem.* iii. 77.

[3] The Kano Chronicle records a raid by Kanajeji (1390–1410) on Turunku, some 20 miles south of Zaria city, then the centre of Zegzeg (MS. p. 34; *Sud. Mem.* iii. 107). Of Amīna we read, 'In his [Da'ūd's] time Zakzak, under queen Amīna, conquered all the towns as far as Kwararafa and Nupe. Every town paid her tribute. The Sarkin Nupe sent her forty eunuchs (*bābani*) and ten thousand kolas. She was the first to own eunuchs and kolas in Hausaland. In her time all the products of the west came to Hausaland. She dominated these regions for thirty-four years' (MS. pp. 38–39; *Sud. Mem.* iii. 109; cf. M. Belo, *Infāq*, p. 18).

Awyo, Hadejiya, Garin Gabas, Gatarwa, Kazurē, Fagi, and Dawa, all very small but in the main of ancient foundation, that of Garin Gabas being the old Biram linked with the legend of Abayajidda. These states survived until the Fulbe conquest when they were embraced within the emirates of Hadejiya and Katagum and ceased to have an independent existence.

Islam was later in reaching the Hausa states than those lying east and west, Kanem and Songhay, both more important terminals of caravan routes. The fact that Muslim geographers had not heard of them indicates that there were not yet any commercial centres whose trade with North Africa was sufficient to excite comment. But there were centres for internal trade and, as elsewhere, the spread of Islam was due primarily to the fact that it was the religion of traders who were allotted quarters in the towns and familiarized the townspeople with its characteristics. Al-Maqrīzī was no doubt writing of these peoples when, after mentioning an expedition of the king of Kanem about A.H. 650 (A.D. 1252/3) against a branch of the Mābina called Kālkīn, he continues, 'Beyond them, westward to Kawkaw, are numerous tribes of which the nearest are Aderma and Dafūmū, among whom are mosques for the use of Muslims.'[1] The tomb of *walī* ḍan Sadaka at Illela in the Washa district who came from Kulun Fardu to preach Islam among the Hausa, is said to date from this period. The Hausa states were regarded as pagan when Ibn Baṭṭūṭa passed through Tākedda and Air in 1353. He says that Tākedda was a centre for Saharan trade and that its 'copper is exported to the town of Kūbar [Gobir?] in the country of the pagans'.[2] He also refers to what appear to be the Nupe when he writes that the Niger, after leaving Mūlī, which is the last province of Māli and belongs to the country of the Līmiyyīn, descends to Yūfī or Yūwī, 'one of the greatest countries of the blacks whose king is one of the most powerful'.[3]

The rulers of Katsina, the town of the desert trade, and Kano, at this time of little importance, adopted a façade of Islam about the same time. The Kano Chronicle states that the religion was introduced during the reign of ʻAlī nicknamed Yāji (1349–85):

[1] Hamaker, op. cit., p. 206. The names of many of the peoples cited by al-Maqrīzī end in *-ma*. This is probably the affix of ownership, e.g. the Kanem Yeri-ma 'Lord of the North'. Earlier he has mentioned the Afuno, the Kanuri term for the Hausa, whose king was called Mastūr.

[2] Ibn Baṭṭūṭa, iv. 441. Gobir was then in Air.

[3] Ibn Baṭṭūṭa, iv. 395–6. Katsina was at war with the Nupe during the reign of its first Muslim king, Muḥammad Korau, *c.* 1320–53 (*Sud. Mem.* iii. 79–80). A new Nupe dynasty succeeded in the fifteenth century.

In Yāji's time the Wangarāwa came from Mayyī (or Mabbī) bringing Islam . . . numbering up to forty in all. When they came they advised the *sarki* to observe ritual prayer and he complied. They appointed Gurdumus as his *imām*, Lāwal his muezzin, and Awta as slaughterer of all the flesh which is eaten. Mandawari was *imām* of all the Wangarāwa and of the nobility of Kano, and Zaite was their *qāḍī*. The *sarki* gave orders that every town in Kano country should observe ritual prayer and they did so. He built a rectangular mosque under the previously mentioned [sacred] tree and the five prayers were recited there.

But the Sarkin Garazawa was opposed to the practice of *ṣalāt* and after they had prayed and returned to their homes he came with his followers and they excreted in the mosque, covering it with filth. In consequence Dan Būji was appointed to patrol around the mosque with armed men from the evening until daybreak, keeping up a constant haloo during the patrol. Whereupon the pagans sought to deflect his company and succeeded in detaching some of them, but he and the rest refused. But the defilement of the mosque continued until Sheshe and Fā-Mōri announced, 'There is no remedy against the pagans except prayer', and the people agreed. So they gathered on the Tuesday night in the mosque and prayed from sunset until sunrise against the heathens, not returning to their homes until the forenoon. God answered their prayer. The leader of the pagans was struck blind that very day and subsequently all who had taken part in the defilement together with their women. After that the pagans were all afraid. Yāji dispossessed the chief of the pagans from his office, saying to him, 'Be thou chief of the blind.'[1]

This affair was clearly a trial of strength between two groups of magicians, the native and the immigrant. The latter's success proved to be only a temporary setback to the old religion for Yāji's son, Kanajēje (1390–1410), was a thorough-going pagan and it was not until the reign of Muḥammad Rimfa (1463–99) that Islam gained any hold other than on the immigrant communities.

The Katsina records state that Muḥammad Korau (1320–53) introduced Islam into that state helped by Ibrāhīm Sura who succeeded him.[2] This apparently refers to the Wangāra dynasty. The third member of this line called 'Alī Murabus began the building of the city of Katsina. Such conversions did not amount to much for al-Majhīlī is said to have converted Ibrāhīm Māje (1494–1520). The rulers of non-trading states who had no need for the link with the wider world were still later in adopting the religion. The most southerly state, Zegzeg,

[1] MS. pp. 24–26; Palmer, *Sud. Mem.* iii. 105–6.

[2] *Sud. Mem.* iii. 79–80. Traditions collected by Landeroin (*Mission Tilho*, ii. 458) also affirm that Muḥammad Korau was a cleric attached to the court of Jabdayāki or Sano, the last Durbāwa, who, by means of a trick, gained the throne and killed the chief.

inhabited by Gwari, whose economy was based on slave-raiding, remained pagan until the Fulbe conquest. Although they added a Muslim name to their other names most of the rulers do not appear to have made even a profession of Islam.

Islamic influence came to the Hausa from many directions, through the pilgrim traffic, trade relations with North Africa and western Sudan, and the political influence of Songhay and Bornu. It gained a considerable hold in certain towns, to the heterogeneity of which the names of their quarters, especially in Katsina, bear witness, but though many of its cultural by-products entered the village civilization Islam left the religious life of the cultivators untouched. The pilgrimage became popular and has ever since played a considerable part in the diffusion of Islamic usages in central Sudan. The arrival of clerics from western Sudan and Bornu in the fifteenth century aided the accomplishment of the urban religious revolution in Kano town. We read that during the reign of Yaʿqūb (1452–63):

> Fellāta came to Hausaland from Malī bringing the disciplines of *tawḥīd* (dogmatics) and grammar. Formerly our knowledge, apart from the Qur'ān, was limited to *ʿilm al-fiqh* (jurisprudence) and *ḥadīth* (tradition). They went on to Bornu leaving a few behind in Hausaland with their slaves and those who were unable to travel.[1]

This sounds like a considerable migration of Tokolor clerics. During the reign of Yaʿqūb's successor, Muḥammad Rimfa (1463–99), the arrival of more missionaries is recorded. According to as-Saʿdī the grandfather of Aḥmad Bābā on his return from pilgrimage (1485) visited Kano and other Hausa towns and gave lectures to students.[2] The Kano Chronicle records:

> During his reign *sharīfs* came to Kano consisting of ʿAbd ar-Raḥmān and his followers. The story goes that the Prophet came to ʿAbd ar-Raḥmān in a dream and said to him, 'Rise and go west and strengthen Islam'.... (He was welcomed by Rimfa) and confirmed Islam in this town for he had brought with him many books. He advised Rimfa to build a Friday mosque. He cut down the (sacred) tree and built a minaret[3] on its site. When he had reinforced Islam and the number of *ʿulamā* had increased in the town and Islam had become universal over its territory ʿAbd al-Karīm (*sic*) returned to Egypt, leaving behind his deputy, Sīdi Fari.[4]

[1] Kano Chronicle, text p. 42; *Sud. Mem.* iii. 111.

[2] *T. as-Sūdān*, p. 37/61.

[3] *Ṣawmaʿ*, Hausa *sūmiya* and *hasūmiya*. This may refer to the building of a mosque-tower rather than a minaret.

[4] Text pp. 43–44; *Sud. Mem.* iii. 111. The ʿAbd ar-Raḥmān first referred to came from Medina.

The Chronicle also states that Rimfa established the custom of *kulle* (wife seclusion) and that 'he was the first to observe the *'īd* prayers at Shādokōn'.[1] The 'Abd al-Karīm referred to was probably that forceful character Muḥammad ibn 'Abd al-Karīm al-Majhīlī[2] and he appears to have had a disciple called 'Abd ar-Raḥmān. He taught *'ilm al-Qur'ān* in Katsina and jurisprudence in Kano, and wrote a treatise on government for Rimfa.[3] He left Kano for Kawkaw in 1502. During the reign of Muḥammad Kisōki (1509–65) many more *fuqahā'* arrived who taught for the first time 'Iyāḍ ibn Mūsā's *Shifā'*, Saḥnūn's *Mudawwana*, Suyūṭī's *al-Jāmi' aṣ-ṣaghīr*, and the books of as-Samarqandī.[4] One of these jurists was made *qāḍī* of Kano.[5] Evidence of an attempt to make Islam the state religion is given in the Katsina record. This states that Ibrāhīm Mājē (1494–1520) 'ordered the people of Katsina to marry' (presumably to follow Islamic practice), mark out prayer-squares, and observe ritual prayer, those who did not comply being imprisoned.[6] As-Sa'dī mentions Berber clerics from Timbuktu who taught in Katsina and Kano.[7] Consequently these two places assumed certain Islamic features like the Friday prayer ceremonial which enhanced the prestige of the ruler,[8] the institution of *qāḍīs* in the chief centres, and the taxation system.

About this time we have the first outside reference to some of these states in the account of Leo Africanus. He mentions after Gago (Kawkaw), the states of Guber, Agades, Cano, Casena, Zegzeg, Zanfara, Guangara, Borno, and Gaoga (the Bulāla state of Kanem?). Leo gives us the only account of Wangāra that we possess. He says that it lay

[1] Text p. 45; *Sud. Mem.* iii. 112.

[2] On this cleric see above, p. 98. He is known in Hausaland as Shaikh al-Baghdādī, but this seems to be a confusion with Maḥmūd al-Baghdādī, an immigrant missionary to Air, killed (*c.* 1640) by the pagan Kel Owey (cf. M. Belo, *Infāq*, p. 16). A *maqām* bearing his name is found at Taghist in Air (see Barth, *Travels*, i. 386–7). Barth also mentions a tradition which ascribes the introduction of Islam into Dawra to 'a man from Baghdad, of the name of Mohammed 'Ali, who killed the dodó, or the old fetish lion' (*Travels*, ii. 560).

[3] Published in Kano by the Katsina Native Administration and translated by T. H. Baldwin, *The Obligations of Princes*, Beyrout, 1932. According to Aḥmad Bābā (*Takmilat ad-Dībāj*, Cairo, 1329/1911, p. 331) it was composed at the request of the ruler of Kano.

[4] Probably Abū'l-Laith as-Samarqandī, *Tanbīh al-ghāfilīn* or *Bustān al-'Ārifīn*.

[5] See Kano Chronicle, *Sud. Mem.* iii. 113.

[6] *Sud. Mem.* iii. 81. During his reign (*c.* 1513) *askiya* Muḥammad sent an expedition against Katsina; *Fattāsh*, p. 77/147.

[7] Among them Makhlūf ibn 'Alī, d. 1533–4 (*T. as-Sūdān*, p. 64), and at-Tazakhtī who became *qāḍī* of Katsina where he died in 1529–30 (op. cit., pp. 64–65).

[8] When Kutumbi of Kano (1623–48) 'went to war or to *ṣallā* he was followed by a hundred spare horses, forty drums were in front of him, and twenty-five trumpets, and fifty kettle-drums' (*Sud. Mem.* iii. 119).

south-east of Zamfara,[1] and until recently had been commercially important and powerful, its king having a standing army of 7,000 archers and 500 horsemen, but at the time he was writing reverses in wars had reduced its influence. It was menaced by the *askiya* (the Kanta?) from the west and Bornu from the east. The latter's attempt at conquest had to be abandoned in consequence of war with the prince of Gaoga. Wangāra must have disappeared soon after this, absorbed by the *kanta* of Kebbi and Katsina.

We are not concerned with the detailed history of these little states, which is in fact very obscure, but it was within the power of any one of them to have built up an empire like those of the West. The only attempt to do so was made by the *kanta* of Kebbi. The Kebbi (correctly Kabi) region lies east of Dendi, between the Zarma and the Hausa, its people according to tradition being a mixture of the two, 'The people of Kabi are descended, according to what we are told, from a Katsina mother and a Songhay father.'[2] At the beginning of the sixteenth century Kotal (or Ṣāliḥ), a local chief of Leka near Gandi, built up an army and succeeded in overrunning many western Hausa states and rendering them tributary. Two years later he assisted the *askiya* to conquer Air (1514–15). When it came to the division of the spoil the *askiya* demanded a third of the tribute of the Hausa states in return for his assistance and the two quarrelled. The *kanta* attacked and defeated the *askiya*'s troops and the latter abandoned any hopes he had of ruling Hausaland.[3] Air (Hausa: Abzen or Azben), the centre of a settled Tuareg polity whose capital of Agadez was founded about 1438,[4] seems to have paid tribute to both the *askiyas* and *kantas* with effective control in the hands of the latter.[5] The *kanta* was also in control of Gurma and the eastern Songhay as far as Tera.[6]

[1] H. R. Palmer suggests (*J.A. Soc.* xxxvi, 1927–8, 218) that it was in Katsina-Laka, north-west of Zaria.

[2] Muḥammad Belo, *Infāq al-Maisūr*, p. 19.

[3] The fragment translated in *Fattāsh* says that the Katsina expedition was in 1512–13, the Agadez expedition in 1514–15, the *kanta*'s break with and victory over the *askiya*'s troops in 1516, and a second victory the following year. In this fragment the *kanta* is called Ṣāliḥ (p. 339), and in the *T. as-Sūdān* as Kotal, chief of Līki (pp. 129–30). Maḥmud al-Kāti says (p. 77/147) that the expedition against Katsina was in A.H. 919 (1513–14).

[4] The Berbers were in control of Air in al-'Umarī's time (A.D. 1342; see *Masālik*, p. 94). The chronicle of Agadez states that Yūnis, the first chief of this line, came to power in A.H. 807 (A.D. 1404–5); *Mission Tilho*, ii. 482; *J. Soc. Afr.* iv (1934), 151. According to Marmol (cf. Barth, i. 459) Agadez was built in 1460.

[5] The islamization of the Tuareg of Air was the work of a succession of migrant clerics from western Adrār. It was so shallow that the *mai* of Bornu, 'Alī b. 'Umar, in a campaign against them in 1658, spared the life of their captured *amīr* on condition that he became a Muslim (Palmer, *Bornu Sahara*, p. 35).

[6] Barth, *Travels*, v. 319.

The *kanta*'s 'empire' followed the usual Sudan lines. The Zarma and Hausa chiefs were left in control of their people with the exception of parts of Zamfara, Ader, and Wangāra which were absorbed into his personal state. He established his capital at Surāmē in his native district and built a powerful fortress at Gungu nearby. The centre of his power was therefore on the western extremity of Hausa country.[1] *Askiya* Muḥammad Bengan attacked him and suffered a disastrous defeat.[2] The *kanta* was killed about 1545 when returning to his country after winning victories over the forces of 'Alī ibn Idrīs of Bornu.[3] The next *kanta*, Muḥammad (d. 1561), was in conflict with *askiya* Da'ūd in 1552 but concluded a treaty of peace the following year.[4]

The successors of the first *kanta* were only able to maintain their power over these states for half a century. Had they been capable they might have built upon the foundation he laid down a power capable of rivalling that of Bornu. Muḥammad Belo writes:

> After *kanta* their power endured about a hundred years without weakening until Sarkin Gobir, Muḥammad ibn Chiroma, rose against them, together with Agaba ibn Muḥammad, Sarkin Ahīr (Air),[5] and Sarkin Zamfara. Each of these chiefs took possession of the towns which were near to him. But it was Sarkin Zamfara who conquered the greater part and ruined the three principal cities [i.e. Gungu, Leka, and Surāmē].[6]

This defeat by the Zamfarāwa led to the abandonment of Surāmē about 1715 and the building of Birnin Kebbi by Tomo as the new capital. The kingdom of Kebbi maintained itself as a reduced state, and, owing to its position and the energy of its inhabitants, enjoyed for a time a peaceful life. They repulsed the Fulbe vigorously and, though they lost most of their territory, were able to maintain their existence in Argungu as a tiny state until the British occupation.

In spite of the constant internecine struggles and the attacks of neighbouring states like Jukun[7] and Bornu, many Hausa states

[1] The Fulbe later chose the same region for their twin capitals of Sokoto and Gwando.

[2] *T. as-Sūdān*, p. 88/146.

[3] *Infāq al-Maisūr*, p. 20. 'Alī reigned one year only and the event may have occurred during the reign of his predecessor Muḥammad b. Idrīs (1529–45).

[4] *T. as-Sūdān*, pp. 168–9, 173.

[5] Agaba won the territory of Adar from *kanta* Sulaimān and was invested by his father as its first chief (1674–87), tributary to Air. The name Adar (Tamāhaqq 'limb') derives from this time. The people of the territory were pagan Hausa-speakers (see *Mission Tilho*, ii. 483–4).

[6] M. Belo, *Infāq al-Maisūr*, pp. 20–21. The *sarākuna* involved were Babba b. Muḥammad of Zamfara, Muḥammad b. Agaba of Ahīr (1687–1720), Aḥmad of Kabi (1700–25), and Muḥammad b. Chiroma (1694–1720).

[7] The Jukun state was situated on the right bank of the Benue with its capital at Pi

advanced in material prosperity through the labours of their cultivators, the justly renowned skill of their craftsmen, and the keenness of their traders. Katsina, the most important commercial town, acquired a reputation for Islamic learning during the reign of Jan Hazo Bakki (1618–48). For a time its power extended over Marāḍi in the north, Zamfara in the west, and Birnin Gwari in the south, but with the rise to power of Gobir its sphere of rule diminished. Kano, noted as a centre for dyeing and leather work, was at this time not very important as a commercial city. It had a very troubled history, eighty years of war with Katsina (1570–1650), devastated on a number of occasions by the Jukun who were at the apogee of their power during the seventeenth century, and subjected to repeated attacks from Bornu, Zamfara, and Gobir. Yet though a tributary state except under a few energetic rulers Kano was stated in 1585 to be as large as Kawkaw which an unofficial census computed as having 7,626 *windi* (family compounds),[1] that is a minimum of 60,000 settled inhabitants. Zamfara which had grown in strength with the decline of Kebbi was steadily weakening during the eighteenth century. Its capital was destroyed by Babari of Gobir (*c.* 1743–62) who founded his capital Alḳalawa in former Zamfara territory (1173/1759). Gobir continued to ravage what was left of it until the Fulbe conquest. Gobir was important as a buffer state keeping the Tuareg at bay after the power of Kebbi declined. When eventually it succeeded in throwing the Tuareg back and relieving the Hausa regions from the menace of their expansion, it turned its attention to the subjection of its Hausa neighbours, and by the middle of the eighteenth century was the paramount Hausa power.

4. THE STATE OF BAGIRMI

When we turn to the country lying to the east and south of Kanem we find ourselves in a region where live small groups of peoples of diverse origins over whom the *mais* of Kanem and their Bulāla successors did not exercise any direct rule though they often levied tribute. In the sixteenth century, through adventurers forming a cohesive nucleus, adopting Islam, and increasing their sphere of influence, two historical kingdoms, Bagirmi and Waday, make their appearance.

South of the Bulāla of Kanem was the Kūka kingdom, formerly

(Hausa: Kwararafa) south of the river. It was a theocratic state with a divine ruler. The first historical mention of it is in the Kano Chronicle in the reign of Yāji (1349–85); see Palmer, *Sud. Mem.* iii. 106.

[1] See *Fattāsh*, pp. 145–6/262.

powerful, centred on Lake Fitri with a capital at Yaw, which levied tribute on the bands of semi-nomadic Fulbe and Baqqāra tribes of northern Bagirmi, the district lying south-east of the Chad. About A.D. 1500–20 pagan Kenga immigrants[1] under a leader called Dokkenge or Birni Besi (1522–36) allied themselves with the Fulbe against attacks of the Kūka of Fitri who suffered a number of reverses. Dokkenge imposed his authority over four small chieftaincies and founded the settlement of Masenya. Gradually the group subdued neighbouring peoples and their authority was accepted by the Arabs and Fulbe. Barth was told that on their arrival they found one Fellāta shaikh living near Masenya, 'who, however isolated he was, nevertheless exercised a very remarkable influence over the introduction of Islamism into these countries'.[2] At any rate in the reign of Mālo (1548–68) we find his younger brother, ʿAbd Allāh, disputing the succession on religious grounds. ʿAbd Allāh (1568–1608) was eventually victorious with the help of pagan tribes. He introduced some Islamic institutions, thus giving the state greater unity, although the people undoubtedly remained pagan. He formed a despotic monarchy, taking the title of *mbang*, and organized a military and administrative system with titled functionaries much on the lines of those of Bornu from whose system he probably drew his inspiration. ʿAbd Allāh also extended the influence of his state, making the Kūka and Medogo pay tribute. Idrīs Alawma made Bagirmi tributary during his campaigns,[3] but after his death the rulers threw off their allegiance. About this time clerics who had caused trouble in Bornu took refuge in Bagirmi, among them Waladaidi (d. *c.* 1600) who prophesied the advent of a *mujaddid* or reformer.[4] Burgumanda (1635–41) was an active campaigner, attacking Sokoro, Mandara, Musgu, and other Chadian tribes and plundering the Arabs. He directed one ambitious expedition through Fitri to Borqu (Waday) and Kawār. This is probably the period when the Bulāla, driven from Kanem by the Tunjur, finally imposed themselves over the Kūka of Fitri and founded Yawo as their capital.[5]

[1] According to Barth's information their former centre was Kenga Mataya, five days east of Masenya; *Travels*, iii. 432. The sacred symbols of the kingdom were a long spear of peculiar make borne before the *mbang* on ceremonial occasions, a small tympanum, and a horn or bugle, which were brought from Kenga (see Barth, iii. 401–2, 432, 609–10).

[2] Barth, op. cit. iii. 433.

[3] Palmer, *Sud. Mem.* iii. 161–2; cf. Ibn Furtuwa in *Sud. Mem.* i. 32.

[4] M. Belo, *Infāq al-Maisūr*, p. 7.

[5] The Bulāla, Muslims in name, claimed to despise the *kirdi* (pagans). They were a ruling class rather than a people and acquired the language of their subjects. They now speak Kūka and all know Shoan Arabic. The Kūka adopted Islam about this time (see Barth, iii. 427–30).

By now the Bagirmians had been formed. They are a mixture of the various groups of aborigines given coherence and individuality by coming under the rule of a small settlement of Kenga. But within the region were also Shuwa and Fulbe tribes, colonies of Kanuri, and many unassimilated pagan tribes such as the Sara, Gabari, Tumok, and Nyellem. In addition, they had acquired a number of tributaries: the country of the Bona and Kirdi (lit. 'pagans') on the right bank of the Shari, Degana towards the Baḥr al-Ghazāl, Dekakire a mountainous region to the west, and Khozām and Debaba bordering on Waday.

As a result of its expansion Bagirmi came into conflict with Bornu and Waday, and from henceforth its history is one of continual conflict with these states and of slave-raiding expeditions among pagan tribes. It recognized in a vague way the suzerainty of Bornu,[1] but *mbang* Muḥammad al-Amīn (1751–85) rejected such claims and carried Bagirmi to the peak of its power. This ruler went on pilgrimage to Mecca and during his reign his subjects were required to make a profession of Islam. The usual legend was acquired that the founder of the dynasty was an Arab immigrant from Yemen. Yet the influence of Islamic law was very weak; his successor, ʿAbd ar-Raḥmān Gwarang (1785–1806), married his own sister, and this was taken by ʿAbd al-Karīm Ṣābūn of Waday as a pretext for an invasion.[2]

5. THE STATE OF WADAY

Waday appears to be the southern part of the region of Berkāmī (Borku) mentioned by Ibn Saʿīd:

> To the south of the land of Kawār is the great mountain range of Lūnyā (Tibesti?) which stretches from west to east. The northern part of this range is occupied by the Berkāmī, a Negro people who inhabit the gorges planted with palms, irrigated, and clothed in verdure. That section of the Berkāmī which neighbours Kānem professes Islam; that which touches the Nubians professes Christianity; and that which adjoins the country of the Zaghāwa worships idols. The Zaghāwa occupy the plains situated to the south of the mountain. The land of Kawār is terminated in the north by the mountain of Ghargha[3] which extends from west to east.[4]

Islam was late in spreading into the Waday region. This was due to some extent to the barrier interposed by the Zaghāwa tribes which

[1] *Circa* 1595, 1650/75, and in 1740.
[2] M. Belo, *Infāq al-Maisūr*, p. 5; Barth, *Travels*, iii. 441.
[3] Ghargha may be Kapka or Gabaga, north of Waday.
[4] Aboulfèda, ii. 218–19; cf. al-Idrīsī, pp. 34, 35, 38.

nomadized throughout all the northern part of the region. At-Tūnisī[1] mentions as the five 'aboriginal' tribes of Waday who could not be enslaved, the Dājo, Maṣālīṭ, Mīma, Kashmara, and Qura'ān, but in fact the population of Waday proper is very mixed, though they belong to the same ethnic group and speak related languages.

Local tradition does not carry us very far back and refers to the existence of a state in the Waday region which was overthrown by Tunjur invaders at the beginning of the sixteenth century. The Tunjur fixed their capital at Kadama (south-west of Abeshe). The Tunjur were probably Nubians who, through contact with Arabs, had become Arabic-speaking.[2] They installed themselves in Darfur about the fifteenth century, wrested the power from the Dājo, and remained in control until their supremacy was overthrown by Sulaimān Soloñ about the year 1630. From Darfur the Tunjur spread into Waday and south to the borders of Bagirmi.

Certain Tunjur rulers had Arabic names and made a profession of Islam, but they made no attempt to force it upon the heterogeneous groups from whom they exacted tribute as did the dynasty which succeeded them. Tradition says that the first to preach Islam amongst the population was one called either Jāmē (al-Jām'ī?) or Ṣāliḥ, whom the genealogists connect with the Ja'liyyīn of the Shendi district of the Nile.[3] In A.H. 1020 (A.D. 1611)[4] a son or nephew of this preacher called 'Abd al-Karīm (also Muḥammad aṣ-Ṣāliḥ[5]) gathered around him Māba and Kodoy[6] who had been converted by his father (or uncle) and, with the help of the Ngalaka, Mīma, and Maḥāmid and other Arabs, waged what was called a *jihād* against the Tunjur. Having destroyed the army of the Tunjur chief Da'ūd[7] he became the first

[1] M. at-Tūnisī, *Voyage au Ouaday*, transl. Perron, 1851, pp. 245–8.

[2] H. Carbou writes, 'The tradition of the Tunjur also mentions a sojourn of their tribes on the banks of the Nile' (*La Région du Tchad et du Ouadai*, 1912, i. 74). Barth also says that they came from Dongola (*Travels*, iii. 430).

[3] Nachtigal, *Sahara und Sudan*, iii. 449 ff. Cf. a different account in Barth, *Travels*, iii. 528–30.

[4] According to the tradition given by Barth, op. cit. iii. 528. But a date around 1630–40 seems more likely.

[5] It was after him that Waday came to be called Dār Ṣāliḥ or Ṣulaiḥ. The word Waday is said to come from an ancestor called Wadā'a (see chronicle in Palmer, *Sud. Mem.* ii. 25). Waday is also referred to as Dār Māba, and the people of Darfur prefer the old term Borqu.

[6] Kodoy, derived from *kodok*, 'mountain', is the name given by the Wadayans to all the peoples inhabiting the mountainous regions south of Abeshe. The centre of the new movement was the mountain of Ab Sunūn whose inhabitants, the Senāwiyya, became the aristocracy (see M. at-Tūnisī, op. cit., pp. 245–6).

[7] The Tunjur moved into Kanem, defeated the Bulāla, and compelled the Arab tribes to pay

Kōlak al-ʿAbbāsī, the title he chose for his dynasty.[1] He made Wāra (north-north-west of Abeshe), the site of Jāmē's settlement, his capital, and his dynasty lasted until 1911. Like former rulers he continued to pay tribute to both Darfur and Bornu which often threatened to restore the Tunjur. Subsequent *kōlaks* attempted to throw off the very nominal suzerainty of Darfur but were unsuccessful until Muḥammad Jawda (1745–95), an energetic chief who also undertook expeditions against pagans in the south. At the end of the eighteenth century Muḥammad Ṣāliḥ (or Sūlē) took possession of Fitri and reached Kanem.

During this period we have evidence of other *fuqahā'* from the Funj kingdom of Sennār teaching in Waday, among them Abū Zaid b. ʿAbd al-Qādir who taught during the reign of *kōlak* Yaʿqūb ʿArūs (Hārūt II, 1681–1707) and Abū Surūr al-Faḍlī who was murdered by his own concubines in Waday.[2] Pupils from Waday also travelled to the Nile to study under shaikhs like Az-Zain ibn Ṣughayyirūn (d. 1675),[3] whilst merchant clerics like Ḥasan wad Ḥasūna (d. 1664) sent trading expeditions to Dār Borqū.[4]

tribute. Later they were subdued by the Bornuans, but regained control for a short time in the nineteenth century with the help of Waday, and finally they were subjected by the Awlād Sulaimān when they invaded Kanem (see Carbou, op. cit. i, chap. 3).

[1] The title of al-ʿAbbāsī is derived from ʿAbd al-Karīm's pretensions to an Arab origin.

[2] See *Ṭabaqāt* of Wad Ḍaif Allāh, ed. Mandīl, Khartoum, p. 32.

[3] Ibid., p. 17.

[4] *Ṭabaqāt* of Wad Ḍaif Allāh, ed. Ibrāhīm Ṣidaiq, p. 47.

4

Islamic Stagnation and Pagan Reaction

I. THE SUDAN DURING THE SEVENTEENTH AND EIGHTEENTH CENTURIES

THE period between the collapse of Songhay and the formation of Islamic theocracies forms an interregnum of eclipse in the fortunes of Islam. The Moorish invasion marks a decisive stage. After it the Sudan returned to its characteristic pattern of small independent states. In religion it was marked by the eclipse of Islamic universalism and the ascendancy of local religions. Islam was neutralized by being emptied of all elements of challenge to African ways of life and Muslims were accommodated into Negro society.

The relative safety of travel in the southern Sahara during the time of the Negro empires had been a great achievement. The attempt of the Berbers under the Murābiṭūn to gain control failed because they were unable to combine; and, for the same reason, those in the west fell under the control of Arab tribes who reduced them to the status of vassals. Its security, broken by the downfall of Songhay, was not restored until the French occupation. For centuries it was a land of warfare where nomad tribes competed for life by pillaging and levying tolls on caravans. Their inroads on the borders drove away Negro cultivators and reduced many areas to desert.

In the Sudan few political organizations embracing many different groups were formed until the nineteenth century. Those of Māli and Songhay split into their constituent sections and the Mossi kingdoms alone remained unaffected by the events around them. It was an age of petty chieftaincies, each striving to maintain its independence and raid its neighbours. In the upper Mande region two Bambara states, Segu and Karta, formed and eventually dominated a wide area, forcing the Islamic centres of Timbuktu and Jennē to pay tribute. Yet in spite of the apparent anarchy and insecurity trade still went on and thousands of new Mande trading settlements were founded through which Islam gained representatives among pagan peoples as far as the forest zone.[1]

[1] Portuguese travellers attest to their widespread activities along the Atlantic coast; they even penetrated the forest and traded with Portuguese on the Gold Coast (see Pacheco, *Esmeraldo*, transl. G. H. T. Kimble, 1937, p. 120). Europeans now begin to influence the fortunes of West Africa though their action was only peripheral. As they set up bases along

Central Sudan was also full of petty states. The Hausa have no historical unity, only a history of mutually antagonistic town states. The attempt of the *kanta* of Kebbi to dominate them failed under his successors. The Kwararafa or Jukun power, so formidable during the sixteenth century, disintegrated rapidly. During the fifteenth century petty states proliferated on the ruins of Kanem. Bornu, to which its old rulers migrated, though only one of many states in the area, gradually stabilized and expanded, reaching the height of its power during the sixteenth century. During the next two centuries it declined gradually, though its appearance of strength and solidarity proved sufficient to deter most invaders. South and east of the Chad were hundreds of small political groupings, among which the Muslim states of Kanem, Bagirmi, and Waday may be distinguished.

A religious revolution during the fifteenth and sixteenth centuries completely transformed the relationship of the Berbers of western Sahara towards Islam,[1] but this was a depressed period for Islamic culture in the Sudan. Islam had touched the cultivators but lightly. Pagan rulers were tolerant of Muslims in their midst. Their form of reaction was not persecution but neutralization. Jibrīl ibn ʿUmar, teacher and forerunner of ʿUthmān ḍan Fodio, writes of the religious parallelism which formed the justification for the *jihād*:

What took place in Bilād as-Sūdān in regard to the intermingling of heathenish and Islamic practices by the majority of the kings of these countries and their subjects was not so much a matter of *bidʿa*, or *taḥrīf*, or *taghyīr*, or following local custom, as the downright heathenism in which they indulged, since it is not related that any one of them ever abandoned such practices otherwise we should have heard. Whether ignorant or intelligent they supposed, when they adopted the enlightenment of prayer and fasting and pronounced the unity of God, that they were Muslims, but undoubtedly they were not.[2]

the Atlantic coast they affected to some extent the commercial currents along west Saharan routes and contributed to the decline of places like Sijilmāsa. As exterior Arabic sources fail us Portuguese travellers take their place, though their contribution is of value for coastal regions rather than the interior for which our primary sources remain internal.

[1] After the expulsion of the Moors from Spain there was a revival of religious fervour in North Africa and 'maraboutism' took its definitive form. Old Berber names were replaced by Arabic names derived from a holy eponym. In the Sahara a Berber counter-revolution against Arab domination caused them to adapt Arabic and make Islam their special preserve by the formation of clerical clans. There was a widespread persecution of Saharan Jews which led to their conversion to Islam. Although the active participation of the Moorish *zwāya* or clerical tribes in Sudan affairs was not very great their Islamic influence has some bearing on the outburst of a new form of Negro political Islam.

[2] Quoted by Muḥammad Belo, *Infāq al-Maisūr*, p. 184. On Jibrīl b. ʿUmar see ʿAbd

The position of the Muslim clerical-trading class within the Negro world should be clearly understood. Dyula formed trading villages over a vast area. They were less attached to the land than other Negroes, their agriculture being done by the slaves their trading activities enabled them to purchase, and could make long expeditions or transfer their whole family with ease. By the fifteenth/sixteenth century they had formed hundreds of settlements all over western Guinea from the Gambia to Liberia (with Kankan as the best-known settlement), in northern Ivory Coast (Mankono, Kadioha, Bong, and Kong), and in the Voltaic region (Mossi, Dafina, Bobo, Senufo, and Gonja countries). They were accommodating and adopted many customs as well as wives from the local people. They were not sharply distinguished from their neighbours but fitted into the framework of their society. They did not regard themselves as living a peculiar life in a pagan environment but as sharing in its life.[1] Consequently they were not a disrupting element. We have stressed this aspect of African Islam because it was just against this spirit of accommodation that the reformers of the nineteenth century set themselves and when the wars of religion began such traders were regarded as *soroṇge*, 'sacrificers'. Muslims were accepted as a natural class, one whose members could carry their religion around with them. They were not proselytizers of Islam, but sellers of protective charms.[2] Although agents of Islamic cultural diffusion they would never have transformed African life. That was the work of an entirely different type of cleric for whom it must be admitted they paved the way. At the time when the remarkable renaissance of Islamic power began at the end of the eighteenth century Islam was little more than the religion of the people of the Sahil and

Allāh dan Fodio, *Tazyīn al-Waraqāt*, in *Der Islam*, x. 16. The technical terms employed are unsuitable in this context, but Jibrīl's vocabulary was limited by the nature of his reading.

[1] At the same time they preserved Islamic characteristics and remained a distinct element. Like griots, blacksmiths, and other occupational groups they were outside the sphere of inter-village warfare. R. Jobson, who travelled in the Gambia at the beginning of the seventeenth century, wrote (*The Golden Trade*, 1623, reprod. 1904, pp. 97–99), 'These Mary-buckes are a people, who dispose themselves in generall, when they are in their able age to travaile, going in whole families together, and carrying along their bookes, and manuscripts, and their boyes or younger race with them, whom they teach and instruct in any place they rest.... One chief reason to encourage their travell, we have learned, which is, that they have free recourse through all places, so that howsoever the Kings and Countries are at warres, and up in armes, the one against the other, yet still the Mary-bucke is a priviledged person, and many follow his trade, or course of travelling, without let or interruption of either side.' Other early European travellers write in similar terms. Mary-bucke is either *mōri-ba* or a corruption of *murābiṭ*.

[2] R. Jobson (op. cit., pp. 63–64) mentions their immense trade in 'gregories', that is, grigris or amulets.

traders, practised only in certain towns and among certain groups: Tokolor in Senegalese Futa, scattered groups of negroid Fulbe as in Futa Jalon and Māsina, western Songhay, Soninke in upper Senegal and the Sahil, Dyula colonies, a few Hausa towns, and by the dominant classes of Bornu, Waday, and Bagirmi.

2. THE COLLAPSE OF SONGHAY AND ITS CONSEQUENCES

Such remote events as the conquest of Granada in 1492, followed ten years later by the expulsion of Muslims from Spain, as well as Portuguese expeditions to the Atlantic coast of Africa, had repercussions in the Sudan. At that time the Mediterranean world was experiencing monetary and economic difficulties, one cause being the draining away of Sudanese gold by Portuguese traders, and Aḥmad al-Manṣūr, Sa'did sultan of Morocco, feeling himself hemmed in between Spain and Algeria under the Turks and obsessed by the mirage of Sudanese gold, turned his ambitions towards conquest beyond the Sahara. The immediate cause of the conquest of Songhay is ascribed to disputes over the salt deposits of Taghāza which lay on the borderland between Morocco and Songhay and were valued by both powers for their importance in connexion with trade. In 1581 Sultan Aḥmad took possession of the oases of Tawāt and Tigūrārīn; in 1585 he seized Taghāza but soon lost possession. In 1590 he raised an expeditionary force of 4,000 men consisting of Moroccan and Andalusian Muslims under Jūdar Pasha. After the remarkable feat of taking this large force across the Sahara in 135 days, a journey our sources pass over almost in silence, they met the Songhay army, which according to a Moroccan source was accompanied by medicine-men.[1] In spite of their superior numbers the Songhay were no match for the brutal disciplined European musketeers. Entering Kawkaw unopposed they found to their disappointment that it consisted of an agglomeration of mud and thatch huts which had been emptied of whatever treasures they possessed by the fleeing inhabitants.[2] Jūdar, therefore, evacuated Kawkaw and occupied Timbuktu without opposition.

A detailed account of the rule of these conquistadors over that limited part of the former Songhay empire they controlled, to which

[1] Al-Wafrānī, *Nuzhat al-Ḥādī*, p. 93/104; cf. as-Sa'dī, *T. as-Sūdān*, p. 102/168. These were no doubt griots or genealogical singers, one of whose functions was to excite the warriors.

[2] Cf. *Hespéris*, iii. 472–3; as-Sa'dī, transl. pp. 220–1.

the relative abundance of historical material might tempt us,[1] would be disproportionate to the scale of this study, but the effect of the rule of a military caste may be judged from the following quotation from as-Saʿdī who points the contrast between the relative tranquillity and prosperity of the country under the rule of the *askiyas* and the disorder which followed the invasion:

The Sudan was one of God's most favoured countries in prosperity and fertility at the time this expeditionary force entered the country. Peace and security reigned in all parts thanks to the beneficient rule of the Prince of Believers, Askiya al-ḥājj Muḥammad, whose justice and firm rule was so respected that orders issued from his palace were executed in the most distant parts of his kingdom, from the frontiers of the country of Dendi to those of al-Ḥamdiyya, and from the confines of the country of Bonduku to Taghāza and Tawāt, as well as in all their dependencies. Now all that has changed. Security has given place to danger, prosperity to misery and calamity, whilst affliction and distress have succeeded wellbeing. Over the length and breadth of the land the people began devouring one another, raiding and war sparing neither life nor wealth nor status, disorder spreading and intensifying until it became universal.[2]

The result of the chaos caused by the invasion was that the old empire broke up into its constituent parts, and the various peoples it had embraced became independent. The Fulbe of Māsina began raiding the Negro cultivators, those of Donko raided the Ra's al-Mā' region, the Zaghrānians[3] devastated Bara and Dirma, the Bambara ravaged the province of Jennē, whilst the Tuareg became ever more and more aggressive against the riverain peasantry of the Niger buckle 'from Gao to Jennē'.[4] Fields went out of cultivation and disastrous famines swept the country. As-Saʿdī describes such a famine which occurred in 1618:

[1] This calamity and the subsequent course of the history of the Niger bend is unusually well documented from both Moroccan, Sudanese, and even European sources. Among them we may mention: As-Saʿdī, *Ta'rīkh as-Sūdān*, 1898 and 1900; Maḥmūd Kāti, *Ta'rīkh al-Fattāsh*, 1913; al-Wafrānī, *Nuzhat al-Ḥādī* (History of the Saʿdian dynasty, 1511–1670), ed. and transl. O. Houdas, Paris, 1888–9; H. de Castries, *Les Sources inédites de l'histoire du Maroc*, serie i, vol. v: Dynastie Saadienne, Paris, 1911; *Tadhkirat an-Nisyān*, ed. and transl. O. Houdas, Paris, 1901; E. Fagnon, *Extraits Inédits Relatifs au Maghrib*, Algiers, 1924, pp. 416–17, 456–7; H. de Castries, 'La Conquête du Soudan par El-Mansour', *Hespéris*, iii (1923), 433–88; E. Lévi-Provençal, 'Un Document inédit sur l'expédition saʿdide au Soudan', *Arabica*, ii (1955), 89–96.

[2] *T. as-Sūdān*, pp. 142–3 (222–3).

[3] Zaghrāna appears to be Soninke *dyō-gorani*, Mande *dyō goro*, equivalent to the Fulbe serf groups known as Dyāwambe in the western and Zoghoran (Hausa Zoromāwa) in central Sudan.

[4] *T. as-Sūdān*, p. 143 (223); *Fattāsh*, pp. 181–2 (317).

The situation became increasingly critical, each day being worse than the preceding. This year the rains failed and the people went out to perform the ritual prayers for rain (*al-istisqā'*). They persisted for 14 days during which the sky remained cloudless, then it rained only a little. A grave famine afflicted the Timbuktu region during which a large number of people died. They were reduced to eating the carcases of dead beasts and human beings. The exchange rate fell to 500 cowries. Then followed a pestilence which carried off many who had survived the famine.[1]

Over the limited region they controlled the Moroccans did not disrupt the basic structure, but like their predecessors applied a form of protectorate. The people observed their own laws and customs, local functionaries were maintained, and they even kept a puppet *askiya* at the head of the native hierarchy. The pasha, nominated at first by the sultan of Morocco, was governor-general with supreme authority only in theory. Alongside him was an *amīn*, a kind of financial secretary, also nominated by the sultan, who limited the effective authority of the pasha since he was in complete control of the finances. Even officers of the army were directly appointed by the Moroccan sultan. Such a system of divided authority could not last long, given the difficulty of communication with Morocco, and the pashas generally acted on their own authority. This led to a sharing of power between two pashas, the commander of the troops and the administrator, and then the *amīn* came into conflict with them both. The result was that the army took advantage of the chaos to elect their own chiefs. The authority of the sultan became purely nominal[2] and the state of the elected pashas took the form of an independent sovereignty with a court and ministers.

The period during which the independent pashas ruled was one of anarchy. Timbuktu remained the capital, but the pressure of powerful neighbours such as Bambara and Tuareg restricted their sphere of effective control to the river. As their military organization weakened, other groups asserted their independence. The *arma*,[3] as the descendants of the invaders were called, became more and more negroid[4] and by the end of the eighteenth century had been absorbed into the Songhay as a superior class. In 1727 Timbuktu became tributary to Mamari Kulubāli, Bambara king of Segu. Gradually the Tuareg

[1] *T. as-Sūdān*, pp. 221–2 (338).

[2] The pronouncement of the *khuṭba* in the name of the ruling pasha instead of that of the sultan of Morocco first took place in 1070/1660; see *Tadhkirat an-Nisyān*, p. 90/145–6.

[3] Arab. *rāmin*, pl. *rumāt*, 'sharpshooter'.

[4] *Tasawdan*, 'sudanized', as the Moors say. Cf. the Arab saying, *turāb al-kuwār taqtul al-bīḍān*, 'the land of the blacks eliminates the whites'.

gained control of the whole of the Niger bend and finally destroyed the last vestige of Arma power in 1737. After raiding Gao a number of times they took it definitely in 1770 and Timbuktu in 1787.[1]

The history of the *askiya* dynasty after the conquest is of only local interest. The disaster was ascribed to the incompetency of Isḥāq who was deposed and later killed by the Gurmanshe among whom he had sought refuge. His successor Muḥammad Gao was murdered by the Moroccans under guarantee of safe conduct. The Songhay leaders then rallied around Nūḥ (1591–9) who became chief of the hard core of Songhay resistance. They began to penetrate down the river into Dendi. All Moroccan attempts to subdue them failed. As a result of old rivalries between descendants of the *askiyas* and *sīs*, aided by pressure from Zerma[2] and Fulbe in the seventeenth century and Tuareg in the eighteenth, the Dendi chieftaincy broke up into small district or village chieftaincies (Ayoru, Tera, Gornol, Namaro, and many others), although neither Fulbe nor Tuareg could penetrate deeply because of the incidence of malaria and the tsetse fly. Some groups, such as the descendants and partisans of the *askiyas*, were Muslim, whilst others, like the people of Anzuru, Tera, and the Sorko fishers who paid allegiance to the descendants of the *sīs*, were pagan.[3]

3. MANDE SUCCESSOR STATES

After the Māli empire had crumbled away, the region west of the Niger suffered from a state of complete anarchy until it was occupied by the French. When the Moroccans destroyed the Songhay state all the northern Soninke states became independent (Dyāga, Bāgana, Dyāra, Gumbu, &c.). Three rival descendants of the Keyta line ruled the central Mande region (Manding, Karadugu, and Bendugu), but its complete disintegration was not arrested and the country became

[1] *Tadhkirat an-Nisyān*, pp. 102 ff. (163 ff.) The Ullimmeden first took Gao in 1682 but were expelled by *qā'id* Manṣūr b. Mas'ūd in 1688. The author of the *Tadhkira* writes (p. 71/112–13) that in 1739 the troops of Fā-magh, the Wankore (Soninke), ravaged the territory of Jennē disrupting all commercial communications. The years 1741–3 were a period of famine when 'the Tuareg were in control of all the land of Takrūr from Hausa to Gurma [i.e. both banks of the Niger], whilst the Fulbe were masters of that part of Gurma which is in the region of islands of Arikun. They had eliminated the authority of the Arma to such a degree that the Arma paid tribute to the Tuareg' (op. cit., p. 75/120).

[2] The Zerma, who seem to derive from three tribal movements of Mande, Songhay, and Hausa, formed in Zermaganda where the tomb of their ancestor Mali Bero is situated. They migrated into the Songhay region about three centuries ago. Their traditions relate that they came from the Lake Debo region, yet their institutions link them with the east and their vocabulary contains from 15 to 20 per cent. of Hausa words.

[3] See J. Boulnois, *Empire de Gao*, 1954, p. 15.

filled with hundreds of village states of which the descendants of Sun Dyāta ruled only one.[1]

It is at the time of the Moroccan conquest that the term Bambara first makes its appearance. It is used of the pagan Mande subjects of the disrupted empire and as-Saʿdī makes a number of references to them.[2] We hear of war-leaders, such as the Sāma-ka (1591–7) who had served in the Moroccan army and learned their tactics,[3] but not of rulers of states. These men were leaders of age-groups who built up armies from captured slaves. Of such was Kaladyan Kulubāli (*c.* 1652–82), a great raider who would not be worthy of mention but for the fact that his descendant *Biton* Mamari Kulubāli (1712–55) founded the state of Segu, whilst an allied group whom he tried to destroy formed the state of Kārta.[4]

Mamari Kulubāli, as chief (*tõ-tigi*) of an age-group association which he welded into an army, gained widespread renown and a vast booty of slaves. He took Kirango (*c.* 1740), the town of the Soninke Boarē who until then had dominated the Segu country. He came into conflict with the rival clan of Māsa-Sī whose chieftaincy was then in Beledugu, taking their village of Sunsana and killing their chief Fulikoro (1754).

[1] The old Keyta dynasty has survived to this day at Kangaba, its birthplace. General Mangin wrote about them, 'Si ses héritiers actuels se souviennent vaguement que leurs pères ont commandés de grands pays et gagné beaucoup de batailles, ils ont entièrement oublié que ces ancêtres ont été des Musulmans fervents et très instruits dont les pèlerinages à la Mecque ont marqué dans les fastes de l'Islam.' Mangin, *Regards sur la France d'Afrique*, 1924, pp. 167–8.

[2] The authors of *Taʾrīkh al-Fattāsh* and *Tadhkirat an-Nisyān* employ the term 'bambara' as equivalent to 'pagan'.

[3] See as-Saʿdī, op. cit., pp. 143/223, 179–81/274–6.

[4] L. Tauxier surveys the material for the history of these states in his *Histoire des Bambara*, 1942. The following table shows the relationship of the two lines:

X

c. 1600–25

Barama-N'golo	Nia-N'golo
Kaladyan 1652–82	Sunsa *c.* 1633
Danfassari 1682–97	Māsa 1650–1710
Suma 1697–1712	Benefali 1710–45
Mamari Kulubāli 1712–55 (Founder of the Segu state)	Fulikoro 1745–54 (War with Segu)
	Sey Bamama 1754–8 (Flight and settlement in Kārta)

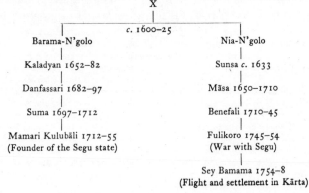

He made frequent incursions into the territory of the *arma* who were forced to pay tribute. After his death civil wars temporarily arrested the expansion of the state, but N'golo Dyāra (1766–90) triumphed over the Fulbe of Kalari and Māsina, and dominated Jennē, Sokolo, and Timbuktu, though he encountered reverses when he attacked the Mossi of Yatenga. His successor Mansong (1790–1808), who was visited by Mungo Park, warred against the Dogon and Mossi, raided Timbuktu (1803), and ravaged Kārta, Beledugu, and Fuladugu. During the reign of Da Dyāra (1808–27) Shehu Aḥmadu freed Māsina from Bambara domination and established a theocratic Islamic state. This event brought about a better relationship between the two Bambara states which had so far been marked only by bloody struggles. This other clan, the Māsa-Sī, after their defeat in 1754 had taken refuge among the Soninke of Kārta. They quickly asserted their independence and dominated the region. They have the usual history of intertribal struggles. They conquered northern Khaso in 1803 and the state reached its apogee under Bodian Moriba (1815–32) about whom Gray and Dochard give some information.

The Bambara kings give the impression of never having freed themselves from the antecedents of the founders of their lineages as chiefs of warbands, for they never developed genuine governments but simply areas of exploitation, and remained military leaders to the end when they were destroyed by an adventurer of a new type called al-ḥājj ʿUmar who entered Nyoro, capital of Kārta, in 1854 and Segu in 1861.

As Ch. Monteil shows,[1] the Bambara ruling clans had no quarrel with Islam on the Sudanese mode. Muslim traders and clerics were found in all their villages. The Soninke and Dyāwara (Kanyāga) over whom the Māsa-Sī asserted their rule were mostly Muslim, and many of the stories about ʿUmar forcing the people of Nyoro to become Muslims are probably without foundation since the Dyāwara from whom it was taken in 1847 would call themselves Muslim. Bambara rulers kept clerics at their courts and adopted Islamic customs, but without any corresponding displacement of their pagan religion upon the observance of which their power depended. Islam was not allowed to compromise the interests of the ruling clan. Thus Turo-koro Mari of Segu (1854–6) was put to death, not for joining Islam, but because he was ready to pay allegiance to al-ḥājj ʿUmar, thus imperilling the independence of the clan. ʿAlī Dyāra, faced with the approach of ʿUmar's army, sought aid from Ḥamadu III of Māsina who agreed to

[1] See Ch. Monteil, *Les Bambara du Segou et du Kaarta*, 1924, pp. 334 ff.

a defensive alliance against ʿUmar if ʿAlī would join Islam, and ʿAlī had a mosque built in Segu as a sign of the change in the rulers' religion, but, as ʿUmar later demonstrated, ʿAlī did not in fact get rid of his 'idols'.[1]

4. FULBE STATES AND THEIR RESISTANCE TO ISLAM

Fulbe nomads, at this time spread throughout the whole of the Sudan belt, were indifferent and often hostile to Islam. In western Sudan two groups in Māsina and Futa Toro are of interest in view of their later significance for the history of Islam.

The beginnings of the state of Māsina go back to the migration around A.D. 1400 of the Dyalo clan from Fūta Toro into Dyā or Dyāga inhabited by Zaghrāna cultivators and Sorko and Bozo fishers. The Fulbe increased rapidly, made Tenenku (ten miles north of Dyā) their centre and gained the ascendancy. Māsina, as the Fulbe called the Dyāga region, was made tributary by *askiya* Muḥammad I of Songhay in 1494. The Moroccan invasion was the opportunity for all the peoples under Songhay to become independent. It was more difficult for Māsina to achieve this owing to its proximity to the Moroccan stronghold at Jennē, but in 1598 the *arḍo* of Māsina revolted. He fled before the advance of the Moroccan army, but returned to Māsina the following year. Subsequent pashas agreed to respect his territory and in 1628 the reigning *arḍo* asserted his complete independence by refusing to accept investiture by the pasha.[2] From small beginnings the Bambara state of Segu had grown powerful and dominated Māsina from 1725. About 1750 the Tuareg Tenegerif, having gained control of a wide stretch of the Niger bend including northern Māsina, also levied tribute on the Fulbe. So far the majority of the Fulbe had remained pagan[3] but a new era came when a Pulo cleric overthrew the old chiefs, defied the Bambara, and founded a remarkable Islamic state.

Soon after the Songhay conquest of Māsina an *arḍo* (our sources say a pretended prophet) called Tengella revolted, but was killed in Dyāra by the troops of the *askiya* in 918/1512–13.[4] His adopted son, Koli,

[1] See below, p. 184, n. 1.

[2] As-Saʿdī, op. cit., pp. 273–4, 278–88, 351.

[3] Of the Dyalo dynasty which lasted for four centuries Delafosse writes, 'Bien que . . . quelques-uns des princes de cette dynastie portent des prénoms musulmans, il semble bien qu'aucun d'eux n'ait professé l'islamisme: ce fut, en tout cas, la raison qu'invoqua Sékou-Hamadou, fondateur de la dynastie des Bari, pour s'emparer du pouvoir' (*H.S.N.* ii. 231).

[4] See *T. as-Sūdān*, p. 77 (127–8); *Fattāsh*, pp. 40–41 (72–74), 76–77 (145–6); Gaden and Delafosse, *Chroniques du Foûta Sénégalais*, pp. 228–9.

who took command of the Fulbe and Mandinka of Bakunse, migrated[1] with other chiefs and eventually conquered Futa Toro with the help of Serer and Tokolor and freed the region from the rule of the Wolof only to impose his own practically pagan dynasty.[2] This dynasty, the Denyanke, remained in power until 1776 when the Tokolor clerical party triumphed over their rulers and founded a theocratic state.

Similarly Islam made little appeal to the nomadic and loosely organized Fulbe of Futa Jalon, Yatenga, Liptako, Gobir, and other Hausa states. But the Fulbe spread as settlers as well as nomads, the Hausa towns for instance were full of negroid Fulbe, and these have been of the greatest significance for the spread of Islam.

5. ISLAMIC STAGNATION IN THE CENTRAL SUDAN

The security of the Saharan routes under Sudanese rule had characterized the central as well as the western region at those periods when Kanem or Bornu were powerful, but now we must take into account the increasing pressure and dominance of the Tuareg over the Sahil from the middle Niger to Lake Chad. They gained control over all Songhay and Hausa settlements in the Sahil, founding settled states in Air and Ader. Teda encampments gradually disappeared from the road to Fezzān as they retreated eastwards. Tuareg pressed deeply into the middle Niger region, mingling with Songhay and producing many tribes of half-castes.[3] In the seventeenth century they menaced the material security of all the northern Bornuan provinces, in the eighteenth century they harassed all the country north of the Yo, and in the nineteenth there was no power to arrest their inroads except their inability to combine.

Bornu attained the height of its power during the sixteenth century during the reign of Idrīs Alawma, but the next two centuries were a period of gradual decline, though its organization presented an appearance of strength and solidarity sufficient to deter any regular invader.

[1] According to João de Barros (transl. G. R. Crone in *Voyages of Cadamosto*, p. 144), Koli (reg. 1559–86) attacked the Mandinka villages on the Faleme and threatened Bambuk. He was so successful that in 1530 the king of Manding sought aid from the Portuguese against the *siratique* (i.e. *sa-tigi*) of Futa, and this was the reason for the embassy which John III sent to the Mande-Mansa, Mamūdu, grandson of the Mamūdu who, tradition claims, was the father of Koli, though he was actually only the adopted son of Tengella, chief of the Yālalḅe.

[2] According to tradition only one of the dynasty, Sule Ndyay (*c.* 1740–8), was a Muslim, converted in consequence of a cure by a Sharīf ʿAbd Allāh b. Maghfūr; see Gaden and Delafosse, op. cit., p. 36. However, as-Saʿdī, in his account of Koli and his first six successors, clearly regards them as Muslims (*T. as-Sūdān*, p. 77/128).

[3] Cf. Barth, iv. 307 and *passim*.

An exception to this freedom from invasion occurred during the reign of 'Alī ibn al-ḥājj 'Umar (1645–85) who had to repel a simultaneous attack of Agadez Tuareg from the north and Jukun (Kwararafa) from the south. The inhabitants were often raided, epidemics and famine took their toll, and the country was in no state to repel a determined invader. Yet there were no strong neighbours. The Kwararafa, once so formidable, disintegrated and at the beginning of the nineteenth century Bornu was still powerful enough to keep in subjection a wide circle of vassal states.

In central Sudan Bornu was the one definitely Muslim state, yet Muḥammad Belo in his *Apologia pro bello sancto* justifies the Fulani *jihād* against it on the ground of its toleration of pagan rites in accordance with the normal Sudanese practice, for, as we have shown, Islam was not regarded as incompatible with paganism until the era of theocratic states. Belo, after recognizing the Bornuans' commendable zeal in studying the Qur'ān,[1] writes:

> But we have been told that their rulers and chiefs today have places to which they ride where they offer sacrifices and then pour the blood on the gates of their towns. They have great houses containing snakes and other things to which they offer sacrifices. They performed rites to the river just as the Copts used to do to the Nile in the Time of Ignorance.[2] We heard that they keep such festivals in which they, their Qur'ān-reciters, their rulers and the populace participated, but no one else, which they designate 'the custom of the country'. They allege that it was *ṣadaqāt* by which they sought prosperity in their work and the repulsion of harmful influences, and that if they did not observe the custom their crops would spoil, their means of sustenance diminish, and their strength weaken. These customs had been transmitted from generation to generation. We have never heard of a single one of their kings or '*ulamā*' condemning these practices although certain Arabs and Fellāta who did not take part in such things continually objected and accused them of paganism. Undoubtedly they were heathen practices, even though their '*ulamā*'

[1] Many *mais* were devoted to Islamic studies, especially the last three, Dūnama (1751–3), 'Alī (1753–93), and Aḥmad (1791–1808).

[2] G. F. Lyon was told that, 'Until a few years ago, when the country became much improved under the mild government of a very religious Moslem [i.e. al-Kanemi], it was the custom to throw into the stream [i.e. the Wobe] at the time of its rise a virgin richly dressed, and of superior beauty. The greatest people of the country considered themselves honoured if the preference was given to one of their daughters, and the learned men augured a good or bad year from the ease or difficulty with which their victim was drowned.' G. F. Lyon, *Travels in Northern Africa*, 1821, pp. 125–6. Burckhardt was also told by Negro pilgrims in Cairo in 1816 that 'at the time of the inundation, which is regular there as in Egypt, it [the Wobe] flows with great impetuosity. A female slave richly dressed is on this solemn occasion thrown into the stream by order of the king' (*Nubia*, App. ii, p. 489).

claimed that they contained no idea of *shirk* or plurality. They were heathens because these idols of trees and waters and places to which they offered sacrifices were the idols of their forefathers before they islamized.[1]

When we turn to Hausaland, and this also applies to eastern Songhay-Zerma country, we are in full heathendom in the eyes of any zealot. Islam was only practised by foreign communities settled in the towns and few even of the rulers made a profession of Islam. As Barth writes: 'It is evident that the larger portion of the population all over Hausa, especially that of the country towns and villages, remained addicted to paganism till the fanatic zeal of their conquerors the Fulbe forced them to profess Islam, at least publicly.'[2]

About 1600 Kano, with other Hausa states, became tributary to the pagan Kwararafa (also called Jukun from the name of their ruling caste) centred in the Gongola-Benue basin. The Jukun also attacked but failed to take Katsina. In 1671 they occupied Kano city but shortly afterwards were defeated by Bornu to which all the eastern Hausa including Kano became tributary. Katsina reached its greatest extent at the beginning of the eighteenth century but was then reduced and superseded by Gobir which by 1764 had gained control of most of Zamfara.[3] The ravages of Gobir and the perpetual hostilities between the Hausa states are sufficient to account for the relative ease with which Fulbe, united by a common cause, were able to overcome them.

Pagan and Muslim rulers alternate in many Hausa states and even if adopted Islam was only a veneer. In Zaria Jatau (1782–1802) is said to have been a Muslim, but his son, Makau, was a pagan and demolished the mosque his father had built. Under his successor Zaria was captured by a Fulbe expedition (1804) and the conversion of the people began. The dispossessed dynasty fled to Zuba among the Gwari and it is evident that the first refugee chiefs were practising pagans.

Fulbe clerics are heard of in the Hausa states in the thirteenth century. By the fifteenth nomads were all over the central Sudan. By the end of the century they had reached the middle Shari where they helped in forming the state of Bagirmi and their clerics converted its rulers. By the end of the eighteenth century both settled and nomadic Fulbe were

[1] M. Belo, *Infāq al-Maisūr*, p. 9.

[2] H. Barth, *Travels*, ii. 118.

[3] K. Krieger provides a ruler-list co-ordinated with the few facts known about Zamfara from relations with other states in an article, 'Zur Geschichte von Zamfara', in *Afrikanistische Studien*, ed. J. Lukas, Berlin, 1955, pp. 51–56. The Zamfara dynasty went into exile in 1764. Its head Abarshi (1805–15) submitted to 'Uthmān ḍan Fodio and his son, ḍan Bako, gained control of Anka (*c.* 1820) where the dynasty survives to this day.

numerous everywhere. The settled had taken wives from the Hausa and adopted their language and cultural characteristics. There were various signs and portents of the gathering storm. In the second half of the eighteenth century two clerics, Mahamman Jobbo and the blind Būbakar Luduji, were engaged in converting the Zerma, and an agitator, Jibrīl ibn ʿUmar, was active in Gobir. In Katsina the opening of the *sacra*, by letting loose the power of the kingdom, prepared the way. Its king-list records that *sarki* Bawa ḍan Gima (1771–1801) 'opened the house which the Hābe had covered with red leather, which was considered the "seat of power", and which the ancestors of the king had not allowed to be opened for fear war would ensue. When he opened the house, *belbēla*[1] came out and filled the whole town.'[2]

In Bornu someone in the time of *mai* Aḥmad (1791–1807/8) realizing the real danger wrote these verses:

Verily a cloud has settled upon God's earth,
A cloud so dense that escape from it is impossible.
Everywhere between Kordofan and Gobir
And the cities of the Kindīn (Tuareg)
Are settlements of the dogs of Fellāta (Bi la'ila)
Serving God in all their dwelling places
(I swear by the life of the Prophet and his overflowing grace)
In reforming all districts and provinces
Ready for future bliss.
So in this year of A.H. 1124[3] (A.D. 1799) they are following their beneficent theories.
As though it were a time to set the world in order by preaching.
Alas! that I know all about the tongue of the fox.[4]

[1] The cattle egret, *bubulcus ibis*, eastern Sudan Arabic *bulbullū*. This is intended to symbolize the Fulbe.

[2] Palmer, *Sud. Mem.* iii. 82.

[3] This must be a misprint for A.H. 1214.

[4] Translated by H. R. Palmer, *Bornu Sahara*, p. 52. Palmer says that the phrase *Bi la'ila*, 'godless', was applied to the Fulbe.

5

The Recrudescence of Islam in the Nineteenth Century: Western Sudan

I. REAWAKENING OF THE FORCES OF ISLAMIC PROPAGANDA

THE nineteenth century was the great century of Islamic expansion in West Africa. In its more remote aspect the reawakening derives from Berber reaction to Arab conquest. Their Islamic zeal thrived on the by-products of Ṣūfism, the religious fraternities, and the cult of saints. The actual expansion was achieved by means of the alliance of the sword and the book. Militant clerics, reacting against the Sudanese accommodation of Islam and paganism, proclaimed the *jihād* and found in the theocratic state a unique means for the attainment of power and the subjection to the state of all the diverse elements incorporated in their commonwealths.

(*a*) *Role of the Moorish Tribes*

South-western Sahara has been thoroughly islamized and arabized. Arabs were not responsible for its islamization, but the form it took was due to their conquest. The Banū Ḥassān and other branches of the Maʿqil who invaded North Africa in the eleventh century asserted their supremacy as a warrior aristocracy over the Ṣanhāja of upper Mauritania in the fifteenth century, over western Mauritania, Waddān, and Tāgant during the sixteenth, and over Adrār and lower Mauritania during the seventeenth. The Berbers tried to shake off the semi-pagan Arab yoke many times, their most famous effort being the uprising known as *Sharr* Bubba (1644–74) under Nāṣir ad-Dīn. Certain sections gained the right of vassal status and subsequently many more were able to assert their independence, among them the Idaw ʿAish, Awlād Delīm, and the Mashḍūf of Tāgant. The result of the Arab domination, however, was profound; not only did the word *zanāja* become the equivalent of tributary or serf, but the western Berbers were thoroughly arabized and only a few sections still retain their language. They lost the use of the *lithām* and many distinctive customary usages. On the other hand, the Berbers of the centre, now known as the Tuareg, retained their independence and consequently their language and customs.[1] Islam took many centuries to win their allegiance, but they did not allow its law to modify their social life. The political role of women was reduced, but they continued to wield great influence.[2] The Tuareg maintained constant pressure upon the central Sahil from the middle Niger to the Chad, but exerted no Islamic influence.

From the Islamic point of view the formation of clerical tribes is significant. During the fifteenth and sixteenth centuries a missionary movement from the Sāqiyat al-Ḥamrā' region completely changed the attitude of the Berbers towards Islam. The influence of the missionaries was such that whole tribes now regard themselves as their descendants. Islam provided a new tribal beginning, a new aristocracy, and a compensation for their loss of political freedom. These clerical tribes (*ṭulba* or *zwāya*), renouncing the use of arms, gained recognition for themselves as tributaries of Arab tribes.

One Arab tribe stands out by way of contrast as a clerical tribe which exercised widespread influence not only in the southern desert and Sahil but upon Negro Islam. This was the Kunta which migrated from the Tawāt region and, by the fifteenth century, were on the borders of Timbuktu.[3] From an original Arab nucleus it grew into a Moorish clerical tribe to whom all the strains of the Qādiriyya *ṭarīqa* in West Africa go back. Through its reputation as a holy family it gained an immense reputation and its leaders became mediators between conflicting forces of Tuareg, Fulbe, and Negroes in the Timbuktu region.

Moorish Islam has been characterized by the inter-related cult of saints and the religious fraternity, and their origins may be briefly summarized since they exercised great influence upon Negroes although Negro Islam did not incorporate their salient features.

(*b*) *Role of the Religious Brotherhoods*

The majority of Sudanese Muslims are linked through their clerics with either the Qādiriyya or Tijāniyya *ṭarīqas*. The great expansion of these orders, particularly the latter, took place during the nineteenth

[1] Some Arab groups have been incorporated and become Tuareg; for example, the noble clans of the Igellād and a sub-tribe of the Ghaṭafān within the Ullimmeden near the Niger in the region of Tilaberi (A. Richer, *Les Ouillimenden*, 1924, p. 41).

[2] In 1475 the Nūnū Ṣanhāja of the Sudan were governed by a woman according to as-Sa'dī (*T. as-Sūdān*, p. 64/104) who gives other instances.

[3] As-Sa'dī, op. cit., transl. pp. 104, 121.

century. The propagation of Islam and internal rivalries within Muslim communities cannot be understood without considering the attachment of the leaders to one or other, for their political influence has been as strong as the religious.

Eastern Ṣūfism was introduced into Spain by Ibn Masarra in the fourth century A.H. (tenth century A.D.) and entered the Maghrib through contact with Andalusian Ṣūfīs. It played a part in the reaction against the Murābiṭūn, and during the Muwaḥḥidūn period the Maghrib produced its great mystics, of whom the most outstanding was Abū Madyan Shuʿaib (d. 594/1197–8). From him, through his pupil ʿAbd as-Salām b. Mashīsh (d. A.D. 1227–8), was derived the teaching of ash-Shādhilī (d. A.D. 1258). Ṣūfī teaching and discipline spread rapidly in North Africa. The danger involved in its development was, in the first place, that it would make the distinction between its teaching and orthodox Islam so wide that it would lead to schism and consequently the loss of its mellowing effect upon those who remained within the bonds of legalistic religion; and, in the second, so enlarge the gulf between the religion of the *élite* and that of the man in the street that there could be little mutual understanding. The first of these gaps was bridged through the work of men like al-Ghazālī who directed the new wine into traditional channels, and the second by the work of popularizers of Ṣūfism such as ʿAbd al-Qādir al-Jīlānī who recognized that all men are not equally endowed with spiritual capacities and sought by the aid of psycho-physical exercises to bring the new insights within reach of the masses.

During the thirteenth century there was a great increase of Ṣūfī teachers who founded *zāwiyas* in rural areas where the 'Master of the Way' lived surrounded by his family, servants, and pupils. From these cells Ṣūfī practices spread throughout the countryside and the Berbers became wholehearted Muslims. During the fourteenth century Ṣūfism was popularized by the *zāwiya*-heads both in their persons and through the organized discipline of the fraternities. The founder of the *zāwiya* was visited by ordinary people, not for his teaching, but to get the blessing of his *baraka*. After his death and burial in the *zāwiya* precincts this process intensified. The direction of the *zāwiya* was continued by his descendants and a holy family was born. The organization of these circles into the cult mysticism of the orders as we know them was rarely the work of the founder whose personal piety and charisma had drawn the circle together, but of the leader who took his place after his death. During the fifteenth century, through the work of men like al-Jazūlī (d. A.D. 1465–70) who attributed himself to the mystical line of ash-Shādhilī, fraternities came into existence displaying the salient features which have characterized them ever since.

Once the conceptions of the saint cult, with its idea of the hereditary continuity of *baraka*, and of the religious order, with its belief in the continuity of mystical teaching and practice, had taken root in the Maghrib, the Berbers inhabiting Mauritania and the Saharan Sahil came under their influence. 'Umar ash-Shaikh (d. 1553) of the Arab Kunta tribe was initiated into the Qādiriyya whilst on pilgrimage and to him all the strains of this *ṭarīqa* in the western Sudan go back. Through this Moorish Ṣūfism of desert and oasis it spread into Negro Africa, first among townspeople and nomadizing Negroes like traders and eventually among the village clergy, but in the process modifying itself to suit their religious aspirations.

We have seen how the Murābiṭ movement which led to the conversion of the Tokolor and Soninke began in Mauritania, and this region has ever since provided missionaries for the Sudan. It was here that Islamic influence became canalized in the hands of clerical tribes. Although only trained pupils were fully initiated, all the members of the tribe were regarded as adherents. These tribal sections eventually became independent and the first head was regarded as the tribal saint and eponym.[1] As emissaries began to spread these allegiances outside Moorish tribes into the Sudan, changes took place. Some borderland Negroes came to revere the living saints as possessors of *baraka*, but this conception did not gain any deep hold. Yet although the orders did not acquire the same moral, social, and political importance among Negro peoples that they had gained among Moors, they provided a label and a ritual link between diverse peoples. The religious society idea appealed to Negro trading peoples like Soninke, Dyula, and Hausa, as well as townspeople and detribalized like the inhabitants of slave villages, but elsewhere than along the trade-routes it was largely in regions where Negro peoples were in touch with Berbers that the orders acquired even this limited influence until they were spread by military adventurers. Apart from this main current coming from the north into the Senegal, Timbuktu, and Hausa regions, another but weaker current came into the central Sudan from the Funj Confederation of Sennār on the Blue Nile.

Before the nineteenth century the religious orders cannot be regarded as an important element in West African Islam, but during that

[1] On the saints of the Sāqiyat al-Ḥamrā' see Aḥmad ash-Shinqīṭī, *Al-Wasīṭ fī tarājim udabā' ash-Shinqīṭ*, Cairo, 1329/1911.

century adherence to either the Qādiriyya and Tijāniyya became equivalent to being a Muslim. It was essential that every cleric should be able to name his initiator with all that implied of linkage with a tradition. The islamization of Futa Jalon and attachment to the Qādiriyya went together at the end of the eighteenth century since the Fulbe clerics and the leaders of the conquest belonged to the Kunta Bakkā'iyya. Among them were also some Shādhiliyya, such as Mōdi Shellu, *alfa* of Labē (*c.* 1760–1813). Later, through the teaching of ʻAlī aṣ-Ṣūfī, this tradition gained considerable, though ephemeral, popularity, since from 1850 the religious and political success of the Tokolor of Dingiray led to the members of both the older orders in Futa Jalon joining the Tijāniyya.

The Qādiriyya spread by means of peaceful propaganda. Its agents, settling in trading centres where they opened Qur'ān schools, were often the first diffusers of Islam in pagan regions. But by the end of the eighteenth and the beginning of the nineteenth centuries new stirrings in the life of Islam revivified some of the old centres and led to the formation of new ones. The Tijāniyya, whose founder Aḥmad at-Tijānī died in 1815, owes its present influence in West Africa to its propagation by al-ḥājj ʻUmar and his followers. Its spread among Muslims has been largely to the detriment of the Qādiriyya, whilst the Tokolor conquerors forced it upon all the newly converted. During the present century it has been spread by peaceful propaganda and has acquired a considerable following in Northern Nigeria, Kanem, and Bagirmi, though the Qādiriyya has retained its hold over Waday.

The revival of Islām during the early nineteenth century owes a great debt to Aḥmad b. Idrīs (d. 1837), but though the movement he initiated influenced the Nilotic Sudan from whence emissaries moved into Waday, Bagirmi, and Bornu, the only direct influence came through the order founded by Aḥmad's pupil, Muḥammad b. ʻAlī as-Sanūsī (1787–1859). His order gained widespread influence in central Sahara and Sahil, but the destruction of the famous fortified *zāwiyas* dominating Borku, Ennedi, and Kanem during the French conquest between 1902 and 1913 has considerably reduced its role in the central Sudan.

About a century ago the Qādiriyya received a fresh impulse through Shaikh Sīdyā 'l-Kabīr (1780–1868) of the Awlād Biri and his grandson Shaikh Sīdyā 'ṣ-Ṣaghīr (1862–1924). A contemporary of the first, Muḥammad al-Fāḍil (d. 1869), founded what amounted to a new order (Fāḍiliyya), and his son Saʻd Bū (d. 1917) gained a remarkable influence among Senegalese Negroes. Another leader who won great success among the Wolof was Aḥmad Bamba (d. 1927), a Wolof-Tokolor, whose branch, known as the Murīdiyya, is a true Negro order and today numbers over half a million adherents.

(c) *Formation of Theocratic States and the Rise of Military Adventurers*

The religious role of nomads has been exaggerated in accounts of the spread of Islam. Even in the early days it was spreading in the Sahil before the brief episode of the Murābiṭūn and the great expansion in the nineteenth century owed less to nomadic Fulbe than is commonly supposed. The Fulfulde-speaking peoples comprise groups of the most diverse origins, red and black pastoral nomads, settled mixed cultivators, and class and caste groups, linked by linguistic and social ties. The history of the nomadic reds is one long attempt to maintain their identity and remain distinct from Negroes, hence their exaggerated racial pride and cattle complex. Only those who remained pure nomads were able to do this. In the formation of the theocratic states which characterize Islamic history during this period the role of the nomadic reds has been secondary. Sometimes, especially in Northern Nigeria, nomads provided the means whereby the aims of the Tōrodḅē reformers were accomplished, but often they have been at enmity with the clerical leaders who tried to make them observe Islamic social custom. It was the mixed Fulbe who produced the great leaders, their lieutenants, and most reliable followers. They are the strongest Muslims in the Sudan and their social custom has been greatly modified by Islamic institutions. In the regions where they succeeded in obtaining power they became an aristocracy and have done more to transform the Sudan than any other people. Once in power they despise the poor red nomads as practically pagans because of their refusal to accept Islamic personal and social law.

Before this era African life had proved impervious to the universalist concepts of Islam and it had survived only by adapting itself to African categories of thought and custom, Muslim clans being accorded their defined place in the social structure like the individual in the African family. This equilibrium was now to be rudely broken by the formation of theocratic states. The word 'theocracy' is used here in the sense of the rule of a man or a clerical organization which lays claim to having a mandate from God. In Islam a theocracy is a state regulated, not directly by God, but by His law and could more correctly be called a divine nomocracy. The initiative and driving force of the new movements came from the Tōrodḅē, the Tokolor clerical class. Though their centre was in Senegalese Futa they had clerical representatives scattered throughout the whole Sudan belt in both Muslim and pagan villages where they were tolerated by the chiefs who made use of them as practitioners of magic and granted them a plot to cultivate, since their activities offered no threat to the position and influence of the ruling lineage or mystery cult associations. The transformation which now took place in the relations of Islamic and pagan societies constituted a religious, political, and social revolution. The religious change brought about by the nineteenth-century reformers lay in the stress laid on the uniqueness of Islam and its incompatibility with worship within the old cults. The political revolution set in motion by the need to impose the religion upon all societies, Muslim as well as pagan, broke the long established social equilibrium. Behind the evolution of the theocratic state may be discerned a class struggle between the Tōrodḅē clerical class and the ruling classes (Denyankē in Futa Toro and the Hausa in the centre). The Fulbe ruling class had always been refractory to Islam, the preserve of a special social category within the framework of their composite society.[1] The clerical reaction led to the creation of a new nobility, the descendants of the leaders of the revolt. The formation of a theocracy or divine commonwealth whose clerics represented the rule of God on earth made the political institution the ruler of all life, and in theory peoples and rulers were associated together as never before. The state claimed the exclusive loyalty of its subjects and no divided loyalties between the law of Islam and the law of the 'fetish' was any longer possible. These attempts at theocracies failed, either through the anarchic method of election based on the analogy of early Islam, or through the adoption of Islamic forms of hereditary succession, to the degenerative effect of which a Fulfulde proverb bears witness: 'the cleric (*tyērno*) begets a chief (*lamḍo*), the chief begets an infidel (*kefero*)'.[2]

This movement was launched in the highlands of Futa Jalon in 1725 by *karamoko* Ibrāhīm Mūsā, and, with the aid of pagan Sōlima Jalonkē, was brought to a successful conclusion in 1776 by Ibrāhīm Sōri who formed an elective theocratic state with himself at the head as *almāmi*

[1] To the old noble Fulbe class the adoption of Islam was equivalent to submission and descent to a lower status. In the Gambia and Casamance the Fulbe noble class who escaped the clerical reaction remain pagan even today, whilst other classes of clients and serfs within their society have adopted, or are in process of adopting Islam.

[2] H. Gaden, *Proverbes et Maximes Peuls et Toucouleurs*, 1931, p. 68.

of Timbo, divided into nine provinces under the authority of clerics having a kind of feudal relationship to the *almāmi*. This was followed in 1776 by the triumph of the Tōrodḅē of Futa Toro led by Sulaimān Bāl over the pagan Fulbe dynasty of the Denyankē, where a similar elective state in which divine law was sovereign was created by *almāmi* 'Abd al-Qādir. In this state the *almāmi* was elected from Tōrodḅē families descended from the 'companions' of the leader of the *jihād*. Its influence deepened the Islam of nominal Muslims and led to the conversion of other peoples of the region including many Wolof. In Bondu also the head of a clerical family, founded in the seventeenth century by a Tokolor cleric called Mālik Si, was affected by the new ideas of militant Islam and adopted the title of *almāmi* about 1775.

From the ramifications of the Tōrodḅē clans came the next three conquerors, 'Uthmān ḍan Fodio, Ḥamadu Bari, and al-ḥājj 'Umar Tal. The country between the Niger and the Chad has always been divided into many little states, more often than not in mutual enmity, at times paying allegiance to the greater states to the east and west. This region was for the first time given a semblance of unity through an Islamic movement inspired by 'Uthmān ḍan Fodio, who from 1786 preached the *jihād* in such a way that it became a racial as well as a religious war, and differs from the other *jihāds* on account of the number of nomads who joined in. These conquests, and later those of 'Umar, though not inspired by nomads, are closely linked with pastoralism as is shown by the use made of cavalry. 'Uthmān and his brother 'Abd Allāh founded the dual empire of Sokoto and Gwandu which led to the definitive conversion of the Hausa to Islam. This empire disintegrated into a large number of separate and often hostile states loosely acknowledging the titular suzerainty of the ruler of Sokoto. When in full decline they were given a new lease of life by the British after their occupation at the beginning of this century. One current stemming from the same initial impulse led to the formation of a different type of emirate, more Pulo than the others, where the Fulbe had become culturally Hausa, on the plateau of Ādamāwa which dominated the numerous weak pagan tribes of the region. Bornu did not escape the attentions of the military theocracy of Sokoto, but it was able to check its forces owing to the fact that the clerical leaders had to rely for military power upon nomads who were only interested in raiding and dispersal with their booty, and also through the resistance of a Kānemī cleric, Muḥammad al-Amīn, who was the effective ruler from 1810 in a less radically based clerical state.

Next came a revolution in Māsina where the Fulbe, whose migrations began in the fourteenth century, had become the predominant population, though tributary at that time to the Bambara. The prophet was the Pulo cleric, Ḥamadu Bari, who freed the Fulbe from Bambara overlordship, overthrew the old pagan Pulo dynasty, suppressed the other Pulo leaders, and founded a short-lived state which lasted from 1810 to 1862 when it was overthrown by al-ḥājj 'Umar, though it was maintained as a successor-state by his nephew at-Tijānī until the French conquest in 1893.

This formidable conqueror, al-ḥājj 'Umar, inaugurates a new type of Islamic adventurer whose vast conquests threw western Sudan into a state of complete anarchy. The imposition of military régimes upset the balanced life of many Negro societies, undermined their social fabric, and undiluted slave-raiding reduced many areas to unproductive steppe. 'Umar was killed in 1864 before he had been able to lay down solid foundations for a state, whilst the rule of his successors coincided with the gradually expanding French conquest of the interior. It is noteworthy that 'Umar made use of firearms bartered for the human booty of his wars and at the same time tried to boycott products of European origin. Through the resistance of these adventurers Islam came to personify resistance and reaction to European penetration, a legacy which continued to characterize the earlier period of European rule.[1]

In 1853 'Umar began a series of proselytizing expeditions which aimed at spreading the Tijānī allegiance among Muslims as well as Islam among pagans, and brought vast regions between the Senegal and Niger under his control. His death in 1864 let loose rivalries within his own family, and his empire split into a number of regions ruled by sons or nephews who paid titular allegiance to the eldest, Amadu Sēku, ruler of Segu. Their position steadily deteriorated in consequence of revolts of the subjected and the advance of the French who finally destroyed their power. Although 'Umar is responsible for the vast expansion of the Tijāniyya *ṭarīqa*, his methods of conversion kindled a hatred of Islam among Bambara and others which led to their casting off allegiance once they were freed from fear. In its Islamic effect his work may be contrasted with that of Ḥamadu Bari of Māsina with his

[1] None of the great leaders claimed to be the Mahdī, but the revolution in Islamic political atmosphere, subsequent anarchy, and resentment against the encroachment of European powers provided end-of-the-world conditions favourable for messianic expectations. It is significant that manifestations were largely confined to Senegal and Northern Nigeria during the period which saw the whole of West Africa fall under European control.

MAP 4

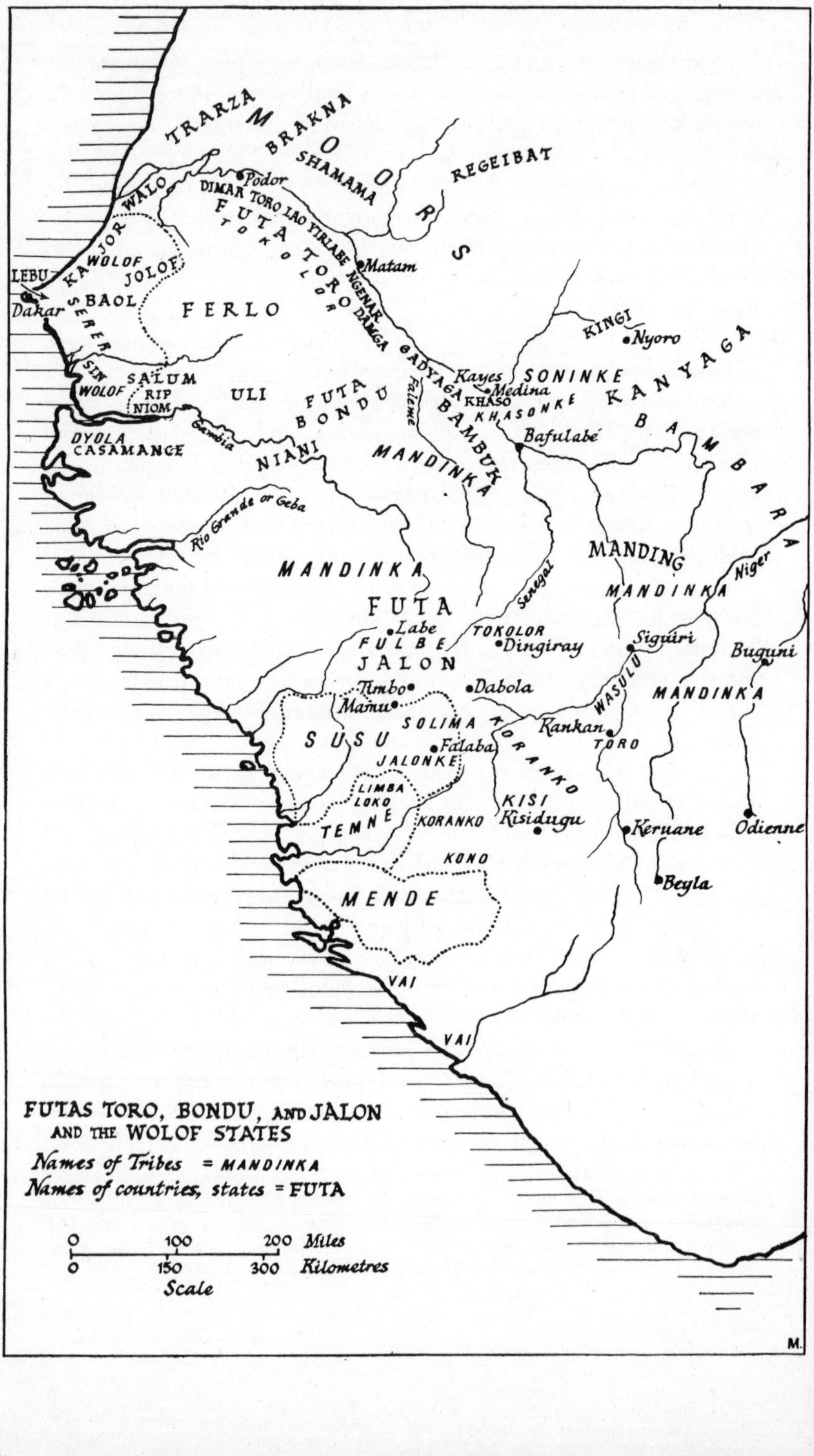
TRARZA
M O O R S
BRAKNA
SHAMAMA
REGEIBAT
Podor
DIMAR TORO LAO YIRLABE
FUTA TORO
TOKOLOR
WALO
KAJOR
WOLOF
JOLOF
LEBU
Dakar
BAOL
SERER
FERLO
Matam
NGENAR
DAMGA
GADYAGA
KINGI
Nyoro
KANYAGA
SIN
WOLOF
SALUM
RIP
NIOM
ULI
FUTA BONDU
Faleme
Kayes
Medina
SONINKE
KHASO
KHASONKE
BAMBUK
Bafulabe
BAMBARA
DYOLA
CASAMANCE
Gambia
NIANI
MANDINKA
Rio Grande or Geba
MANDINKA
MANDING
Senegal
MANDINKA
Niger
FUTA
Labe
FULBE
JALON
TOKOLOR
Dingiray
Siguiri
Buguni
Timbo
Mamu
Dabola
WASULU
MANDINKA
SOLIMA
SUSU
Falaba
KORANKO
Kankan
TORO
JALONKE
LIMBA
LOKO
TEMNE
KORANKO
KISI
Kisidugu
Keruane
Odienne
KONO
Beyla
MENDE
VAI
VAI
FUTAS TORO, BONDU, AND JALON
AND THE WOLOF STATES
Names of Tribes = MANDINKA
Names of countries, states = FUTA
0 100 200 Miles
0 150 300 Kilometres
Scale
M.

effective 'follow up'. Yet these wars with their dislocations led to the formation of new villages composed often of the most diverse people between whom allegiance to the Tijāniyya provided the only link.

Contemporary with the sons of 'Umar were a number of non-Tokolor leaders of ethnic groups who made use of Islam as a rallying cry for resistance against European conquest. These include Mamadu Lamīn, a former companion of al-ḥājj 'Umar, leading Soninke; Tyeba heading the Senufo of Kenedugu; and, most famous of all, a Mandinka named Samōri who (from 1872 to 1898) attempted to form a state in the region between the source of the Niger and Upper Volta. In central Sudan towards the end of the century, Rābiḥ, a slaver from the eastern Sudan, dominated the whole Chad region. These later adventurers used Islam largely as a cloak for their personal ambitions. Their bands, recruited by hope of booty, were formed into regular armies whose striking power was based on horsemen (*sōfa*). They ruined the regions they submitted, sparing neither Muslim nor pagan who resisted. They organized their states along lines different from those formed by their predecessors, since they were purely military régimes. They divided their conquests into provinces and districts having at the head a political chief assisted by a war-chief and a cleric. They formed a *bait al-māl*, and one of their main preoccupations was the maintenance of a commercial link with the coast by means of which they could barter their human booty to obtain firearms. Only those local chiefs who, like Tyeba, the great opponent of Samōri, adopted the same means of raising and training professional troops, were able to resist. They fought one another as well as the French against whose occupation they formed a rallying point, and by whom they were all destroyed. Their conquests, though ephemeral, in some ways prepared the ground for the spread of Islam, for by their massacres and slave-raiding, accompanied by the destruction of symbols, statuettes, masks, and ancestor houses, they broke up the old religio-social structure of many peoples; whilst on the positive side nominal attachment to Islam often led under peaceful conditions to permanent islamization.

2. FUTA JALON

In the heart of the tropical zone lies the mountainous region of Futa Jalon covering some 50,000 sq. km. It consists of vast monotonous plateaux broken here and there by isolated knolls and split by deep valleys. Three-quarters of the whole area consists of *bowal*, poor laterite soil, green during the rains and dry and sterile in the winter when it is affected by the harmattan. Its altitude should make this an especially favoured region, but in fact it has been ruined by deforestation and fire cultivation. Only animal-breeders can make use of these plateaux and it is not surprising to find them occupied by Fulbe superimposed upon Negro cultivators. The earliest inhabitants were such groups as Temne, Kisi, Limba, Baga, and Landuman. In the thirteenth century Susu of the Mande family arrived, the original inhabitants tended to move west and south to occupy more fertile land towards the coast, and the Susu took their place in the still fertile valleys, and then in their turn as they increased began to move towards the coast.[1] In 1534 small groups of Fulakunda established themselves in the western part. From 1675 there took place an extensive Fulbe migration from Māsina and even the Ḥawḍ along the valleys of the Bafing and Tenē to occupy the empty plains of the east over which the Sōlima Jalonkē[2] exercised authority. The second Sōlima king, *Mansa* Dansa (1700–30),[3] gave them permission to settle.

Although only nominally Muslim these Fulbe were accompanied by clerics and during the eighteenth century the new immigrants began a movement for supremacy, adopting Islam as their war-cry. Fifty years of perpetual struggle followed before they finally triumphed over the pagan Jalonkē. This was the work of two outstanding men, one a cleric called Ibrāhīm Mūsā (generally known as Karamoko Alifa or Alifa Ba), the other a war-leader called Ibrāhīm Sōri. Two of the leaders of the migration from Māsina, Sēri and his son Muḥammad Sa'īd (*c.* 1694–1700), although living a semi-nomadic life, had a permanent centre at Fugumba where the tribal assembly met. It was here that clerics settled and opened their schools. The *ardo* Kikala (1715–20) was converted and the two Ibrāhīms, Mūsā and Sōri, who belonged to his family, were both brought up in Fugumba.

Gordon Laing, who travelled to Sōlima in 1821–2, was given an account of subsequent events by the *dyēlis*. He writes that Mūsā Ba, a successor of the leader of the migration, Muḥammad Sa'īd, invited all the Jalonkado chiefs to a great feast at which he performed the ceremony of *tyobbal*.[4] He invited all those who wished for instruction in

[1] Pacheco, writing 1505–8, differentiates between the Jaalunguas (Jalonkē) and the Susu nearer the coast (*Esmeraldo de Situ Orbis*, transl. G. H. T. Kimble, 1937, pp. 94, 98).

[2] *Sōsō sōlima*, 'Susu of the sharpened teeth', was the term by which these Jalonkē were known.

[3] A. G. Laing, *Travels in West Africa*, 1825, pp. 401–2.

[4] See *I.W.A.*, pp. 156 n., 226.

Islam to place their hands on the sacrificial bread and bleeding ram. This ceremony (which took place about 1726) symbolized the cementing of an alliance between the two groups which endured until 1763. Both joined in the *jihād* against the surrounding peoples, especially during the reign of the Sōlima chief, *Mansa* Dansa II (1750–4). But the Sōlima, to whom the Fulbe were tribute-paying pastoralists, grew disquieted at the effect the new religion was having upon the normally irreligious Fulbe. Finally in 1763 the Fulbe cut off the heads of all the Sōlima chiefs in their territory and the Sōlimana joined with the Wāsulonke[1] whom they had recently been fighting when allies of the Fulbe, marched on Timbo, a Fulbe strong point, destroyed it, and then killed all the Fulbe chiefs in their country.[2] The war between the two peoples lasted until 1805.[3]

The foundation of the state came about in this way. The Fulbe in alliance with the Sōlimana gained initial successes, but later underwent severe defeats at the hands of Mandinka of Sangaran[4] and Wāsulu. Karamoko Alifa died in 1751[5] when the *jihād* he had inspired was in complete eclipse. The tribal assembly appointed Ibrāhīm Sōri as war-leader and after severe struggles, first in alliance with the Sōlima and then against the coalition, he succeeded in triumphing in 1776 and emerged as ruler with the title of *almāmi*. The evolution of the title *imām aṣ-ṣalāt* into a political title, *imām aṭ-ṭā'a*, is not clear, but the clerics would know from their legal texts that the political organization of Islam requires an *imām* who has the duty of protecting the Muslim community and extending the domain of Islam. At least three men, 'Abd al-Qādir of Futa Tōro, Ibrāhīm Sōri of Futa Jalon, and Amadi Gayi of Futa Bondu, seem to have become political *imāms* at the same time (1776). Sōri was at first called simply *shaikh*, but Bayol writes that he was granted the title *almāmi* 'on the express condition that he

[1] Wāsulu was Mandinka country into which Fulbe had been penetrating from 1700 and mixing with the people.

[2] On these events see A. G. Laing, op. cit., pp. 401 ff. Timbo was formerly a large Jalonkē village called Gongovi.

[3] The Sōlimana, having lost part of their country, founded Falaba as a new capital farther removed from the Fulbe menace in what is now north-eastern Sierra Leone in 1768. It is unlikely that this name is derived from the Portuguese *palavra* as is generally stated, but that it comes from the river Fala(-ba) upon which it is situated; see A. G. Laing, op. cit., p. 351. Laing says that the Sōlima chief of his time, Asana Yīra (1800–27?), was educated at Labe in Futa Jalon with 'Abd al-Qādir (*almāmi* 1813–25) before the break, and still professed Islam, but secretly because the Sōlimana had reacted against the religion, and that his son and all his subjects were pagans (op. cit., p. 275).

[4] Sangaran is on the opposite side of the Niger from the Solimana country.

[5] A. G. Laing, op. cit., p. 404.

always recognized the right of the council of elders to give their advice on all matters of internal or external policy; and, further, that his successors, elected from his family, will be first recognized as such by the vote of the assembly'.[1] These earlier theocrats, though they were *imāms* of the Muslim community, did not call themselves *amīr al-mu'minīn*, the first to take this title being 'Uthmān ḍan Fodio. The title of *almāmi* (plur. *almabibe*) soon ceased to have any genuine religious significance when pagans like the ruler of Khaso were accorded it upon their agreeing to adopt Islam, that is, become tributaries.[2]

As Sōri became more and more a dictator in consequence of his victories and the devotion of his army, a clash with the assembly of clerics became inevitable. The course of subsequent events is not clear. Mōdi Mada, herald of the assembly who had been largely responsible for getting it to agree to Sōri being proclaimed war-leader in 1751, grew apprehensive of the absolute power at which Sōri seemed to be aiming. He therefore united the partisans of Karamoko Alifa and proclaimed the latter's son, 'Abd Allāh Ba Demba, as *almāmi*.[3] But defeats and especially the invasion of the Wāsulonke and Sōlima in 1763 led to the recall of Sōri, and, as a result of his victory over the Sōlima when they attacked Fugumba in 1767, he became dictator. The shift in power from the clerical to a military party is shown by his making Timbo his capital (*c.* 1780) in place of the holy town of Fugumba, and by his massacre soon afterwards of thirteen members of the assembly of Fugumba. Sōri then formed a new assembly more devoted or subjected to himself and governed the country until his death (*c.* 1784). This event was the signal for the renewal of civil war connected with the question of succession to the throne, an unusual feature of the organization of this state.

We have seen that at one stage a son of Karamoko Alifa was appointed *almāmi* in an attempt to curb the power of Sōri and enhance that of the assembly of clerics. It seems that he was not dispossessed after the recall of Sōri but continued as titular *almāmi* until his death. At any rate, in view of the power of the partisans of Karamoko Alifa, policy

[1] J. Bayol, *Voyage en Sénégambie* (Paris, 1888), quoted by L. Tauxier, *Mœurs et histoire des Peuls*, p. 247.

[2] Mungo Park reports (*Travels*, Everyman edn. p. 59) that 'Abd al-Qādir of Futa Tōro sent a mission in 1796 to Dembe Sega (d. *c.* 1803), the *fankamala* of the Khasonke, ordering him to adopt Islam or take the consequences. He certainly adopted the title of *almāmi* but made no attempt to convert his people. It was not until the conquest of al-ḥājj 'Umar that Islam began to gain ground and in 1912 only a third were Muslim according to Ch. Monteil (*Les Khassonké*, 1915, pp. 364–70).

[3] J. Bayol, op. cit., p. 104.

led Ibrāhīm Sōri to associate with him the former's son as co-*almāmi*. The parties that this division represented were called after the name of their founders, the Alfāya, representing the clerical party, and the Sōriya, the military party. After Ibrāhīm Sōri's death his son Sa'd succeeded (1784–91) and there began the series of bloody struggles for power which characterized the history of Futa Jalon for next century.[1] In 1837 in an attempt to solve the problem a curious arrangement was arrived at whereby in the dual *almāmi*-ship each *almāmi* in turn held executive authority for two years, Sōriya replacing Alfāya, and vice versa. Naturally such an arrangement could not succeed since the reigning *almāmi* often refused to hand over power to his co-ruler when his term of office ended. This revolutionary period was only ended when, after the occupation of 1896–7, *almāmi* Bokar Biro recognized the suzerainty of France.

The political and social organization of the state is of considerable interest.[2] The basis of the political organization was the *misidi* (a corruption of *masjid*) which corresponded to our 'parish' for it consisted of an area of family hamlets (*fulaso* or *marga*) depending on a central *jāmi'*, having at its head a parochial chief assisted by a council of family-heads. The next administrative unit was the *teku* or district, embracing a number of parishes. The *tekus* were originally organized for the purpose of tax-collection and became political divisions having at the head a district chief (*lamḍo teku*) nominated by the provincial governor. The next stage was the province or diocese (*diwal*, pl. *diwē*)[3] under a governor (*lamḍo*) nominated by the *almāmi* or patriarch, and consequently the office alternated between Alfāya and Sōriya according to the party to which the *almāmi* belonged. Each *lamḍo* was assisted by a council on which the *almāmi* was represented by a delegate (*nulal*). In addition there were tributary countries whose number varied according to the power of the provincial governors to exact tribute. Finally, at the head of the church-state were two *almāmis* with the executive power alternating from one to the other. The *almāmi* was nominated by an electoral college consisting of four representatives from the descendants of four cleric companions of Karamoko Alifa and Ibrāhīm Sōri. When nominated he was acclaimed by the general assembly of free Fulbe whose herald or spokesman exercised great influence.

[1] L. Tauxier surveys the material for the history of Futa Jalon in his *Mœurs et histoire des Peuls*, 1937.

[2] This summary is based mainly upon material in P. Marty, *Guinée*, 1921.

[3] The nine original provinces were: Timbo, Buria, Koladē (chief place: Kankalabē), Fugumba, Fodē Haji, Labē, Timbi, Kebali, and Koin. These were later increased to thirteen.

Although elected at the administrative capital of Timbo, the *almāmi* received the turban of investiture at the sacred village of Fugumba.[1] Under his presidency a council of elders decided all political, judicial, and religious matters. The council had authority to depose the *almāmi*, but naturally its exercise varied according to his strength of personality and power, for he was supreme commander of the army.

Futa Jalon was, therefore, from one point of view, a kind of aristocratic religious republic under an elective ruler, or, from another, a federation of small feudal states under an elected *imām*. The dual system of succession, the independent attitude of the provincial governors, and the intrigues of the clerics of Fugumba, rendered any stable political organization impossible. The central authority was very weak and at times governors became masters of territories wider than that of the *almāmi*. The chief of Fugumba village, regarded as the pontiff of Futa Jalon, also exercised considerable power.

Social organization was on hierarchical lines. At the head was a politico-religious aristocracy consisting of descendants of the original leaders who took an active and responsible part in political life. The next stage was formed of less distinguished freemen, various classes of Fulbe and Muslim Negroes, vassals of the nobles, who could attend assemblies but could not normally take part in the debates. These lived in their own villages (*gor*). The third group consisted of free artisan castes such as weavers, carpenters, and shoemakers, who lived in their own groups in the *gors* or their neighbourhood, and could take no part in political life. Finally, came the serf and slave groups. These became very numerous, increasing not merely in consequence of wars of aggression, but also because conquerors like al-ḥājj ʿUmar bartered their prisoners in exchange for cattle. They were divided into categories, domestic serfs who enjoyed some measure of independence, and trade-slaves living a hard life in special villages (*rundē*) under the control of an intendant appointed by the fief-holder. The Fulbe became completely sedentary in consequence of the exploitation of their human booty. A clear social distinction was reflected in the siting of villages. The Fulbe *misidis* and *fulasos*, for defensive purposes and the need to dominate the plateaux, clung to their edges or perched upon isolated hillocks; whilst the slave villages occupied the valleys into which their free ancestors had been forced by the advance of laterization.

[1] A. G. Laing, op. cit., p. 409.

3. SENEGALESE FUTA AND BONDU

A parallel revolution took place in Senegalese Futa, but it began later and reached its climax more quickly for the background was entirely different from that in Futa Jalon. The Tokolor who extend down the Senegal from Dembakené near Bakel to Dagana were thoroughly islamized although pagan Fulbe were in control. Inspired by Tyērno Sulaimān Bāl, who had studied in Futa Jalon, the Tōrodḇē or clerical class overthrew the *tyeddo* or warrior party of the Denyankē and founded a clerical state shortly before his death in 1776 when fighting against the Moors. This emerged as a feudal theocratic elective state under an *almāmi*, ʿAbd al-Qādir,[1] who without great difficulty gained control of the various groups of Wolof, Soninke, Bambara, and Mandinka inhabiting the region. He assigned lands and political authority to the warriors of the *jihād* whose fiefs carried with them the responsibility for defence against enemies, the most dangerous being the Moors who infested the right bank of the Senegal and rendered it uninhabitable for Negro cultivators. His political acumen led him to assign a position to the descendants of the *lām-Tōro* of the deposed Denyankē dynasty, whose chief was allotted a specially created province (part of the present canton of Littama) with the title of *almāmi*, where he had full control subject to the payment of tribute. In fact ʿAbd al-Qādir sought to secure the allegiance of his old adversaries by creating an avowedly pagan enclave where the old practices could be carried out, and to this day the Denyankē have been little influenced by Islam.[2]

ʿAbd al-Qādir attacked and defeated the Trārza Moors in 1786–7, fought the *damel* of Kajōr in 1796–7 with the aim of converting the Wolof to Islam, but in fact ʿAbd al-Qādir himself was taken prisoner though he was allowed to return to Futa after detention for a year. He was deposed in 1220/1805 and destroyed through a coalition consisting of Denyankē, the *almāmi* of Bondu, and the Bambara Māsa Si of Karta. When he advanced to attack Bondu with part of his army a revolt broke out in Futa. Deserted by his followers he was defeated and killed (1806) by the *almāmi* of Bondu with the aid of a Kartan force.[3]

[1] ʿAbd al-Qādir, according to one account, was born at Dyam-Weli, near Buliban, capital of Bondu, but according to another (*Chroniques du Foûta Sénégalais*, 1913, p. 43) in Salūm in 1141/1728–9.

[2] See Mahmadou Ahmadou Ba, 'Notice sur Maghana et le canton du Littama', *Bull. I.F.A.N.* i. 759. The last Denyankē *almāmi* was Diéguéré, 1885–1910.

[3] This is according to the account of Gray and Dochard (*Travels in Western Africa*,

After his death the theocratic assembly elected a cleric called Mukhtār ibn Sirē (Kudeje) as *almāmi*, but he only held authority for one year. The new type of elective system which was adopted on the analogy of early Islam did not lead to political stability, and, in fact, ʿAbd al-Qādir had thirty-three successors, many of whom had several reigns. The theocratic state thus formed was elective from among the companions of the revolt and their descendants, and the government was oligarchic. The Tōrodḇē, the clerical class, became the new nobility and formed an electoral body who chose the *almāmi* from among their number. The state had no capital and each *almāmi* resided in his native village. The state was divided into provinces. Those of Yirlābē, Hebbiyābē, and Boseya formed central Futa; those of the west (Dimār, Law, and Tōro) and the east (Ngenār and Damga) were dependent upon the central authority. Law had its local *almāmi*, Tōro had a *lām*, and eastern Futa had, as local representative of the *almāmi*, the *alfeki* of Damga.[1]

Al-ḥājj ʿUmar gained great influence in his homeland during his tour of 1854 and when he arrived again in 1857 as champion of Islam against Western penetration, he engineered the deposition of the ruling *almāmi*, Muḥammad al-Birān, and, although he did not displace the *almāmi*-ship, put on pressure to get his own nominees elected to both central and provincial offices. The former ruling clerical aristocracy never became reconciled to him, but the Tokolor masses formed the stable core of his army. He led eastwards a great exodus of the able-bodied, and afterwards the young men went each year to Nyoro or Sēgu for enlistment and initiation into the Tijāniyya. The advance of the French made ʿUmar abandon any idea of gaining complete control of the Senegal region, and after his death in 1864 it fell into complete anarchy. Many clerics sought to carve out states for themselves: Tyērno Ibrāhīm (1866–9), Mā Bā (1867), Shēhu Amadu Mahdī (1867–75), Mamadu Lamīn (1885–7), and Amadu Alfa Mūsā (1894–5) are a few of the better known. In 1841 *almāmi* Muḥammad al-Birān signed a treaty of friendship with the French, and gradually Faidherbe won over the provinces severally to accept a French protectorate. When the fifty-fourth *almāmi*, Sirē Bāba Lih, died in 1890 all seven provinces were annexed to the Senegal.

The Fulbe of Bondu, the region between Senegalese Futa and the

1818–21, London, 1825, pp. 193–9) who were nearer to the event than A. Raffenel (*Nouveau Voyage au Pays des Nègres*, 1856, ii. 345–6) who states that he was betrayed by his own Tokolor and killed by the Bambara.

[1] P. Marty, *R.M.M.* xxxi (1915–16), 275–6.

Faleme, also formed a state with an *almāmi* at the head, but it was much less anarchic than that of Futa Tōro, for the choice of *almāmi* was elective within one family which had long been influential in the country. According to tradition the dynasty which ruled in Bondu derived from a Tokolor or Pulo cleric called Mālik Si (hence the family name of Sisibē) who settled in what was then thinly inhabited Mande country with the consent of the *tuŋka* of Galam. He gathered around himself a number of pupils and died about 1680. The inhabitants of the village increased and one of his descendants, Amadi Gaye (1764–85), who lived at the time of the revolution in Futa Jalon, first adopted the title of *almāmi*.[1] The state expanded at the expense of its neighbours, especially Bambuk. Sēga Gaye (1790–4) came up against ʿAbd al-Qādir of Futa Tōro who had him assassinated after having given him a guarantee of safe-conduct. Certainly Bondu cannot be regarded as a theocratic state comparable to the other two Futas. Mungo Park, who visited the capital in 1795, was told that the *almāmi* 'was not a Mahomedan, but a Kafir or Pagan'. His informant could not have meant more than that he was slack in his Islamic observances. He himself writes of Bondu as professing to be an Islamic state:

Their government differs from that of the Mandingoes chiefly in this, that they are more immediately under the influence of Mahomedan laws: for all the chief men (the king excepted) and a large majority of the inhabitants of Bondou, are Mussulmans, and the authority and laws of the Prophet are everywhere looked upon as sacred and decisive. In the exercise of their faith, however, they are not very intolerant towards such of their countrymen as still retain their ancient superstitions.[2]

Major Gray, who writes of the vicissitudes of Bondu as a buffer-state between the Bambara of Karta and the new theocratic states, says that *almāmi* Amadi Isata (1794–1819) embraced Islam in order to gain the support of Futas Tōro and Jalon.[3] As we have seen Amadi Isata killed ʿAbd al-Qādir of Futa Tōro, and, according to Major Gray, the king

[1] Gordon Laing (travelled 1821–2) says that in 1756 the 'slaves' of Futa Jalon (subjected Jalonkē?) revolted and proceeding towards Futa Bondu founded the town of Kundian (op. cit., p. 405). But it seems from a statement by W. C. Thomson (*J.R.G.S.* xvi, 1846, 128) that this was Kundaya, west of Timbo, on the border of Benna and Tamiso. Another statement difficult to assimilate is that of J. Bayol who says (*Voyage en Sénégambie*, 1888, pp. 103–4) that in 1782 Ibrāhīm Sōri invaded Bondu and forced the chief, Maka, to embrace Islam, take the title of *almāmi*, and pay tribute. We do not know whether this is the same or some other Fulbe group.

[2] Mungo Park, *Travels*, Everyman ed., pp. 44–45.

[3] Gray and Dochard, *Travels in Western Africa*, 1825, p. 184; for these events see pp. 193–207.

of Karta (Mūsā Kurabo) made this an excuse to levy an indemnity upon Bondu, the withholding of which led to years of bloody struggles.

In the middle of the nineteenth century *almāmi* Bū Bakar Sa'āda accepted the protection of France. He refused to join the *jihād* of al-ḥājj 'Umar whose army pillaged Bondu in 1856. After his death (1885) a party hostile to his successor, 'Umar Penda, embraced the cause of the agitator Mamadu Lamīn,[1] and Bondu was devastated during the ensuing struggle before the French took over. Since then a great change has taken place in the Islam of Bondu. Formerly lukewarm and opposed to the Tijāniyya which al-ḥājj 'Umar tried to force upon them, their reaction to European influence has made them more fervent Muslims and the Tijāniyya has grown greatly in numbers and influence.

4. THE WOLOF AND ISLAM

Historical events led to the differentiation of the Wolof and Tokolor from Serer. Pressed by Moors and Soninke the Serer had crossed the Senegal and settled along the Atlantic coast before the arrival of the Portuguese. Many of their politically uncoordinated groups paid some form of allegiance to the various rulers of Takrūr until the middle of the fourteenth century when Nydadyan Ndyay[2] founded a dynasty in Jolof which under his successors gained control over a widening circle of Serer groups and part of the Tokolor region. From this time the Wolof differentiated themselves as a separate people. Little by little sections gained their independence. Early Portuguese travellers show that by the middle of the fifteenth century the *dạmel* of Kajōr, the *barak* of Walo, the *tēñ* of Baol, and the *būr-bar-Salum* were independent of the

[1] Muḥammad al-Amīn, generally known as Mamadu Lamīn, apostle of the Soninke and leader of their resistance against the French, was born at Madina in Khaso about 1835/40 (according to others at the old Soninke village of Gondyoro). He studied with various clerics and first makes his appearance among the companions of al-ḥājj 'Umar and Amadu Sēku whom he left in Sēgu in order to perform the pilgrimage to Mecca (1874). On his return seven years later he claimed to be the spiritual and temporal successor of al-ḥājj 'Umar and came into conflict with Amadu Sēku of Sēgu. His ambition to create a Dyakhanke state was frustrated by the French advance. He declared war on them and besieged Bakel (1886). When repulsed he took refuge in Bondu whose *almāmi* he defeated. He fled again when the French entered Diana (Dec. 1886), and the process went on until he was killed at Tubakuta in December 1887.

[2] The desire to introduce an Islamic element has hopelessly confused these legends. These say that about A.D. 1200 a Muslim called Abū Bakr ibn 'Umar (an echo of the Murābiṭ movement), generally known as Abū Darday, came from Mecca to settle in Senegal and preached Islam. He married Fatimata Sal, the daughter of the *lām-Toro*, by whom he had a son called Nydadyan Ndyay (or Aḥmad) who gained control of Walo and later Jolof.

būr-ba-Jolof although they recognized him as suzerain and would seek his aid as arbitrator. The real break-up of the empire followed the conquests of Koli Tengella[1] in the first half of the sixteenth century when the Wolof lost control of Dimār and Tōro. After the revolt of Danki in 1549 Kajōr and Baol became independent. Until the seventeenth century Wolof kept control of the right bank of the river, but by its end they had been driven off by Moors whose intransigence disrupted the ethnic and cultural equilibrium of the region.

During the period of the great Wolof state many small chieftaincies had been formed among the southern Serer. A little before the first Portuguese arrived Mandinka, migrating from N'gabu (Portuguese Guinea) region, settled among them and took over the chieftaincies of Sin, Salum, Baol, Uli, Niani, and N'gabu, which were linked by various political ties with those of the Wolof. The ruling class of Mande origin (known as *gelowar* in Sin and Salum and *garmi*, Ar. *qarm*, in Walo, Kajōr, and Baol) are said to have been Muslims of a sort when they took over the Serer states, but they soon lost their Mande characteristics and became pagan. The most important Serer states were Sin (whose chiefs in Fernandes's time still professed Islam) situated on the right bank of the Salum river, and Salum adjoining Sin inland, whose authority at one time extended to the River Gambia. The tiny Serer states of N'Dukuman, Kungeul, Pakalla, Mandak, Rip, Lagem, and Niombato generally paid allegiance to either Sin or Salum. Rip became independent of Salum and more or less islamized when invaded by Tokolor under a leader called Dabali, and it was in Nioro, its main village, that the agitator Mā Bā began in 1864 to organize resistance against the French.

The adoption of Islam by the Wolof was a slow process until in the second half of the nineteenth century a people's movement developed. Since their territory bordered upon that of Moors and Tokolor, Islamic influence was present among the northern groups certainly before the fifteenth century when Ca ḍa Mosto in 1455 found the chiefs professing Islam.[2] Their attachment, however, was ephemeral, but

[1] See above, pp. 75, 150–1.

[2] Ca da Mosto, *Voyages in Western Africa*, transl. G. R. Crone, 1937, p. 31. Valentim Fernandes (1506–10) also reports that 'The king and all his nobles and chiefs of the province of *Giloffa* are Muslims and have white *bischerijs* who are clergy and preachers of Muḥammad, and know how to read and write. These *bisserrijs* come from deep within the interior, such as the kingdom of Fez or Moroccos. . . . Some of the population or common people believe in Muḥammad, but the great majority are idolaters' (V. Fernandes, *Description de la Côte Occidentale d'Afrique*, ed. and transl. Th. Monod, A. Teixeira da Mota, and R. Mauny, Bissau, 1951, pp. 7–9).

though remaining pagans they adopted a liberal attitude towards clerics, allowing them to settle and form new groupings which often took their name.

The inhabitants of Tōro were the first to become Muslims but completely lost their Serer identity. From the seventeenth century Islam began to gain some of the people of Walo and Kajōr who were exploited by the ruling and warrior classes. The ruling class, whose filiation (except in the *būr-ba-Jolof* lineage) is by the maternal line, were particularly resistant to islamization, though they maintained clerics in their entourage and observed the festivals. The first attempt of a Muslim party to gain control was in 1682.[1] After it failed Islam was in eclipse politically until the eighteenth century. The Tōrodḅē of Futa attempted to wage a *jihād* in Wolof country on two occasions. In 1720 they invaded Kajōr at the invitation of enemies of the *damel*. More formidable was the attack of ʿAbd al-Qādir, *almāmi* of Futa, towards the end of the century. Invading Walo he captured the *barak*, Fara Penda, and his chiefs when they were engaged in a drinking orgy, and had their heads shaved as a sign of their obligatory conversion. Four years later the *barak* revolted and was killed in an encounter with the *almāmi*. Mungo Park gives an account of how ʿAbd al-Qādir invaded Kajōr, was routed and captured by the *damel*, but released after a few months.[2] The history and progress of Islam is associated with a series of internal struggles which brought about the interference of neighbouring Muslims. As long as Islam represented the aggression of Moors and Tokolor, who tried to impose it on allies and foes alike, the religion progressed but slowly. The real influence at work was that of the clerics nurtured in the Mauritanian *zawāyā*. These events and the propaganda of the clerics led to many of the northern Wolof (the thinly populated Walo and many districts of Kajōr, e.g. Ndyambur) professing Islam,[3] though those of Jolof and the Serer states, including Baol whose ruling class was Wolof, were less influenced.

[1] J. Le Maire (*Voyages*, 1695) gives some information about the Wolof and their relations with Moorish clergy. A little before 1685 de la Courbe reports that the Moors profited from the discord reigning in the Wolof states to incite the people to kill the *barak* and expel the *damel* and the *būr-ba-Jolof* from their states. Afterwards Wolof rulers again gained the ascendancy. The *damel*, Ditchiu-Maram, dispossessed chieftainess Yasin, mother of his predecessor, and she offered herself in marriage to a cleric, Ndyay Sal, on condition that he incited his disciples against the *damel*. In the encounter the *damel* was killed and succeeded by his brother under the patronage of Ndyay Sal. The assassination of the new *damel* by the cleric's disciples led to the intervention of the *būr* of Salum and the destruction of the Muslim party.

[2] Mungo Park, *Travels* (Everyman ed.), pp. 261–3.

[3] G. Mollien (*Travels in Africa*, London, 1820, p. 23) wrote in 1818 that, though the

With the arrival of Faidherbe as governor in 1854 and increasing French domination over the Senegal, the old religious foundations of the rulers was wrecked and Islam began to make rapid progress. The ruling class joined it as a basis of resistance to French domination. In this process the influence of Mā Bā (d. 1867), a Tokolor cleric from Futa who gathered around him the forces of resistance by exhortations to the *jihād*, was especially important. The domination of the Trārza Moors over Walo, now completely islamized, was brought to an end by the French in 1855. Makodu, *damel* of Kajōr (1859–62), a drunkard and oppressor of his people, welcomed their influence, but his successor, Lat Dyōr (*damel* 1862–3, 1871–82), a strong partisan of Wolof independence, with the greatest reluctance accepted Islam for the needs of his cause. After 1886, the year Lat Dyōr was killed, the dismembership of the Wolof states and the dispossession of their rulers by the French left the way open for the appearance of a new form of authority based upon devotion to a Muslim saint. Under the inspiration of Aḥmad Bamba Islam was adapted to the needs of the Wolof soul in such a way that it could claim their complete devotion.

5. THE STATE OF SHAIKH ḤAMAD OF MĀSINA

For four centuries since its foundation the ruling clan of the Fulbe of Māsina was that of the Dyālo or Dyālubē. The next most powerful clan was the Sangarē, who were rivals of the Dyālo. Ḥamadu (or Aḥmadu) was the son of a cleric belonging to the Bari family of this clan. After receiving his early education from his father he began his travels. About 1805 he assisted in the initial stages of the *jihād* of ʿUthmān ḍan Fodio in Hausaland. Then settling in a Pulo hamlet near Jennē he was expelled as a subversive element by the *arma*, the descendants of the Moroccan *qā'ids* then in control of the town, whereupon he settled at Sono in Sebera where he opened a Qur'ān school. One day some of his *ṭalaba* were plundered by a son of Gurori Dyālo (or Ḥamadi Dikko), *arḍo* of Māsina (1801–10). They complained to their master who advised them to kill the *arḍo*'s son. When they did this Ḥamadu had to remove his school to Soy to escape the vengeance of the *arḍo*. Ḥamadu's fame and arrogance was now getting out of bounds, therefore the *arḍo* sought the help of his overlord, Da Dyara, the Bambara ruler of Sēgu. Da sent one of his captains to capture Ḥamadu,

ruling class of Kajōr remained attached to their own religion, the masses had adopted Islam. F. Carrère and P. Holle (*De la Sénégambie Française*, 1855, pp. 59, 96) say that Islam had been adopted by the people of Walo and Kajōr.

MAP 5

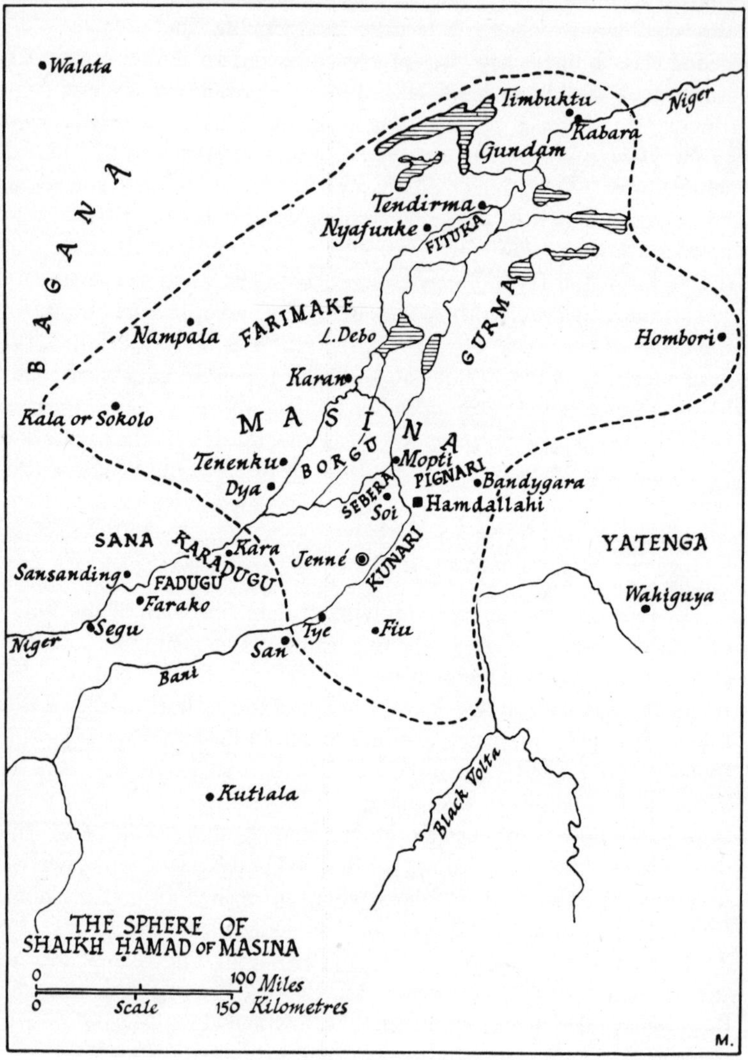

Walata
Timbuktu
Niger
Kabara
Gundam
Tendirma
Nyafunke
FITUKA
BAGANA
FARIMAKE
Nampala
L. Debo
GURMA
Hombori
Karan
Kala or Sokolo
MASINA
BORGU
Tenenku
Mopti
PIGNARI
Bandygara
Dya
SEBERA
Soi
Hamdallahi
SANA
KARADUGU
Kara
Jenné
KUNARI
YATENGA
Sansanding
FADUGU
Farako
Wahiguya
Segu
Niger
Tye
Fiu
San
Bani
Black Volta
Kutiala
THE SPHERE OF
SHAIKH ḤAMAD OF MASINA
0
100 Miles
0
Scale
150 Kilometres
M.

who thereupon proclaimed the *jihād* and won a notable victory over the Bambara near Soy by means of a stratagem. This victory coincided with the arrival of a flag (*tūta*) which he had sent two of his brothers to seek from ʿUthmān ḍan Fodio, but Ḥamadu, now confident in his own ability to carry through the revolution, ceased to have any further connexion with ʿUthmān.

Shēhu Ḥamadu was now able to impose his authority over all Sebera. The Fulbe of Māsina, who had been watching the turn of events before committing themselves to the new leader, took the opportunity to escape from the yoke of the Bambara and in 1810 delivered up the person of Ḥamadi Dikko, *arḍo* of Māsina. Ḥamadu refused the traditional title of *arḍo*, which meant 'leader of the migration', as unsuitable to his pretensions, and like ʿUthmān took that of *amīr al-mu'minīn*, and claimed that he was the last of the twelve *imāms*.[1] The people of Jennē, who were fervent Muslims, now sought his protection, and he sent representatives to exercise authority in his name. These were killed by the *arma*, whereupon Ḥamadu besieged and captured the town. He then crossed the Bani, entered Konāri, and after a long struggle drove out its Pulo ruler, Muḥammad Galadyo.[2] In Konāri, on the right bank of the Bani, he founded Ḥamdullāhi as his capital (1815), and it was here that he was visited by al-ḥājj ʿUmar in 1838 on his return journey from Mecca.

Ḥamadu, unlike ʿUthmān ḍan Fodio, proved capable of controlling his Fulbe and showed exceptional administrative abilities. Once his rule was established he organized the state on theocratic lines, appointing an *amīr* and a *qāḍī* to each province, establishing a system of taxation, a *bait al-māl*, and a form of a military service. Ḥamdullāhi was divided into seven quarters, each with its *qāḍī* and with a *qāḍī al-quḍāt* at the head. The assembly of judges with the theocrat as chairman formed a council of state. The taxes[3] consisted of a tithe on the harvest, of which a tenth went to the collector, a fifth to the ruler, and the remainder to the chief of the province to pay for its administration and the relief of the poor. During its short existence the state founded by

[1] *T. al-Fattāsh*, Introd., p. xii.

[2] Ḥamadu had a long struggle before he was able to subject the Pulo chiefs who had been his allies in the early stages but resented his assumption of authority. Galadyo, the most powerful Pulo chief of the Konāri region, had embraced Islam in the attempt to bolster up his authority. He was forced to retreat eastwards to lands under the control of Abd Allāh ḍan Fodio who gave him a district in Gurma where Barth met him in his old age in 1853 (H. Barth, *Travels*, iv. 253–8).

[3] On his taxation system see Ch. Monteil, *Djenné*, pp. 107–10.

Shaikh Ḥamad was the most genuine Islamic state West Africa has ever seen.

At the beginning of the nineteenth century the majority of the Fulbe of the region were still pagan, but they were all required to accept Islam by Shēhu Ḥamadu. Similarly the Bozo and Somono and those Bambara who came under his jurisdiction joined Islam, and in general their conversion was permanent,[1] though some repudiated it after the fall of the Tokolor state which succeeded that of the Bari founded by Ḥamadu.

When Shēhu Ḥamadu died in 1844 he had extended his authority over all the eastern region from the confluence of the Black Volta and the Suru in the south to Isa Ber and Timbuktu, which he had conquered in 1826–7, in the north. He broke with custom by nominating his son and not his brother as successor. On Ḥamadu's death the people of Timbuktu repudiated the authority of the theocrat, but Ḥamadu II succeeded in getting his authority recognized in 1846 by an agreement with the Kuntī Shaikh al-Bakkā'ī, brother of Shaikh al-Mukhtār, whereby all officials were to be Songhay with the exception of a supervisory Pulo tax-collector.[2] Ḥamadu Sēku II died in 1852 having designated as successor his son Ḥamadu III who had to face the great conqueror al-ḥājj 'Umar. He allied himself with the Bambara of Sēgu and the Kunta, but was defeated by the superior generalship of 'Umar who took Ḥamdullāhi in 1862 and put to death the grandson of the ruler who had received him in 1838. Tokolor rule was now established over Māsina.

But the theocratic state did not come to an end until the French occupation (1892–3). A general uprising instigated by Ba Lobbo, uncle of Ḥamadu III, assisted by al-Bakkā'ī, led to the death of the great conqueror in 1864. But his nephew, at-Tijānī, making Banjāgara his capital, succeeded after years of struggles in reconquering

[1] Ch. Monteil, *Les Bambara du Ségou et du Kaarta*, p. 340.

[2] The austere outlook of Ḥamadu, which was maintained by his successors, bore hardly upon Sudanese Muslims who were deprived of their beer, tobacco, and dances. Barth says that he treated the inhabitants of Timbuktu, which as a commercial city was the abode of many vices, with extreme rigour. In 1831 its merchants sought the aid of the Kunta and Shaikh al-Mukhtār came from Azawād to help them drive out the Fulbe garrison (1844). The Kunta became a third power seeking to hold the balance between Fulbe and Tuareg. But the Fulbe continued to exercise a loose control since they could starve the city, and in 1846 al-Bakkā'ī, brother and successor of al-Mukhtār, concluded a treaty whereby the town was recognized as tributary to the theocracy of Ḥamdullāhi but without being garrisoned by a Fulbe force, the collection of tribute being entrusted to two *qāḍīs*, one a Pulo and the other a Songhay. This was the situation when Barth stayed there in 1853 (cf. H. Barth, op. cit. iv. 433–6).

Māsina, during the course of which the country was devastated. At-Tijānī maintained the theocratic state along the austere lines laid down by Shaikh Ḥamadu, in fact exaggerating some features so that the *muḥtasib* or 'censor of public morals', for example, became a kind of inquisitor. He was succeeded by his sons at-Tafsīr (1888) and Munīr (1888–91) who was dispossessed by Amadu Sēku after his desertion of Nyoro. Amadu was forced to move again when defeated by the French in 1893.

6. THE EMPIRE OF AL-ḤĀJJ ʿUMAR

ʿUmar ibn Saʿīd Tal was born in 1794 or 1797 at Alo'ār (or Halwār) near Podor in Senegalese Futa. As the son of a cleric he received a religious education, and in 1826 he set off to perform the pilgrimage to Mecca where he was initiated into the Tijāniyya *ṭarīqa* and, so he claimed, appointed *khalīfa* for the Sudan. He acquired a considerable reputation during his return journey which lasted many years, by way of Bornu under al-Kānemī and Sokoto under Muḥammad Belo where he remained three years taking part in the wars and acquiring a considerable booty of slaves. After a short stay in Māsina (1838) under Shēhu Ḥamadu he went on to Sēgu from which he was expelled; then Kangaba (Māli) and the Kankan region where he travelled seven years teaching and initiating, and finally he settled at Dingiray at the point of intersection between Futa Jalon, Bambuk, and Bondu. The years 1845–50 were spent in consolidation. His material power began when he broke with Gimba Sakho, the Jalonkē ruler of Tamba (Dabatu) who had permitted him to settle in Dingiray, and during the struggle the Jalonkē were defeated (1852). During 1850 he had been active in Futa Jalon spreading his *ṭarīqa* among the lesser clergy, trying to detach them from the Qādiriyya and allegiance to the *almāmis* and attract them to Dingiray. Although he never attacked Futa Jalon, Fulbe from there formed the solid core of the army of conquest he built up in Dingiray, and the relationship between Fulbe and Tokolor remained cordial.

When ʿUmar felt the time was right he spent forty days in solitary retreat and then proclaimed the *jihād*. He first sought to get control of his native land Futa Tōro, which he had revisited a number of times, by peaceful propaganda; and although the *almāmis* and the Moors held themselves aloof the Tokolor became his strongest supporters. He invaded Bambuk and entered Nyoro, capital of Kārta, in 1854. By then his *jihād* was clearly directed against European penetration, but the

MAP 6

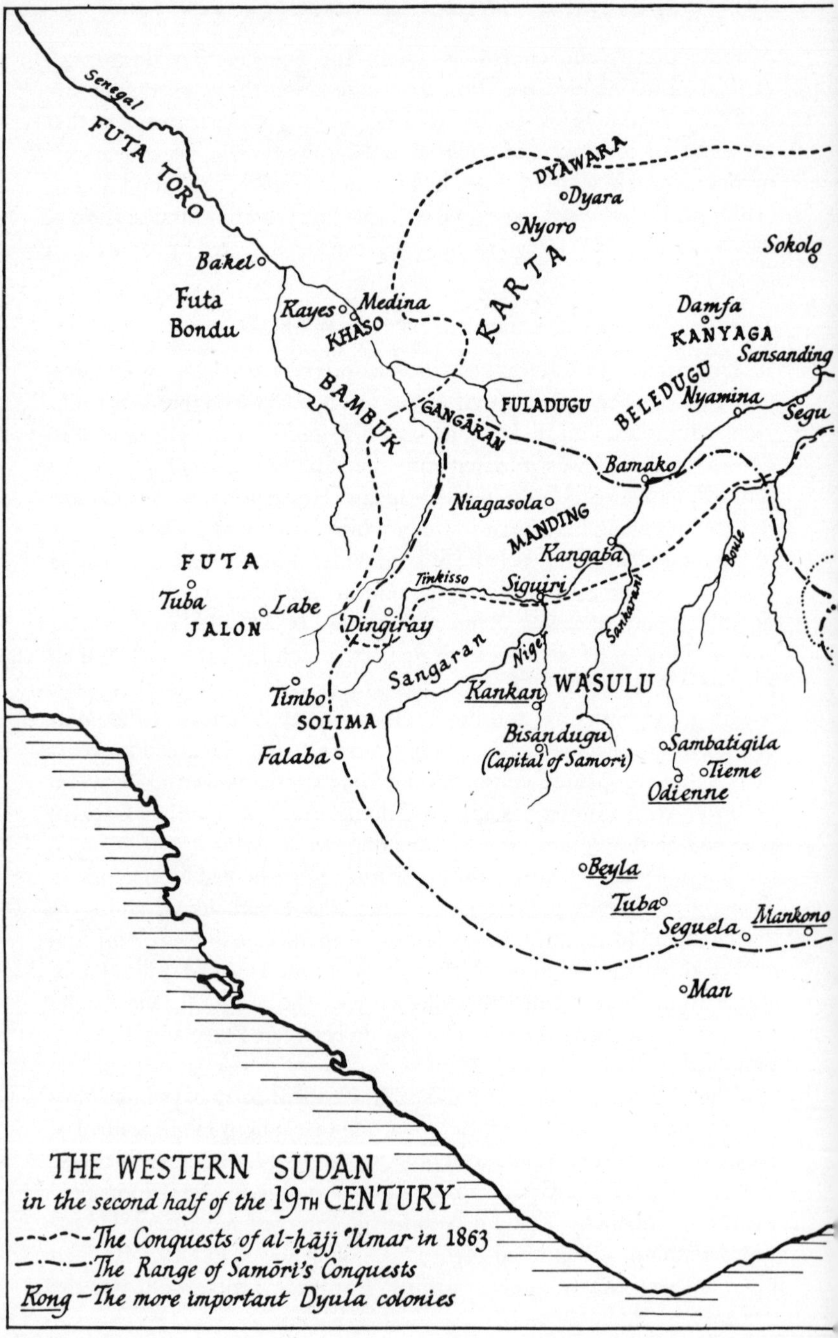

Senegal
FUTA TORO
DYAWARA
oDyara
oNyoro
KARTA
Sokolo
Bakel
Futa
Bondu
Kayes
Medina
KHASO
Damfa
KANYAGA
Sansanding
BAMBUK
FULADUGU
BELEDUGU
Nyamina
Segu
GANGĀRAN
Bamako
Niagasola
MANDING
Kangaba
FUTA
Tuba
Labe
JALON
Tinkisso
Siguiri
Dingiray
Boule
Sankarani
Niger
Sangaran
Timbo
Kankan
WASULU
SOLIMA
Bisandugu
(Capital of Samori)
Falaba
Sambatigila
Tieme
Odienne
Beyla
Tuba
Seguela
Mankono
Man
THE WESTERN SUDAN
in the second half of the 19TH CENTURY
The Conquests of al-ḥājj 'Umar in 1863
The Range of Samōri's Conquests
Kong – The more important Dyula colonies

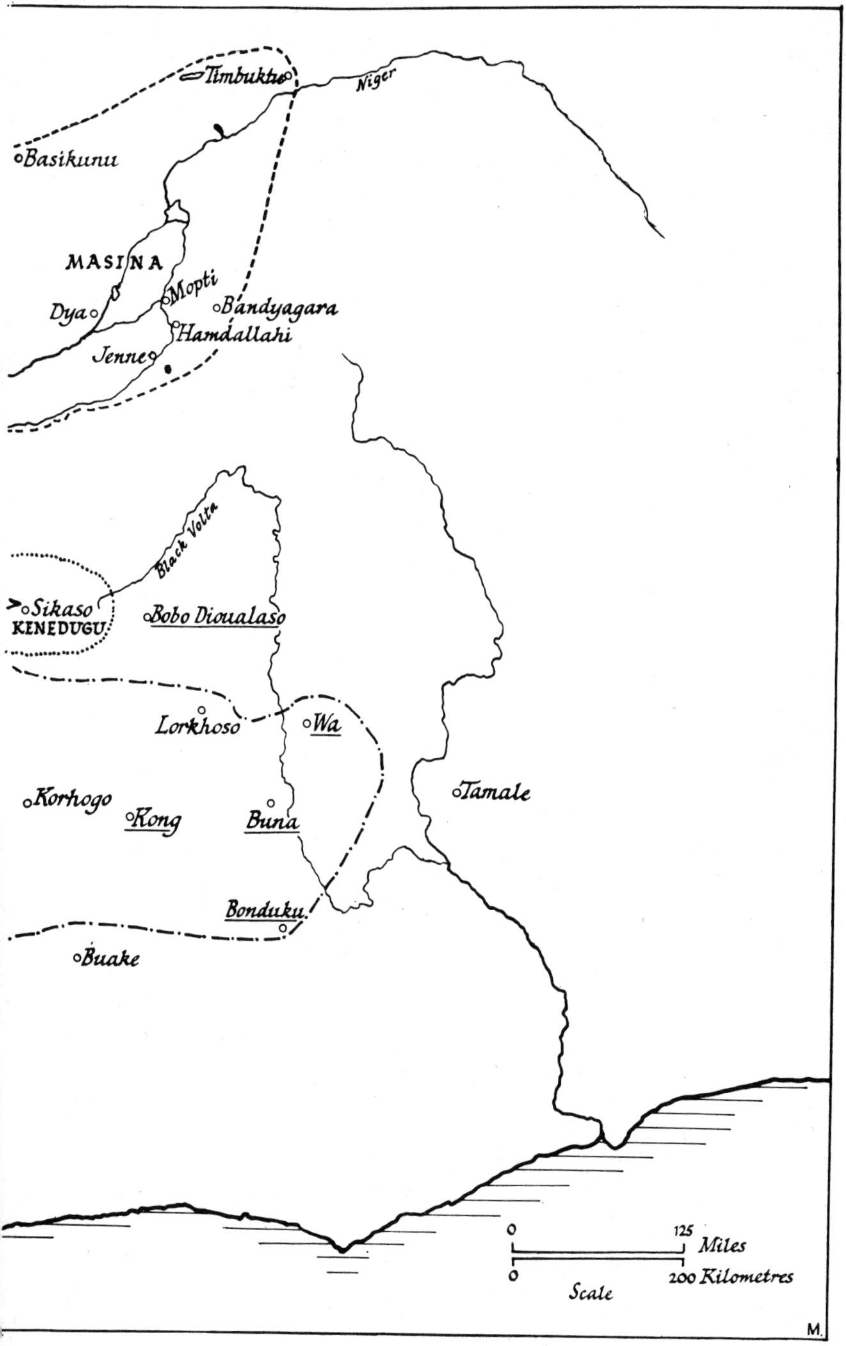

Timbuktu
Niger
Basikunu
MASINA
Mopti
Dya
Bandyagara
Hamdallahi
Jenne
Black Volta
Sikaso
KENEDUGU
Bobo Dioualaso
Lorkhoso
Wa
Korhogo
Kong
Buna
Tamale
Bonduku
Buake
0
125 Miles
0
200 Kilometres
Scale
M.

turning-point in this direction came in 1857 when the French relieved Madīna, capital of Khāso, which he was blockading. When he realized that the encroachment of European powers would make it impossible to build up a state on the Senegal he withdrew eastwards, conquering and enslaving, to form an empire from the Bambara kingdoms and Māsina. Tōro, however, remained his most important source of man-power, and regularly after the rains contingents of young men set out to join his army. After taking Sēgu in 1861 his urge carried him on to the conquest of Māsina and that proved his undoing. The religious revolution the imposition of his rule involved through enforcing Tijānī allegiance upon Qādirī adherents provoked a strong reaction from both the Fulbe of Māsina and the Kunta leaders. Aḥmad al-Bakkā'ī, head of the Kunta, joined forces with the Fulbe and during the struggle 'Umar lost his life (1864).

'Umar was inspired with concern for the spread of Islam merely in so far as it furthered his ambition to form a great theocracy with himself as the divinely appointed ruler. He was acutely conscious that his conquest of the theocratic state of Māsina was illegitimate and sought by various means to justify it.[1] He used the Tijānī link to bind leaders through the oath of allegiance to himself. Among the Tokolor he became a messianic figure and many still cherish the belief that he will come again. Among the Bambara his forcible conversions to Islam did not in general lead to permanent adherence, for once the French gained control the old religious foundations proved to have survived unshaken.

'Umar died at the height of his power, but before he had been able to consolidate his empire, and left his successor to face a vast legacy of troubles, dynastic squabbles, perpetual revolts, and the steady encroachment of the French. In 1862, before he left Sēgu for the conquest of Māsina, he had clearly designated his son, Aḥmad ash-Shaikh, generally known as Amadu Sēku, as his *khalīfa*, and an Arabic account of his life says that he paid allegiance to him as such.[2] Aḥmad's long reign was one of continual troubles. His position was peculiarly difficult

[1] Ḥamadu Ḥamadu of Māsina had allied himself with 'Alī, the *fama* of Sēgu, against the threat from 'Umar on condition that 'Alī embraced Islam and destroyed the symbols of idolatry. 'Alī merely adopted the outward forms of Islam and when he was defeated transported all the symbols of the royal clan to Ḥamdullāhi. When 'Umar took the town he assembled all these idols triumphantly before the *'ulamā'* and declared that Ḥamadu Ḥamadu had been a double-dealer (see L. Tauxier, *La Religion Bambara*, pp. 209, 468).

[2] The phrase is rather unusual: *wa bāya'a lahu 'l-ḥājj 'Umar bi nafsihi*; cf. M. Delafosse, *Traditions historiques . . . du Soudan Occidental*, 1913, p. 84. 'Ajīb b. 'Umar himself related how his father called all his sons together and appointed Aḥmad his successor (see A. de Loppinot, 'Souvenirs d'Aguibou', *Bull. Com. Ét. A.O.F.* 1919, p. 27).

since he lacked his father's great personal prestige to enable him to impose his authority upon Tokolor chiefs who wished to settle down to enjoy the fruits of conquest rather than to engage in perpetual fighting. Once the strong hand of the conqueror was removed, local and partisan ambitions asserted themselves, whilst new men and old ruling families sought after power. During the first years of his reign he was occupied in asserting his control over the Bambara of Sēgu. Although his brothers and other governors recognized his titular succession, they governed their states in virtual independence. Ḥabīb, who revolted against him in 1868, was ruler of Dingiray, Mukhtār had his seat at Koniakari, and his father's slave Muṣṭafā ruled Kārta from Nyoro. After a long struggle Aḥmad's cousin at-Tijānī, probably the ablest of 'Umar's successors, regained control of Māsina after 'Umar's death. In achieving this he was aided by the lack of unity between the Fulbe of Māsina and Sīdi al-Bakkā'ī and received help from the pagan Dogon who hated the Fulbe. He ruled it from a new capital Banjāgara.' In February 1874 in an attempt to reinforce his authority Amadu Sēku assumed the title of *amīr al-mu'minīn*.

The core of 'Umar's armies consisted of the *tālibēs* (Arab. *ṭālib*, pl. *ṭalaba*) who were mainly Tokolor from Futa Tōro. These formed the leaders. After them came the *sōfas* (lit. 'groom'), subject peoples and slaves enrolled into a regular army.[1] The *tālibēs* proved difficult to deal with and their number steadily diminished so that Amadu had not more than five to six thousand left in 1880. The *tālibēs* (together with certain Soninke families of the Sēgu region) formed the privileged class. Exempted from taxation, their function consisted in readiness when called upon to go out to war. All were armed with guns and were expected to provide themselves with horses; these gave them a military superiority over any adversary they were likely to encounter except Europeans. In the later stages Amadu had reason to distrust them; he refused to appoint them to many offices of state, and was forced to rely more and more upon subject peoples, and sometimes *sōfas* (such as the Bambara *almāmi* of Murgula) were accorded positions of authority.[2]

French penetration into interior Sudan began in 1878. At the same time came the rise of the Mandinka adventurer Samōri, and rivalries

[1] *Tyeddo* (pl. *tyebbē*) is the Tokolor name for professional soldiers and mercenaries as distinguished from free Tokolor or Fulbe who were primarily agriculturalists or pastoralists and only warriors when the need arose. Troubles with the *tālibēs* were accentuated because they were living an unreal life away from their home villages and cattle.

[2] See Gallieni, *Voyage au Soudan Français*, 1885, pp. 608–9.

between him and the Tokolor leaders enabled the French to defeat them separately and bring peace to this vast war-tortured region. In 1884 Amadu, feeling his life in danger from discontented elements in Sēgu, transferred himself to Nyoro, dispossessing his brother Munṭaqā whom he had installed there in 1873. The anarchy into which the whole country had fallen gave him no chance of opposing any effective resistance to the French who defeated ʿAjīb, *almāmi* of Dingiray, in 1889; the next year they took Sēgu, and then marched on Nyoro. Amadu fled to Banjāgara, where his defeat in 1893 brought an end to Tokolor dominion over interior Sudan. Moving westwards into Dori, leaving anarchy in his wake, Amadu ended up in the Sokoto state where he died in 1898.

7. MANDE DISPERSION AND COLONIZATION

Since the disintegration of Māli the history of the Mandinka has been characterized by political disunity and they fell an easy prey before the attacks of the great adventurers. Vallière wrote in 1880:

> The Manding nation is absolutely devoid of unity and one must undoubtedly go back far into history in order to find it with a government recognized by all the country. Each village lives separately under its own chief and, although these chiefs all belong to two or three illustrious families, yet in spite of their ties of relationship they have no solidarity of interests. This lack of cohesion between people of the same nation has already produced very bad effects in putting them at the mercy of the Tokolor. . . . Yet strangely enough, these profound divisions and the isolation of each group have not destroyed the ancient national pride and the Mandings speak with emphasis of the Keyta and the Kamara from whom they descend.[1]

Greater initiative was shown by the Mande trading element who were definitely Muslim and spread Islam into upper Guinea and the upper Ivory Coast. This region is peopled by Mandinka in the west (Beyla founded 1763, Kankan *c.* 1690, Kurussa and Odienne region), and Senufo (Sienne or Sienamana) in the centre and east. Other Mandinka migrations came from the west, from the upper Niger and upper Milo (Wasulonke, Futanke, and Dyomande). These immigrants were pagans, but the trading classes among them were Muslims and Muslim Mande spread over the regions of Kankan and Beyla (in the east of Guinea), and in Odienne, Tūba, Man, Kong, and Segela (upper

[1] Gallieni, *Voyage au Soudan Français (1879–1881)*, 1885, p. 338. He enumerates the little Mandinka states, pp. 578–603.

Ivory Coast), Wa and Salaga (modern Ghana), and in Mossi country. Coming primarily as peaceful traders, settling in villages along the trade routes, they brought a measure of prosperity and were welcomed by the pagan peoples among whom they settled. Caillié, who stayed some months at Tienne (near the future Odienne) in 1827 wrote:

> Throughout all this part of the country there are Mandingo villages, the inhabitants of which are Mahometans. They are independent of the Bambaras,[1] as at Timé, Sambatikela, Tangrera, and other villages further south ward. The Bambaras call them *Diaulas* or *Jaulas*, and though they might, owing to their superiority of numbers, molest them if they choose, yet they refrain from doing so, and go to their villages to sell them the superfluous produce of their harvest.[2]

The Dyula married local women and around their commercial centres larger Muslim communities were formed. They had little religious effect upon the local pagans for their primary passion was trading and their Islamic influence incidental. These centres were practically autonomous and Islam reinforced their solidarity. They built mosques in the Sudanese style in their villages and opened Qur'ān schools. Through their commercial activities they gained increasing influence among pagans and during the nineteenth century made various attempts to gain political control and formed small states such as those of Kong (1730–1895) and Odienne (1835–98). The detailed history of these petty states would be disproportionate to their significance in this historical outline, but we may mention one or two which make their appearance in Samōri's career of conquest.

The town of Kong (Kpõ) in the savanna lands of the north of the present Ivory Coast, a region famous for the production of kola, was founded originally by Senufo. At an early date Dyula came to the region for trade and were welcomed by the Senufo as a useful addition to the community. About 1730 the immigrants had gained such power through their monopoly of trade and the art of weaving that, under a leader called Shaiku, they seized the village of Kong and made it the centre of a small federal state. They succeeded in gaining control over a large area from Bobo Dioulasso (under them since 1860) in the north to the borders of the forest in the south. The village grew into an important Mande centre of commerce and Islam, and when visited by Binger in 1888 had 15,000 inhabitants, a very large town in such a region. The Sudanese form of architecture was introduced, its five

[1] Bambara is the term used in this region for 'pagan' Mandinka.

[2] R. Caillié, *Travels through Central Africa*, London, 1830, i. 376.

mosques were adorned with double pyramidal minarets and the houses of the ruling classes with pylons and terraces. It had a thriving and well-stocked market, and its chief industries were weaving, dyeing, and basketry work. Monnier, who visited the town in 1892, found the sight of it rather surprising:

> La ville, surtout vue du nord-ouest, dorée par le soleil couchant, avec les minarets pyramidaux de ses cinq mosquées, les palmiers détachant leur fine silhouette sur le ciel, les terrasses superposées où des groupes de fidèles apparaissent à l'heure de la prière, est une vision inoubliable.[1]

Commerce was the primary aim of its inhabitants and of its religious influence Monnier writes:

> Ici pas plus qu'à Bondoukou, le sentiment religieux n'est exalté. C'est un islamisme à fleur de peau, pour la convenance, par ce que le fait d'être musulman constitue une supériorité. Cela ne va pas plus loin. On fait salam, mais on boit du dolo. Toute cette race Dioula, âpre et travailleuse, dont les caravanes arpentent la route du Niger, a l'esprit trop absorbé par son négoce pour s'attarder dans l'idéal.[2]

In 1889 the chief of Kong, Karamoko Ule (Domba) Watara, accepted an agreement placing the state under French protection. Samōri was soon afterwards active, and, having forced a French force sent to relieve Kong to withdraw, attacked the town and razed it to the ground, mosques and all, in April 1895. Its people today point out the ruins of the old *jāmiʿ* where forty of their clerics were massacred. The Dyula of Kong migrated to Bobo Dioulasso and founded Dār as-Salām and a number of other villages in Bobo country; few returned after the French defeated Samōri and the town has never recovered from this disaster.

Another centre was in the Odienne region. This lies between the Muslim centres of Kankan-Beyla and Kong. One Kaba Tūrē (generally known as *Fa* Kaba), belonging to an immigrant family from Jennē, collected a band of warriors and having devastated Sienko formed a camp which he called Wogyende (Odienne). He and his successor, Mango Mamadu (or Amadu Tūrē), devastated the region and their expansion was only stopped about 1874 by a coalition of Senufo. Mango Mamadu consolidated his power by marrying a daughter of Samōri, who, at the beginning of his career, wished to neutralize a possible rival. The Mango-Samōri coalition imposed itself over the

[1] M. Monnier, quoted by Marty, *Études sur l'Islam en Côte d'Ivoire*, 1922, p. 188.

[2] Quoted by Marty, op. cit., p. 191.

whole region. The French occupation of Odienne in 1898 brought an end to the state, but the result of its formation was that the Senufo supremacy over the Mandinka was lost for ever. Though the pagan element still predominates even among the Mandinka, the islamization of the latter seems to be only a question of time.[1]

Other important trading colonies lived peacefully among pagans. Bonduku, for instance, was founded by Dyula who had abandoned Bēgo[2] after a civil war. The Kulango inhabitants of the region were conquered in the fifteenth century by the Abron who founded a kingdom which still exists. The Dyula of Bonduku remained in good relations with their Abron overlords as a kind of semi-independent chieftaincy. The Abron were attacked by Samōri and Bonduku was occupied by his son, Sarañgye Mōri, in 1895. Today, though the town itself is Muslim, there are only 7,000 Muslims in the whole *cercle*, whilst the people of the country (33,000 Abron and Kulango) have remained pagan.

8. SAMŌRI'S CAREER OF CONQUEST

We have many times mentioned the name of this famous adventurer who attempted to form a Mandinka empire in the region watered by the upper basin of the Niger and its tributaries. Less extensive than that of al-ḥājj ʿUmar it was even less enduring by reason of the French conquest.

Samōri ibn Lāfiya Tūrē[3] is identified with the Mandinka. Born about 1830–5, his father is said to have been a *dyula* of Soninke origin living in Sanan-koro, a village south-east of Kankan.[4] But Samōri is said 'to have become Malinkē in order to stress that he had ceased to be a merchant in order to become a warrior'.[5] Samōri's mother was carried off as a slave by the local chief and Samōri, being very attached to her, enlisted in the chief's army to serve out her release. He acquired

[1] Out of a total population of 114,000 in the *cercle* of Odienne 64,000 or 73 per cent. are Muslims.

[2] Bēgo, according to tradition, was formerly a great trading centre north-east of Bonduku in what is now Ghana territory. It has been suggested that it was the Bīṭu mentioned by as-Saʿdī, *T. as-Sūdān*, p. 11.

[3] For the history of Samōri see E. Péroz, *Au Soudan Français*, 1889, pp. 388–400; A. Mévil, *Samory*, 1899; Delafosse, *H.S.N.* ii. 341–51; and the account in the Dyula dialect in Delafosse, *Essai de manuel pratique de la langue Mandé*, *P.E.L.O.V.*, série iii, vol. 14, pp. 145–93.

[4] Muslim in name only he continued to offer sacrifices in the sacred-grove of Sanan-koro much to the embarrassment of Samōri (see E. Péroz, op. cit., pp. 230–1).

[5] Gallieni, op. cit., p. 599.

great renown as a warrior and eventually became war-chief of Bitikē-Suwanē, chief of Toron, whom he reduced to the status of *roi fainéant*. He conceived the idea of creating a Mandinka empire out of the hundreds of small mutually hostile Mandinka chieftaincies in the region south-west of the vast zone ruled by the Tokolor successors of al-ḥājj 'Umar.[1] He was not a cleric and remained illiterate to the end of his life, but made use of Islam both as a means to conquest and as an aid to organization. Had he lived earlier he might have restored the glories of Māli; as it was he was the expression of Mandinka resistance to European expansion. Having defeated *Fa* Modu, chief of Kuṇadugu, in 1866 he made Bisandugu his capital and extended his authority over Toron, Konia, and the Wasulonke chieftaincies. In 1873 he took Kankan and the following year assumed the title of *almāmi*. In 1882 revolts led to French intervention and wars, during which Samōri gained new territory (Bourē, Bidigas, Siekē, and the Manding of Kangaba), lasting until 1887 when he made a treaty with them. In the north he came into conflict with Amadu Sēku whose son he defeated (1884). His most stubborn adversary was Tyeba,[2] the Senufo chief of Kenedugu, who also had expansionist ambitions. The French occupied Bisandugu in 1891 and Samōri was pushed eastwards from upper Guinea into the upper Ivory Coast where he created a new state. During his ravages in 1894–5 he destroyed Muslim Dyula centres such as Kong, Bonduku, and Buna. Finally, his son Sarañgye Mōri advanced to the Black Volta to try to gain Gurunsi country which

[1] He had the example of the Tijānī cleric of Kankan, generally known as Kankan-Mamadu, a former companion of al-ḥājj 'Umar, who after a quarrel with 'Umar built up a large state based on Kankan which collapsed when he died in 1850 (see E Péroz, op. cit., pp. 382–8).

[2] This dynasty was founded about 1820 in the Senufo region by the Tara-ure family of Dyula origin. For a time it had no fixed centre. During the period 1870–5 there were struggles with Fafa Togora, an old adherent of Shēku Ḥamadu of Māsina, who had founded the chieftaincy of Kinian. Molo Kunansa, then chief, sought aid from Amadu Sēku of Sēgu, who, in return for his help, obliged Molo to become a Muslim, and his example was followed by his family and entourage. His brother Tyeba (Kye-ba) who succeeded (1877–93) established himself at Sikaso where he constructed a stronghold. He came into conflict with Samōri to whose ambitions he proved a serious obstacle. Samōri besieged Sikaso for 16 months until forced to withdraw in August 1887. Tyeba sought to form a Senufo empire strong enough to resist Samōri, and his success was due to the fact that he fortified Sikaso and employed much the same means as Samōri of raising and training a regular army. Tyeba gained control of the districts of Fafa in Kinian in 1891. His expansionist policy was followed by his son, Babemba (1893–8), who was in control of the Minianka and Senufo countries. His struggle with Samōri lasted until 1898 when Sikaso was taken by the French. On Sikaso see Delafosse, *H.S.N.* ii. 373–7; M. Perron, 'Précis chronologique de l'histoire du cercle de Sikasso', *Bull. Com. Ét. A.O.F.* 1923, pp. 497–511.

brought him into contact with the British. His career was brought to an end by the French in 1898 and he died in exile in 1900.

Samōri possessed considerable organizing abilities and powers of generalship. Péroz gives a description of the organization of his empire in 1887.[1] It followed much the same principles as that of the Mandinka provinces of Māli. The first level was the village community. Villages were grouped into 162 districts, each of which rarely embraced more than twenty villages. Each district was under a chief chosen according to Mandinka custom from the collateral line of the principal family. Alongside each district chief were placed two *sōfas*, ostensibly to lend him support, but in fact to supervise his activities. The districts were grouped into ten provinces each under a governor from the *almāmi*'s family or a trusted friend, by whose name the province was known. The central region (Konia, Toron, Sabadugu, and Konadugu), under the *almāmi*'s chief minister, was exempt from taxation. Beside each governor was installed a war-chief chosen by the *almāmi* from among his *sōfas* who acted as the governor's lieutenant, together with a cleric and a griot. Political, religious, and judiciary affairs, therefore, came before the governor only at the third, and generally last, resort, since they were normally settled at the village or district level. Only the gravest matters would be carried before the *almāmi*.

The *almāmi* and the governors had each a core of regular soldiers, called *sōfa kelē*, composed of slaves trained in arms from infancy and volunteers from the villages. Apart from these each governor raised levies on the basis of one out of every ten able-bodied men in each village, and in time of war one out of every two, family chiefs (*lu-tigi*) being always exempted. In time of peace the majority of the levies remained in their home village during the six months season of cultivation and harvest, and constituted a kind of reserve. The *almāmi* had a special guard of five hundred young men who were carefully chosen and trained. All the regulars had a special uniform, varied according to rank and functions, footmen, cavalry, or special guard. The frontiers were divided into eight sections to each of which an army corps was attached, with the task of ever pressing forward, and it was by this means that year by year his domain expanded until he eventually came up against the French expansion.

Islamic law scarcely affected the taxation system. The only tax paid by villages, apart from levies, was the harvest of a special field cultivated for the *almāmi*. Other revenues came from the personal wealth of the

[1] E. Péroz, op. cit., pp. 400–16.

almāmi and his governors, presents which were very considerable, and booty, especially slaves. A tithe levied on the gold extractors of Wasulu served to buy arms from European emporiums on the coast.

Samōri's wars, especially during the last period, devastated vast tracts of country which went out of cultivation when their inhabitants were carried off as slaves. He appears to have had little genuine concern for Islam though it was part of his policy to overthrow the existing religio-political structure by killing priests, destroying protective symbols and sacred groves, laying out a mosque-square, and appointing an *imām* for each village.[1] Such ephemeral conquest sometimes prepared the way for a more positive acceptance, but in general Islam was adopted by the Mandinka only parallel to the old religion, whilst his cruelties and exactions, especially during the last stage, exercised on pagans and Muslims alike, bred a hatred of Islam in the hearts of many he subjected.

[1] E. Péroz writes: 'Quant à l'organisation religieuse, elle est à peu près nulle. L'almamy-émir est chef des croyants et interprète le Coran, dont les préceptes ne paraissent pas préoccuper outre mesure ses sujets. Il est aidé dans cette tâche par un jeune marabout, élève des Maures Trarzas, très doux et fort tolérant, dont il a fait son guide spirituel; grâce à ce conseiller, aussi intelligent qu'aimable, la tolérance est à l'ordre du jour dans l'empire. La construction dans chaque village d'une mosquée plus ou moins rudimentaire, et l'entretien du marabout qui la dessert, sont partout considérés comme une démonstration apparente du culte très suffisante. La seule obligation à laquelle l'almamy contraint strictement les principaux de ses sujets est l'envoi régulier de leurs fils à l'école. Il s'assure lui-même de l'observation de cette règle en faisant venir inopinément, même des limites les plus reculées de son empire, quelque enfant de marque qu'il interroge lui-même. Lorsque son ignorance dénote qu'il n'a pas suivi les cours du marabout, il inflige une forte amende aux parents. Deux fois par semaine, le lundi et le jeudi, il se fait présenter les travaux de ses propres fils; si leurs progrès sont insuffisants, il en rend leurs mères responsables. Malgré ce zèle constant, nous avons rencontré peu d'enfants lisant et écrivant couramment l'arabe; l'incapacité des marabouts, et non le défaut d'intelligence de leurs élèves, m'a paru être la cause de ce résultat peu encourageant' (E. Péroz, op. cit., pp. 414–15).

6

The Central Sudan in the Nineteenth Century

I. INTRODUCTION

THE region between the Niger and the Chad was for the first time given a semblance of political unity through an Islamic movement inspired by a Tōrōdo cleric called ʻUthmān ḍan Fodio. The movement did not lead to the formation of a theocratic state but of a kind of Fulbe Islamic empire. The reformer was recognized as *amīr al-mu'minīn*, but the empire was composed of a large number of separate states nominally subordinate to the new caliph. Although new states were founded, others like Kano, Katsina, and Zaria were continuations of old Hausa states, Pulo kings simply replacing those of the Hausa. The possibility of a theocracy under clerical rule was wrecked when ʻUthmān, in consequence of the vast expansion of the movement he had inspired, allowed his flag-bearers to rule the people they conquered, whilst he himself retired from active administration when he appointed his brother and son as co-rulers of a dual empire. Not only was the hereditary principle adopted but, in contrast to the western Sudan states where the rule of the *almāmis* meant a new beginning, Hausa political titles were adopted together with the elaborate ceremonial and feudal relationships associated with them. The administrative revolution was far-reaching, for the substitution involved the change from sacred to military authority, and to reinforce their power the new rulers placed considerable stress upon Islam. The basis of their authority, however, was primarily right of conquest and the exercise of brute force for there was no community of religion. Islamic law merely served as a source upon which they could draw for juridical justification of the *jihād*, slave-raiding, and new forms of taxation. These states, like that of Samōri, were based on slavery in a different and more inhuman way than in the usual Sudanese state. Organized slave-raiding as an end in itself for stocking farms and export had never before reached such proportions.[1] The widespread adoption of Islam by the varied groups in these slave-states was due to the way the wars and displace-

[1] See C. K. Meek, *Northern Nigeria*, i. 257–8; ii. 10. Clapperton was told by the amir of Kano that the ratio of slaves to freemen was thirty to one (*Second Expedition*, 1829, p. 171).

ment of peoples broke up their basic religious foundations. Unable to restore the normal situation they found in Islam a new safeguard and link with the ruling caste.

Bornu did not escape the new wave of Islamic assertion. Although an Islamic state with a strong tradition of legal study, it was doomed unless it could adapt itself to the new currents. However, the new movement was not set in motion by the Tōrodḇē element as elsewhere. Although there were nomadic Fulbe in Bornu, of whom only groups in vassal states responded to the call, the Pulo clerics who had settled there had become completely absorbed into the Kanuri clerical class and held established positions,[1] and these opposed the reformers in Hausaland who accused the Kanuri clerics of impiety. The failure of the *jihād* against Bornu was due to two factors: the tendency of the nomads to disperse after a victory to look after their cattle, and the fact that reaction to the Fulbe menace threw up a militant Kanuri cleric in Muḥammad al-Amīn who gained control of the ancient kingdom and maintained its integrity against Fulbe, Waday, Bagirmi, and Tuareg alike, whilst his son destroyed the dynasty and formed a new ruling line. In Bornu also a new clerical title, in this case *shaikh*, became the title of the rulers. But Bornu did not become a clerical state since Shaikh Muḥammad did not make a new beginning. He allowed the *mais* to exist as puppet kings with their ancient ceremonial aura. His son, it is true, eliminated the dynasty, but like the Fulbe in Hausaland, he ruled like the *mais*, retaining much of the traditional paraphernalia surrounding the divine ruler. The change of dynasty marked no real break with the past. Islam was the religion of the state, but with no different emphasis from that under the old régime.

The history of the lesser Chadian states, Waday, Bagirmi, and those of the Kotoko, during the nineteenth century was one of unmitigated tragedy, and consists entirely of wars, massacres, and slave-raiding. Bagirmi was torn to pieces between Bornu and Waday, and the final stage before the European occupation brought forth a military adventurer in the person of Rābiḥ, a slaver from the eastern Sudan who devastated the whole region.

[1] The Hausa Chronicle records the movement of a considerable body of Fulbe clerics into Bornu during the period 1452–62 (Palmer, *Sud. Mem.* iii. 111) and H. R. Palmer (*Bornu Sahara*, p. 40) gives a facsimile of a *maḥram* granted by ʿAlī Gaji (*c.* 1476–1502) to a Fellāta cleric, Gabidāma, and his descendants 'on account of the efficacy of his prayers' (*bi ḥurmati duʿāʾihi*). Again (op. cit., p. 34), we read how a Fellāta cleric called ʿUmar ibn ʿUthmān was installed as *imām sabara-ma*, i.e. prayer-leader of the palace mosque, by ʿAlī ibn ʿUmar (1644–84). These and many others became Kanuri.

2. THE EMPIRE OF 'UTHMĀN ḌAN FODIO[1]

The period preceding the *jihād* had been characterized by restlessness and trouble-making among Fulbe in Hausaland. A cleric called al-ḥājj Jibrīl ibn 'Umar, who was expelled from Gobir by Bāwa Jan Gworzo (1768–91), was the forerunner and teacher of 'Uthmān ibn Muḥammad ibn Fūdī, generally known as Usumān ḍan (son of) Fedio (1754–1817). 'Uthmān belonged to a section of Tōrodḅē settled in Gobir.[2] He was filled with disgust at the way clerics compromised with pagan practices, with hatred at the way Pulo clerics like himself were treated by pagan rulers, and with zeal for the expansion of the régime of the divine law. He began his career as an itinerant preacher in Kebbi in 1188/1774–5 and formed a coterie of disciples. Tōrōdo clerics, bringing news of the Islamic revolutions taking place in Futas Tōro and Jalon, fired his imagination to initiate a similar *jihād* in Hausaland. Muḥammad at-Tūnisī, who was in Waday in 1810 and heard the current news of the already successful *jihād*, writes of its motives:

The Falāta accuse all other Sudanese of impiety and heterodoxy, maintaining that only by force of arms can they be brought to repentance. They assert that the other Sudanese have altered and adulterated the principles of Islam, that they have broken the penal prescriptions of the law by allowing pecuniary compensations for criminals, which is illegal and proscribed by the Holy Book. They claim that they have undermined the foundations of religion and perverted the rules of Islam by proclaiming illegal and criminal innovations to be legitimate, by shameful customs such as adultery and incest, the use of fermented drinks, passion for amusement, song and dance, neglect of the daily

[1] The history of the *jihād* of 'Uthmān ḍan Fodio and of the Fulani states has yet to be written. Source material is fairly extensive since it includes both local chronicles and traditions and also the records of European travellers. Most of the local material has not yet been edited. Among more accessible material are: 'Abd Allāh ḍan Fodio, *Tazyīn al-waraqāt* (completed in 1813), partially ed. and transl. by A. Brass in *Der Islam*, x. 1–73; the Hausa Chronicles, ed. A. Mischlich in *M.S.O.S.*: *Afrikanische Studien*, vi (1903), 137–242; x (1907), 155–81; xi (1908), 1–81; xii (1909), 215–74; al-ḥājj Sa'īd, *Ta'rīkh Sokoto*, *P.E.L.O.V.*, sér. iv, vols. xix and xx; M. Belo ḍan Fodio, *Infāq al-maisūr*, Arab. ed. London, 1951, of which the Hausa paraphrase was translated by E. J. Arnett under the title of *The Rise of the Sokoto Fulani*, Kano, 1922; and 'History of Zaria from Fulbe occupation to 1890', in C. H. Robinson, *Specimens of Hausa Literature*, Cambridge, 1896, pp. 102 ff.

[2] Muḥammad Belo distinguishes between Fulbe and the Tawrūd (Tōrodḅē or Tokolor) to which he belonged (cf. *Infāq*, pp. 207–8). This section (Dem clan) had been settled in Gobir for some time since Fodio was said to have been the seventh descendant from the immigrant leader Jaḳolo. Belo also says (*Infāq*, p. 209) that they spoke the Wakore (Soninke) language and were connected with the Sulebāwa (Subalḅe) of Mande stock. They were regarded as *rimḅe*, assimilated free groups, but not as Fulbe proper. Barth says they were numerous in Sokoto and Kebbi of whom those in Zaberma still spoke Soninke. *Travels*, iv 144, 176–7.

MAP 7

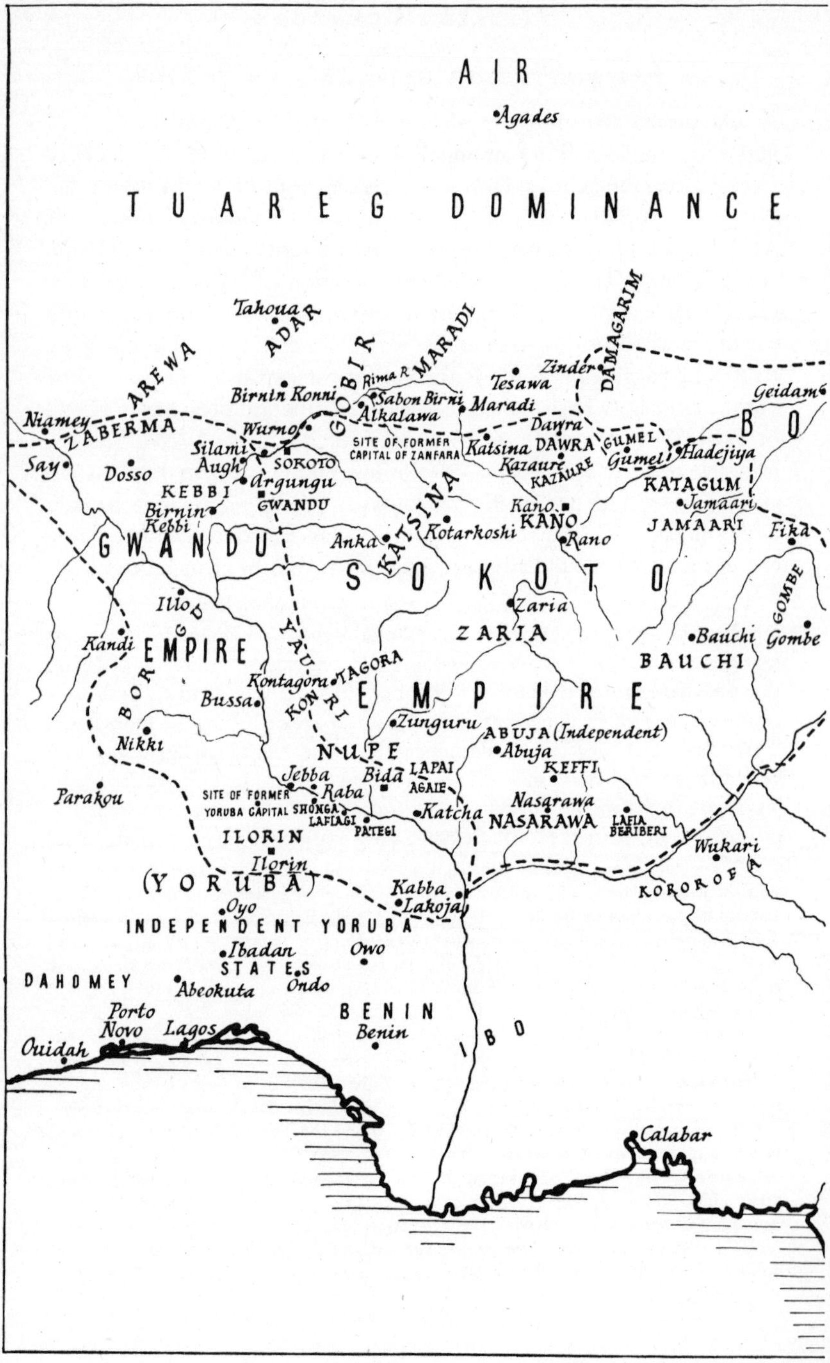

AIR
Agades
TUAREG DOMINANCE
Tahoua
ADAR
AREWA
GOBIR
MARADI
DAMAGARIM
Zinder
Tesawa
Rima R.
Birnin Konni
Sabon Birni
Alkalawa
Maradi
Niamey
ZABERMA
Wurno
Dawra
DAWRA
GUMEL
Gumel
Hadejiya
Geidam
BO
SITE OF FORMER CAPITAL OF ZANFARA
Katsina
Kazaure
KAZAURE
Silami
Augh
SOKOTO
Say
Dosso
Argungu
KEBBI
GWANDU
Birnin Kebbi
KATSINA
KATAGUM
Jamaari
JAMAARI
Kano
KANO
Rano
Fika
Kotarkoshi
GWANDU
Anka
SOKOTO
GOMBE
Gombe
Illo
Zaria
ZARIA
Bauchi
BAUCHI
Kandi
EMPIRE
BORGU
YAURI
Kontagora
KONTAGORA
Bussa
EMPIRE
Zunguru
ABUJA (Independent)
Abuja
Nikki
NUPE
KEFFI
Jebba
Bida
LAPAI
AGAIE
Raba
Parakou
SITE OF FORMER YORUBA CAPITAL
SHONGA
LAFIAGI
PATEGI
Katcha
Nasarawa
NASARAWA
LAFIA BERIBERI
ILORIN
Ilorin
Wukari
(YORUBA)
Kabba
Lokoja
KOROROFA
Oyo
INDEPENDENT YORUBA
Ibadan
STATES
Owo
DAHOMEY
Abeokuta
Ondo
BENIN
Benin
Porto Novo
Lagos
Ouidah
IBO
Calabar

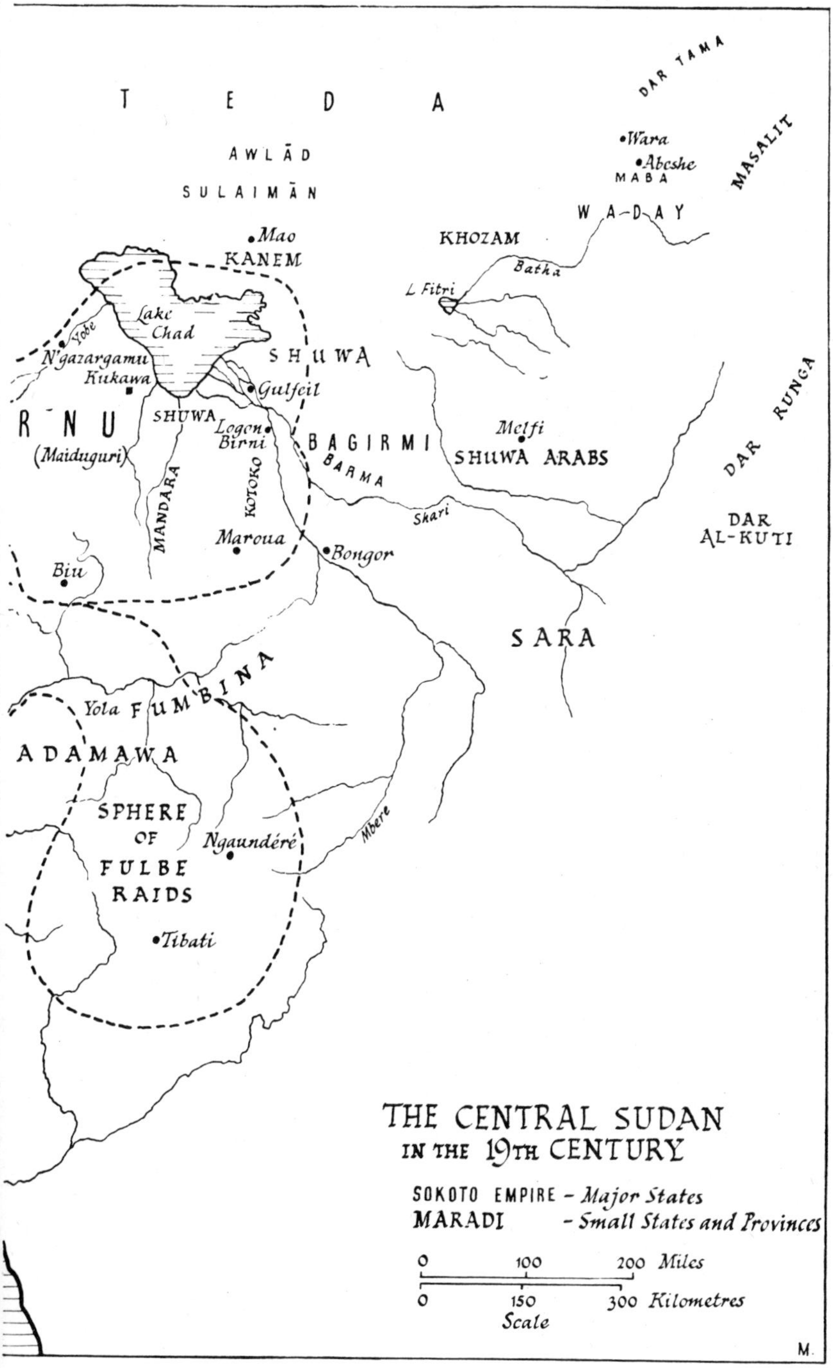

TEDA
DAR TAMA
AWLĀD SULAIMĀN
•Wara
•Abeshe
MABA
MASALIT
WADAY
•Mao
KANEM
KHOZAM
Batha
L Fitri
Lake Chad
Yobe
N'gazargamu
Kukawa
SHUWA
Gulfeil
DAR RUNGA
SHUWA
Logon Birni
Melfi
(Maiduguri)
BAGIRMI
SHUWA ARABS
BARMA
DAR
MANDARA
KOTOKO
Shari
DAR AL-KUTI
Maroua
Bongor
Biu
SARA
FUMBINA
Yola
ADAMAWA
SPHERE OF FULBE RAIDS
Ngaundéré
Mbere
Tibati
THE CENTRAL SUDAN IN THE 19TH CENTURY
SOKOTO EMPIRE – Major States
MARADI – Small States and Provinces
0 100 200 Miles
0 150 300 Kilometres
Scale
M.

B 9533 o

obligatory prayers, and refusal to offer tithes for the poor and unfortunate. Each of these crimes and shameful deeds deserves signal vengeance and calls for a *jihād* in all the states of the Sudan. These ideas fermented for years in the spirit of the Fulān and electrified their imagination, until suddenly there arose amongst them one renowned for his piety and godliness; this was the *faqīh* Zāki[1] who posed as a reformer and proclaimed the holy war.[2]

ʿUthmān's real agitation began in A.H. 1200 (1786) when he embarked on a five-year mission in Zamfara and neighbouring states, at the same time opening a wide correspondence with Pulo clerics throughout Hausaland. His propagandist activities brought him up against Nafāta, Sarkin Gobir, who, according to Belo, took measures to combat his propaganda by decreeing that only those born Muslims should practise Islam and that all recent converts should return to their ancestral religion. He also forbade the wearing of turbans and the seclusion of women.[3] Nafāta's son, Yunfa (succeeded in 1802), a former pupil of ʿUthmān, was openly hostile since he realized that the preacher's activities were subversive to his régime. Hostilities broke out following an incident when ʿUthmān met a party of prisoners of war being led off into slavery and noticing Muslims among them, some his own followers, had their chains struck off. Yunfa marched against Degel where ʿUthmān lived and the date of the latter's flight, 10 Dhū 'l-Qaʿda, 1218 (21 February 1804), marks his *hijra*.[4] From that time he regarded himself as the chosen instrument for the execution of the decrees of the Divine Will, and the courage and steadfastness that engendered gave his followers cohesion and purposiveness. They gathered around him in Gudu and his brother ʿAbd Allāh met and defeated Yunfa's army, composed, ʿAbd Allāh says, of 'Nūba [i.e. Hausa], Tuareg, and Fulāni in allegiance to him'.[5] Thereupon his followers swore to wage the *jihād* against unbelievers and proclaimed him *amīr al-mu'minīn*, in Hausa *Sarkin Musulmi*, a title still borne by the ruler of Sokoto.[6]

[1] This does not refer to Ibrāhīm Zāki, leader of the *jihād* against Bornu in 1808 who became the ancestor of the Pulo emirs of Katagum, but to ʿUthmān ḍan Fodio. *Zāki*, the Hausa word for 'lion', is commonly used when saluting chiefs.

[2] *Voyage au Ouaday*, pp. 290–1. Many of the works of ʿUthmān and his son Belo have political pretensions, seeking to justify their conducting the *jihād* against Muslims, e.g. ʿUthmān's *Bayān al-bidʿa ash-shayṭāniyya* and Belo's *Infāq al-maisūr*.

[3] *Infāq*, p. 67; *Tazyīn al-waraqāt* in *D. Isl.* x. 29.

[4] The coincidence of the *hijra* of ʿUthmān with the taking of Mecca by Saʿūd ibn ʿAbd al-ʿAzīz in A.H. 1217 was noticed by Muḥammad at-Tūnisī, *Voyage au Ouaday*, transl. Perron, 1851, pp. 295–6.

[5] *Tazyīn al-waraqāt* in *D. Isl.* x. 35.

[6] The *jihād* was linked rather vaguely with the advent of the *mahdī*, but M. Belo says

The victory of 'Uthmān's followers over the king of Gobir aroused the Hausa rulers to the peril of a militant Islam. Sarkin Gobir 'sent messages to his brother chiefs of Katsina, Kano, Zegzeg, Dawra, and Ahīr, warning them that he had neglected a small fire in his country until it had spread beyond his power to control. Having failed to extinguish it it had now burnt him. Let each beware lest a like calamity befall his town also.'[1] The various chiefs attacked 'Uthmān's adherents living in their countries, thereby arousing many Fulbe nomads who would have remained quite indifferent to any appeal to Islam, and the whole of Hausaland was plunged into a state of war. 'Uthmān solemnly blessed flags which he conferred on trusted followers and sent them out to proclaim the *jihād*. Belo writes of the use they made of local Fulbe, 'Thus was this *jihād* accomplished. Whenever a king rose to aid his brother kings and attack the Shaikh ('Uthmān) the *jamā'a* affiliated to him took a firm stand against him and made him abandon his purpose.'[2] But the nomads were unreliable. Belo relates how, after the first series of attacks on Bornu inspired by Pulo clerics which led to the sacking of N'gazargamu, they dispersed with their booty leaving the leader Mukhtār with insufficient troops to resist the Bornuan return offensive.[3]

The Hausa put up a strong but uncoordinated resistance and the fate of the *jihād* was often in jeopardy, but Birnin Kebbi and Zaria fell in 1805, Katsina in 1807, Dawra and Alkalawa, capital of Gobir, the most formidable adversary, in 1808, and Kano in 1809. Fulbe invaded Bornu in 1808 and defeated its army, but this success was only temporary since Bornu produced its own militant-religious leader to meet the emergency in Shaikh Muḥammad al-Amīn, generally known as al-Kānemī, who, taking the offensive, finally checked the invaders (1812) at the cost of the abandonment of some western provinces which became Pulo emirates.

expressly (*Infāq*, p. 185) that although 'Uthmān was the *mujaddid* and *quṭb* of his age he was not to be called the *mahdī*. In 1805 he was sent by his father to tell the men of Kano, 'the good news about the approaching advent of the *mahdī* and how the star of the *jamā'a* of the Shaikh will rise and this *jihād* not wane until the advent of the *mahdī*' (ibid., p. 105). This helped to quicken expectations and Belo mentions a number of *mahdīs* who appeared during the early stages of the *jihād*. Many appeared after his time. On Jibrīla or Geni, a Pulo of Katagum who declared himself in Gombē in 1888 and defied the Fulbe rulers until defeated by the British in 1902, see S. J. Hogben, *The Muhammadan Emirates of Nigeria*, 1930, pp. 175–6, 181–2.

1 Muḥammad Belo's letter to al-Kānemī quoted in his *Infāq al-maisūr*, p. 131.

2 Belo, *Infāq*, p. 122.

3 Ibid., pp. 124, 138.

Although the *jihād* cannot be regarded in its initial phases as a racial conflict between Fulbe and Hausa, for the pure nomadic Fulbe did not welcome the agitation of the Tōrōdo upstarts,[1] it did unite for a short time the various groups of Fulbe, red and black, nomads and settled. The leaders, like 'Uthmān, were generally Tokolor or Pulo clerics[2] and it attracted Tokolor from the western Futas Tōro and Bondu.[3] But the nomads could not be aroused by Islam as a rallying cry for they were pagans or indifferent Muslims; to them it was a Fulbe movement with which the measures taken against them by Hausa and Bornu kings made them associate themselves.

By 1810 Fulbe control was established over the Hausa states. Katsina and Gobir continued to resist strongly and though they lost their capitals were never conquered. The early leaders tried to destroy the open practice of pagan rites, a very wide variety of which existed among the Hausa for they had assimilated many small groups and had also set up slave villages as a result of their raiding and wars. Those Hausa who kept Islamic feasts and at the same time indulged in pagan rites were forced to destroy their shrines, although it is said that the Fulbe could not get rid of the famous *gidan tsāfi* called Chōka in Kano city, and that the new town chiefs fulfilled their inherited communal obligation of providing *sadakan iskōki*, animals for 'sacrifice to the spirits' of the locality. The free pagan Hausa or Māguzāwa[4] were not forced to join Islam, but left as tribute-paying cultivators, and at the time of the British occupation half were still pagan. The *jihād* fell much heavier on other pagans whom the Fulbe regarded as legitimate prey.

But the Fulbe drive for domination did not stop at the Hausa states. The Nupe in the low basin between the Niger and Kaduna rivers, who

[1] In the early stages many Fulbe remained loyal to the Hausa. They served in the army of Gobir, whilst the Sarkin Zazzau was warned by Fulbe in his state of a planned rising of the Subalbe.

[2] Even in the east where the armies were composed of nomads many leaders were clerics, among them Gwoni Mukhtār and Ibrāhīm Zāki who led the attack on Bornu and al-ḥājj Ādam who gave his name to Ādamāwa. Belo (*Infāq*, pp. 123–4) mentions nomads waging war on Bornu in the north and Fulbe *mālams* in the south.

[3] Many of these were eventually settled in Zaria; see H. Clapperton, *Second Expedition*, 1829, pp. 159, 205.

[4] The Hausa term *arne* or *azne* = *paganus*, cf. the saying *chinikin azne nōma*, 'farming is the occupation of pagans'. *Māguzāwa* (sing. *ba-māguje*) is derived from *majūs* (cf. Qur'ān, xxii. 17). The jurists adopted this term when they found a formula by which pagans could be admitted among those allowed to retain their religion upon payment of the *jizya*. Saḥnūn (*Mudawwana*, ed. A.H. 1324–5, i. 406) quotes a saying of the Prophet, 'Follow in regard to the *majūs* the same procedure as for the People of the Book.' Khalīl (*Mukhtaṣar*, transl. Guidi and Santillana, 1919, ii. 839, n. 169) regards them as half-way people more linked with the *kuffār* with whom they are to be treated as one *milla*.

can be regarded as entirely pagan although there had been some Islamic influence,[1] were subjected. The Fulbe gained control by exploiting differences within the ruling class. Two rival *etsus*, Majiya (d. 1834) and Jimada (d. 1807), were contending together. As elsewhere there were many Fulbe clerics and cattle-owners in the country. With the aid of his court cleric, *mālam* Mūsā Dendo (d. 1833), Majiya made use of them to defeat his rival (1807), but then found his allies, stimulated by the revolution in Hausaland, for Dendo had received a flag from ʿUthmān, becoming too powerful and was eventually overthrown. *Mālam* Dendo at first retained Idrīs (d. *c.* 1849), son of Jimada, as puppet *etsu* and then changed over to Majiya, but his son ʿUthmān Zāki became the first Pulo titular *etsu*. Another flag-bearer, *mālam* Māliki (d. *c.* 1824), founded the small Nupe emirate of Lafiagi, and even the descendants of the two Nupe *etsus* acquired chieftaincies (Shonga and Pategi). South of the Nupe the Fulbe won a large part of the northern Yoruba region,[2] but as they reached the forest where their cavalry could not operate the Yoruba, forming themselves into defensive confederations based on military cantonments like Ibadan, successfully held up their advance.

Besides emirates founded upon earlier states, individual Fulbe leaders carved out a host of smaller states from other pagan areas: Bauchi, Gombe, Katagum, Missau, and Jamaari on the plateau; the vast region of Adamāwa in Cameroons; and Keffi, Nasarāwa, Lafia, Doma, and Keana in the Benue area. In the west the dynasty of Kebbi, although losing most of its territory, resisted the Fulbe until the forces

[1] The foundation of this Nupe dynasty goes back to an immigrant, Edege or Tsuede, who lived in the fifteenth century. The 12th king, Jibrīl (1730–40, cf. Kano Chronicle, *Sud. Mem.* iii. 124), was the first to call himself a Muslim. Muḥammad Belo writes (op. cit., p. 21) that when Islam began to spread under Jibrīl he was deposed for one who held to the old religion. Islam did not begin to undermine the old beliefs until after the Fulbe conquest.

[2] Islam began to penetrate among northern Yoruba before the Fulbe revolution. Afonja, a northern ruler, rebelled (1817) against his overlord, the Alāfin of Oyo, and invoked the aid of Alīmu, a Pulo *mālam* from Sokoto, and Sologberu, a Muslim Yoruba chief. Alīmu imported bands of Fulbe and Hausa into Ilorin and with their assistance Afonja made himself independent. He adopted Islam and the present mosque of Jimma is on the site of his *matsāfa* or pagan temple. Alīmu died in 1831, but his sons, especially ʿAbd as-Salām, set to work to carve out positions for themselves. Too late Afonja discovered his mistake in encouraging Hausa and Fulbe mercenaries to enter Ilorin. He attempted to destroy them but was killed and ʿAbd as-Salām became military chief and founder of the existing line of *amīrs* of Ilorin. He warred with success against the Alāfin, compelling him to abandon his capital and withdraw southwards to found the existing Oyo. But after the death of ʿAbd as-Salām (1842) the expansion of the new state was modified and the Fulbe, who had seemed under the energy of the founder capable of driving through to the sea, were compelled to expend their energies in continual warfare with Ibadan and other states until the British occupied Ilorin in 1897.

of the initial *jihād* were spent, and it maintained its existence as the small independent state of Argungu only a few miles from Sokoto itself until the British took control. Early in the *jihād* the Fulbe attacked Dendi. Its Songhay, Zerma, and Kebbāwa inhabitants resisted for fifty years, remaining more or less independent, though they were all the same converted to Islam. Tuareg delivered the fatal blow in this region and only a few village states, like that of the Mawri (Arewa), the Jerma of Dosso, and Anzuru under chiefs descended from *sī* 'Alī of Songhay, had the strength to resist. As Barth shows, these former populous and prosperous regions were reduced to a condition of the utmost misery and insecurity.[1] A number of other dynasties survived and resisted the Fulbe throughout the century.[2]

'Uthmān, overwhelmed by the incredible success of the Islamic idea as a means to conquest, thwarted by the ambitions of his flag-bearers in carving out for themselves personal states, and incapable of providing an Islamic system of administration, retired from political life. He appointed his son Muḥammad Belo over the eastern regions with his capital at Sokoto (Sakkwato built in 1809) and his brother 'Abd Allāh (1766–1829) over the western regions with his capital at Gwandu in

[1] Barth, op. cit. iv, chap. 59; and for the independent Songhay see v. 652–4.

[2] Among them we may mention: (*a*) Gobir, the most formidable opponent of the Fulbe. In continual conflict with Belo, who was generally victorious, it gained the ascendancy during the reign of Mayaki (1836–58), who defeated both 'Atīq and 'Alī, when it was able to establish a permanent capital.

(*b*) Adar, west of Gobir and north of Konni, whose people were wholly pagan under Tuareg chiefs originally from Air (Agaba, first ruler of Adar, 1674–87).

(*c*) Katsina, where the Tazarāwa (west of Damagaram), who formerly recognized the suzerainty of Bornu, formed with Katsina the little chieftaincy of Marāḍi (dynastic transference in 1825).

(*d*) The autonomous chieftaincy of Damagaram which recognized the vague suzerainty of Bornu maintained its existence and grew in strength. Founded by an immigrant Bornuan cleric called Mālam (1731–46), it began to grow under Sulaimān ḍan Tintuma (1812–22) who founded Zinder, but it was Tenīm (1851–84) who was its most famous chief, conquering the states of the Sosebakis, Muniyo-Manga, and a part of Dawra (see Landeroin in *Mission Tilho*, ii. 425–43).

(*e*) Dawra. The old dynasty was driven out by the Fulbe and spent a wandering life centred around Zango (Palmer, *Sud. Mem.* iii. 139–41), until Mūsā (d. 1912) was reinstated as Sarkin Dawra by the British owing to the incompetency of the Pulo amir. This seems to be the only instance where the British restored a Hāḅē dynasty.

(*f*) Zaria dynasty migrated to the rock of Zuba among pagan Gwari and Koro, where they founded the state of Abūja, its name being derived from that of the first Muslim king.

(*g*) Other dynasties went into obscurity like that of Zamfara in Anka, sometimes acknowledging the ruler of Sokoto, sometimes in rebellion (cf. Barth, op. cit. iv. 522). Zamfara was divided by the Fulbe into small governorships and ravaged by the continual inroads of the Gobirāwa.

Kebbi. Both capitals occupied an eccentrical position in regard to the territories over which their influence extended.

The organization of the two empires was very loose and government decentralized. ʿAbd Allāh got the worst of the division. His so-called empire of Gwandu was a vague sphere of influence and military action to enforce tribute. Barth gives a list of its provinces as though it were a clearly defined entity,[1] but the Sudanese concept of dominium should be remembered. The authority of ʿAbd Allāh and his successors was exercised directly only over a central core in western Kebbi which had experienced three centuries of administrative tradition and common institutions. If the organized Nupe and Yoruba states are excepted, the sphere of Gwandu extended over non-Hausa peoples split into numerous loosely coordinated village states, divided by dynastic and other internal squabbles and Tuareg penetration. Fulbe military supremacy for a time brought a certain order into the region by supporting the claims of certain lines and exercising the right of investiture, but the disunities were not resolved and after 1850 Gwandu had no control over the western region.

The governments founded upon old Hausa states (as well as the Nupe and Yoruba states related to Gwandu) were more stable. The Fulbe, suddenly exposed to the corrosive effect of power, could not form states based upon the ideals of Islam, but fell back upon the system of the Hausa they had dispossessed. Sokoto, as a new town created in order to symbolize the new dispensation, had a more original character. It was the central parasitic state to which provincial governors were required to forward an annual tribute of slaves and produce, and, when called upon, provide military contingents for particular campaigns. Considerable modifications took place in the boundaries of the old states. Some like Zamfara disappeared and new ones were created since each leader sought to carve one out for himself. Some stress was placed upon Islamic institutions since the first leaders were clerics preaching the *jihād*, but in general the Fulbe adopted the existing state structure with its wealth of dignitaries together with their Hausa titles. Successful flag-invested clerics were recognized by ʿUthmān as fief-holders. The fief, consisting of a *birni* and an unspecified surrounding area, which they sought to increase by taking other towns and setting up slave villages (*rumada*), was not at first intended to be heritable. In the

[1] According to Barth (iv. 203) Gwandu included the western half of Kebbi, Mawri (or Arewa), Zaberma, Dendina, part of Gurma (provinces of Galaijo, Torodo, Yagha, and Liptako), a small part of Borgu or Bariba, the Ilorin region of Yoruba country, Yauri, and Nupe.

early days the theocrat appointed and dispossessed governors arbitrarily, but after a time appointments came to be allotted in the families of the first fief-holders and dynastic lines were recognized. In some states the Sarkin Musulmi chose the ruler from among eligible candidates of the recognized Pulo lineage, in others (including Sokoto) there was an electoral body, though the overlord's approval of the candidate selected was necessary. Some states such as Kano had one dynastic line, whilst Nupe and Zaria had three.[1] Each ruler was independent but not necessarily in complete control of his state. Some were wholly under direct administration, but others had internal independent dynastic spheres which in some cases were directly responsible to the ruler of Sokoto.

The authority of each ruler was centralized in his capital. This was both a legacy from the former state structure and a necessity for his own safety if he were to retain his throne against rivals of his own family and uprisings of subjected peoples. His country was divided into non-heritable fiefs (*garurwan sarauta*) attached to offices allotted among the Fulbe ruling class, native chiefs who had submitted and had been confirmed in their holdings, and powerful officials of client or

[1] The dynastic list of Zaria shows how the various lineages have supplied *sarakuna*:

	Malāwa	*Bornuāwa*	*Katsināwa*	*Sulebāwa*
1804	Mālam Mūsā	..	..	..
1821	..	Yamūsa	..	..
1834	..	..	ʿAbd al-Karīm	..
1846	..	Ḥamad b. Yamūsa	..	..
1846	..	Muḥammad Sāni b. Yamūsa	..	..
1860	ʿAbd al-Qādir b. Mūsā	..	..	..
1860	..	..	..	ʿAbd as-Salām (without dynastic successors)
1863	..	ʿAbd Allāh b. Ḥamad	..	..
1873	Abū Bakr b. Mūsā	..	..	..
1876	..	ʿAbd Allāh b. Ḥamad (second term)	..	..
1881	..	..	Sambo b. ʿAbd al-Karīm	..
1890	..	Yero b. ʿAbd Allāh	..	..
1897	..	Kwassau b. Yero	..	..
1902	ʿAlī b. ʿAbd al-Qādir	..	..	..
1920	..	Dalhatu b. Yero	..	..
1924	..	Ibrāhīm b. Kwassau	..	..
1937	..	Jaʿfar	..	..

slave status. In most cases holdings were scattered so that fief-holders could not count upon a large following in any one locality. Further, they were required to live in the capital where they had their allotted place at the Friday prayer ceremonial and their activities could be supervised. They appointed intendants called *jakādu* (lit. 'messengers') to administer their slave-holdings.[1] Apart from these fief-holders there were within many kingdoms hereditary chiefs of vassal states who lived among their own people and were responsible for collecting and forwarding the block tribute.[2] In areas under direct administration fief-holders were responsible for the taxes from their fiefs and often had power to appoint and depose minor district or village chiefs.

ʿUthmān died in A.H. 1232 (1816–17) and his tomb at Sokoto became a place of pilgrimage. His son, Muḥammad Belo, gained recognition as Sarkin Musulmi by a *coup d'état*, but succeeded in reconciling his uncle and the dual control with ʿAbd Allāh as co-ruler continued. Belo's reign was much taken up with the suppressing of rebellions against Fulbe rule and the survival of the state was often at stake, especially when the Sarkin Gobir concerted widespread revolts of petty Hausa chiefs.[3] Upon Belo's death a split occurred in the family, for his brother Abū Bakr ʿAtīq b. Sh. ʿUthmān succeeded (1837–42) to the disappointment of Belo's son Saʿīd who went to 'Yola where the Adamāwa Fulbe espoused his cause.[4] ʿAtīq, a rigid puritan, attempted some reforms, but the religious enthusiasm of the Fulbe had ebbed, for only ʿUthmān and a few of his original followers were moved by genuine religious conviction. The fruits of power sapped the vital energies that had brought such success and the *jihād* degenerated into undisguised slave-raiding which, together with the perpetual wars, ruined and depopulated vast areas. During the reign of ʿAlī (1842–59) power passed completely into the hands of the provincial governors whose number ʿAlī had increased, and as independent rulers they recognized only the religious authority of the ruler of Sokoto.[5] Tuareg infiltrated

[1] There was originally no allocation of land as such. When, under the British régime, land rather than slave-holdings became important, the jurists asserted that the land was appropriated at the conquest as *waqf* to enable the Fulbe to legalize and acquire any land they desired.

[2] The vassal states of Zaria, which had the widest sphere of all the states, included Keffi, Nasarawan Kwoto, Jamāʿan Dororo, Doma, Kauru, Kujuru, Lere, Fatika, and Durum; some under Fulani, others under native rulers.

[3] Cf. *Ta'rīkh Sokoto*, p. 191 (308).

[4] Hence when his son Ḥayātu adopted the Mahdism of the Nilotic Sudan they also became partisans. After Rābiḥ's conquest of Bornu, Ḥayātu became ruler of the Marua-Mandara region, until Rābiḥ came up against the French when he declared himself to be the Mahdī, but he was defeated by Faḍl Allāh, son of Rābiḥ.

[5] Barth describes the state of anarchy which prevailed when he travelled through Hausa-

into the region of cultivators, notably along the commercial routes leading to the capitals. The Ullimmeden dominated a vast area, penetrating down the Niger and controlling a large part of Songhay. The end of the century was marked by the complete decadence of the Pulo states. The independent Gobir, Kebbi, and Marāḍi states raided them with impunity. Zinder attacked Kano which, in spite of this and attacks by other neighbours, remained the richest and most important Hausa metropolis. No resistance was offered when British troops occupied Sokoto in 1904. Aṭ-Ṭāhir fled and, gathering around himself a few irreconcilables, headed for Mecca, but his followers persuaded him to meet the British forces and he was killed.[1]

Ādamāwa. The Bornu chronicles show that cattle Fulbe were established in Bornu by 1564. A century later they are mentioned in Bagirmi, and during the eighteenth century they were nomadizing among the pagan tribes of the plateau north of Cameroons (these were called by the later immigrants Fulbe Kitije). They were tolerated by the Negro tribes who treated them as vassals. Gradually they gained in influence and Pulo chiefs began to lead raiding parties about the country. Among them was a *modibbo* Ādama who had received a religious education in Bornu and had been on pilgrimage. Hearing of ʿUthmān's *jihād* he went to Sokoto in 1806 to offer allegiance, was invested with a flag, and returned to inaugurate the *jihād*. He succeeded in the difficult task of getting his authority accepted by the Fulbe and unified them temporarily through appealing to their racial and plundering instincts. He began his *jihād* in 1809 and subdued the pagans of the north 'for the religion', as the chronicles affirm, 'and not in order to capture slaves and increase his *ḥarīm*, as was the case with his successors'. He subdued not only the politically incoherent groups, but also Mandara whose rulers had been nominal Muslims for a hundred years. He founded 'Yola on the Benue in 1841 as his capital and died there in 1847/8.

When Ādamu died the Fulbe dominated a region stretching from

land during the reign of ʿAlī: 'Great in extent, but weak beyond description in the unsettled state of its loosely connected provinces, and from the unenergetic government of a peacefully disposed prince; for while one provincial governor [Bowari or Bukhārī of Hadejiya] was just then spreading around him the flames of sedition and revolt, towards the south another vassal of this same empire was disputing the possession of those regions whence the supply of slaves is annually obtained' (*Travels*, iii. 10–11).

[1] In consequence some 25,000 Fulbe migrated. Besides remnants of Amadu Sēku's army, these included Mai Aḥmad, emir of Misau, and Mai Wurno, son of aṭ-Ṭāhir, both of whom became heads of large Fellāta settlements on the Blue Nile. Another was Alfa Hāshim, brother of at-Tijānī and nephew of al-ḥājj ʿUmar, who was recognized as head of the Nigerian branch of the Tijāniyya and settled in Medina.

Madagali in the north to Banyo in the south, and from the River Ini in the west to Lere in the east. The country he unified, though only temporarily, formerly known as Fombina 'the southland', has been known ever since as Ādamāwa. His chiefs set themselves up in settlements within the areas they had conquered, recognizing vaguely the suzerainty of 'Yola, but practically independent. Ādamu's successors and the chiefs of the subsidiary states, who were but nominal Muslims, did not attempt to convert the pagans (Kirdi), regarding them as a reservoir of slaves.[1] They lived in a state of mutual rivalry and their wars and slave raids devastated the whole country.

Barth, who visited 'Yola in 1851, gives a description of the Fulbe state superimposed upon the country. The ruling families were no longer nomadic, but lived on the produce of slave-cultivated farms. The organization was feudal. The nominal chief was the *baban lāmīḍo* of 'Yola, assisted by a *qāḍī* and a council of ministers and representatives (*galadima*) of the different families whose ancestors had participated in the conquest. The provinces were under *lāmīḍos* or *arḍos*, recipients of a turban as symbol of investiture. The islamization of the country was naturally very incomplete and today the Muslims are chiefly the Pulo ruling caste, Hausa traders, Kanuri settlers, Shuwa Arabs, and the inhabitants of former slave settlements.

British, French, and Germans all converged upon this region at the end of the century. When, after the Protectorate of Northern Nigeria was established in 1900, the ruling *lāmīḍo*, Zubair, continued his slave-raiding activities, an expedition was sent against 'Yola. Zubair was deposed, but his brother was installed in his place exercising jurisdiction extending over both British and German spheres of influence.

3. BORNU AND THE SHAIKHUS

At the beginning of the century the relative stability of the Bornu empire with its widespread system of vassal states was threatened by the rising power of the Fulbe in Haùsaland. As the tide of conquest advanced towards the east 'Uthmān ḍan Fodio stirred up the Fulbe groups within the tributaries of Bornu. Abduwa took the little state of Awyo (1805) which by accretion became the Fulbe emirate of

[1] Barth wrote (1851), 'This territory is as yet far from being entirely subjected to the Mohammedan conquerors, who in general are only in possession of detached settlements, while the intermediate country, particularly the more mountainous tracts, are still in the hands of pagans' (op. cit. ii. 503). He gives a list of these settlements (ii. 509–10), some of whose lords owned more than 1,000 slaves and were in open hostility to the *lāmīḍo* of 'Yola.

Hadejiya. *Mai* Aḥmad ibn ʿAlī (1791–1807/8), taking the offensive, defeated another Fulbe leader, Arḍo Lerlima. Fortunes varied at first, but the turning-point came when Aḥmad was defeated, and all the scattered bands of Fulbe were ready to join in.[1] Gwoni Mukhtār succeeded in taking N'gazargamu in 1808, but 'when the Fulbe had gathered up the spoils they returned to their own lands and sought out their families, leaving behind only a small contingent'.[2] *Mai* Aḥmad was able to reoccupy his capital and Mukhtār was killed. This came about because Aḥmad had called to his aid a Kanembu cleric called al-ḥājj Muḥammad al-Amīn ibn Muḥammad Ninga, generally known as Shaikh Lamīnu or Shaikh al-Kānemī, who could raise both his Kanembu partisans and the Shuwa Arabs.[3] Ibrāhīm Zāki now became the Fulbe leader[4] and again N'gazargamu was captured (1811). Dūnama Lefiami, the new *mai* (1807–11, 1814–17), fled eastwards. Again al-Kānemī was called upon for help, and from this moment he becomes the champion of Bornu. He turned to the offensive and defeated the Fulbe without difficulty since the nomads as usual had dispersed. Ibrāhīm Zāki gave up the struggle, contented himself with preserving what he had acquired and formed the emirate of Katagum out of former Bornuan vassal states.

As recompense for his services al-Kānemī had exacted from Dūnama half the revenues of the reconquered provinces. In them he settled his Kanembu followers who became a permanent factor in Bornuan life. From his cantonment at N'gornu he wielded all effective power and in 1814 built a new capital at Kūkawa. He made no attempt to overthrow the old dynasty. The *mai* was allowed to maintain the court ceremonial at Birnin Kabela (or Berberuwa), but was deprived of all real power.

[1] An account of the invasion from the Fulbe point of view is given by Muḥammad Belo in his *Infāq al-maisūr*, pp. 121 ff. In this is preserved his correspondence with Muḥammad al-Amīn in which the latter exposes the pretensions of the leader of the *jihād*.

[2] M. Belo, *Infāq al-maisūr*, p. 124.

[3] Barth writes: 'Of the migration of these Arabs from the east, there cannot be the least doubt. They have advanced gradually through the eastern part of Negroland, till they have overspread this country, but without proceeding further towards the west' (H. Barth, *Travels* ii. 356). They were in Darfur and Waday before 1400 and by the seventeenth century many clans had moved into Bornu. Those like the Salāmāt who moved southwards into regions where the camel cannot live adopted cattle-rearing from the Negroes. They mixed easily with the Kanuri and certain groups lost many of their Arab characteristics. Some thirty tribes are said to have entered Bornu in response to the call of Muḥammad al-Amīn to help repel the Fulbe.

[4] Ibrāhīm Zakiyyu 'l-Kabi belonged to a family long settled in Bornu. His father was *imām* of the pagan chief of Yaiya (Shira). He studied at N'gazargamu and travelled in search of knowledge. After receiving his standard (*c.* 1807) he conquered Shira and Tashena (1809), out of which he created the emirate of Katagum.

This was not accepted without protest. Finding little popular support in his own country Dūnama turned for help to Bagirmi and Waday. He made his first attempt to escape the tutelage of al-Kānemī in 1814. In 1817 he conspired with 'Uthmān Burkumanda of Bagirmi to invade Bornu, but was accidentally killed by the Bagirmian soldiers. The Saifī line continued to exist as puppet kings for another thirty-two years.

Until 1824 al-Kānemī was too occupied with Bagirmi, Kanem, and Waday to concern himself about the Fulbe, but that year he finally defeated the Wadayans at N'gala,[1] and could turn to the west. He harassed the new emirates, but though he gained control of old vassals of Bornu in the north-west (Damagaram, Tesāwa, &c.), the regions of Katagum and Hadejiya were finally lost to Bornu. The Fulbe and Bornu powers settled down to accepting spheres of influence as this letter from al-Kānemī to Muḥammad Belo bears witness:

> We profess the same religion, and it is not fitting that our subjects should make war on each other. Between our two kingdoms are the pagan Bedde tribes, on whom it is permissible to levy contribution: let us respect this limit: what lies to the east of their country shall be ours: what lies to the west shall be yours. As for Muniyo, Damagaram and Daura, they will continue to be vassals of the Sultan of Bornu, who in return will surrender to you all his claims to Gobir and Katsina.[2]

Shaikh Muḥammad was succeeded by his son 'Umar (1835–80). The early years of his reign were marked by little except raids on the Pulo states in the west. But in 1846 his authority was in grave danger of being overthrown when partisans of Ibrāhīm, the titular *mai*, sought help from Muḥammad ash-Sharīf of Waday to restore him to power. The Wadayans took 'Umar by surprise, ravaged Bornu and destroyed Kūkawa, but retired before a reconstituted Bornuan army. *Mai* Ibrāhīm had been executed and 'Alī whom the Wadayans had set up

[1] See Denham and Clapperton, *Travels*, 3rd ed. 1828, ii. 37–39. Denham gives his impressions of their Islam. He says they are 'very particular in performing their prayers and ablutions five times a day. They are less tolerant than the Arabs; and I have known a Bornouese refuse to eat with an Arab, because he had not *sully'd* (washed and prayed) at the preceding appointed hour. In the Bornou towns are many hadgis, who have made the pilgrimage to Mecca, and excel in writing the Arabic characters, as well as teaching the art to others. However strange it may appear, each kafila leaving Bornou for Fezzan . . . carries several copies of the Koran, written by the Bornou fighis (clerks), which will sell in Barbary or Egypt for forty or fifty dollars each. The Arabic characters are also used by them to express their own language: every chief has one of these fighis attached to him, who write despatches from his dictation with great facility'; Denham and Clapperton, op. cit. ii. 161–2.

[2] Quoted in H. R. Palmer, *Bornu Sahara*, p. 269.

was the last of his line. His partisans were hunted out or fled the country and ʿUmar became ruler in name as well as power, though he retained the religious title of *shaikh* instead of assuming that of *mai*. ʿUmar rebuilt the capital of Kūkawa as a twin town (hence its name 'the baobabs'), the eastern part (*billa gediba*) being the royal town, separated from the western (*billa futela*) by an empty space. ʿUmar governed without opposition, except for a revolt of his brother ʿAbd ar-Raḥmān in 1853–4. Confining himself to his palace and devoting himself to religious studies he allowed authority to fall into the hands of favourites, and during his last years the power of Bornu was in full decline. Kanem was under the control of Waday, Zinder and other tributaries in the west had become practically independent, whilst raids from Waday were constant. The decline continued under his successors Abū Bakr (1880–4) and Ibrāhīm (1884–5), until finally in the reign of Hāshim (1885–93) the tottering edifice fell before the adventurer Rābiḥ whose career we shall be considering.

Shehu ʿUmar welcomed to his court the European explorers Barth (1851–2), Vogel (1856), Rohlfs (1864), and Nachtigal (1870), to whose writings we owe so much of our knowledge of Bornu at this period. One of the things which most impressed them was its organization. The dynastic changes which took place in Bornu did not introduce a new order, nor the formation of a new type of Islamic state. Considerable changes were made in organization but they were a continuation of tendencies which had long been in progress. The movement towards a centralized monarchical institution which had been taking place gradually was accelerated during the interregnum. The maintenance of a standing army had long freed the *mais* from dependence upon the old hereditary dignitaries. Shehu ʿUmar maintained a regular army consisting of 1,000 foot and 1,000 cavalry, armed with firearms, and 3,000 men armed with spears and bows. In time of war all the provinces, as well as the Shuwa Arabs, were required to provide levies. Al-Kānemī, although depriving the *mais* of power, allowed them to maintain the trappings of a court and appoint their favourites to the traditional titles which formerly had included fiefs, whilst he appointed his own men to the effective administrative offices. When his son Shaikh ʿUmar abolished the Saifī line in 1846 there was scarcely any real change. The old empty titles were retained in his court at Kūkawa and it is clear from the accounts of travellers that Bornu suffered from having an aristocracy possessing great privileges but no power. The only hereditary feudatory who had any power was the *galadīma*, governor of the western districts. The other fief-holders resided in Kūkawa and farmed out their taxes. The officials who were appointed to frontier districts had the duty of guarding against inroads; for example, the *kāgelma*, governor of the Yo, had the particular charge of containing the Tuareg. An important officer in the entourage of al-Kānemī was the *digma*, a kind of royal secretary who also held an administrative district, but after the changes under ʿUmar his position became merely nominal.

The Shehu was an absolute monarch who appointed as his subordinates men dependent upon himself. He had a council (*nōkena*) whose members consisted of *mainas* (princes of royal blood) and *kōkēnawa* (= Hausa *fadāwa*), the new men. Nachtigal[1] regarded this council as a remnant of the former aristocratic constitution. Although the council itself did not exercise any real power, the *kōkēnawa* who served on it were important since they constituted the new official class. They were divided into the two grades: *kambēs* who were of free birth and *kachelas* of servile origin.

As in other Sudan empires Bornu's influence embraced two types of territory: extended Bornu, often known as Bilād Kūkawa, ruled directly; and vassal states ruled by their own chiefs and subject to a tribute of produce and slaves. The Kanuri country, including its interior tribal groupings, as well as the surrounding country was governed directly by the Shehu's appointees. These officials drew no salary but received grants of lands or governorships, from which they extracted the utmost profit they could obtain. At a subordinate level many subject peoples retained their own chiefs, sometimes subject to the control of Bornuan officials; sometimes represented at court by an appointee of the Shehu. In Makari and Kanem, for example, towns and villages had their own chiefs under the inspection of a Bornuan official called *alīfa*.

The religious policy of the Shehus was little affected by their origins. Stronger emphasis was placed upon Islam as the religion of the state. All the interior non-Kanuri tribes were expected to be Muslims. The chief religious dignitaries were the *qāḍī mainin kihendi*, the *ṭālīb mainin kihendi*, and two *imāms*, the greater and the lesser.[2] The fiscal system was reorganized by al-Kānemī to bring it more in accordance with the *sharīʿa*, but the reforms do not appear to have lasted long. The old empire, as in all Sudan states before the era of theocracies, levied a tithe on the crops of all farmers under direct administration which was collected through village and district chiefs, and received tribute from

[1] Nachtigal, op. cit. i. 347.

[2] Palmer, *Sud. Mem.* iii. 50.

vassals and the booty from their regular seasonal raids. Al-Kānemī attempted to regulate taxes according to the Islamic categories of *zakāt*, *kharāj*, and *jizya*, but soon the *kharāj* gave place to *binemram*, a return to the tax collected by the chiefs of villages, but now a fixed assessment.

The vassal peoples and states in the west and north included the country of the Beddē, N'gizim, Lere, and Keri-Keri; the districts of Gumel, Inglewa (capital Būnē), Muniyo, and Damagaram (capital Zinder). But, as Barth shows, the effective authority of the Shehus scarcely passed beyond the River Yo. South of the Chad the country of the Kotoko (the So peoples) was subdivided into many village states, Logon, Kuseri, Gulfey, N'gala, Makari, and Afadē. Although often obliged to pay tribute the protracted wars between Bornu and Bulāla enabled them to maintain their independence. Each had an hereditary ruler called *miyāra*, with whom resided a Bornuan intendant (*alīfa*). Accounts of their interesting constitutional régimes have been given by Barth and Nachtigal. Denham writes that Wiligi (Midigi?), one of these town states, had walls 'nearly fifty feet high, with watch towers erected on the salient angles, where there are constant sentinels. The sultan also lives in a sort of citadel with double walls, and three heavy gates in each wall, strongly bound with iron.'[1] These village states did not group themselves into any wider political unity so far as we know, and though the towns were old the dynasties then existing were of fairly recent origin. The first *miyāra* of Logon, Bruwa, lived about 1690. Its islamization begins with the conversion of the *miyāra* Ṣāliḥ about 1800.[2] The people of Musgu, south of the Kotoko, remained uninfluenced by Islam except for their chiefs, but to the west, Abū Bakr, 26th ruler of Mandara, accepted it and went on pilgrimage in 1136/1723–4, and the country is now partially islamized.[3] East of the

[1] Denham and Clapperton, op. cit., 1828, ii. 9–10.

[2] Barth, op. cit. iii. 303–4. Ṣāliḥ was visited by Denham in 1823 (Denham and Clapperton, op. cit. ii. 16 ff.).

[3] Mandara Chronicle in Palmer, *Sud. Mem.* ii. 98; cf. Barth, ii. 362–3; A. v. Duisburg, 'Zur Geschichte der Sultanate Bornu Wandala (Mandara)', *Anthropos*, xxii (1927), 187–96; J. Vossart, 'Histoire du Sultanat du Mandara', *Études Camerounaises*, iv (1953), 19–52; M. Rodinson and J. P. Lebeuf, 'L'Origine et les souverains du Mandara', *Bull. I.F.A.N.* xviii (1956), 227–55. Nachtigal writes (op. cit. i. 530): 'East of the Bābir, below the district of Mabani, live the Margi, whose more easterly districts have been won over to Islam and submitted effectively to Bornu. After them, to the east, and south of the Gamergu, is found the small vassal and Muslim country of Mandara (or of the Wandala), and, between it and the western frontier of Logon, stretch the northernmost groups of the pagan Musgu, of whom some chiefs have embraced the religion of the Prophet and recognised the suzerainty of Bornu.' *Wandala* was the royal title.

Chad, Kanem, the cradle of the kingdom, was in a state of complete anarchy during the nineteenth century and cannot be regarded as a tributary of Bornu.[1]

The extent of Bornuan control it will be seen is considerably reduced. Tuareg dominated the regions north-west of the Lake and the Fulbe had carved emirates out of the former vassals west of Bornu. Vassals like Damagaram had become independent and it no longer had any effective power west of the Chad. Bagirmi paid tribute to both Bornu and Waday, but the latter exercised effective control.

4. BAGIRMI

The *mbang* of Bagirmi, ʿAbd ar-Raḥmān Gwarang (1784–1806), provoked both internal and external troubles by his policy. Seeing Bornu preoccupied with the assault of the Fulbe he repudiated her suzerainty, whereupon the *kōlak* of Waday, ʿAbd al-Karīm Ṣābūn, seizing as pretext an appeal from Bornu and the tyranny and moral conduct of the *mbang*, invaded the country.[2] ʿAbd ar-Raḥmān, deserted by his people who had been decimated by a plague, was killed, Masenya was sacked and some twenty thousand of its inhabitants carried off into

[1] Kanem has no history as a separate state from the time of its reconquest by *Mai* Idrīs b. ʿAlī. According to tradition the Tunjur entered the Mondo region from Waday about the middle of the seventeenth century and defeated the Bulāla whose ruling clan went east into the Baḥr al-Ghazāl before conquering Fitri. The Tunjur chief made Mawo (then situated south of the present administrative centre of Mao) his headquarters until he was driven out by an army from Bornu under the command of a Magumi called Dala Afuno (so called because he was brought up in Hausaland). The army settled in Kanem and their chief was appointed the first *alīfa* (*khalīfa*) by the *Mai* to whom he was tributary. At the beginning of the nineteenth century Muḥammad al-Amīn was unable to defend Kanem against the Wadayans. The Dalatwa (descendants of the Bornuans who settled in Kanem under Dala) and the Tunjur were at war, and the latter welcomed Wadayan intervention, by whom they were recognized as rulers of the region. The Dalatwa, aided by Bornuans, soon regained control, but the *alīfa* recognized the suzerainty of Waday and was invested with the title of *ajīd*. The Baḥr al-Ghazāl region was separated and placed under an *ajīd al-Baḥr*. In 1843 large numbers of Awlād Sulaimān arrived in Kanem after their defeat by the Turks the preceding year and soon dominated the region. They were almost annihilated in 1850 by a coalition of Tuareg (see Barth, op. cit. iii. 62–64), and Kanem was in anarchy from this time. The Dalatwa, various Kanuri groups, and the Tunjur were continually at war, until the Awlād Sulaimān, recovering from their defeat, again became masters under ʿAbd al-Jalīl (1870–97). He opposed the increasing influence of the Sanūsī who were strong in Waday and active in Mawo in Nachtigal's time, and it was not until after his assassination that Muḥammad al-Barrānī was able to found in Kanem the *zāwiya* of Bīr Alali. A French expedition arrived in Kanem in 1899 and the region came under their control after the defeat of Sīdī al-Barrānī at Bīr Alali in Jan. 1902, when there began the long process of pacification before Sanūsī power was annihilated in the Chad region in 1913.

[2] M. Belo, *Infāq*, pp. 4–5; Barth, *Travels*, iii. 436; M. at-Tūnisī, op. cit., pp. 122–9.

slavery. From this disaster Bagirmi never recovered. The succession to the throne provoked competitions which resulted in the victory of ʿUthmān Burkumanda over Ngarmāba Beri, the nominee of Ṣābūn, and his confirmation as *mbang* (1807–44) after numerous struggles, though tributary to Waday. The country was devastated during the conflict between Bornu and Waday, each striving to gain control, interspersed with expeditions by slave-raiders from Fezzān.[1] Shehu ʿUmar, whose mother was a Bagirmian, made peace as soon as he succeeded to the throne. Both ʿAbd al-Qādir[2] and Muḥammad Abū Sikkīn tried in vain to free the country from Waday, and once again during the course of the struggles Masenya was sacked and its inhabitants carried off into Waday (1870). As a result of all this conflict and deportations the population was decimated and much of the country went out of cultivation. Finally Gwarang II, after the country had been occupied by Rābiḥ, placed Bagirmi under French protection (1897). This drew upon it the vengeance of Rābiḥ, but his defeat in 1900 at last brought peace to the country.

Travellers, especially Barth who was received by ʿAbd al-Qādir in 1852, have given accounts of the various offices of the government and these descriptions probably hold good for the earlier period. Barth says that the government was an absolute monarchy, not tempered by an aristocratic element as in the Bornuan and Hausa states. The queen-mother (*kuñ-banga*) commanded great respect but did not possess the authority exercised by the *māgira* of Bornu nor the *mōmo* of Waday. The principal officers of the state were the *fāsha*, chief of the army (equivalent to the *kaigama* of the old Bornu) who was also in charge of the royal widows and blinded princes; the *ngarmāne*, the chief eunuch,

[1] Barth was told that the Bagirmians had twice beaten Shaikh Muḥammad of Kanem and the Shaikh only gained the ascendancy after he had called upon Muṣṭafā al-Aḥmar, Turkish commander of Fezzān, with whose help he laid waste the northern part of Bagirmi, carrying off a large number of slaves. This seems to have encouraged Muṣṭafā's deposed predecessor, al-Mukni, to return on a purely slave-hunting expedition together with ʿAbd al-Jalīl of the Awlād Sulaimān, but after quarrelling with the latter about the feasibility of an attack on Bornu, Mukni returned and sent al-ḥājj Ibrāhīm who did some raiding. Then followed in 1824 the Battle of Ngala (see H. Barth, *Travels*, iii. 339, 439–40; iv. 43; Denham and Clapperton, op. cit. i. 118, 126–7; F. Rodd, 'A Fezzani Military Expedition to Kanem and Bagirmi in 1821: Major Denham's Manuscript', *J. Afr. Soc.* xxxv (1936), 153–65; Clapperton, *Second Journey*, pp. 170–1; G. F. Lyon, *Narrative of Travels in Northern Africa*, 1921, pp. 3, 4, 129).

[2] During the reign of ʿAbd al-Qādir (1844–57) a large migration of religious enthusiasts with Mecca as their goal, led by a Pulo from the Niger called Sharīf ad-Dīn (or Dubāba), ended in Bagirmi. They defeated and killed the *mbang* but Sharīf ad-Dīn was also killed shortly afterwards and the scattering of his host added to the disorders of the country (cf. H. Carbou, op. cit. i. 55, *Taʾrīkh Sokoto*, pp. 214–15 (351)).

minister of the royal household; the *geletama* (*galādima*); and the *mbarma*, at one time commander in chief, later marshal of the court. Many of these were of slave origin and eunuchs wielded great influence. Besides the officials of the royal household there were the captains (*barma*) and governors of the provinces; among them the *elīfa Moito* or governor of Moito and the *elīfa ba*, or governor of the water. The chief tribute which the 'pagan' provinces (Miltu, Dam, Somray, &c.) had to pay was in slaves; whilst the people of Bagirmi proper paid a tax in corn, cotton-strips, and butter. Shuwa Arabs and Fellāta paid a cattle-tax.

Of the Islam of the inhabitants of Bagirmi Barth wrote: 'Their adoption of Islam is very recent; and the greater part of them may, even at the present day, with more justice be called pagans than Mohammedans. They possess very little learning, only a few natives, who have performed the pilgrimage, being well versed in Arabic, . . . but not a single individual possesses any learning of a wider range. This exists only among the Fellāta, or foreigners from Waday.'[1]

5. WADAY

At the beginning of the nineteenth century ʿAbd al-Karīm, surnamed Ṣābūn (1803–13), having dethroned his father, ascended the throne. As we have seen al-Kānemī sought his aid in re-establishing Bornu's supremacy over Bagirmi, but Ṣābūn annexed the country himself, an action which al-Kānemī was unable to contest owing to his troubles with the Fulbe of Hausaland. Ṣābūn waged successful campaigns against ʿAbd Allāh, chief of Dār Tāma, a tributary of Darfur. Because of troubles in Fezzān he opened new trade-routes to Benghazi for trade with Egypt and welcomed foreign merchants.[2] His son Yūsuf Kharīfain (1814–29) was also an energetic ruler, but dissolute and tyrannical. After he was killed as the result of a conspiracy there followed a period of internal troubles until a grandson of Ṣābūn, Muḥammad ʿAbd al-ʿAzīz, succeeded (1830–4), though he in turn had to deal with serious revolts. During his last years cholera, followed by famine, drove his people to pillage western Darfur. This served as a pretext for Muḥammad Faḍl, its ruler (1800–1839), to invade Waday and enthrone a brother of Ṣābūn, Muḥammad ash-Sharīf (1835–58), as vassal. Ibrāhīm, the puppet *mai* of Bornu, called upon the new *kōlak* to help him to overthrow Shaikh ʿUmar. He defeated ʿUmar's army at Kuseri, but was bought off with a bribe of 8,000 dollars. He

[1] H. Barth, *Travels*, iii. 451.

[2] M. at-Tūnisī, op. cit., p. 211.

attached himself to the naissant Sanūsiyya, and, since 'bad ghosts had made the old royal town uninhabitable', transferred the capital from Wāra to Abeshe in 1850.[1] The same year he became blind and at the same time had to deal with revolts of vassal tribes. It was he who received Vogel, the first European to visit Waday, who was murdered on leaving it (1858). He was succeeded by 'Alī ibn ash-Sharīf (1858–74), the most outstanding among a series of mediocre rulers. Nachtigal describes him as a just, unpretentious, and sensible ruler. He encouraged the visits of merchants from Tripolitania and the Nile valley. He had expansionist ambitions, enforced recognition from the ruler of Runya and engaged in a long struggle with Arab tribes to the north and east. In 1870 he besieged Masenya, capital of Muḥammad Abū Sikkīn who had refused to pay tribute, and carried off much booty and prisoners. His brother Yūsuf (1878–98) was able to maintain the territorial integrity of Waday, though Bagirmi regained its independence. He maintained friendly relationships with the Mahdī of the Sanūsiyya, but was troubled from 1889 by the invasion of Rābiḥ, who laid waste Dār Kūti and the southern provinces of Waday and installed a Bagirmian slave-trader called Muḥammad as-Sanūsī ibn Abī Bakr as chief of Dārs Kūti and Runya (1890). Whilst Rābiḥ was engaged in conquering Bornu, Yūsuf sent an expedition against Muḥammad as-Sanūsī. Yūsuf's successors had to contend against increasing internal difficulties which were not resolved until the French occupied Abeshe in 1909 and killed M. as-Sanūsī of Kūti in 1911.

The *kōlak* was an absolute ruler of the divine-king type whose name could not be uttered by any of his subjects. Gold similarly was tabooed to all except the *kōlak*. His near relations were usually blinded and denied access to the throne. His insignia consisted of a seal, sword, amulet, and stool, the last being very important judging by the efforts Ṣābūn made to gain possession of it during the *coup d'état* by which he gained the throne.[2] The usual elaborate audience was held in the *fāsher* or court outside the palace[3] or in the pavilion (*qaṣr*) within it, when the *kōlak* occupied a cage (*ligdābeh*), screened from view by sheets

[1] Nachtigal, op. cit. i. 586; Barth, iii. 556. At this time the '*ulamā* of Waday, many of whom studied in the Nilotic Sudan, had quite a reputation. Barth writes that, 'The Wadawy fakihs and 'ulama are the most famous of all the nations of the Sudan for their knowledge of the Kuran, the Fulbe or Fellani not excepted' (op. cit. iii. 560).

[2] M. at-Tūnisī, op. cit., pp. 103–4.

[3] In Wāra on the opposite side of the *fāsher* from the palace was the sacred hill, Jabal Thurayya, where the newly elected *kōlak* kept his seven-days' retreat and where the royal drums and sacred insignia were kept (see the Wadayan Chronicle in H. R. Palmer, *Sud. Mem.* ii. 27–28; M. at-Tūnisī, op. cit., p. 369).

of matting (*shargāniya*). The procedure was regulated by a master of ceremonies (*ajīd al-baṣur*). The palace guard or *ozbān*, which was only on duty at night, was divided into four sections each under a *turgenak* (pl. *tarāgna*), who wore a special uniform, round helmets, and were armed with clubs. The palace had a series of enclosures. The second gate was guarded by *tuayrāt* 'pages' who were also the grooms of the *kōlak*'s horses. Between the third and fourth gates lived the eunuchs under a chief (*ajīd duggu dubanga*) in charge of the royal *ḥarīm*. In Abeshe, the capital which succeeded Wāra, the *kōlak*'s quarters were situated in the centre of the town. Within it was a keep rising by three stages which had been constructed by an Egyptian during the reign of 'Alī. Within the enclosure lived some 1,400 persons and 200 horses. Around it were the compounds of the *mōmo* and great dignitaries. The commercial quarter occupied the north-eastern section and was inhabited by people from Fezzān and *jallāba* from the Nilotic region.

The hierarchical order within the state, although varying under different rulers, consisted in descending order of rank of: (1) the *tanya*, who consisted of four greater and four lesser *kamākila* (sing. *kamkōlak*). The four greater formed the inner council through whom the king ruled and they also acted as chief judges. They were seconded by lieutenants (*andeker*) and squires (*warnang*). (2) The *Mōmo* or queen-mother (sometimes grandmother) who received the tribute of 221 villages. If there were no *mōmo* the *ḥabbāba* or chief wife was the first lady of the state. (3) The chief *ajāwīd* (or *ajawādi*, s. *ajīd*, Ar. *'aqīd*), especially the *Ajīd aṣ-Ṣabāḥ* and the *Ajīd al-Gharb*, governors of the East and the West. (4) *Umanā'* (s. *amīn*), tax-collectors. (5) The *kāmina* who preceded the king when he travelled on horseback. (6) The *tarāgna*, executive officers who executed the royal decrees. (7) *Mulūk al-Jibāl*. (8) The *ajāwīd* of the Arab tribes. (9) Native chiefs of the 'slave' tribes: Birgid, Dājo, Kūka, &c.

The provincial organization was loose but imposing. Each province was under a military governor (*ajīd*) who had at his disposal an army of local levies. Certain *ajīd al-jarāma* were civil administrators with no forces at their disposal. The most important command at one period was the *jerma* who governed Wāra, the Kodoy and the western provinces of Gimer, Sila, Mubi, Korbo, Fitri, Khozām, Bagirmi, and Kānem. Others were the Ajīd al-Maḥāmid (Baqqāra and Zaghāwa tribes north of Abeshe), Ajīd Salamāt over the Salamāt, Dār Haimāt, Dār Kibit, Dār Runya, and Dār Kūti. M. at-Tūnisī says that the Ajīd al-Ja'ātna, who was in full command of this *baqqāra* tribe and had at his disposal a force of 2,000 horsemen and 2,000 footmen, was a palace slave in the time of Ṣābūn.[1] Another slave was at the same date Ajīd aṣ-Ṣabāḥ.[2]

6. THE EPISODE OF RĀBIḤ

In the account of the history of the Chad region we have encountered a military adventurer called Rābiḥ ibn Faḍl Allāh. His twenty years' career of rapine and slaughter is important only in so far as it accounts for the final ruin of the Chad region and the details of his career need not detain us long. Rābiḥ, a *jallābī* of mixed origin but in status a slave, rose to become one of the flag-bearers of the famous slave-trader of the Egyptian Sudan, Zubair Pasha. After the defeat and death of Zubair's son, Sulaimān, by Gessi Pasha in 1878, Rābiḥ took command of the remnant of his troops and remained raiding in Banda and Kreish country until 1885. He became a nominal supporter of the *mahdī*, Muḥammad Aḥmad and his successor, ʿAbd Allāh aṭ-Ṭaʿaishī, and clothed his soldiers in the mahdist-patched *jubba*. In 1889 he went into Dār Runya and built up a powerful slave army, then united Dār Runya with Dār Kūti and installed his lieutenant, the Bagirmian chief, Muḥammad as-Sanūsī, as sultan. In 1891 he embarked on a career of conquest. He occupied Bagirmi, advanced to the Shari, took Logon by surprise, and then invaded Bornu where he defeated the army of Shehu Hāshim at Ngala, sacked Kūkawa his capital and pursued the remnants of his army into Damagaram. Now master of the whole of the Chad basin he founded Dikwa on the Alo River, south-east of the Chad, as his capital. He was preparing to attack Muniyo and Damagaram, vassal states of Bornu, and the eastern provinces of Kano when the arrival of the French in Bagirmi turned his attention back to the Shari. Having devastated the small states of Gulfey, Kuseri, and Logon, where he left strong garrisons, he again swept over Bagirmi and burnt Masenya (1898). His career was brought to an end when he was defeated and killed by the French in 1900. The region which Rābiḥ subjugated was the point upon which French, German, and British expeditions converged, consequently it was split up between the three powers.

Rābiḥ's success was achieved through the disciplined and well-armed army he created which he owed to the training he had received under Zubair Pasha. His army amounted to 20,000 men, of whom 4,000 to

[1] M. at-Tūnisī, op. cit., p. 143.

[2] On the organization of Waday see M. at-Tūnisī, part 2; H. Barth, *Travels*, iii. 547–62; Zain al-ʿĀbidīn, *Das Buch des Sudan*, transl. G. Rosen, Leipzig, 1847.

5,000 were armed with firearms to obtain which he sought to attract merchants having connexions with Tripoli and Benghazi. Rābiḥ had no genuine interest in religion, although he acknowledged the mahdī of the Sudan and repeatedly tried to get into touch with Muḥammad al-Mahdī as-Sanūsī who would have nothing to do with him.[1]

During this period Dār Runya, Dār Sila, and Dār Kūti were more or less islamized in the sense that the chiefs and the trading villages received an islamic orientation. But of this vague religious borderland between the A.E.F. provinces of the Chad and Ubangi-Shari G. Bruel writes:

> In Dār Kūti the mass of the population, though in general understanding Arabic and sometimes dressing like Muslims, have remained faithful to the beliefs of their ancestors who were ignorant of the religion of Muhammad. Similarly, in Kreish country and in the region situated north of 6° (basins of the Koto and Chinko), although the peoples give the appearance of being islamized, a good number even having Arabic names (it is the same in Dār Kūti), they do not practise Islam. Only certain chiefs such as Saʿīd Bandas (brought up in Abeshé) and their entourage were really Muslims, whilst others such as Dabago and Yango Bili, remained fetishists. In the sultanates of Mbomu there are only a few groups of Muslims who are nearly all strangers and reside at Bangasu (about 300 in 1901), Rifai (about 200 in 1901), and Zemio. . . . Such appellations as sultans and sultanates have led people to believe, at least those who go by appearances and have not studied the country deeply enough to see through to realities, that the basin of the Mbomu was an Islamic region, whereas it is nothing of the sort, since the Muslims, nearly all strangers, sedentary or in passage, form only a tiny minority.[2]

[1] On Rābiḥ see J. Lippert, 'Rābaḥ', *M.S.O.S.* ii (1899), 242–56 (a history of Rābiḥ told in Hausa); G. Dujarric, *La Vie du Sultan Rabah*, Paris, 1902; Decorse and Demombynes, *Rabah et les Arabes du Chari*, Paris, n.d.; É. Gentil, *La Chute de l'empire de Rabah*, Paris, 1902.

[2] G. Bruel, *La France Équatoriale Africaine*, 2nd ed. Paris, 1935, pp. 265–6. The number of Muslims in Ubangi-Shari does not exceed 40,000 out of a total population of 1,077,000.

7

West Africa under European Rule

I. THE ESTABLISHMENT OF EUROPEAN RULE

WHEN discussing the fortunes of Islam during the nineteenth century we have been confronted with increasing penetration of European powers into Muslim territory. This chapter will be brief since it is no part of our study to recapitulate the history of the way West Africa was brought within the web of Western civilization.[1]

Until the fifteenth century Europe had no contact with West Africa, but even after contact was made the activities of Europeans were confined to the coast and it was not until the nineteenth century that they began to penetrate into the interior. The reasons for the lack of contact during the first period were both geographical and historical. There were natural barriers to penetration, seas and deserts, problems of navigation, and the unhealthiness of the coastal regions. But without minimizing these factors the isolation of West Africa was due primarily to human factors, the most important being the political spread of Islam and the character of Western Christendom. The spread of Islamic power over the eastern and southern shores of the Mediterranean interposed a barrier between Europe and the rest of the world, not only in space, but in mentality. Eastern and African Christian Churches fossilized and Christianity became the local religion of Europe, creating a cultural system whose mental outlook and psychological attitude was totally alien from that of the African world. Islam, on the contrary, was in continuous contact with Africans. In *Islam in West Africa* I have tried to show the process of reciprocal change whereby Islam as a universal religion moulded African life and at the same time was moulded by Africans in all strands of the triple cord of myth, cult, and fellowship. Islam had become indigenous, a natural part of the West African scene, but Christianity had been severed from African life and when it returned was bound up with secular civilization and an alien view of life.

[1] The changes that have resulted from the impact of the West are discussed in *I.W.A.*, chap. ix.

The age of discovery completely changed the outlook of the west European world, but when, in consequence of navigational advances and the fact that Iberians through having citrus fruits were immune to scurvy, Europeans eventually arrived it was to engage in the traffic in human beings. For centuries this traffic darkened the history of the contact of Europeans and Africans. After Columbus discovered the West Indies in 1492–3 the attention of Spain and Portugal was primarily focused across the Atlantic, but their need to export labour for their plantations linked their exploitation of the Americas with Africa. The period from the fifteenth to the eighteenth centuries was that of the merchant adventurers who had no incentive to penetrate into the interior since Africans brought the slaves to their coastal factories. The accompanying missionary work, tied to the aims of the settlements which sought to attach the convert to an alien milieu, died of the vices of the parent society.

Europeans had to adapt themselves to African conditions. Colonization projects failed owing to the appalling cost in lives and they confined themselves to trade based on coastal factories. They then sought to secure and protect essential maritime links by paying special attention to chosen bases. Finally, they occupied, organized, and exploited coastal territories which, during the nineteenth century, became ever more and more extensive, culminating in what came to be called 'the scramble for Africa'. Thus a process whose first vision was economic gain led inevitably to political action.

West Africa, therefore, remained isolated from Europe until the nineteenth century. The abolition of the slave-trade by Britain in 1807 and France in 1817 led to the abandonment of many factories and the formation of freed-slave settlements, of which the most important were in Sierra Leone Colony and Liberia. Except in the borderland region between white and black around the Senegal, European powers were little in touch with Muslim peoples. The nineteenth century was the most revolutionary in West African history for it was characterized by the letting loose of two great forces—militant Islam and European expansion. No other period had seen the impact of comparable forces, and in the end it came to a contest between the two, a contest which was first seen as such by al-ḥājj 'Umar. The strains and stresses these two forces produced upon a relatively stable African society became unbearable until the European powers finally gained complete control and the process of recovery and readjustment could begin.

The first half of the century was the age of the great explorers, but in the middle a new period opened and the years from 1885 to 1905 saw the rapid occupation of the whole of West Africa. French penetration was planned by military men on continental lines and was entirely different in conception and development from that of the British, planned and developed along lines of economic expediency. The A.O.F. (L'Afrique Occidentale Française) was built up from the base of St. Louis, whilst the English penetrated into the interior along the rivers and made no attempt to link up and coordinate their territorial acquisitions. Under the governorship of Faidherbe, the French made the Senegal the way of access into the interior of the vast Sudanese and Niger regions where Islam was strongest. They also retained or acquired certain bases on the Guinea Coast with a view to an eventual linking up. The highlights of their penetration were the campaigns in the Upper Niger region, the destruction of the Muslim kingdoms and chieftaincies, in particular the overthrow of the successors of al-ḥājj ʿUmar and of Samōri and Rābiḥ, the occupation of Timbuktu, Binger's expedition into the interior of the Ivory Coast, and the conquest of Dahomey (annexed in 1894). The pacification and organization of the central regions, where French occupation for long consisted of little more than a series of military posts, was the work of the early twentieth century.

The French possessions were much the greatest in geographical extent, and they tended to refer to those of other powers as a series of enclaves. These comprised the Gambia, Portuguese Guinea, Sierra Leone, Liberia, Gold Coast (now Ghana), German Togoland (later placed under British and French mandate), and Nigeria. Following the historical accidents of their formation, the ethnic composition of many territories is extremely complex since the groupings, like the physical bands, follow an east–west direction. The British never formulated any unified imperial scheme. Their possessions were acquired largely as a result of political action undertaken in order to protect or consolidate commercial interests and were administered as separate political units. The central region comprised Nigeria, the Cameroons, and the Chad regions of French Equatorial Africa. England, France, and Germany were in competition for the possession of these territories at the end of the nineteenth century. England took over Lagos as a colony in 1861 and extended its influence over the Oil Rivers and the Niger Delta. The Royal Niger Company, founded in 1886 as successor to earlier trading companies, established a protectorate over the Niger and

Benue valleys. The occupation of the northern Fulbe emirates began in 1897. The charter of the Company was dissolved, the two protectorates of Northern and Southern Nigeria proclaimed (1 January 1900), and during the next three years British control was extended over the remaining Fulbe emirates and pagan tribes. Lagos was united to the southern protectorate, and finally in 1914 Lugard amalgamated the northern and southern territories.

The French began their occupation of the Chad regions (which included Kanem, Bagirmi, and Waday) up to the Tibesti Mountains in the Sahara in 1899. Under peculiar circumstances deriving from the scramble for Africa these territories were attached to the federation of the A.E.F. instead of to the Niger Colony of the A.O.F. Germany took possession of Togoland and the Bay of Cameroons in 1884 and ten years later had occupied the plateau of Adamāwa. The powers converged in the Chad region where Bornu was split up between the British, French, and Germans. After the 1914–18 war Cameroons was administered under League of Nations mandate by France and England.

It would be unfair to attribute to the Europeans motives which were solely economic and political and their contact with the Africans to simple exploitation and forget the dedicated service of so many administrators, doctors, missionaries, and others. The reawakening of the Christian conscience led to the elimination of the slave-trade. Christian missionary work recommenced early in the century and played an inestimable part in humanizing the revolution which has characterized the life of pagan regions. The great work missionaries have accomplished is so undeniable that we may be permitted to point out that a true estimate of their influence must take into account the fact that missions continued throughout the whole of the nineteenth century to be marked by the nature of their antecedents, their foreign mentality and individualistic outlook, their aim of spreading Western civilization along with a Western religion, their link with Western imperialism, and the Protestant legacy of divisive sectarianism. Missionaries entering from the sea through the surf and the swamps confined themselves to the pagan coastal communities; the south Sudanese belt with its hundreds of small primitive communities was unattractive, whilst they were warned off the Islamized communities of the Sudanese belt by the colonial governments.[1] Since their evangelism was primarily

[1] An estimate of the effect of Christianity upon West Africa will be found in the writer's pamphlet, *The Christian Church and Islam in West Africa*, London, 1955.

promoted through education, this policy kept Muslim regions in the isolation they desired.

The nineteenth century, and in particular the second half characterized by the formation of Islamic military empires, had been one of the most tragic in West African history. How frequently when perusing the writings of European travellers for the purpose of this study one comes across such statements as this by Vallière (travelled 1880–1), 'The region that we traversed (the plateau of Narena) has become a desert since the fierce wars of the Muslims and Malinkés. At each step we encountered the remains of an ancient and numerous population.'[1] The immediate result of the occupation was to bring peace to these war-tortured regions and allow their peoples breathing-space to recover from their privations. Muslim populations, once authority was properly established, adjusted themselves to the new situation. What both former ruling classes and the general population felt most immediately was the economic effect of such reforms as the abolition of slavery and the imposition of new forms of taxation. But the most important result from the point of view of this study is the way the new conditions favoured the spread of Islam.

2. SPREAD OF ISLAM UNDER EUROPEAN RULE

The traditional state of equilibrium which had been established between Islamic and animistic societies throughout the centuries and the psychological attitude of Muslims and pagans towards each other was upset during the nineteenth century by the founders of the theocracies. Western control, following on this phase, loaded the scales even more effectively against animistic societies than at any other stage of their history. What conquest could only accomplish in a very limited way was carried through by the opening-up of Africa by Western powers. This revolution aided both the consolidation and the spread of Islam.

The immediate effect of European control which brought peace to people who had been living in a perpetual state of insecurity, harassed by war or the raids of slave-hunters, was a slowing down in the propagation of Islam and even a sloughing of the veneer acquired by many who had accepted it from fear. J. Henry wrote:

> When, in 1907, the decree of liberation was promulgated I was not by any means surprised to see, out of nearly 5000 slaves who freed themselves

[1] Gallieni, *Voyage au Soudan Français*, 1885, p. 319.

spontaneously, the greater part return to their homes or to the country of their fathers, to forget the formula of faith and declare themselves fetishists without needing to be initiated, they already were initiated.[1]

On the other hand, the new rulers in the early days of their occupation, not understanding the nature of authority among Africans, confirmed alien Muslim chiefs over the states their predecessors had conquered and even placed others over unorganized peoples. This led to the islamization of many pagans inside their territories as in Nupeland and Ilorin, though outside these states the process was halted temporarily and inside them it was slowed down. During the preceding phase Islam had been spread primarily by political conquest. This in itself only imposed a veneer of Islam, but if the occupation were permanent other factors came into play to deepen it. European conquest ended the era of forcible islamization, but its effects led to its consolidation or its spread into pagan regions.

The establishment of European rule gave an impetus to this propagation in two main ways: through the social revolution brought about by the impact of the West upon animist structures, and through factors which facilitated the work of Islamic agents. The imposition of a new system of rule, the spread of new educational ideals, and the economic impact weakened traditional authorities. Religion and society are so closely bound together that any change in social life means a weakening of religious authority. The spread of European education displaces traditional initiation systems and this leaves the youth without defence against new religions. Secular forces weakened the power of traditional religious knowledge and the old cults and their agents were often discredited. This deflection of the youth from traditional knowledge, the stress placed on materialistic values, and the waning of hereditary religious authority, prepared the way for the acceptance of Islam, particularly among the ordinary people, whilst the 'new men' taught in Western-type schools were attracted by Christianity.

In the second place, the conditions attending European rule, ordered government, peaceful relationships between tribes, free markets, freedom of movement, and rapid development of means of communication, gave a great impulse to the diffusion of Islam. This worked in two ways. On the one hand, young men were attracted to leave their villages to work in towns or groundnut cultivations where they came under the influence of Islam. Many immigrant settlements, such as the

[1] J. Henry, *L'Ame d'un Peuple Africain: Les Bambara*, Münster, 1910, p. 130.

zoŋgos in Ghanaian towns, have a Muslim orientation. On the other hand, the new conditions facilitated the movement of Islamic agents. The trader could penetrate into regions which had formerly been closed. The reorientation of commercial routes from the desert to the coast increased the routes of Islamic penetration. In the early days of European control there were few Muslims in the coastal towns. Today none are without their Muslim quarter. The population of Lagos, for instance, is 50 per cent. Muslim; in Dakar the proportion is nearer 85 per cent. Even in the freed-slave settlements the proportion of Muslims is steadily increasing. In Sierra Leone Colony in 1891 Muslims formed 10 per cent., in 1901 12 per cent., 1911 14 per cent., 1921 19·5 per cent., and in 1931 they numbered 25,350 out of 95,558 or 26·2 per cent. Even sea-routes are utilized and we find Aḥmadiyya missionaries coming from India and beginning their sectarian propaganda in coastal towns. For long this urban coastal settlement affected the sedentary population of the country around the towns very little, but gradually they are being influenced.

Further, the policies of European governments facilitated the work of contact agents and modified background conditions in such a way that many became more receptive to Islam. In the early days government officials showed special consideration for Muslims as people of a higher civilization and often despised the 'primitive' pagans. They not only confirmed Muslim chiefs over pagan communities but gave them greater authority. They set up Islamic law courts. They employed Muslims in subordinate administrative positions which brought them into close contact with animistic peoples. This familiarized animists with the outward characteristics of Islam, enhanced the prestige of adherence to the favoured religion, and provided the Islamic agents with facilities for the exercise of propaganda and various forms of pressure. Marty affirmed in regard to Senegal that, 'through our administration, together with the facilities for communication now open to everyone, we have done more during this last half century for the diffusion of Islam than its marabouts accomplished in three hundred years'.[1]

Brought suddenly into contact with Western civilization and faced with the decay of their hereditary religions many animists felt the need for adherence to a system which would integrate life in a new era, but they were not necessarily willing to pay the price which would bridge the gulf dividing them from their Western rulers, and felt intuitively that Islamic culture corresponded more to their needs. In regions such

[1] P. Marty, *Étude sur l'Islam au Sénégal*, 1917, ii. 374.

as Sierra Leone and south-western Nigeria, where both Christianity and Islam were in competition to claim the souls of animists, the successes of Islam have been striking. Many regions which were regarded as the impregnable domain of animism or open to the progress of Christianity have been won over to Islam. The areas of the greatest advance have been in former French Senegal and Soudan, western Guinea (Guinée and Sierra Leone), the central and northern Mande region, and in northern and south-western Nigeria.

In Senegal the conversion of the whole of the Wolof was accomplished within fifty years. Although the Wolof had been in contact with both Moorish and Sudanese Islam for centuries, it had only gained a small proportion of the people, the noble and warrior classes in particular being opposed to it. Three factors may be mentioned which were responsible for the rapid gains of Islam among the Wolof—the prior conditioning, the French occupation (first by way of reaction as a form of passive resistance and then in consequence of the pro-Islamic policy of the administration), and the Wolofization of Islam under the inspiration of Aḥmad Bamba (d. 1927), the founder of the Murīd movement.[1] The Wolof realized intuitively that their old religion was incapable of carrying them through the next phase of history heralded by the early impact of the West. By adopting Islam *en masse* they were able to preserve their social life and all essential institutions intact and resist the disruptive effects of the legal code of Islam.

The change in the outlook of Aḥmad Bamba was of unique significance for the future of Islam in Senegal. This region had been in a special sense the birthplace and support of militant Islam. Aḥmad Bamba, who received the revelation of his mission in Baol in 1886 when it was in a state of complete anarchy, felt at first that he was called to follow in the footsteps of the old theocrats to restore Islamic authority by waging a *jihād*. But he came too late for that. He quickly won a following and his reputation increased during his exiles (1895–1902 and 1903–7). But he emerged from his last exile to devote himself wholly to his peaceful mission and confined his role to that of saint-head of a *ṭarīqa*. The combination of the revolutionary effects of the French conquest and the reorientation of the Islamic outlook by Aḥmad Bamba not only led to the first appearance of true saint-worship in West Africa and a people's movement into Islam, but resulted in a remarkable bursting of habitat. Under pressure from Moors, Tokolor, and Soninke the Wolof had been pushed back and restricted

[1] See *I.W.A.*, pp. 95, 188–9.

to the Cayor, Walo, and Jolof regions, but security under French rule completely changed the situation and they burst out of their confines. Stimulated by the impulse of the Murīd movement they have colonized and exploited arid lands in Ferlo, forcing the Fulbe who had reduced it to desert to withdraw. They colonized the no-man's-land lying between the various Serer groups, and have become numerous in Sin, Salum, and even Gambia.[1] Small groups of peoples have been absorbed. Many became active traders, founding colonies in all the towns of Senegal. The Islam of the ordinary people, based as it is on Murīdism, is unique in Negro West Africa, whilst the *évolués* exhibit another type of secularized Islam and are very scornful of the saint worship of the *murīds*. Wolof traders in Nyoro in the Sahil supported Muḥammad b. Aḥmad and his disciple, Ḥamāhu 'llāh, against the persecution of the 'Umarian Tijānī shaikhs.

The spread of Islam in western Guinea, French Soudan, and the central Mande regions, although not so spectacular, has been none the less steady. Islam had already been accepted by many Mandinka, and even though large numbers were pagans in practice it was inevitable that under the new conditions most of them would be ready to claim it as their religion. Even the Bambara in French Soudan have been influenced and at least 20 per cent. would claim to be Muslim.[2]

Although Mande traders were active everywhere throughout western Guinea the primary impulse had come from the Fulbe of Futa

[1] Wolof in the Gambia numbered 36,200 in 1950. The Gambia must be linked with the Senegal so far as the spread of Islam is concerned. It is an obvious political anomaly, cut off from its natural hinterland where the main bodies of its people live. The official figures of religious profession are as follows:

Protectorate	*Animists*	*Muslims*	*Christians*	*Total*
1947	46,907	178,000	451	225,358
1948	48,045	180,695	544	229,284
1949	49,236	197,150	500	246,886
1950	19,382	230,649	1,530	251,561
Bathurst				
1946	291	15,866	4,995	21,152

[2]

Soudan Français	*Animists*	%	*Muslims*	%	*Christians*	%	*Total*
1921	1,413,589	57	1,061,000	43	..	..	2,474,589
1940	1,580,000	53	1,370,700	46·5	11,700	0·5	2,962,400
1949	1,438,700	44·5	1,782,750	55	16,230	0·5	3,237,680

Jalon which led to the conversion of the whole of the Susu[1] and smaller peoples during the nineteenth century, but since then the progress of Islam has been steady and has reached the coast. In Sierra Leone it has gained half the Temne and Mende, the two largest tribes. All over this vast area (Portuguese Guinea,[2] independent Guinea,[3] and Sierra Leone)[4] we find today an extraordinary picture of religious change. Hundreds of villages are a mixture of pagans, Muslims, and Christians. The break-up of traditional religions is apparent everywhere, as is the fact that the abandonment of their African religious heritage is only partial and that the springs of conduct of those who have joined one or other of the two available world religions is still that of the old animistic heritage.

Nigeria under British occupation witnessed one of the greatest advances.[5] In the north the traditional confessional neutrality of the British had given way to partiality. Islam appealed to the administrators who were fascinated by the Fulbe state system, and wherever Muslims were found in authority, even over a pagan majority, they recognized Islam as the religion of the state. Through the policy of indirect rule vast numbers of pagans were left under Muslim rulers and insulated against influences such as Christian missions which, though they would not have converted Muslims, would have intro-

[1] The Susu number 320,000 in Guinea and 50,000 in Sierra Leone. The branch known as the Yalunka (Jalonkē) was the centre of Susu resistance to the Futa Jalon theocracy and today the real penetration of Islam among them is relatively moderate. From the Susu Islam is rapidly gaining the Mani on the coast of southern Guinea and Sierra Leone.

[2] In Portuguese Guinea (pop. 510,777 in 1950) the Muslims are mainly Fulbe (known as Fula, 108,000), Mandinka (64,000), Susu, and the majority of the Biafada (12,000). The Manjaco, Balante (except for the Manē who are Muslim), island Bijago, and smaller peoples remain pagan.

[3]

Guinea	*1911*		*1952*	
Muslims . . .	899,400	51%	1,381,000	65%
Total population . .	1,763,000		2,131,000	

[4] In Sierra Leone the 1931 census gave 193,650 Muslims out of a total of 1,667,790, or 11·6 per cent., but the proportion of those who would claim Islam as their religion today would seem to be nearer 25–30 per cent.

[5]

Northern Nigeria	*Animists*	*Muslims*		*Christians*	*Total*
1921 . .	3,278,068	6,686,362	67%	13,685	9,978,122
1952 . .	4,616,000	11,661,000	69%	558,000	16,835,000

duced Western-type education and, if they converted pagans in the Muslim emirates, introduced minority problems. Fifty per cent. of the Hausa are said to have been pagan at the time the British occupied the emirates, today probably 80 per cent. are Muslim.[1] The occupation simply accelerated a process already under way. Not more than one-third of the Nupe were even nominally Muslim in 1880, today two-thirds at least would claim Islam as their religion. Similarly Islam has made great gains among Yoruba and other peoples of Ilorin Province.[2]

The majority of the peoples mentioned had been prepared for the reception of Islam before Western occupation, but the Yoruba region of south-western Nigeria has witnessed a spectacular spread of Islam among people who were previously uninfluenced. The northern Yoruba (Ilorin region) had been subjected under a Fulani emirate, but this only intensified the hatred of the independent Yoruba for the conquering religion, and Islam had to progress under considerable difficulties. It is true that when the first C.M.S. missionary, Hinderer, arrived in Ibadan in 1852 he found Muslim traders active, largely in

[1] C. H. Robinson gained the impression in 1894–5 that, 'about one-third of the Hausa-speaking people profess the Mohammedan faith. This includes nearly all the Fulahs resident in Hausaland; the heathen Fulahs, of whom there are still a considerable number, being found mostly to the west of the Niger' (*Hausaland*, 1897, p. 183). Strongholds of pagan Hausa were the state of Argungu (south-west of Sokoto), the region between Sokoto and Katsina, and the northern regions now in French Niger. The state of Argungu, though so close to Sokoto and continually at war with it, remained independent throughout the last century, but British occupation broke down barriers of resistance to Islam as the religion of the hated Fulani and the state became officially Muslim about 1922, though the majority of the people remained pagan. Islam has been gaining villages between Sokoto and Katsina, though there are still large pagan blocks. Similarly in French Niger territory. The official returns (given by H. Leroux in *Bull. I.F.A.N.* x, 1948, 600) for the sub-division of Marāḍi (mainly Hausa), north of Nigeria, were:

	Islamized	*Animists*		*Total*
Province of Marāḍi .	37,500	19,000	34%	56,500
Canton of Gobir .	35,800	8,200	18%	44,000
	73,300	27,200	27%	100,500

[2] Dr. E. G. Parrinder writes, 'In Ilorin Province the 1921 census gave 66 per cent. Pagans, 33 per cent. Moslems, and 1 per cent. Christians. The latest estimate in 1954 gives approximately 75 per cent. Moslems, from 2 to 5 per cent. Christians, and the rest Pagans. Islam therefore has more than reversed its strength relatively to Paganism. To get some idea of the strength of the Moslem revival one should look at the villages, which are always the most conservative and change to new religions later than the towns. The Resident of Ilorin Province . . . has recently made a very careful survey of villages near Ilorin. In three sample villages in 1930 there were 48 per cent. Moslems, 48 per cent. Pagans, and 4 per cent. Christians. In 1954 in the same villages there were 80 per cent. Moslems, 12 per cent. Pagans, and 8 per cent. Christians' (*West Africa*, 30 July 1955, p. 698).

the slave-traffic, and in high favour with the chiefs, but they were not allowed to interfere with local religion or deflect people from loyalty to it. Islam began to spread after the British occupation and C. H. Robinson wrote[1] of its rapid progress in 1895. Muslims were not allowed to erect mosques in Ibadan until towards the end of the century.[2] 'In the Ijebu country of Southern Nigeria, Islam was introduced as recently as 1893. A few years later one town possessed twenty mosques, and in other towns many were built. In 1908 there were said to be in Ibadan three times as many mosques as there were Christian churches.'[3] In this contest for the souls of the Yoruba the percentage of Christian gains was about 5 per cent. of those of Islam. The reasons for this spread are multiple:

The historical fact of the subjection of the northern Yoruba by the Fulbe, those who became converts acting as agents to their pagan brethren.

The geographical position of the Yoruba on the Niger highway in a region where there was no dense forest.

The political disunity and civil wars between Yoruba communities.

The staleness and fatigue which characterized the Yoruba religion, and its inadequacy as a basis for life under new conditions.

The upsetting of traditional life through the impact of the West. Urban Yoruba changes from folk culture to mixed sophisticated culture.

The nature of their trading economy, density of population and economic specialization, and the vast urban agglomerations which developed independently of European influence, in consequence of their defensive organization.

The hierarchical nature of the Yoruba social and political system.

The fact that Islam was africanized and consequently its suitability to Africans under conditions of great change.

Yoruba have spread into southern Dahomey where they form the largest Muslim element, but Islam has not influenced the Fon whose highly organized religion, unlike that of the Yoruba, has not shown signs of breaking down.

[1] C. H. Robinson, *Hausaland*, 1897, p. 185.

[2] In fact they had their mosques, since a marked-out square or a room in a compound is all that is necessary.

[3] *C.M.S. Review*, 1908, p. 648. In 1913 it was estimated that Muslims comprised 35 per cent. of the population of the group of Ibadan, Ife, and Illa towns (C. G. Elgree, *The Evolution of Ibadan*, Ibadan, 1914). The 1953 Census returned for Ibadan: 60 per cent. Muslim, 32 per cent. Christian, and 8 per cent. animists.

Epilogue

SINCE the effect of Islamic culture upon West Africans has been treated in *Islam in West Africa* we may limit ourselves to a few general observations. In spite of their different forms and endless variety the cultures of the region reveal a definite Negro foundation. In the Sudan zone this is often obscured through the integration of foreign elements into the indigenous structure. The influence of Saharan nomads upon peoples of the Sudan belt has been profound. Cultural interaction has been so complex that it is difficult to disentangle the Negro and indigenous from the foreign and adventitious. Often the elements which stand out most clearly as belonging to a different layer of civilization are the least important in the culture of the people since they belong to the ruling class and the political organization of the Sudan states. Consequently it is easy to exaggerate the influence of northern Hamites and of Islam. Without going to the other extreme and minimizing the efficacy of Hamitic influences preceding Islam in modifying the original data, the broad fact remains that these were Negro civilizations with their own distinctive character, and all the states which arose before the nineteenth century formed themselves upon a solid basis of indigenous civilization. Nor do we want to minimize the effect of Islamic civilization. It is not enough to take the two ingredients, the pagan cultures and Islam, and consider change simply as a kind of quantitative transposition and merging in the form of external evolution, for that would miss the creative and dynamic factor—the two forces reacting upon each other. Neither the African nor the Islamic are static cultures when in interaction, and the process of development, accommodation, co-operation, and ultimate synthesis can only be apprehended dialectically.

The so-called Islamic states in West and Central Sudan were organized on the pattern of advanced Negro societies. Islamic institutions were incorporated and modified these societies, but traditional African society is closed to universalist conceptions like that of Islam. Islam formed merely one element within African culture, the religion of certain classes, but there was no identity of political and religious organization in these states. The 'state' was a family and Islam often became the family cult, but no Muslim chief would have dreamt of imposing the *sharī'a* upon his own family let alone anyone else. Therefore no attempt was made to make Islam the cohesive element of the state overreaching the narrow compass of kinship and initiation.

Through the nineteenth-century revolution Islam was transformed into a social and political force which ushered in a new age because its relationship to indigenous civilization was changed. The theocratic states were new creations, entirely different from anything the Sudan had seen before. They represent an attempt to introduce into the African milieu a concept of the State based upon the universal adherence of all subjects to a common religion. They began as genuine Islamic states. The rulers based their claim to govern upon a mandate from God, and they endeavoured to rule by the *sharīʿa*, the law of God. This new Islam was characterized by the intensity it brought into the former unchallenging Islam, so africanized as to be at the point of losing its identity. This intensity drove Islam into the centre of life as a transforming factor whereby the very equilibrium of society was changed.

The new states foundered, not primarily because they coincided with increasing European penetration, but because they could not transcend the basic African organization of society. The most successful, that of Māsina, was conquered by another theocrat fifty years after its birth at the moment when centrifugal forces within it were heralding its disintegration. These states fell to pieces because they were not based on indigenous institutions, although Sudan elements were incorporated, and Islam did not supply the place of the old ṣanctions of authority. Some, such as the Pulo emirates in Hausaland, reverted to the familiar Sudan pattern with Islam as the state religion or king cult.

After the European occupation Islam ceased to be the ultimate authority for rule and government, in spite of anomalies such as the North Nigerian states. Islam's effect as a civilization, as contrasted with its role as the binding force of a state, is shown by the way it provided the Muslim regions with a high degree of insulation against the penetration of Western civilization. They are now giving way and traditional Islamic culture is regressing. Therefore in considering the influence Islamic allegiance may be expected to exert in those newly independent states where there is a predominance of Muslims (Senegal, Guinea, the Federation of Mali, Niger, Chad, and Northern Nigeria) the effect of the simultaneous spread of secularism must be kept in mind. Secularism will change Islam, not its doctrine or institutions of course, but its religious domain, restricting and narrowing the sphere in which Islam can mould the lives of its adherents.

CHRONOLOGICAL TABLES

1. Kingdoms of Senegal and Gāna

A.D.	
750–800	Soninke state of Wagadu (founded by Magham Dyābe Sīsē).
770	Gāna in existence (Al-Fazārī).
800	States on the Senegal: Ṣanghāna (Serer), Takrūr, Silla, and Galam (Soninke).
	Lamtūna at Awdaghast.
800?	Kaya-Magha (Sīsē clan) founds Soninke dynasty of Gāna.
850	South Saharans (Fulbe?) found dynasty of Dyā-Ōgo in Takrūr.
930	Lamtūna struggles with the Soninke of Gāna.
980	Gāna gains control of Awdaghast.
	Dynasty of Dyā-Ōgo overthrown by Nyakhātē clan (Manna: Soninke) of Dyāra.
1040	Wār-Dyābi, son of Rabīs (founder of new dynasty?), king of Takrūr, joins Islạm.
1054/5	Almoravids take Awdaghast.
1056/7	Lebi, son of Wār-Dyābi, aids Yaḥyā ibn ʿUmar against Godāla.
1076	Almoravids take Gāna. Disintegration of the empire.
	Godāla in the border region.
	Foundation of Soninke dynasties (Sosē) in Kanyāga, Nyakhātē in Kingi (Dyāra), Dukurē at Bakuni, Nono, and other places.
1180	Dyāra Kante gains control of Sūsū.
1090	Soninke of Gāna regain independence.
1100	Berbers form settlement of Timbuktu.
1200–35	Sumāguru Kantē, king of Soninke Sūsū.
1215	Sūsū take Gāna.
1224	Gāna traders transfer their centre to Biru (Walāta).
1235	Sun Dyāta of Māli defeats Sūsū and takes Gāna (1240).
1250	Dispossessed Sūsū dynasty gain control of a region in Takrūr.
1320?	Aḥmad or Ndyadyan-Ndyay, son of a Tokolor cleric and a daughter of the Lām-Toro, founds states of Walo and Jolof. Differentiation of Wolof from Serer.
1342	Al-ʿUmarī says Ṣanghāna subject to Māli.
1350	Manna dynasty in Takrūr overthrown by Wolof called Tondyon who annexed Fūta to a Wolof empire.
1385	Dyāra: Mamudu Dyāwara dispossesses Nyakhātē dynasty and founds that of the Dyāwara.
1390	Dyāra independent of Māli, though retaining a representative.
1400	Lām-Termes (Fulbe) replace Tondyon in Takrūr.
1455–7	Cadamosto, and (1465–73) Diégo Gomez at the Gambia.

1480	Pillage of Walāta by Mossi.
1500	Askiya Muḥammad overlord of Dyāra and Bāghana.
	The Lām-Tāga, a Lamtūna dynasty, displace the ascendancy of the Wolof in Takrūr.
1506–7	Askiya Muḥammad annexes Galam.
1512	Death of Tindio Galadio at Kingi. Koli migration begins, leading to the
1558	Foundation of the Denyankē dynasty in Takrūr.
1596	Conquest of Ḥawḍ by the Banū Ḥassān.
1640	Destruction of Tadmekka by the Ullimmeden Tuareg.
1754	Hegemony of Dyāwara in Dyāra replaced by the Bambara Māsa-Sī.
1776	Takrūr becomes an independent Muslim federation.

2. Māli

9th century	Foundation of the Keyta dynasty of north Māli by Kabala Simbo Keyta.
c. 1050	A king of Malel converted to Islam (al-Bakrī).
?	Baramandāna, a Mande chief, performs the pilgrimage.
c. 1100	Mūsā Alla-koy Keyta.
1150?	Foundation of Jenne.
1200–18	Narē fa-Maghan, father of Sun Dyāta. Capital at Narena.
1218–28	Dangaran Tuma.
1224	Sumāguru, ruler of Susu, annexes northern Māli.
1230–55	Sun Dyāta, son of Narē fa-Maghan, frees Manding (1234) and founds Māli empire.
1255	Ūle, son of Sun Dyāta.
1270	Wātī, son of Sun Dyāta.
1274	Khalīfa, son of Sun Dyāta.
1275	Abū Bakr I, son of a daughter of Sun Dyāta.
1285	Sabakura (Sākūra) usurps the throne.
1300	Gaw.
1305	Mamadu. Nyani becomes capital.
1310	Abū Bakr II.
1312	Mūsā b. Abī Bakr. 1324: pilgrimage.
1329	Timbuktu pillaged by Mossi of Yatenga.
1337	Maghan b. Mūsā.
1341	Sulaimān b. Abī Bakr.
1352–3	Visit of Ibn Baṭṭūṭa.
1359/60	Kamba (Qasā) b. Sulaimān (nine months).
	Māri Dyāta II b. Maghan.
1374	Mūsā II b. Dyāta.
1387	Maghan II.
1388	Ṣandiki.

1390	Maḥmūd (Mansa Maghan III).
c. 1400	*Si* Mādogo of Songhay conquers dependencies of Māli.
1433	Tuareg gain control of Timbuktu.
1445	Portuguese reach River Gambia.
	Mūsā III, king of Songo.
1468	*Si* ʿAlī of Songhay conquers dependencies.
	Manzugal (Mansa Ūle?).
c. 1481	Maḥmūd ibn Manzugal.
1483	Embassy of João II of Portugal.
1498–9	Askiya Muḥammad I annexes Bāghana and in 1500–1 Dyāra.
1534	Portuguese embassy under Peroz Fernandez.
1545–6	Askiya Da'ūd plunders capital.
1591	Moroccan conquest of Songhay.
1599	Maḥmūd of Māli attacks Moroccans in Jenne.

The Keyta Dynasty of Māli (following Ibn Khaldūn)

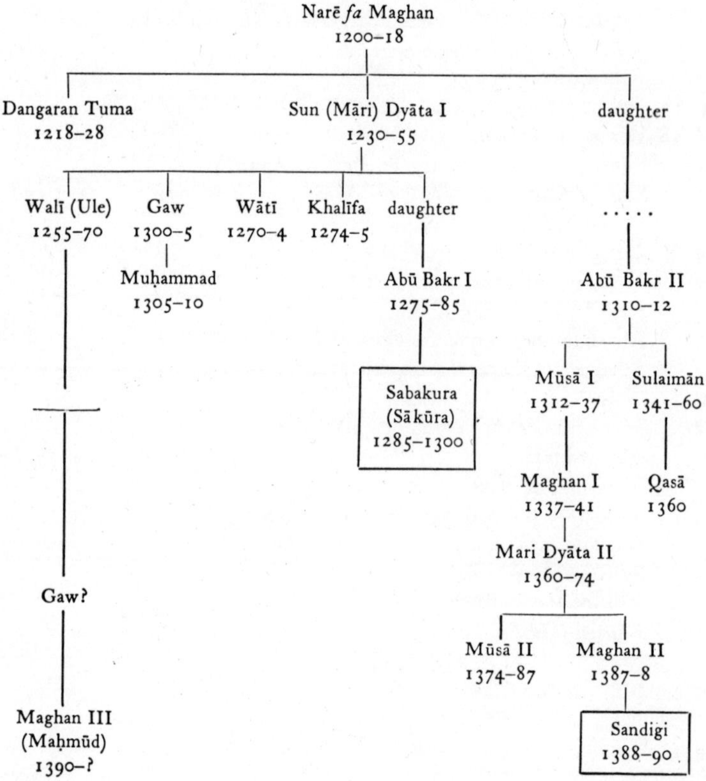

3. Songhay

c. 840	Al-Khwārizmī mentions the existence of Gungia.
860?	Foundation of the *zā* dynasty.
872	Al-Ya'qūbī says 'Kawkaw the greatest kingdom of the Negroes'.
980	Ruling class are Muslims according to al-Muhallabī.
1000	*Zās* in control of Kawkaw.
1009	Traditional date for the conversion of 15th *zā* Kosoy to Islam.
1080	Reconversion of the *zās* to Islam.
1220?	Mossi campaign against *zā* Baray.
1250	Suzerainty of Māli under Sun Dyāta extended over northern Songhay.
1275	'Alī Kolon founds *sī* dynasty.
1295	Sabakura of Māli raids Songhay territory.
1325	Mūsā of Māli visits Kawkaw.
1353	Ibn Baṭṭūṭa visits Kawkaw.
c. 1400	*Sī* Mādogo begins conquest of dependencies of Māli.
1433	Tuareg gain control of Timbuktu.
c. 1460	*Sī* Dāndi pillages Mīma.
1464	*Sī* 'Alī the Great, 18th *sī*. Foundation of the Songhay empire.
1469	*Sī* 'Alī takes Timbuktu from the Tuareg.
1470	Jenne captured. Mossi raid Timbuktu.
1492	Death of *sī* 'Alī and accession of *sī* Bāro (Abū Bakr Dā'o).
1493	Defeat of *sī* Bāro and foundation of the *askiya* dynasty by Muḥammad Tūrē. Consolidation of the empire.
1497–8	Muḥammad I performs the pilgrimage.
1516–17	The *Kanta* of Kebbi becomes independent.
1528	Deposition of Muḥammad Tūrē and accession of his son Mūsā.
1531	Muḥammad Bengan, nephew of Muḥammad I.
1537	Ismā'īl, son of Muḥammad I.
1539	Isḥāq, son of Muḥammad I.
1549	Da'ūd, son of Muḥammad I.
1582	Muḥammad II, son of Da'ūd.
1586	Muḥammad (III) Bāni.
1588	Isḥāq II.
1591	Moroccan conquest. Isḥāq deposed.
	Muḥammad Kawkaw. Killed by the Moroccans (1592). End of the Songhay empire.

4. Dynasties of Songhay

Zā Dynasty

Fragment (*Fattāsh*, pp. 332–5)	As-Sa'dī (*T. as-Sūdān*, pp. 4–5)
1. Alayaman	1. Alayaman
2. Wa'ai	2. Zakoi
3. Kaien	3. Takoi
4. Takai	4. Akoi
5. Mata Kai	5. Kū
6. Mali Biyai	6. 'Alī Fai
7. Biyai Kīma	7. Biyai Komai
8. Bei	8. Biyai
9. Kirai	9. Karai
10. Yama Kalawai	10. Yama Karawai
11. Yama Dombo	11. Yama
12. Yama Janaa	12. Yama Danka Kiba'o
13. Jata-kore	13. Ku-korai
	14. Kenken
14. Kosho Muslim (first Muslim)	15. Kosoi Muslim Dam
15. Kosho Dāria	16. Kosoi (or Kosor) Dāriya
16. Hunabonua Kodam	17. Henkon Wan Kodam
17. Yama Kitsi	18. Biyai-Koi Kīmi
18. Barai	19. Nintāsanai
19. Bibai Kaina	20. Biyai Kaina Kimba
20. Simanbao	21. Kaina Shinyumbo
21. Fanda Jaroa	22. Tib
22. Yama Dā'a	23. Yama Da'o
23. Arkur Juwa	24. Fadazu
24. Barai	25. 'Alī Koro
	26. Bir Foloko
25. Yassi Bo'o	27. Yāsi Boi
26. Bāro	28. Dūro
27. Dūro	29. Zenko Bāro
28. Bisi Bāro	30. Bisi Bāro
	31. Bada

Si Dynasty

Fragment	*As-Sa'dī*
1. 'Alī Golom	1. 'Alī Golon
2. Silmān Nāri	2. Salman Nāri
3. Ibrāhīm Kabayao	3. Ibrāhīm Kabay

Fragment	*As-Sa'di*
4. 'Uthmān Gīfo (time of pilgrimage of Mūsā of Māli, 1324–5)	4. 'Uthmān Kanafa
5. Mākara Komsū	5. Bar-Kaina Ankabī
6. Būḅakar Katiya	6. Mūsā
7. Ankada Dukuru	7. Bokar Zonko
8. Kimi Yankoi Mūsā	
9. Bāro Dal Yombo	8. Bokar Dala Boyonbo
	9. Māri (i.e. Muḥammad) Kiray
10. Mādao or Mā-dogo	10. Muḥammad Dā'o
11. Muḥammad Kūkiya	11. Muḥammad Kūkiya
12. Muḥammad Fāri	12. Muḥammad Fāri
13. Balma or Balam	13. Karbīfo
	14. Māri Fay Koli Jimo
	15. Māri Arkona
	16. Māri Arandan
14. Sulaimān Dāma or Dāndi	17. Sulaimān Dāmi
15. 'Alī (1465–92), son of *sī* Mādao (p. 388)	18. 'Alī, son of *sī* Maḥmūd Dā'o (p. 116)
16. Abū Bakr, named Bāro	19. Bāri, named Bokar Dā'o

Askiya Dynasty

1.	1493	Muḥammad Tūrē, d. 1538
2.	1528	Mūsā
3.	1531	Muḥammad Bengan
4.	1537	Ismā'īl
5.	1539	Isḥāq
6.	1549	Da'ūd
7.	1582	Muḥammad II
8.	1586	Muḥammad Bāni
9.	1588	Isḥāq II
10.	1591–2	Muḥammad Gao

5. Central Sudan

Date (A.D.)	*Hausa states*	*Kanem–Bornu*	*Other states*
c. 800	. .	Dūgū, legendary founder of Kanem	. .
872	. .	Kanem mentioned by al-Ya'qūbī as a district of the Zaghāwa	. .
c. 1000	Abayajidda immigrants settle in Hausa	. .	. .
c. 1050	Bagoda, 1st *sarki* of Kano	. .	. .
1067	. .	Al-Bakrī refers to Kanem as a district of the Zaghāwa	. .
1085	. .	Ḥumē, first Muslim ruler of Kanem. New dynasty?	. .
1097–1150	. .	Dūnama b. Ḥumē builds up power of the state	. .
1150	Gobir dynasty founded in Air. North Katsina village founded (Durbāwa)	. .	. .
1183	. .	. .	Qaraqosh gains control of Zawīla (Fezzān)
1200–50	Wangāra dynasty of south Katsina conquers north Katsina	. .	Foundation of Nupe state
1194–1221	. .	Salma, first 'black' *mai*. Formation of a Sudanese state. Beginning of wars of conquest	Salma conquers Fezzān
1221–59	. .	Dūnama II first Muslim *mai* according to Maqrīzī	Wars of Kanem with the Bulāla
1242–52	. .	Kanembu Muslims establish a *riwāq* in Cairo	. .
1257	. .	Embassy of Dūnama to the Ḥafṣid, al-Mustanṣir	. .
1275–84	. .	. .	*Etsu* Bake of Nupe
1300	Foundation of Birnin Zamfara	. .	. .
1307–43	Tsamia of Kano seeks to control city-cult	. .	Kanembu expelled from Fezzān (1310)
1320–53	Muḥammad Korau, first Muslim *sarki* of Katsina	. .	Katsina at war with Nupe
1342	Berbers in control of Hausa Air	. .	Jukun state in existence
1360–90	. .	Intensification of wars between Kanembu and Bulāla	Jīl b. Sikuma, chief of the Bulāla

1370	Yaji, sarkin Kano, adopts Islam. Turunku dynasty of Zekzek	..	..
1386	..	'Umar b. Idrīs abandons Kanem for Bornu. Beginning of civil wars in Bornu	..
1430	Queen Āmina of Zekzek	..	Nupe temporarily tributary to Zekzek
1438 (or 1460)	Tuareg found Agadez (Air)	..	..
1452	Hausa dynasty of Air settle in Gobir	..	Tsoede gains control of Nupe
1463–99	Muḥammad Rimfa fosters Islam in Kano	..	..
1476–1503	..	'Alī al-Ghāzī stabilizes state of Bornu and founds N'gazargamu	Tunjur in Darfur
1494–1520	Ibrāhīm Maji of Katsina adopts Islam	..	..
1503–26	..	Idrīs Katagarmabe reconquers Kanem	..
1510–45	Kotal, 6th *Kanta* of Kebbi founds a great state, capital Surāmē	..	..
1512	*Askiya* Muḥammad I attacks Katsina	..	..
1514	..	..	*Askiya* Muḥammad attacks Air
1522	Wangāra state absorbed by Katsina and Kebbi	..	..
1536	Foundation of Zaria city	..	Dokkenge founds a state in Bagirmi
1544	..	*Kanta* Kotal attacks Muḥammad b. Idrīs	Tunjur gain control of a state in Waday
1552	*Kanta* Muḥammad (1545–61) at war with Songhay	..	..
1570–1602	..	Idrīs Alawma. Wars with So and Kanem	Bagirmi tributary to Bornu
1580	Kano tributary to Bornu and the Jukun	..	..
1591	..	..	Fall of Songhay
1630	..	..	Sulaimān Soloñ overthrows Tunjur in Darfur. 'Abd al-Karīm overthrows Tunjur in Waday
1640	First Muslim ruler of Zamfara	..	..
1671	Jukun occupy Kano	Bornu attacked by Jukun and Tuareg	..
1674	..	..	Tuareg dynasty of Adar founded
1680	Kano tributary to Bornu	..	..
1710	Power of Kebbi broken	..	..
1730	Foundation of Damagaram	..	Jibrīl, first Muslim king of Nupe
1750	Babari of Gobir conquers Zamfara and founds Alkalawa	...	Bulāla ejected from Kanem by the Tunjur Waday ceases to be tributary to Darfur
1791–1808	..	Aḥmad b. 'Alī	..

6. Eighteenth and Nineteenth Centuries

Date	*Western Sudan*	*Central Sudan*
1675–1720	Settlement of Fulbe in Futa Jalon	..
1712–55	Mamari Kulubali, founder of Bambara state of Segu	Power of Kebbi broken
1720	Invasion of Kajor (Wolof) by Tokolor	..
1725	Ibrāhīm Mūsā launches the *jihād* in Futa Jalon	1723 Abū Bakr of Mandara performs pilgrimage
from 1737	Tuareg in control of Niger bend	Ascendancy of Gobir. End of Zamfara. Foundation of Alkalawa
1751	Death of Ibrāhīm Mūsā. Sori becomes war-leader	Muḥammad al-Amīn of Bagirmi, 1751–85
1754	..	Birth of ʿUthmān dan Fodio
1760–70	Foundation of Bambara state of Karta	..
1763	Alliance between Fulbe and Jalonke Solima broken. Sori becomes dictator	..
1764–85	Amadi Gaye, first *almāmi* of Bondu	..
1767	Solima-attack Fugumba	..
1770	Tuareg take control of Gao and (1787) Timbuktu	..
1774	..	ʿUthmān dan Fodio's preaching tour in Kebbi
1776	Successful conclusion of *jihāds* of Ibrāhīm Sori (Futa Jalon) and Sulaimān Bal in F. Toro. Death of Sulaimān Bal and accession of ʿAbd al-Qādir	..
1784	Death of Sori	..
1784–1806	..	ʿAbd ar-Raḥmān Gwarang of Bagirmi
1786	..	ʿUthmān dan Fodio begins five-year mission
1791–1808	..	Aḥmad ibn ʿAlī of Bornu
1796	ʿAbd al-Qādir, *almāmi* of Futa Toro, attacks Kajor. Khasonke chief joins Islam	..
1800	..	Ṣāliḥ, first Muslim *miyāra* of Logon
1802–8	..	Yunfa, sarkin Gobir
1803–13	..	ʿAbd al-Karīm Ṣābūn of Waday
1804	..	*Hijra* of ʿUthmān d. Fodio
1805	Deposition of ʿAbd al-Qādir (Futa Toro)	Fall of Birnin Kebbi. First Fulbe attacks on vassals of Bornu
1806	Death of ʿAbd al-Qādir (Futa Toro)	Shaikh Ḥamad of Māsina in Hausaland
1807	..	Defeat of Katsina and Kano

1808	..	Defeat of Dawra and Zekzek. N'gazargamu raided. Muḥammad al-Amīn comes to help of Bornu
1809	..	Foundation of Sokoto. *Jihād* of Adama (Adamawa)
1810	*Jihād* of Shaikh Ḥamad in Māsina	Mūsā Dendo in Nupe. Death of *Mai* Aḥmad and succession of Dūnama
1811	..	Second Fulbe raid on N'gazargamu. Muḥammad al-Amīn becomes defender of Bornu
1812	..	Checking of Fulbe invasion of Bornu
1814	..	Building of Kūkawa (Bornu)
1815	Foundation of Ḥamdullāhi, capital of Māsina. Accession of Modian Moriba of Segu	.. ..
1817	..	Death of 'Uthmān dan Fodio. Muḥammad Belo succeeds. Afonja rebels against the Alafin. Death of *Mai* Dūnama and accession of Ibrāhīm (d. 1846) last of the Saifi dynasty
1824	..	Battle of Ngala
1826–34	Pilgrimage of al-ḥājj 'Umar Tal	..
1829	..	Death of 'Abd Allāh dan Fodio
1830	Death of Modian Moriba of Segu	..
1831–42	..	'Abd as-Salām, Pulo *etsu* of Ilorin
1833	..	Death of Mūsā Dendo of Nupe
1835	Al-ḥājj 'Umar in Sokoto	Death of Shaikh M. al-Amīn and accession of Shaikh 'Umar
1837	..	Death of Muḥammad Belo
1838	Al-ḥājj 'Umar in Māsina	..
1841	..	Foundation of Yola
1843	..	Awlād Sulaimān arrive in Kanem
1844	Death of Shaikh Ḥamad of Māsina	..
1845	Al-ḥājj 'Umar settles in Dingiray	..
1847	..	Death of Adama of Adamāwa
1850	..	Tuareg defeat Awlād Sulaimān. Abeshe becomes capital of Waday
1851	..	H. Barth in Bornu
1853	Al-ḥājj 'Umar launches the *jihād*	..
1854	Faidherbe governor of Senegal. Al-ḥājj 'Umar preaching *jihād* in Futa Toro, invades Bambuk, and captures Nyoro (Karta)	..
1855	French free Walo from Moors	..

Date	*Western Sudan*	*Central Sudan*
1856–7	Al-ḥājj ʻUmar besieges Medina (Khaso)	..
1861	Al-ḥājj ʻUmar takes Segu	..
1862	Al-ḥājj ʻUmar conquers Māsina	..
1864	Death of Al-ḥājj ʻUmar and accession of Amadu Seku	..
1879	Samōri takes Kankan	..
1880	..	Death of Shaikh ʻUmar of Bornu
1885–93	..	Shaikh Hāshim of Bornu
1886–7	Samōri besieges Sikaso	1885 The Mahdī takes Khartoum
1889	..	Rābiḥ in Dār Runya
1890	French take Segu (Amadu Seku)	..
1891	French take Bisandugu (Samōri) and Nyoro	Rābiḥ occupies Bagirmi
1893	French take Jenne. End of Tokolor empire	Rābiḥ conquers Bornu
1895	Samōri takes Kong	..
1896–7	French take Futa Jalon	British occupy Ilorin
1898	Final defeat of Samōri	Rābiḥ devastates Bagirmi
1900	..	Defeat and death of Rābiḥ. Occupation of Gwandu
1902	..	Defeat of al-Barrānī (Sanūsī). Occupation of Bauchi
1903	..	Occupation of Sokoto and Kano

INDEX

Both the Arabic definite article *al-* and *b.* (for *ibn*) have been disregarded in indexing.

PRINTED IN GREAT BRITAIN
AT THE UNIVERSITY PRESS, OXFORD
BY VIVIAN RIDLER
PRINTER TO THE UNIVERSITY